Two Years with the Chinese Communists

PLATE I

[*Photograph by the authors*

A study in quietude. Temple court in the Western Hills.

TWO YEARS
WITH THE
Chinese Communists

BY

Claire and William Band

NEW HAVEN
Yale University Press
1948

To the Peasants of North China
who at grave risk to their own lives
sheltered us from the Japanese
for two years

To the Officers and Men
of the Chinese Eighth Route Army who protected us
and escorted us through more than
a thousand miles of enemy occupied territory

To all Chinese Students
striving quietly and with heroism for the building up
of the New China, strong, unified
and Democratic

INTRODUCTION

THIS book is our war-time baby. It germinated among the highlands of Hopei on Christmas Day in 1941, while we were hiding from marauding Japanese in a poor peasant's mountain hut.

In embryo it was at first a simple story of our escape from the enemy in Peiping after Pearl Harbour. Nourished on thoughts and reflections among those secluded valleys, the story grew into a narrative of our experiences in China, more especially since 1939; and now that it is fully fledged, it has become something more comprehensive.

With a full story of our own exciting adventures as a frame of reference, we have tried to give an all-round picture of China and her victory in the fight for freedom.

Because our experiences have in many ways been unique, we have given a somewhat unconventional picture with emphases that will be unfamiliar but none the less significant. We have tried throughout to be unbiased in questions political, and in all things reasonable and scientific. We trust that the general effect will be accepted as fair and generous.

The book is not intended to be a learned treatise. We have given few if any statistics, for we believe that to be truly scientific we must also be truly human. *Dragon Fangs* is chiefly concerned with Chinese people, not with China's "millions". We have chosen the title because we like to think of the dragon as a symbol for ordinary Chinese men and women: he has always been a friendly symbol, quite unlike the fiery dragon of Western fable.

Nevertheless the Chinese dragon has been growing up; during the inner conflicts of adolescence he has been developing new powers; his youthful fangs have brought disaster to his enemies; the promise of maturity is great.

We have been privileged observers of this development; in a sense we have taken part in it ourselves. With our Chinese friends we have shared thought and feeling, joy and hardship, through fifteen years of struggle. What we have done here is to record our own experiences in order to portray as accurately as may be the spirit of these happy and industrious folk. We hope that this book will help towards a clearer understanding of China's human problems, and that through a better understanding there may come a deeper sympathy and a lasting bond of friendship.

The greater part of this book deals with areas still, at the time of writing, either under enemy control and occupation or liable to sudden raids by enemy ground forces. Much of the information given in the book had therefore to be smuggled through enemy lines.

The names of many places were therefore omitted. To give fictitious Chinese names to actual villages would lead to unnecessary confusion, and to omit names completely would sometimes make the description of local incidents unduly clumsy. We resorted to the device of giving fictitious English names to some Chinese villages, and where these occur the reader is asked to understand that the English is not intended as a translation of the actual Chinese names. When a Chinese place-name is given in Chinese (Wade or conventional geographical Romanisation), it is the actual name.

The names of certain secret agents have been given in fictitious Chinese. When a Chinese personal name appears as one word only it is, unless the context makes the contrary obvious, fictitious ; when it appears as three, or occasionally as two, it is the actual (Romanised) name of the person : his family name always appears first, and his given name, or names linked by a hyphen, follow.

With the above exceptions every word of this book is, to the best of our knowledge, absolutely true.

CONTENTS

ix

ILLUSTRATIONS

Chapter I

OASIS OF FREEDOM

OUR academic year 1939-40 began in a spirit of subdued gaiety : the wire-haired terrier next door gave birth to five sprightly little pups.

Optimistically we expected German totalitarianism to collapse from inner rottenness once it was brought up against real military opposition. We were sure that Japan could do nothing, exhausted as she was with the China " incident ". We could therefore afford the luxury of a detached philosophical point of view in the new conflict in Europe. The purpose of the war was ostensibly to save culture from the ravages of barbaric German Hitlerism ; so ours was a useful oasis of sanity in a crazy world.

The sense of conflict tended to raise our spirits. The year 1939-40 turned out to be a year of picnics and holiday trips to the western hills. Most popular resort was the Empress Dowager's Summer Palace about a mile from our campus.

While the majority of visitors would frequent the dainty restaurants in pavilions overlooking the lotus-laden lake, we would more often take a stroll around the willow-lined banks, beyond the promenade and the long arched bridge over to the rocky islet and the swimming pool. At the far end of the lake where it emerges into the stream that used to take the Dowager's barge to the Forbidden City, is a spot haunted by wild birds in great profusion.

There also is a tiny islet among the shrubs of which nested a pair of brilliant golden sheldrake, and in the upper branches of one large tree, perched in comic formation, large and awkward-looking cormorants keeping a watchful eye on the fish below. Warblers, bramblings, woodpeckers, finches, they were all there among the willows and the reeds ; a paradise of song.

Over the high-arched marble bridge we would amble on round to the little-known area that is still rice-paddies, and admire the lines of silent heron standing on the banks of irrigation channels. Every now and then one heron would gently rise, and with a single sweep of his graceful wings, glide to a point of greater vantage there to renew his vigil.

We would gaze in rapture across the blue waters of the lake at perfect gems of temple architecture snuggling up against a pine-clad hill. And brooding over all, the lovely western mountains. Nowhere in the world can one drink so deeply of so serene an atmosphere of peace.

These wonders were hallowed by the memories of more than four thousand years of civilisation, but in the year of grace 1939 they could not be tasted without adulteration.

At the outer gates of the Summer Palace we would discover a fleet of buses and automobiles, most of them arranged by the Japan Tourist Bureau, cheap excursions to the famous beauty spots of North China.

Approaching a pretty tingtze that would make an ideal picnic site, strains of frightful music from a tin phonograph would strike discordant beats upon the air. A party of Japanese, petty officials from some monopoly organisation in Peiping, would be seated in a circle round the floor of the pavilion with the din-box at the centre, bottles of Japanese beer lying untidily about, and gaudily painted females of the species at the banks of the lake washing large shoots of garlic for the party.

Let us search instead the less familiar northern slopes of the Palace hill, where the ruins of the older palace still suffuse an air of dignity and mystery among the ancient pines and winding streams. Alas we would be met by three " potatoes " staggering down the path, the middle more drunk and hilarious than the others ; boisterous laughter from above giving sufficient warning that more of a similar condition could be expected shortly.

The imperial colonisers could hardly have chosen a more vulgar or less congenial gang of oafs from all Japan than the crowd that set up their shops, hotels and brothels in Peiping, and who spread their filth over those lovely monuments of China's ancient culture.

We had to choose our time and place with care, and when we did succeed in discovering sufficient quiet, its enjoyment came to us with a peculiar relish. We came to look on life as a precious series of moments snatched from fate. We came dangerously near to an epicurean philosophy ; shall we put it this way : Make full use of each day's opportunities, they may be our last !

And following out this line, strange as it may seem, we thoroughly enjoyed our academic work. Our Chinese colleagues were our best and most intimate friends, and we carried out our scientific researches with zest and enthusiasm. There was no artificial dignity about our relations with each other or with our students and assistants ; we all approached our " work " with the same anticipation of enjoyment as we would a feast of Peking duck. During this period the output of original results from our laboratories reached its highest peak, comparing favourably with that from any similar-sized institution in the world.

1940

But when the crash came in May, 1940 it was a severe shock to our morale. Norway had been a warning, but it was too remote and we had let it pass without registering. We were all completely unprepared for the blitz on the Netherlands, and it knocked the bottom out of our shallow philosophy.

We fell wallowing in the sloughs of despondency ; all energy, even desire, for playing around with advanced physics and mathematics evaporated. Only one circumstance remained upon which we could legitimately congratulate ourselves ; our academic enthusiasms had not been merely a psychological escape from " reality ", and we were not prepared to accept them as such now that this reality was beginning to stare us in the face.

Class work practically ceased, beyond the mere formality of counting attendance ; research apparatus collected dust ; crowds milled around the bulletin boards ; we clustered in each others' offices to discuss the latest reports from Europe. There was no getting away from it, the whole world was " up against it " in a way we had never realised.

Escape we must. We took our first vacation in three years at Wo Fo Ssu, temple of the reclining Buddha in the western hills, June 20 to 24. Sleeping beneath stately pines and cedars, listening to the curoo-cuckuroo of turtle-doves and the nasal squeak of drongoes streaking among the branches, we quickly forgot the mad world outside in a spiritual relaxation which would do justice to any religious discipline.

But not for long. On the 22nd some visitor from the city brought the local newspaper and left it lying about ; and in headlines that fairly screeched we saw

" FRANCE CAPITULATES ".

That rag was edited by a German in pay of the Japanese ; we just did not believe our eyes ; surely it was one more of those vile Transocean propaganda stunts to demoralise the Reich's opponents ? But it was too true. And it began to rain, a cold dismal steady downpour.

The stone-lined swimming pool behind our court began to fill with water, and the frogs began to croak, with a sound that reverberated through the night. They seemed to say : " Laval ! Laval ! Petain ! Petain ! " Those almost human toads !

England had her back to the wall ; yet we were assured that man-power was no problem. We still cannot see how they worked that out, but there was at that time nothing else for us to do but to " stand by " as requested.

We again entered into the University programme with all the sublimated emotion that would far more easily have been used in open conflict with the local totalitarians. Defeat was as inconceivable to us as it was to the Chinese, and our becoming sharers in national adversity made our mutual understanding more complete.

News of Britain's air victory over London, during the opening days of that semester, we greeted with mixed pride and shame. Proud of the heroism of our folk at home, ashamed that we were not taking part, ashamed of our quiet nights and our comfortable home, our peaceful lives. Our earlier rationalisations began to sound hollow. The partition between " sublimation " and " escape " became so vague that it was no longer clear whether our academic work was an outlet of real value or merely a personal escape from an unpleasant, indeed disastrous situation.

It was Hitler's declaration of war against Russia that restored our mental equilibrium. Unable to form our own judgment, we remained satisfied that the Chinese should be unanimously confident that the Russians could hold out and that Hitler had made his one big mistake. In this the Chinese proved better prophets than many observers much nearer the scene of battle.

Germany's failure to beat Britain was nevertheless no guarantee that Japan would finally lose. So far as our local situation was concerned therefore, while we were merely inconvenienced, our Chinese friends suffered. There was some censorship of mails from abroad, and we lost about half the magazines addressed to us either because they contained anti-Japanese material or illustrations that pleased the censor. But letters addressed to Chinese were surreptitiously steamed open—an espionage system by means of which the Japanese hoped to keep watch on dangerous characters. The cost of living doubled itself within the year, and again this hit the Chinese more than it did us.

SKELETON MACHINERY OF OPPRESSION

But to get an idea of the real grimness of the prospect for our Chinese friends, we must know something about the puppet government organisations set up in Peiping by the Japanese after 1937.

Until 1943 the Peiping organisation remained quite independent of the Wang Ching-wei show in Nanking ; the latter was operated from Tokyo for international political purposes with the idea of proving to the world that China was then an independent member of the Great East Asiatic fraternity, and Chiang Kai-shek a mere mountain bandit.

The Peking outfit had no such purpose ; it was operated directly by the Kuantung Army, the brigands of Manchukuo, as a military supply base for armies in Inner Mongolia and Northern Manchuria. The puppets and their offices were installed merely for convenience of local administration, and perhaps for the entertainment of the Japanese at home.

While they were " only for convenience " we must not underrate either their complexity or their importance in the general strategy of total warfare in the Orient. The Peking puppet show was decked out with every conceivable department, each department having its puppet head and its Japanese adviser.

Nominally subsidiary to this system of government departments was a series of special military organs with more or less well-defined but obscure purposes.

Parallel with these was the semi-political " Hsin Min Hui ", or literally " New People's Association ". For this remarkable body there were no entrance or membership fees ; members drew salaries and received commissions ; its budget was met by the Kuantung Army. In return for these emoluments members of the Hsin Min Hui acted as voluntary thought-police among those with whom their everyday occupations threw them into contact ; they became busybodies interfering with the functioning of private institutions.

The Hsin Min Hui offered a sufficiently powerful protection for the ever-present section of society that lives by its wits, by blackmail, confidence trickery, playing upon the fears of the ignorant. Wearing a badge of membership of the Hsin Min Hui was sufficient warrant for any one of these blackguards to make a sudden search of any private residence, even cause the arrest of any citizen suspected of anti-Japanese sentiment.

Under the auspices of the Hsin Min Hui classes were held for the training of spies, special agents for an Oriental gestapo.

In general the Hsin Min Hui, under its Japanese advisers, was responsible for engineering the spiritual slavery of the Chinese people. The methods employed were almost unimaginably vile. Lies and deception, blackmail and extortion, graft and corruption, torture and terrorism, narcotisation, prostitution and obscenity ; all conceivable vices were cultivated in a bedevilled drive to undermine popular morals and morale.

The more positive side of this enslavement programme was handled by the "Great East Asia Culture Bureau", a branch of the puppet government nominally under the Department of Education but actually in control of the said Department's policies. By censorship of all publications, textbooks and broadcasts, by conducting thought examinations of all candidates for teaching jobs, and all candidates for graduation from school and college, and for employment in any of the puppet civil services, this bureau was intended to preserve the form while killing the spirit of higher education for the Chinese.

Then the "Great East Asia Development Company" was an analogue, on a grander scale, of the old "East India Trading Company". All industry in the new colonial area of North China came under its control, all enterprises were financed and operated under its monopoly, private Chinese businesses being either purchased or confiscated, usually with the assistance of some intrigue arranged for by the ever-willing Hsin Min Hui.

Complementary with the Development Company was the Labour Association, responsible for recruiting and transporting all labour supplies demanded by the Development Company. The Labour Association's methods varied all the way from mean trickery to crude press-gangsterism, but the result for the labourer was uniformly the same—abject slavery to his Japanese employers.

The Labour Association published figures during 1942 which

demonstrated their claim to have provided the Japanese industrial machine with no less than a hundred thousand new labourers per month ; the implication intended was that Japanese industry in North China had been expanding at a tremendous rate. The truth of the matter seems rather to have been that total disregard for the health and life of the slave labourers produced the need for slave replacements at the rate of about a million a year.

But that was after Pearl Harbour. Before then all this machinery of oppression was held in check ; for the benefit of Western observers, it was maintained in an apparently tentative, more or less humane condition.

Very thorough spade work was, however, carried on during the two years 1939-41. All residences were regularly inspected and a fairly thorough census was taken. Every citizen was registered with the police and his fingerprints recorded. Every one was put through a thought examination in which he or she was required to write down answers to such questions as : " What are your ideas about the Great East Asia Movement ? "

Strict inspections were made of all travellers through the various city gates, partly as a check on the census, partly to enforce the blockade against the guerrillas ; and, the one constructive step, to enforce anti-cholera and anti-typhoid prophylactic measures upon all travellers in and out of the city.

On the other hand, during these two years preceding Pearl Harbour, the local Japanese behaved well enough as individuals. They were biding their time and disarming their enemies.

OSTRICHES AND SAND, PHILOSOPHERS AND CLOUDS

After New Year 1941, in spite of increasing tension over the Pacific, we continued in an ostrich-like attitude. Perhaps because depreciating local currency gave the University a much greater purchasing power in terms of local goods and services, we embarked upon a programme of material expansion, the only real justification of which was, as it happened, as a booster of morale.

During the spring and through the summer we were constructing new roads, erecting new faculty residences, enlarging the gymnasium building, and making detailed plans for expansion of the Science College.

Then in September we admitted a larger student body than ever before in the history of the University. But even with the help of so much enthusiasm, it became increasingly difficult to ignore the dangers of our situation.   American faculty with families had mostly evacuated at the urgent advice of their government, and some of the British families had done likewise on their own initiative.   But there was no panic among us, those of us remaining had decided that we could take whatever was coming.

Our Chinese friends were definitely hoping that Japan would be drawn into war with America.   Their gravest anxiety was that Japan might be weaned away from the Axis by some secret deal at China's expense.

The Chinese had absolute faith on the one hand that Russia could hold Germany, and that on the other hand America could smash Japan.   And while a declaration of war across the Pacific would remove their means of livelihood by closing down the University, it was their only hope for national salvation.

We shared in these hopes, although the consequences of a Pacific war would be far more severe upon us than upon them. Indeed these consequences promised to be so ugly that most of us were far happier with our heads shrouded in academic clouds than contemplating terrestrial realities.

Chapter II

YELLOW PERIL

WHEN the United States of America issued the last ultimatum to Japan to declare her intentions in the Pacific we came down to earth with a bang.

On Tuesday evening, December 2nd, we held a secret meeting of some of the Western faculty members, should any of us care to take to the hills at the last minute. Fifteen of us agreed to make the attempt.

We had it all worked out in detail. The Japanese were to begin by a direct attack upon Thailand, say some time between December 15th and 20th, and then on the day following, America and Britain would honour their pledges and declare war upon Japan. This would give us twenty-four hours in which to make a tidy get-away.

Our President would declare the University closed immediately news came through of Japan's attack on Thailand, and we should have the satisfaction of knowing that the Japanese had never been able to interfere directly with our institution. The fifteen of us could take a picnic trip to the western hills and be well into guerrilla areas before our governments declared a state of war to exist between ourselves and the Japanese.

The Japanese made fools of us, but in that we were in good company.

Some of the prospective evacuees were anxious to get straight through to Chungking and out home. Others had jobs awaiting them in Chengtu. A few declared for staying with the guerrillas for the duration. All the experts in Peiping, at both the American and British embassies, had made no secret of their opinion that Japan could not stand more than six months or a year of all-out warfare against Britain and America in the Pacific. We were quite equal to a sojourn of that duration among the mountains, trying to be useful to the guerrillas in their technical work ; and what could be more pleasant than a triumphant return to Peiping with the Chinese armies of liberation ?

Theoretically all this seemed very fine ; but personally we must

admit that, although our optimism was unshakable, the suggestion
of escape into the mountains, abandoning our home and all that
was in it, and working with the guerrillas, came to us as a great
surprise. To say the very least, it demanded a very fundamental
reorientation in all our thinking. Of course things actually happened so suddenly that it would hardly be true to describe our
decision, finally, to escape as due to processes of thought at all.
It was in fact an impulse even more unreasoned than the one which
had urged us on to Peiping in 1937.

Two Worlds

From the time of Tuesday's secret meeting we began to live in
two unreal worlds : the academic world of the past and the
adventurous world of the future. The present was just a hazy
dream.

On Wednesday we did a little surreptitious packing of clothes
to try out how many things we could get into a comfortable haversack ; most of the stuff had to be unpacked again because we were
using the things, but remaining at the bottom of the bag were two
mosquito nets. Also we settled in our minds what we would wear
when we left—as much warm underwear as possible and our
strongest outer garments. Since we were not in the habit of camp-
ing out in the hills we had nothing particularly suitable.

Meanwhile more from inertia than from any real interest we
carried on with proof-reading of a new theoretical physics text
being printed by the University Press for our local use. And on
Thursday evening we had our regular research discussion on the
theory of liquid helium, but the transition temperature kept getting
mixed up in one's mind with the declaration of war and the
freezing of bank credits in the Orient. On Friday we did some
shopping, laying in food supplies to be sent out by underground
contacts into the hills to await our arrival there ; two sacks of canned
goods, sugar, cocoa, dried fruit, etc. And all the while Bill had
to behave normally at the office, giving lectures and attending to
department business just as if nothing were happening.

On Saturday morning Bill went to our Bursar's office to ask
for some cash with which to defray expenses during our journey.
But the cash situation was bad. All credits had been frozen for
some months, and after paying salaries there was practically no
cash left in the safe. Our President had gone that very morning

to Tientsin to try to work out some better arrangement for releasing cash for current expenses. We were advised to wait for the week-end after which the total amount available could be divided fairly among those needing special funds. So it came about that when we made our escape we had practically nothing in hand : in actual figures it was just $250 local currency, or roughly equivalent to £5 between us. And our President was still in Tientsin.

On Sunday the conflict between past and future became painfully acute in the present.

Right after breakfast, Lindsay comes over to discuss possibilities. He says :

"The others all seem to think they're going to have time to get out a University bus, take along their stuff and pretend to be a picnic party. If they get stopped they would not get into serious trouble. But you see I cannot afford to run the risk of being stopped !"

We know, of course, that he has twice visited the guerrilla areas since 1938, and that among the Westerners in Peiping he was most active in getting material aid to the guerrillas, and so is a chief offender in the eyes of the Japanese. We are therefore sympathetic to his feeling of insecurity. But when he makes a direct proposal :

"How far would you be willing to go to get away ?"

Bill hedges with : "How do you mean exactly ?"

Lindsay : "Well, I mean to say, how about a shooting party ?"

Bill : "Good Lord ! I've never handled a gun in my life !"

Lindsay : "Oh ! Well ! Never mind that ! The theory is, don't you see, that if the enemy is under fire, he is much less likely to shoot accurately even if your fire is quite inaccurate ; it gives you a much better chance to escape !"

It is the first time that Bill has ever really let himself visualise being shot at, and it gives him a nasty feeling in the stomach. He replies :

"Well, give me time to talk it over with Claire !"

Lindsay then dashes off on his bicycle while we have a private talk about the desirability of risking a desperate shooting party. We know that the Japanese have nothing serious against us, and that to be found along with Lindsay, armed, would mean the loss of our present good chances of being treated as respectable internees.

It might mean much worse. The fifteen evacuees had divided naturally into three groups of five, each of which was making its own plans for escape. We know that the other groups will certainly attempt no fireworks; if war comes too suddenly they will accept internment peacefully. Why shouldn't we?

And yet? Claire says she is game for anything that Bill is conscientiously willing to take her through. The one thing we are not going to face is the possibility of a separation that would put us into opposite camps. We either escape together, or remain together. Should a woman risk a shooting party? And on the other hand, a woman and the Japanese?

It is one of those decisions that are made for you. If we hesitate long enough to calculate all the alternative possibilities, there will be no time to act either way. So when Lindsay comes back, somehow we are ready with our answer: "Okay! We're with you!" And Lindsay starts to show Bill how to use the revolver.

A few minutes after this episode, we were due over at the gymnasium for a meeting of a group of faculty who were planning a joint "At Home" for the students on Christmas Day. We were all intimate friends, but the others were nearly all Chinese and knew nothing of our evacuation plans. Under their influence it was a thoroughly lighthearted affair, and all kinds of pleasant little schemes were laid for ourselves and our students during the festive season. It was only upon coming out of the gymnasium and strolling peacefully under the weeping willow trees on the banks of the "Nameless Lake" that we realised, with a jolt, that we had for one brief hour jumped completely out of one world into another. The Christmas party was a plan about the future, but it was unreal, fantastic, belonging completely to the world of the past.

We were due out to supper that evening at M's. At half-past six we had an unexpected caller in the person of Number Five in our shooting party. He came to show us the neat medical kit he had secured. We told him that according to the University's plans we were to be provided with a medical kit by our medical office, but that nothing so far had been done about it as far as we knew. As usual we had nothing in the house. We admired his kit and wondered whether the medical office would serve up anything half as handy, then jumped on our cycles and rolled gaily round to the other compound for the evening meal.

Our hosts were not supposed to know about the secret evacuation plans, but we sensed that an indiscreet friend had been gossiping. Instead of making a clean breast of it, we kept up the farce of pretending there was nothing in the air at all. Most of the evening was taken up by Bill arguing that Japan would never dare to make war with America, that the whole Pacific tension was a war of nerves waged aggressively by America, and that Japan would not take the plunge. Things would gradually cool off.

While Pearl Harbour was already being bombed, we had talked ourselves into such a state of optimism that we overslept ourselves next morning.

DASH FOR FREEDOM

It was about five past eight, Bill had just finished shaving and was still in his pyjamas, Claire was just getting out of bed when a terrific banging fell upon the front door.

" Quick, Bill ! It must be Michael ! " said Claire in breathless excitement. Bill jumped to the door of the bungalow, and even before the door was opened, Lindsay was already shouting :

" Japan and America at war ! Give you twenty minutes to get ready ! Here's your pistol ! "

" Show me again how you work it ! " said Bill in a daze.

" That's the safety catch ; here, I'll pull out the magazine. You pull that back to set it for shooting. D'you remember now ? "

" Yes, O.K. ! We'll be ready ! "

Lindsay dashed off, leaving Bill, still in his pyjamas, trying to collect his wits, with the unfamiliar weapon in his hand.

Claire was already pulling her ski-suit out of the drawer.

" Hurry, Billy ! Can we make it ? "

" Sure ! " said Bill, trying to prevent Claire from sensing the apprehension he was feeling like an electric current in his spine. No time for words. Dressing took ten minutes. Packing some clothes into knapsacks another ten minutes. Claire ran across the compound to Lindsay's place while Bill made a tour of the breakfast table, pocketed the fruit, and, from the pantry, lifted a fresh ginger-cake the cook had made the day before. He then went into the kitchen and told the servants that the Japanese would soon be arriving ; we two were leaving in a hurry, leaving everything for them. He then followed Claire over to the car Lindsay had waiting outside his house.

Our servants came out with a pan of hot milk they had had ready for our morning coffee. Claire swallowed a glassful, but Bill's mouth was so dry he could not manage to swallow even a mouthful. Meanwhile the Lindsays were about ready; their servants were helping to bring out the sacks of food that had had no chance of going on ahead, and there were several cases of radio equipment for the guerrillas.

We waited five more minutes for Number Five, but he did not turn up in response to Lindsay's message. We finally got started about eight-forty and made for the power-house to look for one of the Chinese staff who had promised to come. Lindsay is a fast driver in normal circumstances. This time it was unnerving. On the sharp bend at the bottom of the slope out of our compound he nearly overturned the car. On the right-angle bend at the end of the tennis courts he repeated the performance.

Screeching to a stop outside the power-house, Lindsay jumped out of the car, dashed into the control room. But in a moment he came tearing back alone, the man was not there. Lindsay swung the car round and sped back towards the compound, discovered the missing lad on a cycle by the tennis courts, face as pale as death : his family would not let him go with us.

Another hair-raising turn-about in the car, and then a race for the east gate.

Would the Japanese be there already ?

What was the use of trying to shoot ? We'd all get caught anyway, and shot.

Anyhow this east gate is a better chance than the front gates ; guards likely to arrive there first.

Thank God ! The gates are clear ! We're out !

We bumped north along the dusty track that connected with the main Tsing Hua road, and turned west into that thoroughfare past the north side of our campus. As we neared the junction where the main road comes from Peiping past our campus front gate, the traffic policeman signalled us to stop.

A Japanese military truck came out from Peiping and turned west towards the Summer Palace along the road we wished to travel. The traffic man signalled us to proceed. He didn't even look at us as we passed him. Phew !

But the truck was too slow for Lindsay ; he swerved the car out and made one sweep past the truck, almost knocking down a pedestrian Japanese officer on the other side of the road.

We reached the Summer Palace gates : would the guards stop us ? The guards were not on duty !

To avoid the village of Chienlungchiao where there were always armed guards on the road whose special duty was to inspect traffic and prevent smuggling to the guerrillas, we took a short cut off the main road, dashed over a narrow bridge and nearly knocked over a hay-cart that was approaching the bridge from the other side.

Rejoining the main road beyond the village we were beginning to breathe more freely when at the foot of a small hill to our left we noticed a party of Japanese soldiers round a field gun. On the right, farther along the road, was a target. Our hearts sank. What's the use of pistols now ? One shell from that thing ?

We slowed down almost to a standstill. But the party took absolutely no notice of us. We crawled along until we lost them round a corner ; then Lindsay stepped on the accelerator and we flew along at full speed, springs touching bottom at every bump.

In a few minutes we reached the entrance to the Black Dragon Pool Temple, where Lindsay's contact man had promised to meet us. Here we were to inquire for Old Number Seven, the person responding to this password would be trustworthy. The car drew up right in the doorway and we all tumbled out expectantly.

A ragged old priest happened to be coming down the steps at the moment and we hailed him hopefully ; but Old Number Seven meant nothing whatever to him.

Then through the temple doorway we espied two soldiers, they might be puppets or they might be Japanese. Our apprehension mounted as, turning towards the west we saw on the top of a hill just across the main road, a Japanese sentry outside a small shelter, with a rifle on his shoulder, standing watching us with apparent interest.

In the car were our respective haversacks of clothing, two flour-sacks of tinned foods, and about five suitcases of radio-equipment ; should there be a search . . . well we could hardly afford to wait for that. Failing any proper contact, the only alternative would be to abandon everything but our own haversacks and strike across country blindly for the mountains.

How long should we wait in hopes of the contact man turning up ? How long would that sentry be content just to stand and watch us from his perch ? Would the bus party be following from the University ? And above all, how far behind was the search party that the Japanese would be sending out after us as soon as they discovered our escape ?

For about ten minutes we remained in suspense, trying to look like casual visitors. Then three coolies with shoulder-poles and empty manure baskets came along one of the foot-paths among the rice-paddies. They knew nothing of Old Number Seven either, but were easily persuaded to carry our suitcases and the sacks of food, which we proceeded to remove from the car without daring to look up at the Japanese sentry.

Away marched our little caravan, disappearing as rapidly as possible round the walls of the temple and out of sight, trying hard not to seem in too great haste.

We had not gone very far before the coolies realised that there was something very queer about the expedition. In the first place we were most anxious to avoid the larger villages where there were most likely to be Japanese units. This involved us in crossing tilled fields where the footpaths had been lost under the autumn plough. Scrambling across a deep ditch, one of the men caught the metallic sound of rattling in his burden.

It does not sound quite so familiar in Chinese, but what he said in effect was :

" Here ! What is all this stuff anyhow ? And what kind of business are you up to, eh ? "

Mrs. Lindsay had to employ her most persuasive fluency in the local dialect to pacify the men.

" That's only tinned food and we're going to the hills for a picnic. We are a party of Frenchmen and Germans. You just keep straight on, there's nothing to worry about ! "

But by the time we had by-passed one garrisoned village and come to the outskirts of another where there was no garrison, no amount of persuasion would get them to go an inch further.

Two of the carriers were father and son ; the son was inclined to continue but his father vetoed it :

" It's too dangerous ! Besides, our identification cards don't. permit us beyond this point, and if the Japs find us out of bounds, you know what that means, curse it ! " He picked up one of the suitcases and rattled it in front of his son's face, repeating : " Too dangerous, I tell you ! "

We had come to a stop by the side of a great manure pile, and some fellows shovelling the muck into barrows and baskets had stopped to listen to the argument. We enlisted their help to find a new set of carriers, and in about fifteen minutes we were off again. These new boys seemed more alive to our predicament, and more willing to help us dodge the local military.

Towards midday we began to feel reasonably safe from capture. The sun was hot—as it can be even in the depth of winter on the Peiping plain—and with all our winter clothes on our backs we were sweltering in the heat. This did not tend towards clarity of thought, but our exhaustion gradually took the edge off our excitement, and we began casting about for some definite plan for the first night's rest.

Some of the fruit from Bill's overcoat pocket helped a bit. Our first idea was Miao Feng Shan, well-known pilgrimage centre in the mountains, which, according to our latest information, was a guerrilla strong point. But the carriers thought otherwise ; they told us that the Japanese had maintained a garrison there for some months already. We trudged on wearily for another hour or more hoping against hope that there would be some kind of a lead out of the blue. At last Lindsay got it.

Because the man may still be there, we must leave his name out of this account. What, in effect, Lindsay exclaimed with a sudden emphasis was :

" Hao —— ! ! That's the man ! He has a house somewhere round here, and he was reputed to have supplied the guerrillas with medicines. Ask the men if they have heard anything about him ! "

They had heard of him, but did not know exactly where his house was ; that it was somewhere in this direction they were, however, fairly sure.

At each little village we passed through we now made discreet inquiries, received only vague instructions to proceed in the same general direction.

As we were nearing the foot of the first big range of hills— the one running north from Ta Chueh Ssu—the carriers sighted a man with a mule and asked us if we would object to transferring our baggage to the animal. We had not been long with the muleman when he volunteered to take us right up to Hao's house —he knew the man well. He would not be at home, but his housekeeper would be able to help us. Mr. Hao had a very high reputation among the poor peasants in the neighbourhood.

We realised later that our carriers had known far more than they had admitted ; known even that the muleman was in fact waiting for just such an emergency as our arrival—with the radio parts. At the time we were too excited to realise this ; our good fortune seemed more an act of providence than the result of years of careful secret organisation under the very noses of the Japanese.

With renewed energy we marched straight at the face of the mountains, and after about a half-hour's stiff climb emerged upon a small prominence on the summit of which had been built a delightful summer residence. The caretaker was at home and, with such supplies as he had on hand, he bustled to prepare us a meal. It was about three p.m. and we had had nothing to eat since getting up that morning.

Fried vegetables, a little grilled meat, some noodles and some walnuts. They certainly tasted good.

Meanwhile we had been trying to win the confidence of the caretaker ; but he would not own to knowing anything about the guerrillas. At last we had to own the truth that war was on between the Japanese and ourselves, and that it was a matter of desperation that they help us.

" Could we possibly stay here one night while you send someone out to look for contacts ? " we pleaded.

" No ! Certainly not ! The Japanese inspect here every day and they would surely find you ! "

We thought he was lying to us, and asked sceptically :

" How far away are the Japs from here ? How can they inspect every day, there are so many little places like this ? "

" They have a garrison only about three *li* away ! "

Our hearts sank. Here we were after marching all day into what we thought was going to be safety, and we were only one mile from a Japanese fortified point.

" What can we do ? "

" Now, I have a relative acting as caretaker in another summer residence further north. You go there, he knows more than I do, and might be able to help. And anyway his place is that much further from the Japanese."

Passing the buck, we thought. But luckily—or was it purpose-fully?—the muleman was still hanging about, and by about four-fifteen p.m. we were clambering again down the gully, out on to the lower slopes of the hills, no doubt in full view of the enemy. Skirting the foothills for about half an hour, we then struck up into the mountains again, arriving at another pleasant villa just as twilight was threatening.

There was no one at home here either, and the caretaker lived in a small farm-house a little further on. We sat on the steps of the front gate while the caretaker's wife sent a young carpenter to look for her husband. There were several other labourers hanging about, waiting for their evening meal. The woman urged us to come inside, but this time we refused, and asked the muleman to stay with us in case we still had to keep moving on. We had given up hoping for safety, and were blankly prepared for marching on all through the night if necessary.

RESCUED !

It was almost dark by the time the caretaker arrived. He was quite excited. He wanted to be sure the rumour was true that the Japanese were at last being beaten by Britain and America. He treated us like heroes, so elated was he by our news. We could do nothing but accept his pressing invitation to come inside. He would certainly do something for us. We began to relax for the first time that day.

The couple ushered us into a room of the cottage ; it was fantastically furnished ; upholstered chairs and a settee from the neighbouring residence were arranged around the family shrine, with a Buddha, candlesticks, incense urns, hanging silk scrolls and other trappings of a pious, Buddhist family. The woman lit an oil lamp and left us to our thoughts. They locked the door from the outside.

We were on the whole inclined to optimism. But why that locked door? Had they simply kidnapped us to be ransomed back to the Japanese? Peiping was so full of rumours about irregular bandits in the hills ; no, surely they were not true ? We were too tired to contemplate such unpleasant possibilities for long.

It must have been about an hour and a half later that we were awakened from our drowsiness. Almost as silently as a ghost, our host tiptoed into the room, followed by a little wizened-faced old fellow with a beard and a long gown, and after him the care-taker's wife ; she closed the door behind them silently.

The host went quickly to the lamp, turned it down so low that it all but went out, muttering to himself how dangerous such a bright light was at that time of night.

The old man broke the silence with a half-whisper :

" Ah ! So these are our international friends ! "

Host : " Yes ! They have been resting here waiting for you ".

Old beard : " Tell me what it is you want and I will do what-ever I can for you ".

As spokesman for the party, Mrs. Lindsay explained briefly what had happened, and asked him if he could find any way of putting us in touch with the Eighth Route Army.

The old man nodded and turned to our host. There followed a half-audible but animated conversation, interrupted by many suckings-in of breath through the old man's beard ; it seemed to continue almost half an hour before he even looked at us again.

Satisfied at last, the old man turned around, and with a long whistling intake of air, he leant forward to pronounce his verdict :

" You know you could not have come to a better place than this. I am the magistrate of this county ! The Japanese think they rule this place, but the people have elected their own government and I am the head. We have now selected a safe place for you to hide, and I shall immediately send my messenger out to get in touch with the army. I am sorry you were not here two days ago ; a large unit of men were then spending the night under my roof. You could have joined them. As it is you may have to hide here for several days before we can arrange everything properly. However, rest assured we shall do our best. You are now in safe hands ! "

They quietly deprecated our heartfelt protestations of relief and gratitude, bade us instead prepare for the journey to our new hide-out.

" Now we are only going a short way. There will be an armed guard ahead, and you will follow in single file. Never mind your things, we shall carry them for you. You must tread as lightly as you can, must never speak a word or even cough. You must not smoke, nor show any light. If you want us to stop for anything, give a low whistle like this " : and he imitated the call of a night bird.

It was pitch dark as we crept spookily up the little winding footpath, over rocks and under shrubs until the dim form of a temple nestling in the tiny valley brought us to a stop. We were taken in through a side door and round several corners into an inner court where a dim light was shining through the once-papered windows of one of the rooms.

Here we found a family just disturbed from sleep on their kang—a brick bed heated from below. They had a candle lit. At the other end of the room was a similar kang, empty. There was no furniture in the room.

The men dumped our baggage on the brick floor, told us to take our choice of kangs; the one with the family was warmed, the other was cold; if we preferred the warm kang the family would move over to the cold one.

They were dressed in flimsy rags; padded with cotton wool no doubt, but pitifully inadequate. The old man let out a church-yard cough, the baby began to wail miserably, a couple of cats stood up and stretched themselves before settling down again on a warm spot of the kang. No! We four agreed. The cold kang for us. We would not dream of disturbing the family for worlds.

"Well, just as you please!" the magistrate had replied. "Really it is no trouble. They will willingly move over if you want warmth. They are good folk". He explained that this family would accept responsibility for our safety while his messenger was scouting for the army contact. Look-out would be maintained, and should there be any sign of a search party, the peasant family would hide our baggage somewhere among the rocks in the valley and a man would be at hand to guide us out of danger.

"Leave your things all packed up ready for any emergency; do not stir outside of this courtyard until you receive definite instructions." And with many expressions of goodwill the old magistrate took his leave.

We spread ourselves out on the dusty brick surface of the kang and tried to relax with all our clothes on; we had no bedding and were warned to remain prepared for instant flight.

We had been too warm all day in the sun, but after dark it had become bitterly cold. The cold from the kang struck through us like a knife; an icy blast whistled through the torn-out paper windows. By morning we were stiff with cold and had had precious little sleep. It seemed to take almost half the day before the sun climbed high enough to shine into the little court; and then we sat on the door-steps trying to get unnumbed.

There was plenty of time to take stock of our position. First of all, what exactly was our evidence that the war had started? How could we explain why the Japanese had not tried to stop us on the way, when they had so many perfect chances to do so? Have we been fools escaping from nothing but a false alarm?

There was, in fact, not very much evidence. The Lindsays had been trying to tune in on the usual eight o'clock news broadcast from the British station in Shanghai but failed. Then, searching the dial, they were just in time to hear the tail end of a German broadcast from Shanghai:

" . . . must therefore conclude that a state of war exists between America and Japan!" And that was all. Lindsay had immediately run across to our place, delivered the revolver to Bill, dashed off to warn Number Five, and then broken into the garage and forced the starting-key of the University car and raced it back to the house. While he had been gone his wife had received a telephone call from someone who had heard the same German broadcast: but there were no details. No one knew for sure what had happened.

Even supposing Japan and America were at war, and even supposing Britain became involved, why so much haste? Surely Japan was regarding North China as an independent state; perhaps North China would be permitted to remain neutral, and we would have been quite safe in Peiping.

Fond speculation! Had we but known it at the time, we would have felt more grateful for our freedom. Not more than eight brief minutes after we had left the Yenching campus the Japanese had entered by the front gates. One party made straight for Lindsay's house to arrest him, found it completely empty. The main party entered the Administration Building, called a mass meeting of the entire community and announced closure of the institution. While we were wondering about our nervous excitability, our colleagues were already in the hands of the enemy.

Early in the morning we had given some cash to the farmer, and someone had gone down to the nearest village and bought some rice. This formed the basis of our food during our stay there, and a large group of labourers joined us in sharing it. We thought they were a little free with our supplies, but after all, they could not expect a chance like that more than once or twice in a lifetime.

Two or three times that day there were alarms, and we were preparing to decamp in haste only to discover that our over-careful guard had spotted Chinese peasants coming down from the mountains carrying bundles of brushwood that made them look like soldiers in the distance. Once or twice we peeped out through a crack in the side door that looked out over the wide plain across which we had trailed the previous day, and wondered what all our friends were doing over there in the direction of Peiping.

As evening was coming on a messenger came with a note written in Chinese on a small scrap of paper. Its contents translated, ran something like this :

" Greetings to our anti-Fascist international friends ! Welcome to Free China ! We are ready to protect you from the cruelties of the Japanese. At midnight to-night our guide will come for you. Until then, sleep peacefully.

" Comrade An."

Great rejoicings ! The old magistrate had made his contact in double quick time ! We prepared forthwith to sleep in readiness for the strenuous night in store for us.

One last long look through the gate, over the plains to the city lights of Peiping. Good-bye Peiping ! Peiping, city of compromise and peace ! Tsai-chien ! We shall be with you once again, a city reborn, purified and free ! Until then, tsai-chien !

Chapter III

FUGITIVES

FLOATING on calm silvery waters, beneath the shadow of a perfect conical peak of emerald green towering into the blue sky, strolling leisurely along the avenue at Yenching that leads to the South Swallow courts, Bill's cycle struck something and the whole scene vanished. Voices were teasing us : "Are you real ? We thought you were in the mountains ; is this just your ghosts ?"

The voices faded out. It must have been a dream. But what was that bright light ? In a moment we were wide awake, a flashlight shining in our faces, and behind the flashlight a familiar figure. It was Ho, the young mechanic whom Lindsay had taken out to the guerrillas two years before. Ah ! At last ! But Ho suppressed our sudden impulse to shout for joy.

Before awakening us Ho had already prepared everything for the night's journey, and within about ten minutes we were out on the trail. There were two or three armed guards with rifles, and Ho was armed with a business-like automatic. And there were quite a few carriers. The whole group seemed vaguely familiar. We took a closer look in the dark ; yes ! they were none other than those harmless-looking labourers who had been feeding at our expense during the day. Here they were armed to the teeth, hand grenades sticking out on all sides from specially made rag bags hanging from their shoulders. During daylight, harmless farm labourers ; at night, hardy guerrillas. Ho was a responsible officer in the organisation that maintained liaison between the mountain base and the secret underground agents in Peiping ; and these were his henchmen. The day before they had not admitted to us the slightest knowledge of guerrilla affairs.

They were now as keen as mustard to show us their "stuff" : our arrival was evidently quite a break from their usual routine of smuggling supplies and information through the Japanese blockade.

We all filed through the back door of the temple and out on to the steep slopes of a narrow ravine. The path was very tricky in the dark, and in spite of Ho's earnest warnings regarding the necessity for complete silence, Bill dropped his walking-stick on the rocks with a clatter that echoed among the cliffs. At once there was a quick movement of something shadowy down on the opposite side of the ravine, and there came a low whistle like the call of a bird. The noise had alarmed one of Ho's sentries; it had alarmed Bill also; it was our first lesson in the art of night marching over rough country.

We passed through a large courtyard, apparently attached to another old temple of considerable size and at each gate was a sentry on guard. In a few moments we came out on to the open mountain side and climbed rapidly up a pilgrim path paved with slabs of rock. Here we had the help of brilliant moonlight, but it seemed to make the escort nervous. At several bends we were commanded to halt in a shadow while Ho went ahead, crouching under the hill, to climb slowly up on to a rock, rifle at the ready; each time there was a Japanese sentry-post visible from the rock, well within shooting range. We were not allowed to pass the bend until the Japanese sentry was known to be asleep, or dead.

Before long we were taken away from the paved path, and we began climbing at great speed through dried grass, slipping on sharp bits of rock, date shrubs tearing holes in our trousers. These were the trackless slopes of Miao Feng Shan; we climbed them for three solid hours before coming to a pass, almost completely exhausted, and began at once to scramble down the other side without pausing for relaxation. At last we struck a narrow footpath, a mere goat track, and here we were told to lie down and rest while two guards went ahead to scout. In less than fifteen minutes we continued the walk, and soon came up with the van-guard chatting with a couple of peasants from further down; everything ahead was clear.

Continuing down the path, we came at dawn into what once had been a thriving little village, now lying in utter ruin. We had entered the Japanese "no-man's land". Here we turned up a little valley overgrown with wild date shrubs, and in a few minutes came to an isolated farm dwelling. This was built on a small walled terrace overlooking the ruined village, and had apparently escaped the Japanese devastation. Within the court were a dozen or more Chinese soldiers in uniform, wearing the Nationalist twelve-pointed blue button on their caps; they were

Eighth Route Army guerrillas, and were as surprised to see us as we were delighted to see them.

Ushered immediately into the main cottage room, we were warmly welcomed by a fat and jolly, middle-aged woman who was tending an immense cauldron of steaming, millet gruel. In the dark recesses of the room we could make out a large kang, and on the kang were the dim forms of half a dozen more Chinese soldiers with their uniform coats unbuttoned. Along the back of the kang and round the walls of the room were stacked their rifles and their packs, hanging from wooden pegs stuck in the clay walls.

The fat woman, leaving a soldier to stir the cauldron, took us into her private inner room, and there, on a much smaller kang was the whole family, including the cat. The room was full of smoke from a bowl of incense and charcoal embers that the old mother used to light her pipe; and there was no trace of ventilation. We were cordially invited to share the family's bed, but after the fresh air on the mountain all night, we were almost choking with suffocation, and as politely as we could, we gently but firmly insisted upon returning to the outer room. We went to bed instead with the soldier boys.

We shall never forget the luxury of that kang. Yes, hard though it was, it was luxury to us. The kang was heated from below by the smoke exhaust from the fire under the cauldron; and after our exhausting night on the mountain, where we had walked and climbed over ten miles of wild and trackless slopes since midnight, the hot brick surface, padded with our overcoats, was sublimely and deliciously relaxing.

In half an hour or more, the fat woman served us with bowls of millet gruel for breakfast, the same as she was giving the army boys. There were no condiments, no sugar, no greens; just plain millet gruel. Yet how delicious! And outside, the army boys were singing one of their popular marching songs, like a grace before their meal.

By five in the afternoon we too were marching on, once more down along the mountain trail. Some time after dark we had already climbed over a fairly high mountain pass; ahead dim lights glimmered, and the barking of dogs echoed eerily among stone walls. Almost at once we found ourselves in a stone paved street with high walls on both sides. Here was a prosperous, country town. We were called to a halt outside a school building, and as the carriers dropped their huge basket-loads on the stone floor of the main schoolroom, we climbed up on to the children's desks and tried to sleep.

A tiny oil lamp was lit at one end of the room which had at first been empty. We had not been more than a few minutes in the place when, looking around us, we saw the room filling rapidly with village people and their offspring. Presently began an ear-splitting hubbub. Our guides were bargaining with the village representatives about the rate of payment for fresh carriers. Ho had already assured us that from now on we were guests of the army, and we should on no account trouble about expenses ; he had assumed full responsibility for all such details. Here the hubbub mounted to such terrific proportions that the crowd began to lose interest in us, queer and spectacular though we no doubt were in their eyes.

At the climax of all this bother, a village man who called himself a representative of their village congress, but who, to us, looked exactly like any of the other farmers in the place, called us to come away. We were a little hesitant about making a move without specific command from Ho, but this man assured us that it would be quite all right, and that Ho would follow later. So we were marched off down the street in a great hurry to the end of the town and on outside it to an isolated temple building. Here we discovered ourselves quite alone with the villager, no escort, and no Ho. The villager had to give some mysterious signals before he could get into the temple, and then we were taken through to an inner room. It was all so mysterious and irregular, that we were apprehensive ; and to crown all, the villager left us in the room and locked the door on the outside as he went. Fairly trapped !

Ten anxious minutes, and then, to prove what nervous fools we were, in walked Ho himself with a happy smile on his face, followed by the village representative with some cups and a kettle of boiled water. He explained to us that we were in this way avoiding the publicity in the school house, which might have started a leakage of news back to the Japanese. A little late, we thought, to hide now, when the whole village had already seen us, and witnessed the squabble over porterage fees. We suppose it was good diplomacy on Ho's part, first to please the public, and then give plenty of face to the town's security officers. Anyhow we were moving so rapidly that a little news leakage couldn't do us any harm ; if there was any trouble coming it was for the villagers. The Japanese would most certainly take revenge upon them for assisting our escape.

After a short rest and a few cups of hot water we were all off again in the darkness. Through a long valley, by two more villages, until about midnight when we arrived, dog-tired, at the village chosen by Ho as our next sleeping place, having walked a total distance of about fifteen miles.

Our arrival here was certainly more secret than at the place where we had changed carriers. No advance warning had been sent ahead, and at the end of the village lane we just piled over a broken-down wall into a private courtyard and presented ourselves to the startled peasant family within. The peasants jumped to the conclusion that because we were in Western style clothes —which just meant " foreign " to them—we were a Japanese press-gang. Alarm was raised, and the entire male population had beaten it up into the surrounding hills, where they stayed until dawn.

For our part, we were over-tired ; we cared nothing so much as to get to sleep, but our nerves were too jumpy to relax. Soon after climbing on the kang, an old woman of the family came into the room and began fooling around with some straw and brush-wood. After she went out Bill, in an irritable mood, got up and bolted the door behind her, hoping by that means to prevent further disturbances. He was almost dropping off to sleep when the old hag came again, pushed, and then began knocking at the door. She made far more noise this way, so Bill got up again to let her in. She fiddled around so long this time that Bill gave up waiting for her, climbed back on the kang and tried to find a softer spot that wouldn't hurt the bruises he was getting on his hips. We were both black and blue in odd places after two or three nights of kang riding.

The hag left eventually, and Bill was too tired to get up to refasten the door. At last sleep came, and then almost at once there were four men in the room ; and it was not a dream either. They were picking up our baggage and dropping them in their baskets. They were our carriers. Bill called to them in some excitement :

" Hey !   What's that for ? "

" You've got to be ready to run !   The Jap devils may come here any time ", they replied in loud cheery voices.   Apparent it was that they had not the least sympathy with our jumpy nerves. We had given the villagers plenty of alarm earlier in the night ; perhaps they were getting one back on us.   Still, we received no orders to get up, so we held on to the packs we were using for pillows, and continued even more desperately in our efforts to relax. But we were anything but bright and breezy in the morning when breakfast was announced by Ho who seemed as fresh and happy as if he were out for a pleasant picnic.

To avoid publicity we had to stay in the courtyard all morning. There was a light fall of snow.   At eleven we set off as inconspicuously as possible in broad daylight.   The fresh moisture in the air, the enchanting scenery in that little glen decorated with silver-barked poplar trees, and the relief at being able to walk in daytime instead of at night, all helped to soothe our jagged nerves. We felt more like sleep than we had done all through the night. We walked in a half-awake state through lovely country, and seemed to recapture for a brief moment that early childhood's romantic feeling of being lost in fairyland.

Shortly after midday we were welcomed at the next village, by the village chairman.   His home was clean and well appointed, and we reclined upon his spacious kang in marvellous comfort while tea was served with all the courteous formalities known only to the Chinese.   The family members stood respectfully around the room listening to Ho's account of our journey up to date.

After one of those moments when one practically dozes off to sleep, we glanced up to see a group of new faces looking at us ; and a few moments later, still more.   At length the room was simply packed tight with faces all gazing open-mouthed upon us in quiet concentration.   At the back of the crowd little children had been helped up by their parents on to the tops of cupboards and chests to see overhead.   Suddenly a little peep-hole appeared in the paper windows beside us, and a dark brown eye ;   then another peep-hole and another dark brown eye ;   and another.   We made one ourselves with the moistened tip of a forefinger and looked outside ;   the whole courtyard was thronged with youngsters who could not possibly squeeze inside.

Our imitating them in the peep-hole business had started them off in merry peels of laughter.   But we were too tired to do any-thing more to entertain them.   At first Ho had tried to keep them out, but we assured him we did not mind in the least being looked at if it afforded them all amusement.   This relieved Ho immensely.

" It is really impossible to keep them away without being exceedingly impolite ; they have never seen a Westerner before ", he explained.

As we took our leave, the whole village was out to bid us good-bye ; the children ran in excited clusters in front of us, stood on the banks of the path to watch us pass, then ran ahead again to line up for another look.   It was a hilarious send-off, with no attempt at secrecy.

The snow had ceased, and we climbed over a hill and down into another valley of very different aspect.   It was much deeper, huge boulders, no water, no trees.   We clambered down through this barren scenery and before long came to a widening of the valley in the centre of which stood a good-sized village in utter ruin.   Every cottage had been gutted by fire, most of the walls razed to the ground by shelling.   Not a single inhabitant remained. This was our second sample of Japanese methods of pacification.

A few miles farther down we came upon another, still larger burnt-out village.   But here, all round the hill-sides overlooking the ruins, were Chinese guerrilla troops on manœuvre ; and there were one or two cottage rooms still with roofs intact.   There seemed to be at least one peasant family in residence, and other broken-down rooms had been taken over by the soldiers as a temporary field headquarters.

Our guide Ho at once made contact with the company's captain —Chang Wen, and we were assigned a room in fair repair for the night.   There was not much paper left in the windows, the cooking cauldron was missing and the fire-place was a wreck.   However, the kang was in good enough condition and the roof was sound ; we were better off than most of the soldiers.

While the army scoured the village for a spare cauldron, Lindsay and Bill built up the fire-place with stones and clay from the broken-down walls outside, and collected straw and brushwood for the fire.   In about an hour we had boiling water in a cracked cauldron and a roomful of smoke.   Pretty soon we were boiling some rice our carriers had brought for us from the temple where Ho had picked us up.   A meal fit for a king ; plain boiled rice and, from among the things we had brought out from Peiping, a tin of Japanese sardines.

The bitter cold was increasing, so we patched up the windows and let the fire burn through the kang-draught to try to get more warmth with less smoke, but there must have been something wrong with the chimney. While we were battling with the smoke in our eyes, the soldiers of the company began to pay us courtesy calls. They came in groups of four and five, some groups just standing still for a few minutes staring at us without a word, others passing the time of day with proper formality, several entered into a reasonably interesting conversation about our journey and the Pacific war. The most astonishing thing about them all, to us, was their mild politeness ; it was such a contrast to the rough and brutal outlook of the classical Chinese soldier who had been such an unpleasant element in the pre-war Peiping scene.

Next morning four soldiers came marching into our room and placed a box on the kang, without uttering so much as a word, and disappeared in haste. In a moment Lindsay had recognised the box, it contained a portable radio receiver he had made in Yenching and had sent out to the guerrillas the previous summer. Here it must have been hiding in the mountains ever since, a major Japanese campaign raging around it. In great jubilation we pulled the antenna out of the box, strung it through the window, tied half a brick on the end and slung it up into a date tree, turned on the switch, adjusted an I.F. transformer, and there she was ! We were listening to the B.B.C., London.

That afternoon we listened to the news bulletin. We learnt only that Italy and Germany had declared war on America, and inferred that Japan had already done the same. We had to listen to several bulletins before we could reconstruct the recent course of history, but it was immediately obvious that the new war in the Pacific was the real thing, and that we had dashed for freedom on no mere wild goose chase.

We supped on boiled rice and corned beef. But the B.B.C. announcer's polished cadences reminded us that civilisation continued just around the dial. We could almost see his immaculate suit of clothes, and smell the good strong coffee he must have had for breakfast. To save the dry batteries, we indulged only in news broadcasts ; any more would have made us home sick anyhow. When Captain Chang Wen called with some of his men that evening to hear what news we had picked up, we were still optimistic about Hongkong.

HIDING IN A PEASANT'S HUT

That night Ho came with two items of information. First, that the Japanese had come out with search parties so that our continued journey was unsafe ; secondly, he had arranged for a safe hiding place where we could wait until a proper convoy could be sent to bring us to the Ping Hsi subdivisional headquarters, where all guerrilla activity in the western mountains is organised.

In the gathering darkness we left the village and the main valley, started on a narrow trail up a long winding tributary. Across small terraces of corn stubble, with date shrubs and walnut trees growing in wild confusion, we climbed steadily for over an hour, and came at last to a tiny hut. Inside this hut, except for a passage of two feet wide along one side, there was nothing but a kang, big enough for about five short people. When we tried to lie on it our legs dangled over the edge ; if we had tried to lie with our heads on the outer edge to use the wooden beam as a pillow in the way the Chinese peasant does, we would have looked like a shipwrecked crew trying to be seasick.

All our baggage—including Lindsay's radio cases—was thrown on the kang, and the four of us crowded round the edge, sitting or half lying over the baggage. Ho disappeared and there seemed no one in residence. It was pitch dark.

After about half an hour Ho came back with a farmer, and from their conversation it appeared that this had been intended as our hide-out, but Ho was conscious of having seriously under-estimated our aggregate recumbent area and was anxious to improve matters for the party. Meanwhile another peasant brought us in a kettle of " kai hsueh " and poured it out into some greasy rice-bowls. " Kai hsueh " is boiling water, mixed with the flavour of whatever had been cooked in the cauldron for the peasant's previous meal.

Thus refreshed, and a plan of action decided upon by our guide, we climbed for another half hour, the last steps being up a slope so steep that we could hardly make it, in the blackness of the night we literally lost grip of the ground and slithered back upon the carriers. At last, breathless, we arrived at another peasant's hut, and were ushered inside without further ceremony.

PLATE II

[*Photo by Michael Lindsay*

The heroic Kong family who, at the risk of their own lives, sheltered us for two weeks from Japanese search parties. They are here seen standing on the narrow footpath outside their mountain hut, December 26, 1941.

This room seemed much more spacious. It was at least nine feet by twelve, and the passage at the head of the kang about three feet in width, with some chests of grain occupying still more space around the door. That was all we noticed about the room that night. As we began to climb on the kang to go to sleep, the whole place suddenly became alive with small roaches. They swarmed up the walls, and the straw matting that covered the kang's clay brick surface was alive with the creatures. Ho encouraged us with the assertion that they would not bite. We started swatting them, but it made no impression; there were too many of them.

H. : "I'm very sorry, but there's no other place!"

Farmer : "They are really quite all right; they won't bite!"

L. : "We'll inflate our rubber mattresses; maybe that'll keep them off!"

B. : "Fugitives can hardly be choosers; we shall have to make the best of it, that's all!"

Claire : "I'm sorry, I just can't lie down on the things!"

B. : "Oh! Come on! They can't do you any harm!"

Claire : "No! You go ahead if you want to, I'll just stand up here; I couldn't sleep there!"

The Lindsays were practically asleep before Claire finally gave in. But we were disturbed once during the night; one of them had crawled down Mrs. Lindsay's ear. But they didn't bite. We slept with them for two weeks, and there was nothing on the kang that could bite—perhaps the roaches were good friends after all.

Getting up in the morning consisted merely in putting on our shoes and adjusting our collars. We slung the antenna out across the little glen and listened to the news from Australia; the Germans were retreating from Moscow, and Hongkong was stabilised; co-operation between China and Britain in the defence of Hong-kong was making history!

In the daylight the room seemed larger than it had at night. Coming in through the door, which was made from kaoliang canes, the kang stood at the right, a good nine feet by six, filling that end of the room. The passage directly ahead of one had ample width to allow two people to pass each other; at the back of the room at the end of this passage was the cauldron and stove, the draught from which passed under the kang before going through the chimney. Against the wall on the left of the passage was a large grain chest, in the wall above it a small latticed window, on the window sill an old oil jar and a teapot. A little oil lamp hung from the wall near the window. Above the cauldron was a hanging basket to hold all the simple gadgets for cooking—wooden spoons, an iron scraper for cleaning the cauldron, a wire sifter, and chopsticks made of rough twigs from which the bark had been peeled. Front wall of the room on the right hand as one entered the door, was all paper latticed window coming down to the surface of the kang. Overhead was suspended a couple of heavy wooden planks roped up to the beams of the roof, a large basket containing some old clothing, and stuck between the rafters was an old umbrella and a dilapidated straw hat.

Everything was grimy with smoke and dust. When we came to make some hot water for a wash, and also to drink, we had to clean the cauldron—sweep out the scrambling cockroaches; they kept dropping in in spite of the wooden lid. Before we could drink the boiled water, we had first to sift the insects out with the wire sifter. The " kai hsueh " had a characteristic taste of straw which may or may not have been beetle.

Coming out into the crisp morning air we discovered that the little footpath along which we had come the previous night, passed right along by the front of our hut, and overlooked a narrow glen in front of us; the ground dropped sheer away from the side of the path which was hedged by a rough, date-twig eyebrow. A few yards further along the path was a tiny hut with a straw roof; and there was the family who had vacated the room we were now occupying.

They were simple peasants, Mr. and Mrs. Kong and their two children, aged two and five. Their real home was down in the village we had just left; they had escaped up here to their walnut grove when the Japanese burned their home; now they had vacated their " summer cottage " for us, and gone to live in their wigwam which was really meant for a donkey and two pigs. They had the two pigs in with them. The donkey had gone to live next door, another hut wherein dwelt an old couple and their young daughter, refugees from the same village. By the front door of this hut a terrace crossed to the other side of the gully, and over there was a tiny spring with delightfully fresh drinking water bubbling into a cleft in the rock.

We were so high up among the sheer mountain peaks that the sun shone into the glen only a few hours each day. A lonely eyrie, fascinatingly aloof; in and out among the twigs enchanting little tomtits flitted, daintily acrobatic.

The warm-hearted Kong family made us really welcome. They gave us free access to the family supplies of brushwood fuel for the fire, which father Kong had to replenish daily, scouring the mountain side. And when we had trouble lighting the fire, mother Kong would come in and help. The first evening a local scout came in with Ho to warn us that the search column of Japanese were operating rather near, so that all our baggage must be well-packed ready for instant removal to hiding places in the glen. Father Kong would be responsible for carrying our things to safety while the guide would conduct us to a place of safety should an emergency actually arise. At night we were to leave nothing out, and sleep fully dressed.

We remained in this state of tension for a whole week, although Lindsay insisted upon keeping the radio receiver handy for the daily news, packing it up only for the night. Then on December 20th we heard the crack of a revolver shot down the valley. The guide was not with us, so Kong dashed off to the shoulder of the mountain to pick up information from a neighbour according to some routine arrangement. In ten minutes he was back to tell us it was a false alarm.

But next day, shortly before noon, the guide himself turned up in some excitement; the Japanese were headed in our direction, and we must decamp immediately. We left all our stuff with Kong, and tore up the mountain.

The footpath climbed steeply from terrace to terrace, disappeared into nothingness at the base of the last escarpment. It was a hectic scramble up the last steep slope over the pass. On the other side the country was more open, like a high plateau; there seemed no place to hide and we felt far less safe than in Kong's little glen.

We wandered down the gentle gradient to a lonely little cottage that stood out on the barren plateau like a beacon. The peasants here seemed rather scared of us, and we sat just inside the door, gazing out at their tiny threshing floor and listening apprehensively to intermittent firing of machine-guns somewhere off down the slope.

Late in the afternoon we sneaked back again—just to see if there was anything left. If the Japanese had actually come up as far as Kong's place, and if they had found the slightest evidence that the Kong's had been succouring army men or assisting refugees, the place would have been burnt to the ground. We began to realise what it meant to the Kong family to have us on their hands.

As we reached the ridge, the guide bade us pause while he went on ahead to make sure the enemy were not in ambush awaiting our return. But we were too impatient to get back home— yes ! it was already home to us, that wretched little hovel ; home, because there dwelt therein a spirit mightier than all the evil demons of Japan. We followed slowly down in a straggling line, the ladies bringing up the rear. As we made the last bend, there were the little huts just as we had left them, snug under the terrace ; the two pigs were nuzzling in the rubbish heap, and the children were playing on the steps of the hut. The Japanese had not come up the valley so far.

Making an early supper we retired to sleep as soon as it was dark, expecting more emergency trouble on the morrow. Instead of the Japanese, we had forty Chinese army boys and Captain Chang Wen with us for a meal ; they were keeping out of the direct path of the enemy, following his flanks. When they left in the evening, they entrusted a couple of ponies and a hostler to the good offices of the other family.

The hostler slept with the family on their kang, and the Kongs told us that there was no objection to this arrangement except that the hostler was dirty—he had lice. We looked at those poor grimy little children and wondered whether the hostler was the only victim.

On Christmas Eve we had a call from Comrade An who had signed that first written welcome we had received from the guerrillas. We were not a little surprised to find that Comrade An was a girl, an officer in the Women's Mass Association ; she brought us good news ; the enemy had passed out of range and in a day or two we should be able to continue our journey.

The two weeks we spent at the Kongs' eyrie were perhaps the most memorable period of our lives.

On our third day there the local county magistrate had paid us a visit, and had followed up his visit with gifts : an army rice-

bowl apiece and a pair of chopsticks each ; a cabbage or a few
potatoes and turnips every three or four days from an enemy-
patrolled village several miles away. Besides these, we were able
to buy walnuts from Mr. Kong, who, in peace-time, used to depend
upon the sale of his nuts in Peiping. By direct route, that city was
within an easy day's journey from this place. Then Kong kept
us informed of the meat situation ; whenever his friends were
slaughtering an animal we would get first choice of the best cut.
We were able in this way to buy a pig's liver one week and a leg
of mountain goat the other week. And of course we had with
us a few cans of beef or fish, a little cocoa and some sugar and dried
fruit from Peiping.

At the time we felt the diet was inadequate, and there was no
variety in possible ways of cooking with only the cauldron to
work with. But looking back upon it, the list on our menu
sounds epicurean compared with the dietary rigours through which
we later had to pass.

Then in the matter of personal toilet facilities the two weeks
were even more memorable. The Kong family had one small
and badly dented brass wash-basin which they let us share with
them when we wanted to wash our hands or faces. Other than
this our toilet activities were completely in suspense. Both men
had forgotten their razors, and that simplified matters even further.
We had one comb between the four of us.

There were a great many other things we had forgotten, and
we had plenty of time in which to remember them. Objectively
the things we had remembered to bring were probably just as
surprising, but at the time we were more impressed by the things
we had not brought. We had no shaving outfit, no mirror, no
medical supplies. We had brought the current five-year diary,
1939-44, but had left behind the two previous volumes covering
the period from 1929 to 1939. Our new graphlex camera was
still sitting on Bill's desk in the study.

The loss that distressed Bill most of all was his collection of
theoretical research notes. On Saturday, December 6th, Bill had
collected the more important notes together in a neat set of three
folders, one for statistical mechanics, one for relativity, and one
for his manuscript text on theoretical physics. In each set there
were several items almost ready for publication, and as a whole
they represented four years' study and research. Bill was planning

to bring them to the house, pack them into the haversack ready for the emergency. But on the Saturday he had too many other things to carry and left the notes on his office desk at the laboratories ; and on Monday morning it had been too late.

Before we left the Kongs' shelter we had made from memory a complete inventory of everything we had left behind : a whole household in excellent running condition with over ten years' accumulation of the most attractive furnishings and equipment, linen, bedding, crockery, silver, cutlery, clothes, embroidery, Chinese works of art, and our personal library. And here were these Kongs with absolutely nothing, happy to share their all with us. They shamed us out of regrets for what was gone. To indulge in self-pity in the face of these people's heroic fortitude would have been impossible ; we were free, was not that sufficient ? After we had come through the dangers and hardships of the journey we should be back again in civilisation, we would accumulate again more up-to-date impedimenta, but these people would still be happy with their poverty, their interminable struggle. Their generosity humiliated us.

But the most memorable part of our two weeks was Christmas. We had already heard from Miss An that the Japanese search party no longer threatened us, so that we were eagerly anticipating a resumption of our journey. Then down in the gully right opposite our door Mr. Kong slaughtered one of his two pigs, and gave us the choice of a cut for our Christmas party. For their own use they cleaned and cooked the pig's head on the fire in our room and this took most of the afternoon of Christmas Eve.

Meanwhile a Comrade Lee called upon us, a secret agent just out from Peiping on his way to the Ping Hsi headquarters. He had been detailed to guide us on the next leg of our journey, and while the pig's head was stewing in our cauldron, he told us what had happened in Peiping after our escape.

Christmas Eve ! When the day's work was done, the local menfolk came into our room with their pipes and a pot of mountain tea. There were five of them : Kong himself, a younger brother and an uncle from down the valley, another relative who had come to help Kong slaughter and clean the pig, and another friend from over the mountain. Sitting or squatting on the bed, all nine of us spent a light-hearted evening singing Christmas carols and patriotic Chinese songs.

During Christmas Day the Kong family cooked all their meals on our fire, because the fire in their own room was busy with the remains of the porker. On top of that was our own cooking. The room reeked with a rich mixture of smells ; pork liver gravy, wood smoke and rank tobacco. And it began to snow outside, hoar frost forming on hedge and cottage thatch. Another grand community bedtime sing-song with cups of cocoa all round ; it was a perfect old-fashioned Christmas party.

JAPANESE BLOCKADE ZONE

Early on the morning of Boxing Day came a message to tell us that we should be moving on that afternoon. The Kong family joined us in a farewell breakfast of boiled pork, potatoes and rice. After breakfast the county magistrate came to say good-bye and to receive our heartfelt thanks for his hospitality and that of the people of his district. Lindsay took some pictures, one of which —the heroic Kong family—faces page 32.

Before four in the afternoon we were off down the little glen the way we had come up two weeks before. In addition to the four "passengers" our caravan now included ten carriers and two donkeys. During the two weeks a large quantity of stuff had been collected from hide-outs in the hills around, stuff that had been awaiting a suitable convoy to headquarters after having been smuggled out from Peiping during the previous five or six months. The convoy of troops was waiting for us at the burnt-out village below, and under Captain Chang Wen whom we had met when we had first arrived. With the captain was his wife, a regular soldier in his company ; they had been through the whole campaign together.

In the gathering darkness we filed out of the burnt village, about half the company in front, passengers and freight in the middle, the rest of the company following, all in single file along the narrow mountain trail.

By about half-past seven we had climbed to the top of a pass and after fifteen minutes' rough scrambling down the other side, which was quite trackless, we were collected together and warned that in about half an hour's march we should be within sight of a Japanese fort, and then for another half hour we should still be within range and must therefore be ready for any emergency. No coughing, no smoking, no talking, and while in sight of the fort, no noise of footsteps—we must be like ghosts in the pale moonlight.

Shortly after eight we came out on to a wide sandy terrace, and as we tiptoed across this exposed area we could see the fortress dark against the hillside not more than five hundred yards away. Stretched out in a long line in full view of the fortress's embattlements, we felt like perfect targets for a wakeful machine-gunner. In a few breathless moments we were jumping down a steep slope off the flat and out of sight into a large dried-up river bed. From the stars we could see we were going due north as we tramped at a good pace over the loose shingle up this river. It was very heavy going for two solid hours, before we turned unexpectedly up a side trail, passed under a surprising old pailou like the monumental gateways of Peiping main streets, negotiated several more corners around clusters of ancient conifer trees, and marched right into the walls of a great castle-fortress, built in massive stone.

This castle, we were told, was Chen Pin Ch'eng, literally Protect Regime City; it had evidently been a frontier outpost in former times. It was about a quarter of a mile square, with a huge gateway in each of its four side walls, and a great four-faced archway at the centre where the traversing highways crossed. Instead of government troops, there were peasants living in the barracks now; it had become a " city " by nature as by name.

Unfortunately we were in no mood for appreciating the place as an historic relic. We had made at least fifteen miles, all hard slogging in the darkness. We were freezing cold, and while the convoy was looking for suitable quarters for the rest of the night, we stood for a full half hour helplessly shivering in the street, too exhausted to keep warm.

At about midnight there was a meal of " lao-bing " and boiled water. Lao-bing are flat pancakes, more strictly, fried dough made from wheat flour and water; for variety they are sometimes made of kaoliang flour; and the wealthy folk can even add some chives to flavour them. Ours were just wheat flour dough fried to a nice pale brown, a bit soggy in the middle, but very, very satisfying. So satisfying that we were able to fall asleep on the cold, hard kang.

Aroused before dawn in the morning, we discovered to our dismay that our limbs were paralysed with cramp. As we climbed down off the kang we had to lean heavily against the walls to avoid tumbling over, and as we stepped down the door-step out of the hut, the agony was excruciating.

How could we possibly resume the march? Yet almost miraculously, during the breakfast half-hour—plain boiled flour noodles and hot water—our legs limbered up perfectly, and we were able to get on the march with the convoy at seven.

It was a new convoy. Captain Chang Wen and his company were to leave us, to continue north up the long, dry river bed, detailed for guerrilla activity in the so-called Ping Pei area north of Peiping. The new convoy was to take us across the Yung Ting River, on the other side of which there was another local unit awaiting us. We marvelled at the secrecy and efficiency of all these arrangements.

Little guessing that we should meet again we bade good-bye to Captain Chang and his brave spouse, and set out in high fettle for the peaks. The fortress city was surrounded by the most amazing scenery. Towering above our heads, huge precipitous peaks were catching the rays of the rising sun, gleaming green and gold through the crisp, clear morning air.

Up among these golden peaks climbed the winding trail. An hour and a half of exceedingly stiff climbing brought us to a pass between two giant tops; in spite of our exertion and the brilliant sunshine, it was icy cold. Little icicles had formed all over Bill's beard, and Lindsay, who had developed a slight head cold, had a three-inch icicle hanging from one nostril; and the pass was not the top. Instead of going down, we skirted along the precipitous slopes of the mountains for miles, and again climbed up on to a great plateau. It was half-past ten before we reached the highest point of the journey, and here, probably three thousand feet above the castle-fortress, we were actually looking down upon the golden peaks that had towered over us earlier that morning.

And in the midst of all that wilderness, in a woodman's tiny cottage, we were able to rest and get something to eat.

In the afternoon we started to drop down off the plateau; the initial descent as usual being a hectic scramble over trackless slopes almost too steep to keep a foothold. How the carriers were able to keep up with the convoy with their heavy loads was a miracle; but there was worse to follow.

We had just come down on to a valley bottom and picked up a goat track when the entire armed convoy, with the exception of a couple of advance guards ahead of us, veered off to the right along a track which skirted the sides of the mountain. We were told to follow the guide down and that the army would join us later. No explanation was offered, or if it was, it was lost in the increasing distance across which the messages were being shouted. In less time than it took to think, the whole company had vanished round the corner, and very soon it became quite obvious that the guide —our Comrade Lee—did not really know this part of the country much better than we did. He had been relying on the excellent intelligence service of the convoy.

For a while there was really only one way down, but shortly the valley divided ; to the left appeared the best path down, but the company had gone to the right, and if they were to rejoin us further on, it was obvious that we should have to turn down to the right here. This we did, and soon found ourselves completely lost. We were in a great ravine the sides of which hung over ominously ; in its bottom a tremendous earthquake had flung at precarious angles huge blocks of unweathered rocks over which we had perforce to scramble.

We four passengers were by this time well ahead of the carriers, and even of the two armed guards and the guide. The baggage men were trailed out in a groaning line behind us as far as we could see towards the top end of the ravine, cursing audibly. We had come to a full stop ; there was a sheer drop in front of us of some fifteen feet ; and while we could probably negotiate it, the baggage men obviously could not. Then an excited cry came echoing down the canyon :

" Come back ! Wrong way ! Japanese fort down there ! "

It took us a gruelling half-hour to regain the point at which we had gone wrong, and there was the convoy captain laughing at us. He explained that his men had never intended to join us ahead, but that after collecting some grain from an isolated farm-house they were coming back to catch us up, which they had now done, only just in time to see the last carrier stumbling over the rocks out of sight on the way down to the enemy's stronghold ! He seemed to think it was all a huge joke ; but our sense of humour was not equal to the occasion ; after that thin noodle breakfast we were not feeling equal to so much waste of energy.

The remainder of the afternoon we were winding down another great ravine with enchanting scenery at every turn ; it gradually widened out into a grand canyon which would eventually have taken us down to the main Yung Ting River, the one that runs under Marco Polo Bridge. Before reaching this main valley, we veered off to the left along a well-worn trail that skirted the vertical sides of the canyon in hair raising unconcern. This trail soon brought us out on to more or less open country showing signs of cultivation, and by four p.m. we had arrived, after covering at least seventeen strenuous miles, at a small hamlet named after the Buddha.

This was our resting place for the night. After an excellent meal of cold pork liver and boiled rice, materials we had brought with us from the Kongs' place, we retired early in the expectation that we should be making the river crossing before dawn on the morrow.

There was a Japanese patrol route along the main valley and it was better to cross before daylight. To our inquisitive questions about how we should cross, they replied mysteriously : " Yu fah-tse ! " " There is a method ! " But there was no bridge, and there were no boats, the river was too deep to ford ; it was frozen, but not solid enough to walk over.

When we were roused about four next morning there was the same pantomime as on the morning before. Our legs were again so stiff with cold that it took about an hour for them to thaw out. But by five-thirty we were ready for the trail again, with a meal inside of us. But the carriers were not ready. During the previous day's climbing several of them had injured their feet. A search party was sent out for fresh carriers, but the sparse population made it an unpromising hunting ground. It was half-past seven before we eventually set out, and broad daylight by the time we dropped down into the bed of the Yung Ting River.

Jumping down the rocks on to the stretch of sand by the river's edge we emerged upon an unforgettable scene. Behind, we seemed to have come out of a solid precipitous wall that stretched from one bend in the river to the next. On the opposite bank were more gentle slopes and a great jumble of boulders abutting the mountains farther west. Up on these slopes little knots of our convoy were already collecting at look-out posts watching for the possible approach of an enemy patrol.

Upstream to the right the river came from round a corner through a deep gorge, and just at the foot of these cliffs we espied a tiny coracle at the water's edge, where the ledge of ice fused off. Three soldiers were getting into it, and a peasant punted it across to the other side. So that was how we were to do it ! The basket—for that was all the coracle was—was kept secretly by a farmer up on the plateau, brought out only at night, or when an army convoy could guarantee its safety. This patrol route was supposed to be one of the Japanese blockade lines preventing the movement of supplies and personnel in the guerrilla areas.

As we were lining up for our turn one of the soldiers drew our attention to a column of smoke that had started rising to the sky from a point somewhere down stream :

" That ", he said, " must be the Japanese burning down a hamlet ; it might be my own home ! This is their regular patrol route ; we had better be quick ! "

They got us across fairly rapidly, but we had to wait on the other side, just out of sight of the river, for the whole convoy to get across and reassemble. It was a tantalisingly slow business at the time, but thinking back we can now realise that that little basket, five feet square had had to make something like twenty-five crossings each way, a peasant on either bank with a boat-hook, and one in the basket with a punting pole. The stream was running with full force, and there was a heavy ice-flow ; they carried three passengers, and did each double crossing at an average of three or four minutes, which, to say the least, was no mean acrobatic performance.

The convoy had a couple of transport mules, and these waded through the river under their own power after being encouraged in the usual way with plenty of verbal instructions from both banks. But the two donkeys that they had brought along in case either of the lady passengers got too tired, refused to take the icy plunge, and were left behind.

A Narrow Escape

It was almost ten before we got started. Almost as soon as we had climbed well out of sight of the main river, our vanguard started shouting at the tops of their voices :

" Women shih paluchun puyao pao ! "

" We are Eighth Route Army, don't run away ! "

And in a moment we turned a corner and came within sight of a small hamlet set on an outcropping shelf of rock. The peasants were already dashing up the sides of the mountain, and only after repeated assurances were they dissuaded from flight.

When we finally climbed up on to their terrace the whole family clan were out to meet us. The housewife had been surprised in the middle of cooking their morning meal: "Japanese raiders approaching!" and in her excitement had spilled the gruel all over her front as her daughter had thrown a pail of water on the fire. They had had no breakfast, and we could hope for no drinking water. The Japanese were there almost daily, and they naturally had thought we were the same party. We felt terrible at having caused them unnecessary fright, but there was nothing we could do but apologise and hurry on.

The climb became still steeper; there was a small brook up whose bed we were working. It was frozen solid, and nearing the top of the climb the footpath crossed and recrossed the ice, passing perilously near the tops of slippery, frozen water-falls. On one particularly bad crossing we held hands to make a human chain. As well we did, for at this one Claire stumbled and fell, her legs dangling helplessly over the icy edge, hundreds of feet sheer chute below.

By about midday we reached the top, came upon a fine old temple farmstead built of stone, commanding a tremendous view of the surrounding country. We piled into the courtyard, the convoy clamouring for hot water to drink. In about fifteen minutes we were served with boiling fluid. We were just about to help ourselves to a second cup when an alarm was raised:

"Better leave at once. The Japanese came here yesterday at about this time, and we expect them to come again; any sign of your presence here will be made an excuse for additional atrocities by the enemy!"

We knew this was no false alarm; had we not already seen that ominous column of smoke as we crossed the river? So we did not try to drink the second cup, thirsty though we still were, but hurried off at once over the shoulder of the mountain and round across the top of another valley farther north. In less than an hour we had come down into a wide valley, climbed over another ridge and arrived at a small village hamlet teeming with fresh troops. We had completed the scheduled day's march, logging only seven miles, but crossed the river and climbed about 2000 feet into the bargain.

As we had come within sight we had seen the men scattered all over the hillside, and when they had seen our column approaching they had begun streaming back to their base. They had three machine-guns with them, and were a remarkably business-like unit. Introductions completed, feet, hands and faces washed in warm water, we were just relaxing before supper when the company was surprised by the precipitate arrival of a breathless messenger.

Just ten minutes after we had had that last drink of hot water a party of Japanese had come upon the temple, had surprised a meeting of peasants, arrested a dozen and shot one man. Our guide Lee was very much shaken up by the narrowness of our escape, although the captain of the escort seemed sorry to miss a chance for a scrap. The guide was mopping his brow and muttering to himself for a good half hour after ; he was in no mood to risk a fight on this trip. And the alarm meant that our manager had to spend all night looking for fresh carriers for the morrow.

The next day was comparatively easy going with glorious views over countless ranges of mountains losing themselves to sight in a magnificent series of shades of blue. At one place we were on a level trail winding around the top of the world, with a hawk's-eye view of ominous depths below.

" Down there ", said the guide, " so far below us that you can't see them, are the Japanese forts. From here you could almost throw a hand grenade on to them."

In another section of the day's march we were tramping along a peaceful glade where flocks of sheep and goats were grazing. And again we scrambled over sandstone ridges in deep-worn footpaths twisting among stumpy scrub oaks and tall silver-barked poplar trees.

It was here that Claire was persuaded to try riding a donkey. Much against her inclinations she mounted, protesting meanwhile at the insecurity of her position. Presently the path took a sudden turn and dipped to a lower level. The donkey, following the usual laws of its own motion, suddenly lowered its head, crouched low on its forelegs to take the gradient, the rear end rising like an ocean breaker and pitching Claire headlong over the creature's neck, head first into the arms of the startled donkey-man.

The donkey may be sure-footed, but it is the animal's back you have to sit on. One can be quite sure the donkey will come to no harm no matter how dangerous the trail, but that is no guarantee that in order to save its own skin it will not at a pinch, jettison the rider.

We were actually on the march that day for a solid seven hours without more than a five-minute rest at midday, and covered more than twenty miles. Breakfast had been nothing more than boiled noodles and hot water. A half-hour before the end of the march Bill collapsed from fatigue : it was "hungry knock". He was saved by nibbling two small pieces of chocolate that we still had left from the meagre supply we had brought out from Peiping.

Having painfully learnt the lesson that one has to eat a great deal more noddles than one's unaccustomed taste would suggest, we dragged ourselves over the last hill and arrived dead to the world at our destination. Here there was a semi-permanent army garrison, with a political director who could speak a little English. He told us that there was only one more blockade point to pass and that the "Ping Hsi" headquarters was just two days' march away.

Next morning there was some excitement among the team of village carriers : the wife of one of them tried to keep him from going with us, she felt it was too dangerous, specially as the men would have to find their way back home next night without armed escort ; and the Japanese were out every day. We were just assembling for departure when the officers called a halt. A wireless message was coming in from the headquarters about our journey, and we must wait for it to be decoded. Japanese movements were reported across our path, we had to double the strength of our escort, and proceed with due caution. Scouts were sent out ahead, and we waited until eleven-thirty until one of them returned with the all clear message, before starting.

Since it was going to be a long march, we encamped at one p.m. and had a light meal. The next village, which we were expecting to pass after dark, was controlled by a Japanese block-house. A steady afternoon's climb brought us out of the valley, which had been surprisingly well wooded, up again into barren mountainous country. Just before sunset we reached the pass over the other side of which was the enemy strong point. And by seven-thirty we had come within the danger zone of the garrisoned village.

Our guide repeated all the warnings as to silence that we had followed on the previous occasions, and added that we must keep at least two strides apart in single file to avoid presenting a solid target to a machine-gun. The greatest danger was of our arousing the village dogs ; if any dog barked there would be a chorus in the village that would disturb the Japanese in their slumbers, cause them to dash hysterically for their machine-guns.

As we approached the village we could just make out the form of the block-house on the opposite side of the little glen. Our path entered the outskirts of the village, climbed up behind it and continued in full view of the block-house over the roof-tops. There was a brilliant moon.

At the approaches to the village our escort mounted their machine-guns, trained them directly on the block-house, ready to draw the enemy's fire. Otherwise our safety depended upon keeping a ghostly silence.

The steep slope that took us up behind the village was of loose shingle, deliberately prepared that way to make silent progress almost impossible. One of the carriers, no doubt tired with his heavy load, slipped on the slope. A sprinkling of stones slithered with a rattle down the path. From the village came up to us a muffled bark : " WOOF ! " But it stopped short in the middle.

We were posed in a long line across the back of the village in full view of the enemy. Hearts stood still for a long moment. Then the ghostly procession continued in serene silence.

At the top of the next pass the track had been destroyed and we made a perilous circuit in the misleading moonlight of a huge ragged crater torn from the mountain's face. A land mine had been placed there for the benefit of such parties as ours. The peasants had seen it, had detonated it a few hours previously, and reported to the Japanese its success in destroying a fictitious guerrilla unit.

A half-hour later we rested for a few moments, and the guide explained what they had done to prevent the dog-barking hazard. The escort had sent on ahead a liaison officer to contact with the underground patriotic movement in the village and warned them to keep their dogs indoors that night, and to throttle any animal that got restless as the guerrilla unit passed by. Perfect co-operation between the peasants and the army had made all the difference between safe convoy for us, and an ugly death at the hands of the Japanese.

To get out of this danger zone we had another stiff climb, and by midnight we had arrived at the village originally chosen for our night's sleep. It was pitch dark by now, but we were warned

PLATE III

This is how we crossed the Yung Ting River—in a basket.

against using the least glimmer of light ; it was here that the Japanese had raided at dawn that very morning. The baggage had to continue while we ourselves remained for a meal of steamed oatmeal noodles and hot water served at two in the morning.

The village had been badly burned, and the few villagers who had returned during the day were still badly shaken up. We were allowed a few hours' rest so long as there was no immediate news of Japanese returning. But at five in the morning we had to get a move on to be out of range before dawn—which was the enemy's favourite time for surprise raids.

We reached the next village, which was considered safe enough for a semi-permanent Eighth Route Army garrison, in good time for breakfast, the total distance we had come since the previous evening being about seventeen miles. Here we found ourselves in telephone communication with the Ping Hsi headquarters.

Guerrillas and telephones ? It seemed incongruous. Yet there was the machine hanging on the clay-brick wall of the cottage where we were devouring a good breakfast of rice and fried vegetables with bean curd for flavouring. The telephones are all machines captured from the Japanese, the wire is a single line strung up on trees or bits of broken branches stuck in the ground of field or terrace ; the ground serves as return conductor. The system does not make for clarity of reception, but it saves material and increases speed of packing-up in an emergency.

While we were having breakfast the people at H.Q. were told of our arrival and sent back a reply urging us to hurry on : " There are only fifteen miles more, you can get here this evening ready for the New Year celebrations to-morrow ! " We realised that it was New Year's Eve already. But we had been on the go for nearly twenty-four hours with no more than a couple of hours' sleep, and we were frankly not interested in New Year celebrations.

However, after a cup of our cocoa to cap the meal we set out on the journey. The local garrison provided us with mules and ponies, but because we two could not ride, the animals were more ornamental than anything else. Of course we took a "lesson" in riding them, but that did not help to make the journey any easier. We continued arguing with our guide that we would prefer to have the journey split into two stages to give us one good night's sleep in preparation for arriving at the headquarters. We felt that would give us a better stomach to face the celebrations.

But what happened was this : we had been going for little
more than an hour along a well-beaten track in a wide open smooth
river valley, without escort—which was considered no longer
necessary—when there came galloping towards us from ahead a
horseman, surely a messenger from headquarters to welcome us.
He started to wave excitedly to us, and as he drew up who should
he be but Charlie, a graduate of Yenching.

It was a thrilling reunion, and the happy conversation that
followed served to dispel our fatigue, and Charlie was a persuasive young man. We quickly succumbed to his reassurance
that we could easily make the whole journey. He had himself
just come from there since receiving the telephone message during
breakfast. After the " hungry knock " experience, Bill insisted
however, upon first having a snack for lunch before attempting
the one mountain pass that separated us from the headquarters.
At the nearest hamlet we bought persimmons and peanuts and
made some cocoa with water boiled by one of the villagers, enjoyed
a break sitting on a grindstone in the sunshine.

Unfortunately Charlie had under-estimated the difficulty with
which we could make the trip on foot. It was well after dark
when we actually arrived, almost dead beat. The last hour or two
had been hard going on soft sand, which, of course, made a perfect
pony-riding surface ; but try it on foot after two days and a night
of climbing and starving without sleep, and you will understand
how we finally collapsed on the benches in the little village hut where
our welcome feast had been awaiting us for some hours.

The General and his Chief of Staff and other officers came out
to the edge of the ruined village to meet us as we came up out of
the river bed, and we had just about enough energy left to be polite.
In a vague dreamy way we felt we had closed the old year well.

Chapter IV

GUERRILLA BATTLE GROUND

COMMANDER of the Ping Hsi guerrilla area was General Hsiao K'e, a small-statured, wiry young man with deeply penetrating dark brown eyes, small features; his husky voice had a very marked southern accent and an excitedly rapid diction. Only by his personality, zest and energy could we distinguish him from his junior officers; there was no difference between their uniforms, and there were no formalities connected with differences in rank.

Speaking of this lack of rank-distinguishing ornaments among Eighth Route Army uniforms, we heard a good story told by the guerrillas about another of their Western guests. Fatigued with his travels, this gentleman was more than irritated by the persistent curiosity of the soldier boys, the peasants and the children. Held up by bad weather at one point for several days, he insisted that the local unit provide him with a special guard to keep out inquisitive intruders. But such was the camaraderie among the Communists that it was almost impossible for this guard to function properly. The guest's temper mounted to bursting point after several interruptions. An old peasant woman—actually his hostess —tiptoed to the window of his room and peeped through a hole in the paper; he had spotted her; the old woman saw the irate "foreign devil" leap to the floor with an energetic oath, and she beat a hasty retreat as fast as bound feet would carry her.

The next intrusion was an army man who came boldly into his room. The Westerner's knowledge of Chinese was quite limited, and when in a temper, even more limited.

He asked: "Now what do you want?"

Soldier: "Wo lai kan ni!" (I have come to see you!)

"Well get the hell out of here!" exclaimed the gentleman, and pushed the boy backwards through the door.

Next day the same Chinese soldier called again. More sparks flew, but the soldier this time held his ground. Suddenly the Westerner got an uncomfortable idea. He reached for his dictionary and turned to a list of military ranks. Pushing this in front of the soldier he asked:

" What are you ? "

The army boy looked at the Chinese characters on the list, and his finger rested unmistakable at the word for " general ".

Fortunately for us, exhausted though we were, we were not let in for any such embarrassment. Ours was a different kind of trouble. The warmth of General Hsiao's welcome to us seemed to have been partly measured by the number of charcoal braziers brought into the room where the feast was served on New Year's Eve. The feast itself was most astonishing ; it would have been judged good even in a Peiping restaurant ; yet about half-way through the meal we suddenly lost our appetites and failed entirely to do justice to the meal. We put it down to being over-tired, but it must have been the charcoal gas. It was our first experience of these time-honoured toe-warmers. Next morning we had splitting headaches.

Neither of us could take a very appreciative part in the New Year celebrations, at which the four new arrivals were a star turn. Banners were up on the walls of ruined cottages and round the open-air meeting place :

WELCOME TO OUR ANTI-FASCIST FRIENDS
MR. & MRS. B. AND MR. & MRS. L.
DOWN WITH HITLER, MUSSOLINI AND JAPAN !

The personal touch was very affecting ; done in English specially for our benefit, it made us feel proud to represent China's new Allies in the war against Japan.

At the meetings were speeches, more speeches and still more speeches ; it astounded us how these peasant soldiers sat there and drank it all in with apparent enjoyment for hours at a time, sitting either on the clay ground, on rocks or pieces of log, while one after another of their leaders stood up on the improvised stage and harangued eloquently and otherwise in all the dialects under the Chinese sky. At every strategic moment cheer leaders would leap to their feet and shout well-worked-out slogans for the audience to take up and re-echo with clenched fists thrusting in the air.

This was the beginning of a new era of hope for these stricken people ; this New Year was the happiest they had seen for ten years. At last the world democracies were fighting with them against a common foe. There was much hardship to come, but with this new hope, a world-wide, anti-Fascist united front, the final victory at last was sure. As tangible evidence of this new international united front, we came in for more than our fair share of notice in the speeches and the slogans ; we blushed to feel the warmth and enthusiasm those poor boys put into their roaring welcome.

What could we do to help ? It seemed obvious to us that the helpfulness was to be entirely the other way round. But General Hsiao did his best to reassure us in a special personal interview and succeeded at least in convincing us of the breadth of vision of these so-called guerrillas.

Up there in the wilds, cut off from all amenities of modern civilisation, it seemed like a voice from another world to hear the General saying :

" We know well that science is the foundation of modern industrial civilisation, and the hope of future technological progress for the benefit of mankind ; we are therefore more than happy to welcome the first British scientist to visit our areas, see our anti-Fascist work and witness our struggle against the Japanese invaders. We are not only a military organisation ; we pride ourselves also on our educational work, our cultural work among the people of North China behind the enemy's lines, and in our rear base at Yenan."

To us, just such sentiments had begun to degenerate into artificial rationalisations when brought up against the tense situation of actual warfare at our own door-steps ; yet here, among the men in actual combat, fighting a desperate campaign already in its fifth year, these same ideas were still fundamental guiding principles. Perhaps we had not been so far wrong after all ! We felt instinctively at one with our hosts with the certainty that we were entering upon a real and lasting friendship which would endure through any number of divergencies of opinion and differences in manners of life.

Such were our feelings after our talk with General Hsiao, but with some of his junior officers we were not quite so happy. They seemed to think that, like their troops, we needed educating too. On January 2nd we were submitted to a series of formal reports on their political organisation, their secret underground work in Manchuria, Japanese taxation in occupied areas, and so on. The reports were verbal, and in Chinese ; they started early in the afternoon, broke off for about an hour for the afternoon meal, and then continued all evening by the light of a small vegetable oil lamp.

There was more of a similar kind the next day; Bill did not make a good impression as a student of guerrilla affairs. On the fourth day they expected us to go by horseback to visit the communication department some ten miles away, to stay the night there and listen to some more reports and lectures. That is where we went on strike; we let the Lindsays go without us, and stayed at home in the broken-down cottage at General Hsiao's headquarters, and did our best, in two days' quiet rest, to recover some of our exhausted energy.

Appropriately enough it was a Sunday, and the army officers actually let us alone. So after a lazy morning we took a quiet stroll up the river bank until we came to a secluded patch of clean sand, surrounded by steep rocks; here we relaxed, watched the wild ducks playing in the foam and skimming over the large white stretches of ice that half covered the stream; we drank in the healing music of the rippling waters and basked in the beauties of the mountain landscape.

In the midst of our reverie we were surprised by a young peasant emerging upon the sand from some hidden cleft in the cliff behind us, and drawing water from the river; he returned the way he had come and disappeared from view after a brief glance in our direction. It seemed our presence caused him no great surprise; no doubt he had been at the New Year mass meetings.

But a few minutes later, just as we were thinking it was nearly time to go back, an old man's voice hailed us from away up above the cliff. Getting up and turning in that direction, we espied a funny little old chap beckoning us with all his might to come up his way. We were in the mood for the unexpected, and very soon found the hidden trail that the young water-carrier had used. The old fellow did not wait for us to catch him, but nimbly sped up the steep slope every now and then turning about to throw us a friendly smile and encourage our speedier progress.

After about ten minutes' walk we came out upon a little farmstead, with cornfields on the slopes, and a neatly made threshing floor banked with stacks of cornstalks and rushes. The old chap beckoned us to come within, welcoming us as callers to his home. Inside we found the young water-carrier and his wife, they were son and daughter-in-law to our host.

Their dialect was not easy for us to understand, but we got along famously. The old father spent most of his time, he said, around the farm working with his son, while the old mother, who was out at the time, spent her days down at the village selling walnuts to the army boys. The daughter-in-law was ill, and they had hoped we might have medical supplies or at least be able to give some advice ; but there was not the slightest suggestion of mendicity in their attitude ; they were treating us as equals and felt sure that if we had been able to help we should have done so purely out of comradely friendship—which we should ; our regrets at being unable to help were well taken.

After all the usual formalities had been correctly observed, we took our leave, accepting a few walnuts from them as a parting gift ; the old father showed us the best way back to the village. About a week later we saw the young peasant in the village and asked after his wife.

" Oh ! She died a day or two after you called on us ! " he replied. And to our expressions of distress he replied with a grin of unconcern :

" There was nothing we could do about it ! "

We began to realise what a grim life these poor people had been forced into by these years of war and struggle. All the year round they subsist on the same inadequate diet of corn, walnuts and dried turnips ; helpless in the face of disease and epidemics, defenceless almost from Japanese marauding raids and subsequent famine ; and yet their human spirit triumphed over all, a happy smile upon their weather-beaten faces even for us Western strangers in their midst.

It was the day after we had visited the peasant family that we experienced our first air raid alarm. There was a bugle call that we hadn't noticed, and then one of the service boys came excitedly into the room telling us to run out of the village in a hurry, a Japanese plane was coming over. We personally did not see the point of getting so excited, we had had Japanese planes over our heads nearly every day for more than four years, and they had never meant a thing beyond the fact that we were sorry they were not Chinese planes instead. So we sauntered out into the open space that did for a courtyard among the ruins and gazed up at the plane which was by now well in sight. It passed overhead without apparent interest in the village. The service boy probably thought we were brave indeed ; but it is amusing to look back on that first incident and contrast it with the reflex actions we acquired after the first time in a real raid.

The chief engineer, Dah Yang, of the local radio station attached to General Hsiao's headquarters, was in a little village about one mile from our quarters ; he held a welcome party for us at the workshop ; mountain potatoes, meat balls, fried ham, wood-ear fungus, meat soup, rice and other dainty delicacies, cooked in the genuine Peking mode. Surrounded by wireless condensers, valves, dry batteries, switches, bits of wire and sticks of solder, ebonite and an old bottle of flux, it was more like home to us even than the meal, except that the various atmospheres were rather more mixed that we were used to. And round the walls of the laboratory, which was just another of those re-built ruined cottages, were the inevitable posters, this time with a faintly original note :

" We are hungry and thirsty and need knowledge for refreshment. Assist us, dear professors ! "

" Be the good students of Lenin, Stalin and Mao Tse-tung ! "

" Following General Hsaio K'e : March on ! March on ! "

It was while strolling among the different sections of the radio station that Claire's fur coat for the first time attracted the attention of the peasants. A crowd of people gathered around the inspection party asking us all kinds of questions of an obvious kind ; conversation was just straightforward interchange. But Claire was stumped when they wanted to know what kind of fur she was wearing. In Peiping it had been sold to us for unplucked marmot, but what that was in Chinese we did not know. The word " mah " means horse, so when Claire told them it was " marmot " they thought she was teasing them :

" No, it certainly isn't horse-hide ! " they exclaimed. We had the same joke many times throughout the three winters we were among the peasants, and we never could explain to their satisfaction why she wore the fur outside. They always wore skins with the hairs inside ; the way we did it was the way the horse wore it !

But the richest fun we had at the Ping Hsi headquarters was with the service boys, the orderlies who looked after the chores. Simple-minded peasant lads, they had hungrily assimilated the comradely spirit of the Communist Army, a wee bit too well for our peace of mind. When one of them brought into our room a truncated petrol-can of hot water to wash with on rising in the morning, he would stand by to see the fun ; and when Claire wished to get a good wash down it devolved upon Bill to push him gently through the door and to stand guard, for otherwise within a few minutes the boy would return and barge right in on operations. It was, of course, cold outside, and after we had washed, he would do likewise with what water remained.

We were undoubtedly receiving specially favoured treatment ; the boy would not himself have hot water to wash with his comrades outside, and naturally took the chance of a hot wash in our room. Far be it from us to discourage such laudable efforts at personal hygiene !

Their habit of expectorating on the clay floor of our room was something of which we were not able to cure them during the four weeks we were there, but fortunately we found no difficulty in dissuading them from brushing the dust into the air each afternoon. One afternoon, finding time free, one of the boys wanted to compose a letter to his mother. We were happy to see that he could actually write, a rare accomplishment for China's peasantry ; but we were taken aback when he sat down on our bed-kang and borrowed Claire's Swan fountain pen. The letter was asking his mother to send him a cat's skin to line his winter hat.

Claire had been feeling below par ever since our arrival in Ping Hsi headquarters, probably due to the charcoal gas ; and when she complained of an irritation on her chest, Bill diagnosed the spots we discovered as "a nervous rash or something". There was nothing else within the gamut of our previous experience that could account for them.

But a few days later Claire found a little grey thing crawling on the neck of her underwear.

"Bill ! Look ! What's this ? " she exclaimed in horror.

Bill rose to the occasion with alacrity and, a sure stroke of genius, pronounced the verdict :

"That must be a louse ! "

There were seven of them on a first count. At night she had more trouble and next morning a thorough search discovered twenty more. Nervous rash indeed ! They had been breeding in bliss for several days. And we remembered then that just before the rash had appeared we had been sleeping under some army officers' overcoats when we were out on one of those information lecture visits that we had been unable to refuse, in another village.

We spent that day boiling Claire's underwear—her only set —over a charcoal fire, while she kept under cover on the kang. And next day Bill made his own personal discoveries, scoring six only. But the service boy spotted Bill, and forthwith started to follow suit. Lice is trumps but not in our bedroom, thank you. Communism or no Communism, out you go, quick march!

But these were trivial matters after all. Outside in the crisp sunshiny air the boys were singing one of their favourite marching songs. They drilled, marched, sang songs, attended classes from five in the morning until nine at night ; they have withstood the mighty onslaughts of a powerfully mechanised enemy, endured flood, fire, starvation and disease without material relief in any form ; and all on a diet of corn and turnip, two meals a day, and nothing stronger than hot water to drink ; they had been doing all this for more than four years already with prospects of another four years more. What other race on earth could do the same ? It was an honour for us to have those lads borrow our fountain pen, for us to share their wash-basins, and be accepted by them in all respects as equal to themselves.

During our stay at General Hsiao's headquarters we shared the officers' mess—two meals a day. They ate a good deal better than the ranks so far as variety was concerned. Rice was the basis, and there was almost always some meat : pheasant or wild duck, sometimes a little goat meat, once in a while a turtle from the river, and even as a special delicacy, dog meat. Bean curd, fungus and green peppers were popular, but there was little else in the way of vegetables.

From our later experience of the army's feeding habits, we have concluded that the Ping Hsi menu had been specially improved for our benefit ; normally the officers, while they do retain the services of the best cooks, feed very little better than their men except when they have special guests to entertain.

In addition to all this excellent fare, General Hsiao provided us with ample bedding (cotton-wool padded blankets), padded winter uniforms and cloth-soled marching shoes. It took us a long time to get used to ourselves in this outfit, especially the padded trousers, but they were light and warm, and completely eliminated the need for wearing our overcoats while marching.

We felt badly about receiving so much in return for so little. Lindsay had, using some of the accessories he had brought out from Peiping, embarked upon a series of technical improvements in the radio station that promised to take some considerable time, but we had done nothing much more than appear at their public meetings and given a series of lectures on the theory of radio oscillations to the leading service-men of the radio station. So when a telegram came from General Nieh, commander-in-chief of all guerrilla forces in the Hopei region, welcoming us to his headquarters farther south, we asked General Hsiao's Chief of Staff to arrange for our journey.

This trip could be done on horseback in a week ; in fact General Hsiao had just done it in five days. But for us there were places and organisations to be seen on the way, we should take it very leisurely ; we were no longer refugees, but tourists.

So on January 29th the staff officers arranged a farewell break-fast for us in the best Chinese style. We spent the morning fixing our baggage, by now quite bulky with the bedding and the extra clothes ; and we were introduced to our ponies which we were expected to ride with all the baggage fastened over the saddles first. In fact we tried riding them in the village, and one of the officers took a snap of us with a captured Japanese camera. But that was the last time—walking was so much more comfortable.

During these preliminary pleasantries we were beginning to get anxious about the time, expecting a day's trip of at least fifteen or twenty miles. It was not until half-past twelve that we actually got started, and after an easy walk over a couple of passes covering no more than seven miles, we arrived at our destination for the night by half-past two in the afternoon !

Here was the headquarters of the department responsible for liaison with the underground patriotic movement in occupied cities. We met some Yenching students who had been brought out of Peiping since the outbreak of the Pacific war, and they told us what had happened at Yenching the morning we had escaped, the gist of which we have already given.

There were several other mild surprises in store for us in this village. First one was the way in which the noodles for supper were served in a wash-basin. We found later that this was normal practice throughout the guerrilla areas ; the enamel basins were captured from the Japanese Army stores, were easily carried around on manœuvres. We supposed, being naturally optimistic, that the particular wash-basins were reserved for such use ; there was no real guarantee.

The second surprise was how the service boy produced a new wick for the vegetable-oil lamp by the light of which we went to bed that night. He just pushed his fingers through a hole in the seat of his padded trousers and pulled out a little cotton-wool, twisted it a few times, and there was the wick.

It was amusing also to sleep that night in the same courtyard with our ponies and the guide's mule ; they were vigorously munching straw all night, and stamping heavily on the ground. The noise disturbed us then, but we had so much of it in the months that followed that it seemed uncanny to sleep without the animals.

But our biggest surprise was next morning when we were presented with an autostrop safety razor and six double-edged blades. The razor was made in Japan, the blades in Germany. There was a similar set for Lindsay. The outfit had been purchased at General Hsiao's request three weeks earlier by the army's secret agent in Peiping. Those six blades were still not finished when we arrived in Chungking two years later.

After a marvellously clean shave Bill felt much more equal to the rigours of the road. We put in seventeen long miles that day, up the Chu Ma River. We passed through one village where an election was in full swing, the village heads, the hsien magistrate and other officers were being chosen. At another village we were able to buy two eggs—a rare treat, since the Japanese had carried away most of the poultry of the region during their last autumn offensive. We sucked them for lunch while on the march.

It was a regimental headquarters where we stayed the night and all next day. The officers had a bicycle, and were trying to repair a puncture ; it seemed strangely out of place in that roadless district ; and the room they assigned to us actually had some glass windows.

The village had not suffered too badly from enemy action, and it felt like luxury to be in a comparatively undamaged place once more. But our glass windows were more attractive to the rank-and-file of the regiment than to us. There was quite a contingent of men living in the same courtyard as ourselves, and we had to find something to cover up at least the lower portion of the windows before we could decently prepare for bed. Our soldier friends were quite undaunted by that, however. There came a half-suppressed tittering by the crack of the door, and as Bill went to investigate matters, a hasty scuffling through the hallway. They left us alone after that, and on the whole behaved most courteously.

ONE MORE BARRIER

During the last day of January we waited for the formation of a convoy. One important Japanese blockade line had to be crossed, the one that separated the Ping Hsi guerrilla area from the central district of the Border Region, running along the Chu Ma River above the occupied garrison town of Tze Chin Kuan.

In the morning the Colonel took us a walk round the village to inspect the look-out posts in the surrounding hills; he claimed that ten days previously a party of two hundred Japanese had come out to attack them, but had been driven off. He pointed out exactly where they had come into the valley, and how he had both outnumbered and outmanœuvred them. Our ideas about this being a pleasure tour were a little jolted by this, but only momentarily; it was easy to forget the threat of surprise attacks in the happy company of these young enthusiasts.

There was feasting at the officers' mess here too; chicken, egg soup, chiaotze (boiled pie), fruit, rice, potatoes and a little local wine. It was farewell not particularly for us but for three colonels who were coming with us to attend conferences at a subdivisional headquarters through which we should have to pass.

It was not until four in the afternoon of the first of February that we finally left the village, with the object of getting to within the shortest safe distance from the blockade line just after dark, keeping our arrival somewhat secret from the local population. Our guides did not wish too much leakage of information that might risk our intended crossing becoming known to the enemy.

It was a lovely twelve miles walk through glades of birch trees; but it was dark before we reached our destination and we could hear the wolves howling. A glimmer of light welcomed us at the tiny hamlet in a little valley; everybody in the neighbourhood seemed to have heard about us in advance, and was out to see us come. The guide remarked with a grin that it didn't really matter because we would be across the line on the morrow anyway, and there would be no time for the Japanese to do anything about it.

The complete convoy formed next morning, and the officers gathered in the room where we had slept to share breakfast with us, sitting on our kang. A girl worker dressed in a black outfit supposed to imitate the peasants' style, one of the travellers in the convoy, invited herself into the room to share the officers' meal ; she had already had a couple of bowls of ordinary breakfast outside, but was still well able to stuff down huge mouthfuls of officers' fare on top of that.

Many of the women in the guerrilla organisation were similarly addicted to over-eating. There were innumerable thin and undernourished men, but we never saw a thin woman among the Communist workers with a few outstanding exceptions. They contrasted sharply with the peasants in this ; it was probably a compensation for the loss of those subtle feminine pleasures that can only be found in more civilised family surroundings.

There is an amusing point in this connection. In many units boys and girl workers all feed together ; they bring their own bowls and chopsticks to the place of assembly, and a service boy brings out of the kitchen the huge bucket of millet ; at a signal they all fall to and take a bowlful. One bowl is insufficient for the majority, and the faster eaters can get as many as three bowls before the ration is exhausted. This means that the slower eaters often lose their chance to get even a second bowl that is strictly their share.

This would seem to have put the girls at a disadvantage in the co-feeding units. We asked one of them how she managed the situation, and she told us the trick. Slow girls take only a small bowlful for the first helping, finish it in plenty of time to get a second helping which they make piled high enough to bring the total meal to two level bowls.

Theoretically, Communism is " each for all ", but in this and many other little ways that crop up in everyday living, it seemed to work out quite differently. But we can hardly blame their Communism ; there is the same drifting away from normal standards of mutual helpfulness in circles that would vigorously deny Communistic tendencies. We must put it all down to the fact that " there's a war on ! " Our natural capacity for mutual co-operation seems to be definitely limited ; all our routine lives we are herded together in co-ordinated operations ; there are few times when we can express our own individuality, and one of these is when we can swallow a bowlful of gruel more than the next fellow.

But to return to our trip. We did not get started until nearly midday, and we reached the river, with its Japanese patrol route, by four in the afternoon. It was a very different proposition from the crossing of the Yung Ting River. Here we could almost have jumped across, but were advised not to make the attempt; the current was fierce; and there was a bridge. Two logs supported at the centre by a high truss; it took a considerable effort of will to get started up at all, and a miracle to prevent us from falling off in the middle. We climbed on all fours up one slope to the peak at the centre, and slithered down the other log with a horrible propensity to roll off one side or the other. Once across we indulged in laughter at the antics of the soldier boys, many of whom seemed just as awkward as we had felt.

Half an hour's walk from the river was deemed safe enough to stop and have a picnic—the second meal of the day, in celebration of having crossed the last Japanese blockade line. But there was a geographical barrier which was even more formidable, a tremendous mountain range.

We climbed continuously from five-thirty to nine that evening. For the first two hours our route lay up a frozen river bed, crossing and recrossing the ice a hundred times in the gathering darkness. Before we reached the top of the range the moon came out. For most of the time we were passing under the base of great dinosaur-shaped masses of rock that cast their shadows on the moonlit mountain wall across the valley.

As we came out on top to a barren wilderness under the moon, even the guide seemed momentarily to have lost his way; he had to make several trials at the proper place to go down on the other side. And when we did start down it was like descending into a bottomless pit. The glaring moonlight of the summit had dazzled our eyes, and in the fierce shadows we could see nothing for a long time.

Yet the convoy, once fairly started, began to scramble at top speed over the barren slope. To keep pace with them we had literally to leap from rock to rock down the face of the mountain. Wherever the moonlight picked out a pinnacle of stone, there would we jump; if it held beneath our weight, well and good; if not, we were in the air again before we had lost our balance, some less fortunate one zigzagging below would receive a pelting of slithering rock and stone. A wild and frenzied escapade.

At last the country eased out and we found a path, but the pace never slackened for a moment. On and on down the valley, barren rocks and precipices rising on all sides, weird and awe-inspiring. It must have been after midnight when, away up a side ravine we could see a few spots of light and hear the sound of a dog barking hollow among the overhanging cliffs.

When we finally climbed up into the village, it seemed in a normal state of repair, but everywhere was boarded up for the night, and the convoy's manager had a deal of trouble trying to get any response from the inhabitants. For half an hour we sat on a log in a corner of the lane, surrounded by men and mules, stragglers of the convoy that kept coming in and crowding around.

We had covered thirty miles of terrific country, but it was only then, when we started another of those shivering fits like the palsy, that we realised how thoroughly fatigued we were. Even with our heavy overcoats on top of the padded uniforms we were still cold. And half an hour later they found an empty room for us which proved to be even colder, from long disuse ; the kang was icy damp. The small straw fire one of the soldiers put under it did not seem to make a scrap of difference. Even after a drink of hot water, we lay shivering on the kang for half an hour or more in our padded uniforms, with half the bedding under us, half on top, and the overcoats piled over that, trying to keep each other still. Then someone in the convoy brought us each a bowl of hot rice gruel to serve as the evening meal, and after sipping that, we were at last able to get the better of the palsy in our muscles.

We were disturbed once by a peasant woman who insisted upon bringing in a sick relative for us to cure. She seemed to be suffering from advanced pulmonary tuberculosis. Finally we got about two hours' sleep. The temperature can be judged from the fact that on rising at dawn we found the ink in Bill's fountain pen frozen solid. Looking back at that night, it is always amazing to us that neither of us came down with sickness ; we must have been tougher than we knew.

After that frigid night, it was a relief to see the sunshine next morning lighting up the wisps of cloud, at least a promise of warmth to come. The air was biting dry and cold as we crept outside and walked down through the still half-awake village to the room where the three colonels were calling us for breakfast. We

PLATE IV

Guerrilla snipers in the Wolf Tooth Mountain Range.

discovered them just getting up off a large warm kang after a good night's sleep.

" Well, I'll be darned ! " we both exclaimed.

" Why ? What's the matter ? " asked the colonels.

" We nearly froze to death last night ! And here you are snug as a bug in a rug ! Why didn't you . . . ? "

" We were warned that you preferred privacy for hygienic reasons, and that was the only private place in the whole village. We are very sorry if you've caught cold. Didn't the service boy make a fire for you ? "

They looked as though there would be trouble for the service boy if we made a real complaint.

" Yes, he did, but the fire didn't seem to make any difference. But never mind, we haven't caught cold. Please don't trouble now about that, we're quite all right now ! "

But how we envied them their warm kang, and we almost cursed that hygienic reputation we seemed to have picked up from somewhere.

After a delicious breakfast of millet gruel and sweet potatoes, we got started down the ravine early enough, and before noon had descended into a broad cultivated valley that reminded us of the plains of Peiping. The weather was almost spring-like, and with the sudden change from the previous night, we fairly sweltered in our padded uniforms and woollen underwear.

These sartorial handicaps notwithstanding, we were still able to outwalk the three colonels. They were in high spirits after passing the last barrier, and spent the morning teasing each other. Colonel Hsiung was " baby " because of his short stature, Colonel Huang was " bandit " because of his beard, an unusual appendage for the Chinese youth, Colonel Wang was " turtle " after his name-sake Wang Ching-wei : " turtle " is a term of derision applied to anyone of despicable character although originally meaning a man whose wife is unfaithful to him.

All three colonels were itching to get on top of their mules, and kept urging us to ride our animals so that they could do like-wise without being discourteous to us. In the end we succeeded in persuading them to waive the formality, and they mounted their steeds with obvious relief. It was amusing to see them, perched, it seemed, so precariously, atop their bedding on the saddles, go trotting ahead of the convoy in great glee.

Soon after noon we arrived at a sizable little town, and found that one of the colonels had already been shopping at the market buying some special delicacies for lunch. They had bought rice, peanuts, dates, and bean curd, and we contributed a large tin of sardines from our rapidly diminishing share of the supplies we had brought out from Peiping.

Although there was plenty of time to make another stage of the trip, the three colonels decided that we had done enough the night before, and that the whole party should take a rest until next morning. In fact " bandit " Huang had badly blistered his feet, and after lunch we discovered him, an object of mock-derisive teasing from his comrades, washing his feet in wine.

The courtyard they had found for us was pleasant but far from private ; they had taken to heart our morning's complaint. Crowds of villagers came to see us during the afternoon. Donkeys and mules, including our own animals, were stabled along one side of the court, the peasant family were in residence along two other sides, and our room occupied the fourth. Outside the window of our room a huge sow with eleven recent arrivals was snuggling on a heap of straw. There was an atmosphere of peaceful serenity about the place that did us a world of good. By simple contrast with the previous night, this was like being back in civilisation.

During the first three hours next morning we walked through no less than fourteen villages, none of them in ruins ; a little world of rural quiet, sheltered from the stormy world outside. There were seven more villages in the afternoon, and then down through a narrow gorge cut by a river in the foot-hills of the Wolf Tooth mountain range we emerged by four o'clock upon a broad sandy valley.

Here, strategically placed to defend the area through which we had just come, was the first subdivisional headquarters of the guerrilla war base, one of the most strongly held bastions in the area. The village is but one day's march from the city of Paoting on the Peiping-Hankow railway, which city can be seen on a clear day from the tops of the Wolf Tooth mountains. Our own log for the day was twenty miles.

Chapter V

WELCOME TO FIELD HEADQUARTERS

THE village was clean and well-appointed, thanks to the routine attentions of the garrison. At every approach there was a look-out post of hard clay sunk in the ground, from which any attacking party could be covered with machine-gun fire. The village commanded a magnificent view of the whole Wolf Tooth range and stood at the junction of two broad valleys, the one running east being very fertile.

Our arrival had evidently been expected, and we were taken at once to a private court which, we were told, was to be our residence during our stay at this headquarters. Two rooms to ourselves, a private toilet, a stable, all in the one court, a special entry at the gate and a bright youngster to act as service boy. He had a well-trained treble voice, and it was he who first sang us the song of the Wolf Tooth Mountains, variously known as " The Five Braves " or " Chess-board Rock ".

This song refers to an incident during the Japanese campaign of the previous autumn when the enemy successfully occupied the mountain range for a short period. A rear-guard of five men held a small temple built at the " Chess-board Rock " until the main body of Chinese troops had retired to safety, and finally, these five men had leapt over the precipice, two surviving with injuries. The chess-board is carved in the living rock, and the priest who lives there wears a gown chequered like a chess-board. The origin and history of this quaint shrine we have not discovered, but it is probably connected in some way with Taoist magical cults. The old fellow was a loyal helper of the guerrillas, who regularly used his place as a strong point.

The moment we had arrived at the headquarters, the chief of the supply department had exclaimed :

" Look at your shoes ! You must have a new pair at once ! " and forthwith ordered one of the attendant service boys to run to his office and fetch some. Within five minutes we were fitted with excellently made cloth shoes. The next question he asked was :

" How long since you had baths ? "

This question was not as embarrassing as it sounds ; it was in fact just under two months.

" Well ! well ! You shall have baths to-morrow ! We have a bath-house not far from here, and we shall reserve it for you. We shall have ponies ready for you to ride there."

This sounded too good to be true ; guerrillas and bath-houses ? We had always thought of the bath-house as a preserve of the larger cities.

And again :

" What kind of cakes have you been eating since you left Peiping ? " He knew well enough, and derived great pleasure from our thunderstruck expressions at the arrival in our room of plates of pears, apples, oranges and—dainty little sponge-cakes ! These sponge-cakes were a real mystery. We were variously informed that they had been made by General Yang's own cook, and that they had been bought in Paoting by one of their secret agents specially for our welcome party.

In any case, the cakes were evidently quite an unusual feature to them, judging by the way they enjoyed eating them along with us. They must have laid in a very plentiful supply, for a fresh series of dishes would be produced with great gusto, like rabbits from a conjuror's hat, for our refreshment at each meeting, party and drama show that we attended throughout the week we were there.

Our bath-house expedition was an historic event, both for us and for the bath-house. The date was February 5th, 1942. Spring was in the air ; we had lost the feeling of being fugitives, at last we were tourists, even explorers. And we set out in the early morning on ponies in high spirits.

No, the ponies were not in high spirits ; they seemed singularly disinclined to proceed. No sooner had we gained the open country outside the village, than they seemed to realise where they were going, and started at once to take exception. They knew well enough that we were absolute novices at riding, and at the first crossing of paths they deliberately headed off in the wrong direction —one that would bring them back home.

No amount of pulling at the reins would stop them ; the most we were able to do was to make them go in circles ; the guide —the Q.M.G. himself—was well away along the proper path when he looked around to discover our comic plight. Turning back and seeing us in an hilarious state, he nearly split with mirth.

Finally he had to dismount and catch Claire's animal by the nose, lead it a few yards in the proper direction ; with this control the pony was obedient enough. But no sooner had he let go and caught hold of Bill's animal, than Claire's at once turned back and made off on its homeward trail again.

This circus went on for several minutes amidst roars of laughter from all concerned. As each pony was turned in the proper direction, the other would shy off home. We cannot recall how the problem was finally solved ; it seemed something like the simultaneous measurement of position and momentum of the electron ; but in the end we all got started in the right direction with sufficient momentum, and the brutes thereafter contented themselves with more passive methods of resistance, trading upon their reputation for being " lao-shih "—old and gentle.

Claire's steed had been selected specially with an eye to her safety, and was reputed to be the oldest and most gentle pony in the camp. Hitherto when riding the baggage animals at odd moments, we had been anxious to avoid going at more than a slow walking pace ; but to-day we were in the mood for taking a lesson in riding. But could we persuade that animal to get a move on ? It continued adamantly to promenade in the most sedate manner imaginable. Even the other animals seemed to get impatient, and nosed into the rear of the slow creature in an effort to urge it into better speed.

At last Bill discovered a trick. Riding close in behind, he poked at it just above the tail with a stick ; and there was just one spot that seemed to act like a self-starting button. Each well-placed poke produced a definite increase in momentum ; and by catching up behind before the increase had been lost, repeating the poke, Bill was able to build up quite a respectable speed in Claire's animal. It was like a Pavlov reflex. Three or four successive spinal stimuli, and we were going at perhaps seven or eight miles an hour ; the ponies had actually to trot. But that was where our riding problems really began. We ceased entirely to worry about the animal's rear, and had to pay attention to our own.

In theory we knew all about it ; the correct grip with the knees, the correct slope forward to take the impact off the spine, and all the rest of it. Our guide kept shouting these instructions to us as we sped along, but it didn't make a bit of difference. Either we had to stand up in the stirrups to prevent the saddle from knocking the guts out of us via the seats of our pants, or else we had to try and grip the animal by the belly with our heels to stop being thrown off the saddle at each jerk of the animal's back. There was no mercy whatever.

Our discomfiture made the officer's hilarity even more boisterous, but our own mirthfulness gradually deteriorated into a sense of futility : we should never learn our lesson, unless it be the lesson that guerrilla horse-flesh had no love for us.

Then our guide, sensing this disappointment, gleefully tried to convince us that if we would urge our animals on still faster, say to a real gallop, then our discomfort would vanish, we should find ourselves floating along with a gentle swinging rhythm at ten or fifteen miles an hour. The idea was breath-taking ; and who knows whether the ponies accepted the rule ? None of the army boys ever seemed to get their seats bastinadoed even when riding slowly, and we felt sure that our animals were serving us with a special kind of medicine reserved for novices ; and what might they not have in store for us at higher speeds ?

However, spring was in the air, and we were out for fun or nothing. So it was not long before there was a race on between the guide's animal and Bill's which left Claire's lazy animal contentedly ambling far behind. We put it that way deliberately— the race was between the animals, not the riders. Bill was a mere spectator who happened to be sitting on top of one of the animals, at first. By the time the officer brought the creatures back under control, Bill was hanging on to the thing's neck for dear life, slipping gradually round under its belly in a most undignified posture.

About half-way to the village with the bath-house a party of army officers passed us at a gallop, also on their way to the bathhouse. And when we arrived, there were the officers waiting impatiently for us, because the General had issued strict orders that no one should use it before we had finished.

Such preferential treatment made us feel most foolish, but there was nothing we could do about that now. We were taken into a long room fitted out somewhat like a railroad dining-car ; it was the dressing-room, and the baths were off the other end. A curtain of cotton cloth hanging in the entrance was all that separated the dressing-room from the crowd of waiting officers outside.

It was comfortably warm in the dressing-room, and Bill decided to try it out. But the boys outside kept peeping round the curtain to see how we were getting along, and Claire decided that privacy was distinctly inadequate. The baths were large enough to hold at least a dozen people at once and looked tolerably clean. But there was a sickly odour of goat's meat about the whole place that undermined one's confidence in its hygienic condition. Bill was not really sure whether he was cleaner after the lonely bath or not. We learned a long time afterwards that the soap they used for cleaning out the bath-house was a local manufacture the basic substance of which was mutton fat from the mountain goats of the guerrilla area.

After the bath, we were taken to a large restaurant in the village operated by an army co-operative, and we had an excellent lunch in the best Peiping style.

The return trip was relatively sedate ; the animals behaved well and we could concentrate on the scenery. By the time we had got back we had ridden twenty miles, just for half a bath. This kind of thing is a regular routine with the army boys. Wherever there is a bath-house available, officers and men from fifteen miles around will use it in turn ; each day being reserved for some particular department in strict rotation. Personally we never adapted ourselves to the idea of public ablutions, and even though later we had a standing invitation to join General Nieh's party at the Hopei headquarters, we preferred the private wash-basin routine.

The second morning at General Yang's place we had visitors at our private court-yard. Five young army officers and two young women party workers, one a nurse and the other a political propagandist. The political lady did not seem more than about nineteen years old, but confessed to having two children. She did not mention her husband, and at the time we felt it better not to inquire about him : these Communists were supposed to have some rather advanced ideas and we wished to avoid embarrassment.

The girls themselves were very much at home ; their behaviour generally made us think how much we preferred seemly respectfulness from junior members of society. When the Q.M.G. called in near lunch time, the girls hailed him with delight, invited the whole group to stay lunch with us, and demanded chiaotze on the menu. We were amazed at the easy way in which the Q.M.G. took all this chaff, and equally surprised that their requests were granted without hesitation. We all had a very happy lunch together, during which the girls made fun of the Q.M.G.'s propensity for absorbing wine by filling his little wine-cup with soup while his back was turned. After the meal the girls took us to see the local unit's wireless station, and the political propagandist mother of two stayed supper with us too.

It was only later, after they had all gone, that the young service boy happened to refer to the young ladies, and we learned from him that the young mother was none other than General Yang's wife. We accused him of not having introduced us properly so that we could be appropriately courteous, to which he cheerfully replied:

" Oh ! That's nothing to worry about ! The Eighth Route Army are always like that ! "

During the late afternoon a welcome drama performance began. They had a great pit dug out of the loess earth, and side tunnels leading into it from all directions that made excellent air raid shelters. At one end of the pit was a raised platform for their open-air theatre. It was down into this pit that we were taken for the meeting.

Crowds of people, all in uniform, were already seated in the pit on logs of wood, or just on their own packs. In the front of the audience we saw a pair of straight-backed, hard-wood chairs stuck right between the audience and their view of the stage, and in front of the chairs a square hard-wood table. To our horror we were conducted straight to these two chairs, and asked to seat ourselves thereon.

We protested vigorously, and after they thought we had been exhibited well enough to the audience in this undignified procedure, the chairs were removed and we were allowed seats on a comfortably low stool. Charcoal braziers were then brought in to warm our feet, cups of tea to keep us warm inside, and pears and sponge-cakes to warm our hearts.

There were welcome speeches to which we had briefly to reply. Then singing, dancing, and drama of first-rate quality were produced on the stage by the army's amateur dramatics association. At about ten, after it was all over, they served us another excellent meal, and presented us with a little paper packet containing real coffee grounds—so that we could make our own brew in the morning.

The following afternoon we were invited to join in a banquet at a neighbouring village in honour of the officers who were in conference with General Yang. General Yang himself walked over with us, and we were seated at his table. Altogether there were about ten tables in two separate courtyards ; it was a very high-spirited gathering.

During the earlier part of the meal conversation was conventional, chiefly centred around the war news, which by then was none too happy. But this was suddenly changed when a note was handed from one of the colonels in the other court to General Yang's Chief of Staff, conveying a challenge from the colonels' basket-ball team to play a match against any team chosen from the staff officers. Pandemonium at once broke out on all sides, challenges and counter challenges were flung hither and thither in great glee.

Zest was added to the situation by the fact that the Chief of Staff was very fond of alcohol and well-known to be able to hold more than most. Supporters of the colonels' team launched a campaign ; they played the finger game with the Chief of Staff —the loser to drain his cup at every round, until in a very short while the meagre supply of wine was exhausted and water was added surreptitiously by a staff officer.

It took quite a time to get the company moving from the festive board towards the basket-ball ground, and when we did get there it was occupied by rank-and-file soldiers at their regular play hour. Chief of Staff, who was very stout and nicknamed " Fatty tank ", was quite unconcerned over this, and strolled jerkily on to the field as if there was nobody there. The crowd of colonels laughed and cat-called at him, cheering him on until suddenly the ball, tossed by one of the soldiers, dropped vertically just in front of his nose. Either by direct impact or by being shaken off, his spectacles were dashed to the ground and broken. " Fatty tank " was very short-sighted, and this accident effectively put him out of action amidst delighted roars from the colonels' cheering squad, and hair-raising roars from the opposing side.

Leader of the staff cheering squad was political commissar, equal in rank to General Yang. During the meal he had been at our table and we know he had not touched a drop of wine, but at this point he leapt out of the side-lines into the middle of the field and, feigning drunkenness, began a pantomime show jeering and laughing, doubling himself up with mirth, making all manner of comic gestures in ridicule of the colonels' team, to the great delight of his own.

These light-hearted preliminaries continued for the better part of an hour, when suddenly everyone realised that if the actual game did not begin soon it would get dark before they could finish it. At once the field was cleared and the teams settled down to business.

We are no judge of basket-ball, and would not like to say whether the standard of play was high or otherwise. But the spirit was great. They derived no end of fun from the game. At one point when the score was even, a penalty was pronounced against the staff team, and the colonels scored a basket; there was tremendous cheering and hooting in response, and a great argument about whether or not the penalty should have been granted. Before things could develop into anything unpleasant, General Yang dashed on to the field and shouted at the top of his voice:

"Penalty for the staff team! Colonels' captain is discussing strategy with Baby Huang!"

But Baby Huang was so obviously not an expert in basket-ball that this set off the whole works into so much mirth that, when the staff took their penalty shot, they missed the basket by a mile. However, it squared the "face" account, and the game continued in good spirits.

The final score we have long since forgotten, but we still remember the certainty that these young men, between guerrilla operations, get the most out of the simplest things life has to offer. No crowd anywhere could have behaved in a more light-hearted way; and the complete absence of formalities, even almost of respect for their senior officers, made it all the more significant that their leaders should be able to handle the men so perfectly. A complete mutual trust and confidence regarding the fundamental things for which they all were fighting was at the bottom of this, but as yet we were only dimly beginning to understand.

In another nearby village was the headquarters for the local counties' government supervisory office. At this office we were guests of the supervisor with General Yang and some of his staff. It was here that we realised who the referee had been at the famous basket-ball match—the supervisor himself. At the government headquarters the feast was of better quality, but the atmosphere was much more sedate. There was a similar contrast between local government groups and army groups all through the guerrilla areas.

On Monday we visited the soldiers' drama club room and inspected a drawing class. General Yang presented us with a set of snaps of activities of their army organisation. In the evening we had a supper with the General and after supper attended another dramatic performance. And we departed next morning.

All travel arrangements were in the Q.M.G.'s expert hands. We had been given maps, ponies and a guide for the day, and after a thirty-mile walk we arrived at the Resist-Japan Union University. But of this more anon. On Friday we walked another stage to the third subdivisional headquarters of the war base, under General Huang.

Our welcome to the Border Region was in reality a series of welcomes, each welcome outstripping, if possible, the previous one. At the third subdivisional headquarters they had their army drama club out in force by the side of the path at the approaches to their village, with a great banner held by two standard bearers, inscribed with the startling word

WELCOME

and as we came over the brow of the hill in sight of this demonstration of cordiality, we were met by General Huang, Commissar Wang and their chief secretary, Jack Shih. The drama boys struck up some patriotic songs, and at the end, the fist-raising slogan shouting. It made us feel ridiculous. But Jack Shih quickly put us at our ease.

Jack Shih was a 1934 graduate of the Peking Customs College. When the student agitations were at their height, he was already working in the Shanghai customs offices, enjoying the high life of that city, with a good salary, augmented by generous seizure benefits. The students' call to arms found specially sympathetic response among the customs officials, for they were coming continually in contact with the results of appeasement in their daily work. Jack had once tried to seize a shipment of silver being transported by Japanese *ronin* against customs restrictions, but was beaten up for his pains.

Jack was a real gentleman with a clear understanding of Westerners' whims and fancies that seemed almost uncanny out there among the guerrillas. He was homesick for news of his family ; his wife had stayed behind in Yenan where she was teaching in a Resist-Japan middle school. Jack happily exclaimed to us :

"There are going to be many joyful reunions after this war is over!"

But not for Jack; he was killed by enemy action just fifteen months later.

General Huang's headquarters had been set up in an abandoned Roman Catholic Church building. Erected in 1937, this building had been abandoned when the Japanese came through the area, and it had not been damaged in any way.

It was in this auditorium, for that is what the army did with the main church hall, that Bill opened his mouth too wide and, as it were, put his foot into it. At the head of the church hall they had built a stage for dramatic performances. Over this stage in red letters cut in paper pasted on a white ground was the glaring banner:

WELCOME TO MR. AND MRS. WILLIAM BAND

The whole show was to be our star turn. Bill was expected to make a speech, and because among the audience were the intellectual elite, medical and military "big shots" of the district, something more than mere padding seemed called for.

So he prepared something along the lines that the four allies, China, Britain, America and Russia, though all different in their concepts and standards of democracy, were all striving towards the same ideals, all equally opposed to Fascist dictatorship. There was no checking over the manuscript notes beforehand; they expected the thing to be genuinely extempore.

Everything went well at first. They were quite happy to hear that America's democracy was imperfect because of the monopolistic powers of the great trusts, and that Britain's system was still far from perfect even though her democracy was the oldest. The interpreter had a grand time, and his words came forth most eloquently; it seemed almost as though he had said the same kind of thing many times before.

But when Bill went on to say that in Russia, too, Stalin had powers that were far greater than were consistent with true democracy, the interpreter boggled hopelessly. He was a young English teacher at the Resist-Japan Union University, and Bill thought at first perhaps he had not quite understood, so he repeated the statement so clearly and slowly that there was no possible cause for doubt. With a look of agony on his face, the interpreter turned to the line of officers behind us on the platform, received Jack Shih's nod of the head, and proceeded with the translation in third person reporter style.

The sudden hush that came over the meeting was terrific. The audience was too polite to do anything but applaud, but there was no enthusiasm in it. Claire's speech of appreciation helped to ease the situation, and the dramatic performances that followed the speeches were so superb that we quickly forgot the little political *faux pas*. The drama club was the one connected with the Union University ; the acting, the costumes and the scenery were marvellous. The play was that masterpiece of the Russian stage : " The Inspector ", by Gogol, depicting the corruption of Russian Tsardom during the early nineteenth century. As they may have intended, it was an education to us. Between the scenes we were served with tea, peanuts and dates.

The performance ended around three in the morning, and President Cheng of the Union University, with his wife, came back with us to our rooms for a meal of delicious Cantonese gruel. It happened to be New Year's Day on the old lunar calendar, and the village streets were decorated with hanging paper lanterns. Our rooms, a suite of two, were provided with a good coal stove and a captured Japanese gramophone with recorded American music. These guerrillas !

Our education continued next evening, when Dr. Kotnis came to have supper with us. Kotnis was the Indian medical who succeeded Dr. Norman Bethune in his work at the front among the Chinese guerrillas. A most charming young man, he had been introduced to us earlier at the Union University reception, and he had captivated our imaginations. The meal had not gone on for long before the real subject came up : we had guessed it would as soon as we saw him arrive.

Kotnis : " About your speech at the meeting last night. We welcome criticism, but it ought to be based on knowledge. Have you studied the Russian Constitution ? Do you know what powers Stalin has ? You have said yourself several times that the border peoples here have achieved a new democracy which is perfect in principle ; did you know that our Constitution here is an almost exact copy of that in Russia ? Stalin has no more power than a perfect democracy will grant him : his power is delegated as the peoples' representative."

Bill : " I must confess ignorance of the Russian system, but I find it hard to believe what you say about the limits of Stalin's power. Hitler was, after all, elected by the people and his dictatorial powers have become quite unlimited. Some say he is even yet supported by the majority of the German people, yet the fact remains, as I said last night, that the German system is essentially and explicitly opposed to the democratic ideal. Stalin, on the other hand, does preach the gospel of democracy, and in this all the four allied nations are united. But I do not agree that you have any right to claim that Russia is more perfect either than America or Britain in respect of its actual realisation of a democratic way of life : even our King has less authority than Stalin ! "

And so it started. We kept it up ding-dong all evening, going through the whole range of arguments. In the end Kotnis gave up, and a few weeks later demonstrated effectively enough that Bill had not shaken his convictions by formally joining the Chinese Communist Party. Kotnis must naturally have reported the gist of this argument, but it did not appear to make the slightest difference. As they claimed, they stood for a United Front against the Japanese, and differences in political theories were not allowed to interfere with the main business at hand. Of course Bill was marked in the Border Region as a sympathiser, but not as a " fellow traveller ". The courtesy they showed towards us was, if anything, increased.

They were the more anxious to create a good impression, when they knew that we were not politically inclined to accept their doctrines.

During one of the afternoons at the third subdivisional headquarters we were taken over to visit their local military hospital. Of the hospital itself we shall talk in more detail later. Here we want to tell of the children of the village who piled out on the path to see us set off. They thronged around us so closely and so boisterously that our guide—a journalism student from Yenching, named Lin, resorted to a ruse to clear the path.

" What would you like to do ? Sing a song for these foreign guests ? " asked Lin. There was a lull in the excitement, as a sufficient proportion of the youngsters became momentarily self-conscious. Taking advantage of this pause in the hubbub, Lin commanded :

" Run away home anyone who doesn't want to sing a song ! "

and to a few doubtful ones on the edge of the crowd : " Come on in and sing, or else buzz off ! "

Then catching hold of a likely looking one in the front : " You lead ! What do you want to sing ? "

In less than ten seconds they had chosen their song, and a chorus of gleeful voices, obviously well drilled in such performances, sang praises to the guerrillas and brought down blood-curdling curses on their Japanese enemies. Framed by the mud-walled cottages, stone pigsties and a village grindstone, this crowd of eager little children gave us a heartening picture of China's unconquerable resistance, clear promise of the re-birth of a nation securely rooted in the good earth.

Our trip from the third subdivisional headquarters down to the central headquarters of the Border Region war base was exceedingly leisurely, and it began in a typical manner. On Tuesday, February 17th it was, and we were up betimes all ready for an early start, forgetting that as usual there must be a farewell feast. We were not given any breakfast until nine, when we were ushered into the General's private suite and discovered the whole H.Q. staff there to do us honour with the best delicacies imaginable. Not until eleven were these formalities over and did they allow us to emerge upon the village lane to look for our baggage mules.

The mules were in fact there, but they had not been made ready. Army hostlers were thorough realists : what is the use of being ready for people who are eating a feast ? So it was well after noon before we actually got started. It was a lovely spring day, and we were scheduled only for a four-hour trip, so why rush ? In guerrilla areas there are enough occasions when haste is a matter of life and death, why should we waste nervous energy rushing about when it isn't necessary ?

Lin, the journalist, was delegated to accompany us all the way down to the central headquarters, and as we walked along, towing the mules by the nose, he told us what had happened to him since he left our University.

How Lin Joined up with the Guerrillas

We bought a pocket full of dried Chinese dates each and, lacking other facilities for cleaning them, just rubbed the dirt off them on to our hands. While we were chewing these delicious morsels Lin narrated :

" You may remember how Nanhua was helped to escape from the campus by Miss H ? She got him safely into the Central Hopei guerrilla base, and within two weeks I received his letter urging me to proceed immediately without waiting for Mr. L. as originally planned.

" That was in July 1938, and there was a whole group of us planning to come out. Besides myself there were two other boys and two girls. The girls chose to go first. That was because we felt they had the better chance of being allowed through by the Japanese, disguised as young school teachers going to take up posts in primary schools in their native villages.

" The girls prepared bogus letters of appointment. The boys arranged to be at the railway station when the girls left to see how things went with them at the inspection. Of course we avoided any contact while we bade this silent good-bye. They got through all right, and sent another letter back urging us to make all haste to follow.

" Remarkable how efficient the communication system is between the two sides ! We forthwith arranged our disguise in consultation with the Communist Party contact man in the city, and within three days we in our turn took the plunge. I was the most trouble because of my southern accent : I could not possibly pretend to be going back to my native village ! The other two boys were both from the North, and could therefore pass for local villagers ; but I had to set myself out as an insurance tout, a line of business that the Japs didn't seem to mind in the least.

" We got on the train all right, and successfully survived the half-dozen inspections on board. Disembarking at Hsu Hsien, one station north of Paoting, we had to face the last and most difficult barrier. On the platform was a bedraggled looking unit of puppet Chinese troops who seemed obviously to have been worsted in battle not many hours before. Their officer overheard our replies to the local inspector and exclaimed :

" ' What ! You going to Hei Lung Kou ? '

" We : ' Yes ! Why ? What's up ? '

" He : ' You can't go there, the Reds are there ! '

" We : ' But that's our home village, we must go ; we don't know anything about the Reds ! '

PLATE V

[*Photo by E. R. Lapwood*
View of Lang Ya Shan (Wolf Tooth Mountains) from 1st Base H.Q.
Guerrillas in Chin Cha Chi.

" He : ' You don't know anything about the Reds ? Phew ! We just had a fight with them ; if you go there they will surely kill you ! '

" We : ' We don't believe you ; our families are there and we are going home anyhow ! '

" He : ' Come on now ! You can't fool me ! I know you are college students going to join up. Anyhow, go ahead, do as you please, I won't stop you ! '

" To say the least, this officer's attitude was a surprise to us, and we breathed a sigh of relief as we were allowed to pass through the barrier. Had there been a Japanese officer supervising affairs, as there often is, we would certainly have been apprehended.

" We made our contacts, as arranged, in Hei Lung Kou, and in a day or two arrived safely at the headquarters for the Tientsin area : in fact we found ourselves within thirty miles of that city. And imagine our surprise the day after we arrived, to be introduced to a new convert whom we recognised as none other than the puppet officer who had let us past the barrier at the railway station. He confessed to having made up his mind to follow us at the very moment he was questioning us, after his ignominious defeat at the hands of the guerrillas that morning.

" After our sheltered hygienic life at Yenching we found the rough conditions at the guerrilla camp very trying. I came down with dysentery within a few days, and was laid up for three weeks with it. During that time the people there decided that I had better proceed to Yenan for a period of training : our school life had been quite inadequate as preparation for the work we now had in hand.

" So on September 19th, things moving rather slowly, all six of us started off on the long trek to Yenan with a small armed escort, carrying all our worldly possessions on our backs. We walked forty miles one night across the Peking-Hankow railway —the one we came down when we escaped from Peking. When we reached General Nieh's headquarters we learned that the Japanese had an offensive in full swing along the Shansi railway running between Tatung and Taiyuan.

" We waited for three weeks hoping for conditions to become more normal, but in the end were advised to alter our route. We crossed the Taiyuan Shihchiachuang line instead, into S.E. Shansi and then crossed the Yellow River into Honan, where we entrained on the Lung-Hai line for Sian.

" At Sian we registered at the Eighth Route Army offices there and were told that it would not be possible to go direct to Yenan because the Nationalists were blockading the region we wished to reach. Instead, we had to walk away to the north-west up into Kansu and come down south again into Yenan from Yulin.

" The whole journey took us four months' time. After a thoroughly practical training in methods of mass education and political principles I was assigned to my present position here with the army in Hopei."

The many interesting visits we paid on the way down to General Nieh's place under Lin's guidance will be described later. Our " royal tour " came to its grand climax on February 25th at the village where General Nieh's headquarters were then located, about fifty miles west of the Peking-Hankow railway, and nearly due north from the important railway junction Shihchiachuang.

Our total time from Ping Hsi was just four weeks, and it had been a most memorable four weeks. The total log stood at about 365 miles walking from the point at which we had abandoned the car at Black Dragon Pool on December 8th. We were, of course, much less distance than that from Peiping by a direct line. On the map it looks about 150 miles as the crow flies.

As we have just said, our royal tour came to a grand climax. As we entered General Nieh's dining-room, we rubbed our eyes in amazement. On the large table spread with a white cloth and set for about sixteen people were laid out all manner of Western-style delicacies, complete with all the recognised instrumental facilities for their enjoyment. A variety of cold meats, but specially sliced ham and chicken salad with eggs, tomato and lettuce salad, touched us most of all. Then there was milk and butter, bread and toast, and real coffee, sweetened with sugar ; and fish, boiled and fried ; and apples, pears and oranges ; and large, beautifully iced cakes.

Were we dreaming ? Was this really just a guerrilla encampment ? It reminded us of one of our happy picnic parties in the good old Peiping days ; and the officers were much more like a college group than a gang of bandits as the Japanese would call them. General Nieh himself impressed us as more like a scholarly university president than a great guerrilla strategist.

Chapter VI

COLLEGE SCIENCE FOR GUERRILLAS

DISCUSSING our future plans, General Nieh told us that conditions for travelling through to the interior were too dangerous at that time because of Japanese activity along the Shansi railway between Tatung and Taiyuan, across which they would have to smuggle us if we wished to continue. We were, of course, entirely in the hands of the Eighth Route Army and, as before, ready to do anything which they thought would be useful. General Nieh promised that there would be some valuable work in connection with their wireless school training programme if we would patiently wait for a few weeks for the scheme to be properly organised.

During that time we were installed in another village in the central headquarters group. An undamaged courtyard that had formerly been commandeered by the army for a branch of the headquarters organisation was assigned to us as our permanent " war-time home ". There were four rooms for the residents, one for the headquarters representative, Roger Liu, a room for the cook and his assistant and the service boys, and a kitchen. Roger was a 1936 graduate from Yenching, acted as interpreter and guide to all the Western guests who lived or stopped over in the Border Region.

The court was paved with stone, and the rooms were well constructed with bricks and had plaster-cement flat roofs. We were provided with collapsible furniture—chairs, tables, bedstead and desk. On the wooden bed a canvas mattress stuffed as thickly as we pleased with straw. Round the walls, which were plastered with whitewash, were stuck enlarged photographs of scenes and activities in the guerrilla areas. The kitchen was well equipped with cooking utensils, and the cook was good enough at producing both army style Chinese food and Western style dishes, according as the appropriate raw materials were available. There was nothing " marvellous " about the regular menu, compared with the feasts, but it was definitely good compared with what one would have expected. For war-time, it was a "home from home", and almost in the lap of luxury.

The L.s arrived at this court—which we now call the "International Peace Hotel"—about a week later, and with them were other Western evacuees from Peiping and Tientsin; two Frenchmen, a Dutchman and an Austrian Jew stayed there for varying lengths of time during that spring; and the following summer an American banker and a German woman; all went through to Chungking after some weeks' delay, except ourselves and the Lindsays. The Austrian Jew, as a medical man, settled down to work with Dr. Kotnis in the army service.

It was just one month after our arrival that the formal opening of the Radio Teachers' Training School was held. There were upwards of a dozen former university students from the cities of Peiping, Tientsin and Tsinan, and a larger number of boys who had been ready to enter college when the war broke out in 1937. These were the young wireless engineers. In addition there were roughly sixty youngsters with rather less formal education who were being trained in wireless communication procedures by the college boys.

The college boys seemed eager for a refresher course covering the things they had forgotten during their four years of active service on the guerrilla front, and Bill was therefore slated to give them a complete series of lectures on college physics and college calculus, with special tutorials in advanced calculus, theoretical electromagnetism, vector analysis, etc., to the more advanced men.

The whole wireless school, together with their cook and service staff, lived as a self-contained unit in a village about a mile south of our place. A reconditioned village house that had been destroyed by enemy action was used as a schoolroom; the roof had been re-made by the boys themselves, with clay patted hard on wooden-board ceiling; when it rained, the roof leaked in twenty places. There were no desks: the boys sat on boards or logs and worked at benches supported on clay pillars that they had set up for themselves. The windows were merely holes in the walls.

They had almost no library, they had only what they could carry on their own backs along with their bedding, their toothbrush, rice-bowl, spare uniform and extra pair of cloth shoes. There was one mule for carrying the school's equipment—a mimeographing machine, stocks of paper, cooking utensils, and so on.

The paper they used was Japanese newsprint sheets. Their chalk, pencils, ink, pens and other consumable supplies were all captured by the guerrillas from the enemy.

With the opening of the teacher training classes the army sent back an order through their underground organisation for a set of textbooks to be purchased in Peiping stores. In a few months they arrived at our International Peace Hotel, and there were great rejoicings as we unpacked the parcel : wireless radio, physics and mathematics texts, over a dozen volumes in all; our college library.

Enthusiasm for the new courses was a real inspiration. In addition to the first-rate boys already attached to the central headquarters wireless department, there were a half dozen promising young students brought over from S.E. Shansi across the dangerous Shihchiachuang-Taiyuan railway specially to attend the classes ; there were others brought down from the guerrilla base to the north of Peiping ; wherever there was a college boy who had escaped into the mountains in 1937 and who had proved himself worthy of the cause by his courage and devotion, and whose academic ability was regarded as above average, he was called back to headquarters and enrolled in our school if he could possibly be spared from his war work.

In addition to the science work, we had many informal contacts, talks, discussions and rambles through the villages with these boys. As part of their English conversation lessons, some of them gave us outlines of their personal adventures, and this would seem to be the most appropriate place to relay some of those remarkable life stories.

DAH YANG

Dah Yang had been the chief engineer at the Ping Hsi radio station when we were there, and had been transferred to the central headquarters radio station shortly after. He was put in charge of the educational work of this station, and we might call him the Dean of Studies for the Wireless Teachers' Training School. Like many of his former classmates, Dah Yang had been brought up in an intellectual atmosphere of great depth and vision in a highly cultured home. His father had been educated in Tientsin and Tokyo and, before the 1911 Revolution, had held an important cultural post in Peking.

In the republican regime Dah Yang's father was appointed head of one of the important government departments, in which position he could have made plenty of opportunity for graft. But the old man was a sincere believer in Christian ethics and remained uncorrupt. He baptised Dah Yang as a child in one of the Christian missions. The family lived a very comfortable life in a Western style house tastefully decorated and equipped with a private library chiefly devoted to works on economics. The father was attracted by the economic theories of Marx, but would not agree that they had any application to China.

Dah Yang entered one of the great national universities in 1935 and took an active part in the student movement during the following two years. After the Japanese invaded North China and occupied Nanking, their home became a centre of secret resistance. Instead of continuing his education under Japanese auspices, Dah Yang stayed at home to help teach his young brother and sisters. He also helped some of his former classmates in private wireless studies. His home became a rendezvous for patriotic underground activity and for the dissemination of reliable news. They eventually established liaison with patriotic guerrillas and organised the escape of fugitives from the enemy's secret gestapo.

During the first year of the occupation most of his fellow patriots went out to join the guerrillas, and he himself planned to go out with the last batch. They dissuaded him, however, asserting that the life would be too hard for him after the comfort of his home; and at last they had slipped secretly away leaving him alone with his thoughts.

But not quite alone; he had a girl friend, and they married in August 1938, going to live in the British Concession at Tientsin. Before their marriage the girl had already been a patriotic worker, one of her more spectacular feats being to plaster the Japanese Occupied part of Tientsin with posters announcing the arrival of the Eighth Route Army in East Hopei, almost completely surrounding Peiping; and early in 1940 the pair of them made contact with the Eighth Route Army organisation and escaped into the western hills from Peiping to join up with the Hopei guerrilla war base.

" I shall never forget my mother's parting message. We had in the past had many heart-to-heart talks about the need for serving our country, and at the last she had bade me farewell in these words :

" ' Don't worry about me when you are gone. I shall always remember that you are doing your best for your country ! ' "

When Dah Yang was put in charge of the wireless station at Ping Hsi, the commander there offered Mrs. Yang a chance to study wireless so that she could be with her husband. But she, being a qualified teacher, begged to be given some constructive work instead. They made her principal of a primary school in a neighbouring village. Within a few months the Japanese embarked on one of their regular mopping-up campaigns in the area and all the units had to pack up and move around dodging the enemy.

Some of Mrs. Yang's colleagues were hiding with peasants because they happened to be sick, and unable to stand the arduous marching. One day Mrs. Yang decided to pay these colleagues a visit, as her unit was passing through the village. She stayed an hour too long : some smart espionage work on the part of the enemy had disclosed the presence of party workers in the village and Mrs. Yang was captured along with her colleagues by a unit of puppet Chinese troops in the pay of the Japanese.

Dah Yang had a melancholy disposition, but an utterly unselfish devotion not only to the cause for which he was fighting, but towards all his friends and fellow-workers. It seemed hard for him to forgive himself for the death of his wife, but was proud beyond words for the sacrifice she had made, and more than willing to make the same sacrifice himself. Hardship and suffering meant nothing to this child of luxury ; he was roughing it with the hardiest toughs in the toughest army in the world. He had been down with malaria several times, suffered three months from typhoid, and yet persisted in working himself to the last ounce of energy all the time.

It was with great difficulty that he told us about his wife, and when he had finished he pulled himself together again and said :

" But I have had my revenge ! That unit of puppet troops were encountered later by a stronger force of our army and were completely eliminated by us ! "

Dah Yang was a delightful, perfect young gentleman, a typical representative of China's scholar gentry at their best, working himself to death for his country in the great United Front against Japan.

"IRON OX" HAN

Han was nicknamed by his fellow-teachers the "Iron Ox" because of his tendency to obstinacy; he found it harder than most to submit himself to their regular democratic group disciplinary methods. But he was a first-rate technical man in the wireless service station, and an excellent student in advanced mathematics. The story he gave us is worth quoting in full:

"My first contact with the Japanese was when I was only nine years old. Our village home in Manchuria was on the Korean border, and there had been a Korean uprising, the exact nature of which I understood nothing. But the Japanese held a public ceremony at which they brought twenty-eight Korean suspects and buried them alive. The dreadful thing so upset me that for three nights I couldn't sleep a wink.

"Four years later Marshal Chang Hsueh-liang was at war with the Russians over the rights of the South Manchuria Railway, and I remember clearly the public rejoicings in November 1929 when the Russians agreed to sell out their rights to Marshal Chang and called off the battle. We Chinese in the North-Eastern Provinces were naturally anti-Japanese and pro-Russian. The Japanese murder of the young Marshal's father in 1927 had helped to stimulate this sentiment, and this railway deal inaugurated a great wave of liaison activities aiming at full cultural *rapprochement* between Russia and Manchuria.

"When I was fifteen I went to Mukden and entered a military school, commenced training in machine-shop work in connection with the arsenal there. But this was just one month before the Mukden Incident closed everything down. The school ceased functioning and I went back home, staying there for six months in a very depressed atmosphere. There was shooting and looting every night in the villages. The 'bandits' were Chinese volunteer anti-Japanese units deliberately trying to upset the Japanese-imposed regime of 'law and order'.

"Four of these patriots demanded shelter in our home which was one of the largest in the village, and in return they guaranteed our safety from molestation. During the day they would sleep under our protection. During the night they went out hunting, and brought back silks, money and fire-arms. They had been policemen under the Chinese Government and were specialising in raiding the police stations now under the puppet regime. They succeeded in securing great quantities of ammunition, and even a number of machine-guns were smuggled into our house.

"Japanese efforts at installing a completely new police organisation were at last successful in the larger towns, and after six months conditions in Mukden itself had so far returned to normal that schools began to reopen. I returned to the city and entered an industrial school for mining. But although the schools were open, they were very different. I found that in my industrial school I could learn nothing but the techniques of manual labour. And after my 'graduation' in 1934 I was able to apply only for coolie jobs because I had not learnt the Japanese language.

"Dissatisfied with this state of affairs, I took the first chance to evade emigration restrictions and left for Peking and entered the newly reorganised North-eastern University, refugee institution from Mukden. The great majority of students were, like myself, escapees from the Japanese regime in the North-east. We formed a strong anti-Japanese organisation and devoted much time to propaganda for national resistance.

"During the 1935 demonstrations our University had a strong contingent out, and taking part in the general activities at that time we had a team of two hundred boys and girls touring the countryside lecturing to the peasant population on the necessity to resist Japan's aggression. This experience was a great eye-opener to us also. We were appalled by the state of ignorance in which the vast majority of our peasant people were doomed to pass their lives. Many of the people whom we met, only a few hours' journey from the cultural capital of the nation, had never even heard of the Japanese.

"Most of our propaganda team were arrested by the local military authorities as disturbers of the peace and forcibly sent back to Peiping. I escaped their clutches and decamped to Paoting where my sister was living. Those who had been sent back to Peiping were threatened with death if they continued in such 'Communist activities'. Did you ever hear of such stupid nonsense ? It made students think that you cannot be patriotic without becoming a Communist.

"It was in fact the first time I had ever given a thought to Communism, and because of it I began to study some of the literature of the Chinese Communist Party. I found it very impressive, but I am still not a Communist. Scientists should remain neutral.

" After hiding some weeks, I eventually returned to Peiping in time to start the second semester of class work, but found the school in no mood for studies. The place was in a turmoil over a suggestion that the institution should move farther away from the Japanese and establish itself in Sian, where there was already a fairly strong anti-Japanese organisation and less likelihood of police interference in the interests of appeasement. It is interesting that Sian should have been the centre of both the most violent anti-Communist organisation at the same time with the quite distinct anti-Japanese organisation. The two conflicting aims came to a crisis with the kidnapping of the Generalissimo almost a year later. The anti-Japanese parties won.

" Although this move to Sian was, for our University, a purely internal one, there was such an obvious connection with the fundamental problem of national security that our excitable students very soon became unreasonable. Those who supported the move began accusing the opposition of lack of patriotism, and incensed them so much that an open brawl ensued in which some of the students were knocked unconscious. The University authorities forthwith decided to act at once to avoid further dispute. The local military authorities provided us with a special train and we all embarked for Sian. We travelled so leisurely that, as the train passed through Paoting I was able to get out and pay a fare-well visit to my sister and catch the train again by cycling down the line.

" We finally got settled in the south-east suburb of Sian, but our troubles were by no means ended. The authorities had sent a new Dean along, the old one wishing to remain in Peiping. This new Dean proved unable to maintain proper discipline, and there were student agitations for his removal in which I took part. As a result the old Dean was sent up from Peiping and he at once set about punishing those who had been active in the disturbance. As a native of the North-east I had had the privilege of free tuition and free board ; but these privileges were now removed as punish-ment, and being on my own I could no longer afford to stay at the University. Instead I resigned and came back to Peiping where it was easier to find means of support. I entered the National Peking University and enrolled as a student of geology. But I had only one year there before the Marco Polo Bridge Incident again interrupted my studies.

"In the course of our military training at the University we students had made contacts with patriotic officers of the 29th Route Army, and one of these officers had prepared a volunteer group of students as a nucleus of resistance to the invaders should the crisis come. So that summer we were not unprepared, and, escaping from the city, we gathered under our officer in the grounds of the Yuen Ming Yuan—ruins of the ancient Summer Palace that was sacked by Western troops during the Taiping times.

"With about twenty rifles between us we raided one of the Peiping prisons and three hundred of the four hundred prisoners we rescued joined our volunteer army. We then organised a thorough search of the villages and the towns all round Peiping for arms and ammunition abandoned by the retreating Chinese troops, succeeded in salvaging no less than a thousand pieces, including some field guns.

"But we were terribly short of funds, and no satisfactory way of feeding our ranks. Our General, as we now called the officer who had organised us, therefore decided to approach the French Catholic fathers in the mission near Wenchuan for financial help. Unfortunately for our reputation our General was not very far removed from the old style bandit, and under the stress of circumstances was reverting to type. We found ourselves therefore with no less than eleven Frenchmen on our hands as hostages ! There were, of course, a majority of old-style soldiers in our unit, because of the large number of such people we had released from the prison, and others who had joined up with us since. But we students were aghast at the kidnapping and tried our best to persuade the General to release them, but to no avail. He replied that the capture of the missionaries would bring him in much needed funds and also ensure our safety from direct attack by the Japanese. So bandits we had to be as the price of patriotism !

"We had encamped at the summit of 'crow's nest', that ruin on the top of the sharp-pointed hill not far beyond the Black Dragon Pool, and from there we were able to harass the Japanese on the main road towards Miao Feng Shan. One day we opened fire on a Japanese staff car, but two of its occupants escaped and in two hours they returned with forty men armed with rifles and a machine-gun. But from our perch we were able to keep them at bay for more than three hours after which they withdrew with heavy losses. However, within another hour a new party arrived with a field gun and began shelling our position which therefore rapidly became untenable. So we quietly withdrew with our hostages to a safer place about two miles away.

"After the publicity given to this encounter by the Japanese in the Peiping Press as part of their efforts to secure the release of the French priests, more students escaped from the city and joined us. They had not believed the Japanese story that there were Frenchmen kidnapped, but had been just waiting for definite information that anti-Japanese guerrillas were operating. When they discovered that we had kidnapped the Frenchmen they at once joined us in a campaign among the former soldiers and the jail-birds to convert them away from the kidnapping policy. Just as if we were still in college !

"But the ' general ' was too smart for us. While we were busy campaigning against him, he had secretly effected a ransom and secured his funds before releasing the captives.

"It was not long after this incident that the regular Eighth Route Army representatives reached the environs of Peiping and made contact with us. We gladly abandoned the bandit group in favour of the new organisation. I volunteered for active service with these guerrillas and spent some time fighting in Chahar Province before being withdrawn to the Ping Hsi headquarters where my technical training was turned to use in radio repair work.

"After the war I am hoping to be able to return to college training and complete my study for an engineering degree so that I can take an active part in the industrial reconstruction of the country."

Liu Shuang

Liu's father was one of the leading railway engineers in Free China. Liu had passed the entrance examinations for the science college at Yenching University, was planning to become one of the physics students in the autumn of 1937. When the Japanese invaded North China, Liu's family dissuaded him from coming to Peiping, and he entered the University at Tsinan instead. Within a few months, however, the family moved from Tsinan to Hankow to avoid the enemy's advancing hordes, and Liu went with them.

In Hankow he entered the National Military Training College along with a few hundred other patriotic students hoping to be trained for commissions in the army. The teachers in the college were old-time militarists without the least idea how to handle the high-spirited youths, and discipline was conspicuous by its absence. Their training was frequently interrupted by rioting ; and even what training they received was useless. The boys used to sing songs of derision about their teachers, and at times the school authorities called upon the military to quell disturbances by means of machine-guns. There was one typical teacher who, when supposed to be lecturing on guerrilla strategy, spent his time boasting of the escapades he had taken part in during a campaign for the suppression of a peasant uprising.

Shortly before the Japanese occupied Hankow, the school abandoned the idea of training its students for army work. The whole group was transferred to Nanchang and a new body of students, including girls, were started on a course for political leaders and cadres to work among the people in organising them for war and reconstruction.

This was hardly more successful than the military training had been. In the first place there was no very clear idea of what the students would be actually doing after their graduation from the course, and no field work for them to put into practice their principles while still in the school. And in the second place the school was under the control of the C.C. clique, a pro-Japanese faction within the Nationalist Party. Here is what Liu had to say about the affair :

" We had all enrolled as patriotic students, but were disappointed to discover that none of the courses of study mentioned anything about anti-Japanese resistance. How were we going to preach patriotism to the peasants in any other terms than on a programme of resistance to the invaders ? We became critical again of our teachers, and many of the students abandoned the school.

" Then a rumour began to grow among the students that some of us were being forced into the C.C. clique, that faction of the Kuomintang that has a bad reputation for subversive pro-Japanese activity. More of the students deserted the school. And before very long the rumours were verified. The secret agent of the clique made the mistake of trying to get hold of one of the girl students to join the clique.

" The first the rest of us knew about it was a wild scream from the office of the Dean, and a bunch of us rushed in to discover this girl student being interviewed by the school officer who had a revolver in his hand. The girl told us that she was presented with a wad of notes at the point of the revolver, and had been ordered to sign a declaration form which swore loyalty to the clique.

" The victim had to declare his or her willingness to obey the Generalissimo, to obey Chen Li-fu and his brother Chen Kuo-fu, and finally to obey without question the immediate orders of the clique's local officers. No doubt the first two obediences were merely blinds to trap patriotic students into signing. But this girl had had courage enough to raise an alarm when her natural resistance to signing away her freedom had caused the officer to threaten her with a revolver.

" The incident of course spread further apprehension throughout the school and the great majority of us abandoned, or rather deserted, the school. This meant that most of us did not feel safe from the attentions of the clique's secret agents. We knew too much about their illegal methods to be safe. Without telling my parents I left secretly for Yenan and joined up with the United Front Movement there ; it seemed the best way to serve my country as there was no possible opening in the area where the C.C. clique was operating."

Like the other two men, Liu was no politician. All he wanted was an outlet for patriotic instincts such that he could be of use as a scientist, and this united front movement was his " spiritual home ". As a physicist, Liu was brilliant, inheriting the gifts of his father.

There were other stories equally informing, but these three will serve as typical examples. The thing that surprised us was not so much the enthusiasm with which these youngsters settled down in the uncongenial surroundings for advanced study, remarkable though that was ; it was rather the fact that the Eighth Route Army headquarters deliberately diverted them from their normal army work so that they could spend a considerable part of their time studying things like differential calculus that could not possibly have any remote connection with guerrilla warfare.

PRE-ENGINEERING PROGRAMME FOR GUERRILLAS

General Nieh explained this to us as quite simple. The Eighth Route Army is not merely a guerrilla fighting organisation, it is primarily an educational enterprise through which to lead the people of China in cultural reconstruction. This policy of requiring their personnel to spend whatever time they could in study was most fundamental in their whole outlook. The leaders of the Army were fully conscious of the great sacrifice which these university boys had made when they abandoned their college careers in Peiping and other cities for the sake of the national cause, and were anxious to make full use of the opportunity which they now had for study.

During the reconstruction after the war China will need all the engineers she can muster ; and not only engineers, but patriotic engineers with a devotion to duty far more complete than one might normally be able to hope for. These boys had proven their devotion and their loyalty ; from this point of view they were the cream of the nation, and it was a shame if their present guerrilla life was going to destroy their future usefulness as technical men. Our educational programme was, therefore, planned as a pre-engineering refresher course.

The boys were a delight to teach. Although they had been away from studies for four years or more so far as mathematics was concerned, yet within three or four weeks they had got back into the swing again, and we sailed along at full speed as thoroughly as any first-rate university class.

At various times through the course there were alarms and news of Japanese campaigns of which more will be given later. We had to keep pretty well packed-up and ready for sudden raids most of the time, but on the whole we stayed in the one village for over a year, and the group got some solid work done. In spite of the almost complete absence of laboratory equipment, outside of that for wireless communication, we got through the whole of college physics in a way that would probably horrify more orthodox professors ; and they really did master college calculus. We tested them thoroughly : weekly quizzes, monthly written examinations, and every quarter a comprehensive test, all up to the best college grade.

It all seemed queer and incongruous, surrounded as we were with normal peasant life : pigs and poultry, donkeys and grindstones and old women sitting on the steps of the classroom door twisting hemp into string on their bare shins.

Back in Yenching University we had often talked about how remote we were from the real China. What was the use of all this modern science to the poor peasant, and how can our luxury-spoiled students fit into their future environment? But these guerrilla boys had no such qualms. They were so close to the real China that they shared no such illusions about the need for cultural work and higher education. To them it was painfully obvious that China's real need was for more and still more advanced scientific work, coupled with intensive education for her poverty-stricken masses.

When you have lived several years under the same roof as the poorest of the farmers, eaten the same food and scratched the same species of louse-bites, arm-chair discussions about the need for fitting China's youth into China's own present economic and social environment become just so much reactionary nonsense. Our real mission is to fit China's youth to change their country, to stimulate them in their revolutionary endeavour; and that is what these guerrilla boys are getting out of their advanced study in that mountain stronghold.

PLATE VI

[*Photo by E. R. Lapwood*

View of Sha Ho 3rd Base H.Q. Guerrillas in Chin Cha Chi.

Chapter VII

DRAGON VERSUS OCTOPUS

OUTLINE HISTORY OF THE BORDER REGION

TAKING a look at the map, one can see the tentacles of the Japanese octopus stinging deep into the flesh of the Chinese dragon. For six years they had been pumping devilish poisons into the life-blood of their victim. But the people of North China had been generating an anti-toxin so effective as to threaten the life of the octopus itself. The dragon's fangs were ready very soon to strike back.

At the outset of the China Incident, the Japanese mechanised forces made an uninterrupted advance along the main railway lines in North China. During August and September 1937 they reached Nankow, Kalgan and Tatung and entered Suiyuan on the road to Mongolia; along the Peiping-Hankow line they arrived at the junction Shihchiachuang and turned west along the railway to Taiyuan as far as the pass at Niang Tze Kuan. The Chinese provincial forces were completely routed and abandoned their equipment all over the countryside.

In front of the enemy's rapid advance people abandoned their property in the towns and fled to the hills, or evacuated along the railways. Local government officials with the necessary resources were the first to make their get-away. The whole province of Hopei was reduced to chaos, police ceased to function, disorderly gangs of demoralised soldiery roamed the valleys and started to terrorise the peasants. Japanese special agents began setting up puppet regimes in all the larger cities and the county towns, and their influence threatened to reduce the entire area to colonial status, repeating the process that had already been successfully completed in the North-Eastern Provinces of Manchuria.

To prevent this debacle from materialising, the headquarters of the Chinese Communist Party at Yenan decided to despatch troops to the defence of Shansi Province, in co-operation with the Nationalist forces there. These troops met with spectacular success. The first Chinese victory over the invaders in the North was that of the Communist Army at Ping Hsin Kuan, on September 25th, 1937, where the Japanese were thrown back in their advance across the country.

On another front the Japanese threat to Taiyuan caused the 115th division of the Eighth Route (Communist) Army to be sent across the railway to the south to defend that city, leaving only a small detachment in N.W. Shansi consisting of one regiment, one cavalry unit and two companies under General Nieh Jung-chen. General Nieh was instructed to build a guerrilla base within the Great Wall, the base which became the Border Region now known as " Chin Cha Chi " : Chin, an old name for Shansi, Cha for Chahar, and Chi for Hopei (Chihli). The full name of the war base is, in English, The Shansi-Chahar-Hopei Border Region War Base.

General Nieh was no amateur strategist. He had worked in the Schneider-Creusot arms factories in France, the Renault motor works, and the Thomson Electric Co. He had been active in the Labour Movement in Europe, studied in the Labour University of Belgium, and received political training in Moscow and practical fighting experience in the civil wars in his own country.

His headquarters were set up on November 7th, 1937, in the county of Fuping, of which the county town was the only county town not occupied by the enemy in the whole province.

From this centre, party workers were sent out to stimulate the formation of anti-Japanese associations, arrange for the setting up of local self-government in the villages. Mobilisation committees sprang into existence in every district in a great popular movement in support of the anti-Japanese programme.

The mountain war base had a mushroom growth, but its roots went down deep into the ground : it was something the people were waiting for, were already well prepared for, and welcomed with enthusiasm as their one hope of salvation from abject slavery at the hands of the Japanese. Its spectacular success was due in part to this popular awareness of its messianic character, but not less to the skill and ingenuity of General Nieh and his staff. The base had become a formidable obstacle to the designs of the enemy even before the Japanese realised what was happening. In the winter of that same year the enemy attacked the area with 20,000 men concentrated in eight converging routes ; they were defeated in as many pitched battles.

In the spring of 1938 local guerrilla units in the plains of Central Hopei east of the Peking-Hankow railway, were linked up with the main base and rapidly became a wealthy adjunct of the war base. Guerrilla warfare on the plains became a permanent reality, calling for courage and skill surpassing even those called for among the mountains.

During the summer of 1938 the Eighth Route Army opened a general offensive on the two main railway lines on either side of the Central Hopei plain—the Peiping-Hankow and the Tientsin-Pukow lines. This offensive coincided with the Japanese drive southward towards the rail crossing at Hsuchow, and, by disrupting their communications materially contributed to the defeat of the enemy at Taierchuang—which was the first big Nationalist victory over the Japanese in their southerly advance through Shantung.

In retaliation for this, the Japanese concentrated 12,000 men in an attack upon General Nieh's headquarters at Fuping. Greatly outnumbered, Nieh withdrew from the town, resorted to continuous flank attacks upon the enemy and so effectively cut him off from his supplies on the railways that the Japanese were obliged to withdraw after suffering heavy losses in men and equipment, and having achieved nothing of military value except a bitter experience.

During these summer campaigns the Eighth Route Army were successful in liberating the mountain area north of Peiping, which they called " Ping Pei ", establishing popular anti-Japanese associations, mobilisation groups and village self-governments. At the same time Eighth Route Army agents spread all round Peiping, and established strong connections with local patriots on the plains of East Hopei between Tangshan and Tientsin, where the puppet Yin Ju-keng was nominally the head of the Japanese administration.

In the autumn of 1938 the North China command of the Japanese Imperial Army gave evidence of having realised what was happening under their snub noses. No less than 50,000 men were deployed in seventeen concentrations to " mop up " the main base around Fuping county (hsien). Thanks to the superior intelligence service of the guerrillas, they were able to evade completely the fire of the enemy, and to make it so hot for the Japanese through the month's operations that he was obliged again to withdraw to his original positions, leaving behind an estimated ten thousand casualties, including several high officers.

The spring of 1939 saw a Japanese campaign against the guerrillas on the plains of Central Hopei, but again they were too late ;

co-operation between the local population and the armed forces was already so close that the Japanese failed to break the organisation of resistance. During the remainder of the year 1939 there were nothing but local encounters, both sides were consolidating, and building up political offensives.

During 1940 the Eighth Route Army launched what they called a " hundred regiments' campaign ", simultaneously on all the main railway lines in North China. Military stores, arsenals and factories, puppet organisations were raided, damaged or destroyed all round the Border Region. The campaign permanently changed for the better the whole military situation in North China, establishing the Eighth Route Army as the superior force in the area outside of the immediate neighbourhood of the railway lines themselves. The invaders were forced into an essentially defensive position from which they have never fully recovered.

During this hundred regiments' campaign the Ping Pei areas were extended a hundred miles north of Peiping, and the contact with East Hopei was so materially strengthened that that district became a fully organised part of the whole war base.

In a hastily planned retaliatory campaign, the Japanese sent 50,000 men on the rampage throughout the region, burning down villages, slaughtering the people, and carrying off all the movable property they could get away with. They called it a " San kuang " policy, literally " Three clearances ", supposedly clearing away the three main supports of the guerrilla forces. At the end of this campaign the Japanese announced that the Eighth Route Army had been wiped out of the region, and that General Nieh had gone to Yenan to apologise for his failure to Mao Tse-tung.

As a matter of fact by the end of the year 1940 a map of the operational area of the Eighth Route Army in North China looked something like a huge dragon's head with the Japanese life-lines clamped securely in its closing jaws.

Through the year 1941 the Japanese made continuous and frantic efforts to liquidate the threat to their hold on North China, apparently in preparation for their Pacific adventures. Every section of the Border Region was attacked in turn, climaxed by a great assault upon the main base around Fuping through the two months of September and October. No less than 70,000 Japanese and 30,000 puppet troops took part in these operations. Again carrying out their " San kuang " strategy, they certainly did great material damage to the people, but their main objective of regaining the initiative in their struggle with the Eighth Route Army was completely missed. We arrived in the region just one month after the end of the campaign, and found the Japanese so weakened that they were not in fact able to repeat the performance until two years later. The region was left in comparative peace the whole time we were there and we watched its recovery from the devastations on every hand.

During 1942 the Japanese embarked on a new purely defensive campaign on all fronts round the Border Region. In their propaganda to the Chinese in Peiping, the Japanese claimed to have built 10,000 miles of blockade ditches round the guerrilla bases—five times the length of the Great Wall—to serve the double purpose of protecting the railway zones from the attentions of the guerrillas, and of impeding the mobility of the Chinese in their communications between the different sections of their war base.

Within the areas protected by the ditches, the Japanese built block-houses, three to the mile in all directions, connected with telephones and linked by motor roads. Having established this system, they proceeded to dig, under cover of strong armed protection, another line of ditches a few miles further out into the guerrilla areas. Ditch digging by day and counter ditch filling by night became the order of the year, until finally the Japanese were forced to change their strategy again.

They now first made a raid in considerable force upon a strategic point, erected a fort, garrisoned the point and protected it against the Chinese by a sufficient number of heavy machine-guns, large supplies of ammunition and reserves of food. Only after a line of such strong points had been secured was the ditch digging undertaken to consolidate the area newly marked out for block-house control. The success of this method depended entirely on the fact that the Eighth Route Army had no heavy artillery, and had no way of reducing a fort without first capturing it in hand-to-hand fighting.

This fortress strategy caused the Eighth Route Army command serious trouble. It was essentially the same strategy as had been used by Chiang Kai-shek during his final campaign to dislodge the Reds from their soviet in Kiangsi. But the speed of progress of the Japanese was exceedingly slow. During the two years we were there, the enemy did succeed in advancing a distance something like ten miles up some of the main valleys into the mountains around the main base in Fuping, and in building fortresses uncomfortably near to the headquarters at several points.

The Chinese christened the method " caterpillar-eating-leaf strategy ", and devised their counter strategy on the " bird-eating-caterpillar " idea. This succeeded excellently in the main base west of the Peiping-Hankow railway, but on the plains of Central Hopei there were too many caterpillars for the birds.

During the spring of 1942 the enemy actually succeeded in erecting forts and block-houses all over the plain, making a complete network of strong points linked by roads and telephones and garrisoned by at least 30,000 men as a permanent force of occupation. To establish this stranglehold, 50,000 armed troops supplied with tanks and airplanes were employed for three months ; and the result was to oblige the Eighth Route Army to remove their regular forces and their supply services out of the plains and back into the mountains near Fuping. From that time on Eighth Route Army work in the plains was limited to underground infiltration, secret mass organisation continuing the former open anti-Japanese activities among the peasants. A continual struggle is being maintained preventing the Occupationists from taking full advantage of their conquest, and causing a perpetual drain upon their man-power and resources. Completely underground, and operated from the stable mountain base close by, these activities are completely proof against all attempts at suppression.

From their main base in the mountains, the Eighth Route Army's counter strategy was based upon the fact that with the extended block-house area, the Japanese garrison forces were spread out so thinly in small units that the Chinese Army could go at will through the whole railway zone without fear of meeting superior forces. The Chinese made a greatly increased number of raids on occupied cities within the railway zones. Puppet officials were arrested and shot, prisoners taken, stores captured or destroyed by fire, military dumps exploded, the population encouraged to resist the demands of garrison forces for taxes and food supplies. Underground resistance movements were established in all the large occupied cities. From East Hopei the region of influence under the Eighth Route Army was extended to three hundred miles north-east of the Great Wall at Shanhaikuan into the heart of Manchuria.

At the end of 1942 General Nieh was able to report that in spite of the Japanese determination to encroach upon his area at all costs, the Eighth Route Army had been able not only to maintain its power and initiative, but had also enlarged the area within which it operated and increased the population voluntarily co-operating with the Border Region democratic government.

During 1943 the Eighth Route Army intensified their bird strategy, capturing forts and block-houses, raiding the building parties and rescuing conscript labourers employed on fort-building campaigns. It was estimated that to every fort built the enemy lost sixty men and that several thousand Chinese labourers made good their escape into the Border Region. The Eighth Route Army command felt confident that they could so delay the enemy's plans by these methods that the Japanese could not accomplish their purpose before the larger problems arising in the Pacific would reduce them to impotence. Nevertheless the struggle was bitter and continuous ; for the Japanese were determined to complete the job in the least possible time regardless of cost.

The Japanese did succeed in establishing enough forts at the valley entrances near to the Chinese centres of command to make it easier for them to spring surprise attacks on the Chinese. But not until the autumn of 1943 did they feel in a position to repeat major operations on the scale that they had used in 1941. And since then they have apparently been obliged to remove a great part of their China forces down south to open up the land route to Indo-China. This has left the Eighth Route Army free enough to consolidate in preparation for the great land offensive on the Japanese positions defending North China and South Manchuria, called for in the final stages of the war.

Chapter VIII

PEN, SCALPEL AND SWORD

WE had walked no less than thirty miles the day we arrived at the Resist Japan United University. A telephone message had gone through to the third subdivisional military headquarters asking them to inform President Ch'eng Fang-wu of our impending visit, but it had not been relayed. Our guide in consequence had some difficulty in finding the right place. In the village where he had expected to find the President, there was only a small unit of girl students who came tumbling out of a cottage to see us. They were all dressed in the same padded cotton uniforms as the boys.

It was nearly dark by the time we located the village where the administrative staff of the University were living, and well after their usual meal time. They used to eat twice a day, at about ten and four, and when travelling, one aimed at arriving at one's destination in time for the second meal, otherwise it made trouble for the kitchen—or more often for the traveller. Unless one was high enough in rank it meant one had to go hungry until next morning.

Fortunately for us, our " rank " was honorary enough, apparently, to rate a feast at whatever time we arrived. And at the University, it was no exception. Their cook produced a first-class Chinese feast in less time than it took to get through the formalities of introductions and polite conversation with the President and his wife.

President Ch'eng was wearing the same kind of uniform as his students, practically identical with that of the fighting men of the Eighth Route Army. But there was nothing military about his personality, which was as scholarly as one would expect of a college president. A well-known Leftist writer, his most famous work was his translation into Chinese from the German of Marx's *Das Capital*. From 1924 to 1926 he had been a teacher of physics and mathematics in Canton, so we had no difficulty in understanding each other.

Sun Yat-sen's historic speeches on the Three Peoples' Principles at the Canton University had stirred Ch'eng's interest in things political. From 1926 to 1928 he was a leader of a Leftist literary group in Shanghai, and from 1928 to 1931 he studied politics in Germany. Returning to China he joined the Hupeh Provincial Soviet as chief of that government's committee on education. Between 1932 and 1933 this soviet group was driven by Chiang Kai-shek's forces from Hupeh into Kiangsi, and Ch'eng Fang-wu almost died of starvation during the campaign. For six months his staple diet was roots and dried leaves ; when once they found an ox, they ate the whole thing, including the leather and the hairs. Malaria got him, too, and at times during the civil war he had to be carried from village to village. His sufferings continued through the long march from Kiangsi to Shensi, 1934 to 1935. But once in Yenan he settled down again to constructive work, founding the so-called " Communist Academy ".

In 1937 when the Chinese Communists declared war on Japan, Ch'eng Fang-wu was no longer satisfied to remain in safety. He had twenty thousand students in the academy at Yenan, studying cultural warfare against the Japanese : they had already started a thorough war-time educational programme in response to popular demand throughout the country, and the majority of patriotic students in China who had no family ties to hold them back, had flocked to the call, trekked to Yenan. The Japanese were quick enough to realise that Yenan had become the centre of student resistance, and ruthlessly bombed the place until hardly a stone remained above another. The old city of Fushih (Yenan) was razed to the ground.

The Communist organisations literally dug themselves in at Yenan ; by living in loess caves they immunised themselves from damage by air raid. And instead of disbanding the students—there were plans for admitting a total of 60,000—President Ch'eng decided to move right in behind the Japanese front lines, make his institution a thoroughly guerrilla one in immediate touch with the scene of battle : his students would study cultural warfare in the firing line itself.

No less than 10,000 students went over the lines with Ch'eng Fang-wu in a mass attack upon the ignorance of the country people—their weakest line of defence against the Fascist invaders. Marching across Shansi after being ferried over the Yellow

River, the party divided into three groups before jumping the Shansi railway. The first group succeeded in getting over without mishap, but they roused the railway patrols, and the second group had to wait until things quieted down again. Even so, some of the stragglers got caught when the second group went over, so the last group was given a strong armed escort. A pitched battle ensued as the students crossed the line, and before they could make the hills on the other side, Japanese planes came over and machine-gunned them from the air.

Arriving in Hopei Province, the students were divided between two groups of villages, one being organised into a purely military training school for army officers, familiarly called "Kangta", which means Resistance College, and the other group became the college for cultural and civil service cadres. with schools for arts, education and jurisprudence. It was this group who were now known as Resist Japan United University, or for short, just Lienta. Because there is a "Lienta" at Kunming, namely the South West Associated University, we shall refer to the Communists' Lienta as the "Guerrilla Lienta".

The library of Guerrilla Lienta was a collection of some twenty thousand volumes that they had carried with them, a few books in each student's pack. Classrooms, they had none other than disused barns, open-air arenas, peasants' threshing floors, sandy stretches in little mountain glens. Dormitories and dining-rooms were also lacking : they were billeted on the villagers in the same way as the Army, and ten or more students would sleep together on a single kang. Their dining-room was the village square, and they gobbled up their meals guerrilla style, seated on their haunches round the millet pail.

There was nothing that the Japanese could bomb, and when the enemy launched a mopping-up campaign, the students packed up their kits and just kept moving around, keeping the enemy out of sight over the other side of a hill. Whenever they could find an hour or so to spare they would unhitch their portable blackboard from the donkey's back, and hold their classes under the trees.

It was a hard school, but it was a living school where principles and practice went hand in hand—they lived as it were from hand to mouth with their political and sociological theories. There was nothing high-brow about their studies. They could ill afford Utopian imaginings.

Through all this hard living, President Ch'eng stayed with his students as one of them ; and all his colleagues maintained the same spartan tradition. The Chancellor was one Chang Lung-chi who, as a student in Peiping, was as early as 1920 expelled from college for anti-Japanese activities, and chose, of all places, Japan as refuge from the pro-Japanese clique in China. Here he joined a secret anti-Japanese group of Chinese students in Tokyo to study the enemy's psychology. On returning to China he was again arrested for participating in student agitations against the compromising policies of the government. This time his health was affected, and in 1931 he decided to go to Germany where he studied economics for five years before returning to his own counry. He joined up with the Yenan group just before the Sian Incident, December 1936.

On the morning after we arrived, February 11th, we had breakfast with the President and his wife, and were then taken to a big welcome meeting of all the students and the staff, a great mass of uniformed people assembled out in the open under a clear blue sky. A long session of speeches and discussion ; they asked more than fifty questions in writing, for us to answer, about our impressions of the Border Region, about life in Occupied Peiping, but chiefly about the international situation, at that time very grim.

In the evening there was a banquet at which we met the local leading people. With the President and his wife were the professor of pathology of the Bethune Medical College, the chief of the government supervisory district, the Dean of the college, and the Dean of the medical school. In high spirits, they drank their wine to a Chinese finger game ; to help out, Bill competed with the professor of pathology who drank his wine without the least objection to Bill eating " mantou " instead. He was so adept at losing the finger game and being " obliged " to drink his wine that in the end he cried quits because of a class in pathology he had to give at five in the morning.

In the evening they assembled about a dozen of the key people of the University for a round table discussion. One could not tell from their appearance who were professors and who were students ; both groups were represented. There was the general secretary, chairman of the student association, director of student welfare, two or three deans, two important professors, and others.

They never used their titles in conversation, and they all looked like rough farmers except for a slightly greater attention to personal hygiene.

The room was illuminated only by a couple of small vegetable oil lamps set on the table. An atmosphere of eery secrecy and grim seriousness enveloped the group ; it was by no means a detached academic calm that these educationalists believed in ; theirs was a great enthusiasm for their cause.

Their college syllabus was probably the most remarkable in the world, centred entirely around mass resistance to Japanese Fascism through cultural reconstruction of the peasant population. One was surprised first at the absence of all artificial regulations and restrictions that worry the hair off students in ordinary academic institutes of higher learning. Admission was by recommendation, not by examination ; any young man or woman who could present acceptable evidence of being sincerely patriotic and sufficiently intelligent, would be admitted. College was a call to battle not an invitation to a leisurely course of study. After admission the student was provided free tuition and free food, clothing and lodging of the type available among the peasants in the villages, and was given a small amount of pocket money to buy little comforts from the village pedlars.

Students felt themselves to be volunteer members of a cultural army, and worked with immense enthusiasm. They do not attain pre-war academic standards, because they do not study pre-war academic subjects. They study biology only in connection with nursing and medicine. Agriculture is a matter of testing for one's self new varieties of seeds, and selling new ideas to the peasants ; Art, of publicity for progressive programmes and popular morale ; Jurisprudence would leave out any study of Roman Law in favour of the probable bones of contention in a farming community in village units. What they do learn they use and test in the daily struggle against the Japanese.

Because of the urgent need for local leaders, the first class of graduates from the Guerrilla Lienta were given only three months' training, and were immediately placed in local government work and mass movement organs to combat the influence of infiltrating Japanese agents. For six months these youngsters held the front with an absolute minimum of preparation while the second class was being given a more thorough training. When we arrived the third class was receiving a whole year's education in the meaning and practice of militant democracy in the war against Fascist imperialism.

SCALPEL

Next morning President Ch'eng walked with us across the Tang River to meet Dr. Kotnis and the Bethune Medical College group at the village of Ko Kung; there was another welcome meeting there, and we had to address a gathering of over a thousand students and teachers, nurses and doctors.

In 1938 Dr. Norman Bethune had started the first training class for nurses with only eighteen students. The Border Region school of hygiene was formally opened on September 18th, 1939, eighth anniversary of the Mukden Incident. Norman Bethune died on November 11th of that same year, from sepsis due to a self-inflicted wound sustained while operating on a wounded soldier. The International Peace Hospitals were founded in Bethune's memory early in 1940. In association with these hospitals are now the Bethune medical colleges. These institutions are now operating in every border region through North China.

Chief of the International Peace Hospital in the Hopei area was Dr. D. S. Kotnis of Bombay University. With four other Indian delegates of the Indian National Congress, Kotnis came to China in 1938 to help China's war of resistance; they brought with them equipment and medical supplies, and reported to the Chinese Red Cross Society for an assignment. They were sent first to work with the National Army at Wuhan, and stayed to within three days of the fall of those cities to the Japanese. They then came to Chungking via Ichang and awaited more ambulances and supplies from India. At this time the Chinese Red Cross Society decided to move the whole group up to Yenan to work with the Communist forces. They went with the Eighth Route Army through South Shansi, South Hopei, Central Hopei, Ping Hsi on all fronts of the guerrilla war. Three of the doctors then returned to India, one stayed in Yenan with the Communist headquarters, and Kotnis elected to stay with General Nieh's headquarters in Hopei, to follow in the footsteps of Dr. Bethune.

President of the medical college in Hopei at the time we visited them, was Dr. Chang I-chen, a graduate from the Kiangsi Soviet medical college, and co-worker with Dr. Bethune. In his college there were fifteen teachers with full medical training in modern schools. There were more than seven hundred students, 35 per cent. of them being girls.

At the beginning of the school's history the first class of nurses were graduated after only eight months and sent out to serve with the troops. The second class received a year and a half before graduation. The third class was just beginning a three-year course which should turn them out as practical doctors of great value in actual operational conditions on the guerrilla front.

Students of the medical course mostly came from the peasants' children in the primary schools. The training they received was intensely practical. Four hours' instruction every day in class was followed by three hours in actual work around the hospital. The teaching programme was so arranged that each day's lessons could be reviewed and digested either on the same evening or the following morning, because of the uncertainty of guerrilla life. If they studied at full speed for a week, planning for a general review at the end, there might possibly be a Japanese raid, and they would have to pack up and move around, probably forget the whole week's lessons. They got their subjects of study by the scruff of the neck as it were, and kept them under control the whole time from the beginning of the course to the end.

Altogether seven hundred graduates of the school had already gone out among the soldiers as medical officers and nurses. In every unit there were youngsters well enough trained to do a good first aid job in dressing wounds and providing simple treatments for the more common ailments, and knowing enough about medicine and surgery to recognise when a case required hospitalisation. Each main subdivisional area had a good branch hospital headed by well-trained doctors and staffed by trainees from one or other of the Bethune colleges. No wounded man was more than fifteen miles from one of these hospitals, and everywhere were willing peasants ready to act as stretcher-bearers under orders from the local military nurse or doctor.

We have visited several of these subdivisional hospitals and were amazed at the ingenuity with which crude facilities were turned to good use. Beds were for the most part just broken doors from ruined cottages, or unnecessary doors from cottages still inhabited, sometimes mounted on a few clay bricks at each corner, a good wad of straw for a mattress. Drug stocks were scarce.

Powders and pills were kept in canvas pockets hanging on the walls, bottles were mounted in specially made folding boxes which, when closed, fitted on to the saddle of a mule. Instruments were always kept in their packing cases when not in actual use. At a signal the whole hospital unit could be packed up and on the move within half an hour, and in another half hour the "demolition squad" would have cleared away every possible trace of their presence, leaving nothing but empty cottage rooms in case the Japanese arrive and seek to punish the villagers for co-operating with the Eighth Route Army organisation.

The central hospital of the Hopei region under Kotnis was on a larger scale than the subdivisional units. He had 180 beds spread among the various village buildings. Two rooms were set up as operating theatres, one for general surgery, one for eye-operations. They were equipped with folding beds that had been imported by Dr. Bethune. An idea of the scale of the work can be gathered from the fact that during 1941 there had been 450 major operations and 800 eye operations performed in these two small cottage rooms. And this period included the Japanese autumn offensive when their work had to be considerably disrupted. In fact the village itself was occupied once during the campaign and their operating theatres had to be rebuilt after the campaign was over.

In addition to the regular work for the Army, the hospital staff ran a free outpatient department for the villagers.

A portable X-ray outfit was available for T.B. diagnosis, but the supply of film was not adequate to admit of any serious work outside of fluoroscopy, and with no tube replacements, they could not afford to use the machine for therapy. Nevertheless it was a very valuable piece of equipment, and all medical students went through a short course in X-ray techniques in connection with the routine fluoroscopic tests.

The major problem was that of drug supplies. The Army's department of hygiene, under which the hospitals are all administered, was conducting experiments in the use of native remedies, and many such were actually put into circulation by the hospitals with considerable success. Also large numbers of drugs used in Western medicine were being locally manufactured : alcohol, chloroform, ether, sulphuric acid, dover powder, and so on. The two most important ones, however, iodine and quinine, could not be so produced, and no substitute was available. A certain amount was smuggled in from Occupied areas, and much was captured from the enemy by the guerrillas. But because the Japanese were themselves short of quinine, the shortage of that drug in the guerrilla areas was exceedingly acute. Almost the entire personnel of the Eighth Route Army were carriers of malaria, and during times of stress or emergency large numbers of them came down with attacks of the disease. Fortunately it must have been a comparatively mild type, because the death rate was remarkably low.

The magnificent work of these medical institutions in an area that had never before known medical services of any kind, is beyond praise. They politely asked us for advice and criticism of their medical educational policies and of their experimental research work. But we could only express our sincere admiration and highest appreciation of the success of their heroic labours.

Cut off and blockaded by geographical barriers, by Japanese fortifications, and even by political barriers from their own National Government, there was no way whatever by which they could receive substantial help from outside. To a very great extent they were cut off even from expressions of sympathy from their Allies.

There is an amusing incident connected with our first visit to Dr. Kotnis' hospital. They had a bath-house in his village, and Dr. Kotnis insisted upon our planning to take a bath while we were there. After our experience at General Yang's headquarters, we were not too keen about it, but it seemed impossible to refuse—we could hardly claim that we did not need a bath! So a message was sent to the manager of the bath-house to have the place reserved for us some time during that morning.

Our conversation was presently interrupted by a messenger to say that everything was ready for us, we were to please go right away. So along with Kotnis we strolled through the village to the baths. After admiring the iron pipe connecting the outside furnace with the bath, we entered the courtyard to discover about twenty soldier boys squatting and standing about, either just finished bathing, or waiting to bathe.

We were then ushered into the dressing-room which, as at General Yang's place, was made private only by a flimsy cotton curtain draped in the open doorway, and there they left us to our own devices.

PLATE VII

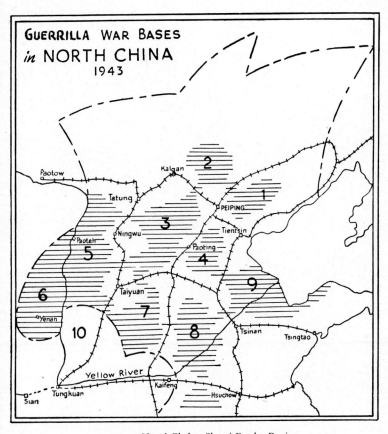

I, 2, 3, 4 : Hopei-Chahar-Shansi Border Region.
5 : N.W. Shansi Border Region.
6 : Shensi-Kansu-Ninghsia Border Region.
7 : Shansi-Honan Border Region.
8, 9 : Honan-Shantung-Hopei War Bases.
10 : General Yen Hsi-shan's Special Area.

To bathe or not to bathe ? At least we could pretend to bathe, so as to avoid hurting their feelings ; they seemed very proud of these facilities ; but if the water smelled anything like it did at the other place we should be cleaner dry than washed.

Just to see what the prospects were, Claire drew aside the curtain at the other end of the dressing-room, and to her horror saw a man in the bath.

"I can't have a bath there ! They said it was ready ; what do they mean ? " She exclaimed indignantly. We forthwith came out into the courtyard to look for Kotnis, but he had gone. We followed out into the village and caught him. We told him how Claire had been going into the bathroom and seen a man already having a bath there.

"Impossible ! " exclaimed Kotnis ; "they told me it was ready for you ! " Kotnis went back immediately and discovered that the man had been in the bath to clean it out especially for our use. But we got out of having one—it was too late, and, privately, we thought a nude man standing in the bath-tub to clean it out did not sound too healthy anyway !

During the autumn of 1942 Kotnis began suffering attacks of epilepsis, although at first they were not definitely so identified. They were put down to simple fatigue. He had mastered the language well enough to lecture regularly in Chinese. He had been strenuously engaged in both hospital practice and teaching for a period of four years without a respite in front line conditions. The only kind of break he had had was when the Japanese came out to "mop up" the area, which could hardly be counted as a picnic for him. So it was considered desirable to give Kotnis a holiday from hospital administration. The. army headquarters decided to transfer him to our place, let him live in comparative comfort, and do some writing about medical work both for the Communist propaganda department at Yenan, and for medical extension work in the Border Region.

Before he could complete his teaching work and wind up the business of administration to hand it over to his successor, Kotnis suffered his final series of attacks, passed away on December 9th, 1942.

We had known Kotnis only ten months, but from the first we felt an immediate attraction which we believe was mutual. We became fast friends at once, and were planning for many happy adventures together in the future. But our personal loss was far less than the flood of feeling that swept the Border Region with his death. Friend to all his colleagues, and to his hundreds of patients, Kotnis was mourned by all. Though death is a daily risk in guerrilla areas, there was not a valley in the whole war base where Kotnis was not mourned with a sense of personal loss.

Kotnis was an efficient and able young doctor, and snobbery was as foreign to his make-up as selfishness. He recognised no artificial barriers of race, class or creed. For him the supreme value was human friendship through a courageous life.

Officers and men of the guerrilla war base mourned Kotnis as a friend, but they also mourned him as a symbol of international sympathy for China in her struggle against Fascism. But they mourned him most of all as a doctor : there was no one to take his place.

THE SWORD

What Guerrilla Lienta was doing for the civil service, " Kangta " was doing for the Army. At the very birth of the Border Region war base it was decided that the anti-Fascist army must be an educated army fit to give a cultural lead to the people from among whom its personnel was recruited.

The peasant population was in fact being educated and revitalised culturally through the army. In addition to their specifically military training, which was specially adapted to the guerrilla nature of the warfare for which they were being trained, every officer received at Kangta both political and cultural education. In fact every soldier in the army was receiving the same three types of training—military, political and cultural ; and upon the graduates of Kangta devolved the responsibility of educating the army as well as leading it in battle.

Cultural leadership is in fact the key to the army's true significance. We were at first slow to realise· this fact, perhaps remembering too vividly the amusing experiences we had had with the service boys at the guerrilla headquarters in Ping Hsi.

The Army accepted youngsters as volunteers at the age of fourteen, merely on the strength of a physical examination and an oral test on the " Ten anti-Japanese oaths " drawn up by the Border Government. As often as not these lads had had no formal education before enlistment, primary education had started in the

egion, but it was by no means universal. They were mostly
poor farmers' children whose experience embraced only the everyday routine of life among the crops and animals on their parents'
farms, and the season-by-season visitation by the Japanese and
their atrocities. In contrast with the Ping Hsi boys, those at the
headquarters under General Nieh had already been two years
with the army, and a more courteous and high-minded group of
youngsters would be difficult to find anywhere.

When they reach the age of eighteen or thereabouts, if they
have proved proficient at their studies and exemplary in behaviour,
they are promoted to full membership in the Army, either as
fighting men or assigned to some service department for specialised
training. One condition for promotion of the boys who were
enrolled before 1940 was that by the end of 1941 they should know
at least 500 Chinese characters, and be able to read the soldiers'
bi-weekly newspaper.

Their education continued in the army proper, up to approximately middle-school level, in the subjects of natural science,
social science, history, geography and general knowledge. Every
soldier, when not in actual battle, spent two hours a day in study.
In addition to this regular class work the boys were encouraged
to go in for hobbies. There were soldiers' clubs to encourage
members in performing drama, singing songs, drawing and painting,
writing stories, essays and verse. All these hobbies were used as
media to stimulate patriotic sentiments, not merely for relaxation
for the troops. Democratically operated, their charters had been
nevertheless drawn up specifically to channel their activities into
the war effort. We were privileged to visit several of these clubs
and ascertained the very creditable quality of their art work.

Our visit to Kangta was as memorable for the things that
happened incidentally as for the things we saw and were told about
the college itself. To get the whole story we have to go back to
one day previous to the visit. It was on Saturday night, February
21st, that we arrived at the village called Wentang, "hot springs",
in Fuping county. Chang, the guerrillas' clerk of works, was
then stationed there engaged in supervising the erection and fur-
nishing of the bath-house facilities for the use of the soldiers. These
baths had formerly been operated by the monks of a temple in
whose court the hot springs were to be found.

On the way in to Wentang we had had to cross the Sha River.

There were wild geese and heron over the stream. Lin's horse decided it wanted a bath. Just at the deepest part it started to rear up on its hind legs trying to disengage the rider, and finding this impossible, it sat down and rolled over on its side. Lin and his baggage got decidedly the worst of the encounter.

We reached Wentang early in the afternoon in time to book a bath. While this was being prepared—they had the place specially cleaned for us—Chang took us up the hill where army men were excavating a site for the large auditorium which was to be the Congress meeting place for the Border Region Congress ; and on our return the bath-house was ready, and clean spring water was just coming into the bath as we entered the building. Normally the spring water was too hot for comfort, but because it was flowing in fresh on to the cold stones, it was just right for enjoyment. It was only afterwards that we heard why they had specially cleaned it for us : they knew that the whole Eighth Route Army personnel used it regularly as treatment for "itch", there seemed to be quite a lot of dermatitis of various kinds, including "Hongkong foot".

We had walked over twenty miles that day, and after the bath we were more than ready for a meal and a good night's sleep. Chang was over courteous on both points. He insisted on giving up his own room for us, and on providing special heating under the kang. A blazing fire of coals was already going strong in the bedroom before we returned from the bath. And when we protested that we preferred a smaller fire, he replied : "Yes ! Yes !" and after our backs were turned on went more coals. He thought we were only being polite. Then for supper he asked us whether we would like sugar ? We had been offered sugar as a special treat all the way down the trail, and it had been served up in all kinds of queer combinations. Sugar had been one of the more conspicuous shortages in the Border Region, because it had to be either smuggled in or captured from the Japanese. It was therefore a special delicacy reserved for honoured guests. We told Chang with considerable emphasis that we did not care for sugar. But again he thought we were only being polite. There was sugar on almost everything that came on the table, even the fried eggs, and there was a separate plate heaped with sugar alone.

There were many months later on during our sojourn with the guerrillas when we were even more hungry for sugar than they were, and even sugared fried eggs would have been delectable. But just then we had had more than we could stand. Fortunately for Bill his stomach seemed to have been fully-fashioned leather; Claire was always the sufferer in such awkward situations.

Whether it was the coal-gas in the bedroom, or the sugar and onions, or the heat of the kang, Claire was thoroughly unwell all night. The heat was terrific; we could smell the straw mat singeing. We tried limiting ourselves to half the surface, baring the clay of the other half to cool it off, and then transfer just before the covered half began to smoulder; we did not achieve a wink of sleep all night; and in the morning when Chang came to the room to see how we had fared, he was so beautifully polite we could only say the kang was a bit too warm, and he again took it as a compliment to his hospitality. It had certainly been warm.

Before breakfast—which again was thoroughly sugared—half a dozen little schoolgirls dressed in army-style uniform came crowding in to seek our autographs and encouraging words in their school-books. Their farewell songs made the welkin ring.

On the way down from Wentang to Kangta we met a long line of over a hundred Kangta students marching to Wentang for their turn in the round of engagements at the bath-house. When we arrived at Kangta, President Sun of that college confirmed the bad news that Singapore had fallen.

There was an open-air supper in our honour, and a great mass meeting to welcome us to Kangta, at which their dramatic club gave a special performance. The loss of Singapore did not seem to have upset them over much; and that night, after another fifteen miles' walk, we made up for the previous bad night, a thick wad of straw on wooden boards made a much more comfortable nest than an oven-hot kang.

On Monday morning we made a tour of the students' billets. Our guide was an English teacher whose language he had learned in the Chinese labour corps in England and France during World War I. We saw the boys at class in the open air. It was beginning to snow but that did not seem to upset them either. After supper a little service boy gave us some excellent stories about how he had escaped from the Japanese in occupied areas and joined up with the Eighth Route Army.

Next day we toured the three villages that made up the billeting quarters of the college and its associated preparatory school. The commissar was so courteous as to let Bill ride his private pony, and the difference between riding this beautiful creature and the wretched animals we had tried to ride before was astounding. Evidently officers' privileges are not to be sneezed at !

The preparatory school classes were not in session, the children were busy re-building a Japanese ruined village house for their classroom, mixing their own mud-cement and carrying their own stones and bricks that they gathered from the ruins. A perfect object lesson for the youngsters in Japanese atrocity, and a useful training in the ancient art of building your own home, an art that every North China peasant must know.

The President of this officers' training college was one Sun I, but no relation with Dr. Sun Yat-sen. He had been educated in the old style primary school, but his family had not been wealthy enough for him to go beyond that into the new college system. Instead, he joined a military school and became a petty officer in the Christian General Feng Yu-hsiang's private army.

Impressed by the Leftist doctrines disseminated among his men by General Feng, Sun tried to put them into practice in his relations with the peasants of the province of Shansi where the army was at that time stationed. But so bad was the general reputation of the soldiery that Sun was quite unable to establish confidence, failed entirely to allay the suspicions that poisoned the relations between army and people. Later, when Feng's army suffered defeat in a civil war, Sun escaped with a fellow conspirator and joined up with Chiang Kai-shek's revolutionary national forces in Honan. Here they were still dissatisfied, and when sent on anti-Red manœuvres, they deserted, with some thousands of their men to the Communists. That was 1931 in Kiangsi ; Sun had been with the Communists ever since.

Another interesting member of the staff at Kangta we met was Lin Chun-yeh, vice-chairman of the department of political education. The thing they themselves thought was surprising about Lin was that he had never been in any military action, never been to Soviet Russia, and yet knew by heart all official Russian statistics and history. He had been in former times a Communist underground worker or Red agitator in non-Communist areas of China.

Assistant chief of the Higher Rank Officers' Training College was another remarkable individual, called Liu Ch'ang-hui, only twenty-eight years of age. He had been educated only in the Communist Armies for fifteen years since his first enrolment at the age of thirteen. He had been wounded five times in the civil wars, spent altogether twelve months in hospitals, and actually been twice abandoned by his comrades for dead. His first resurrection was during the long march, the second during the 1935 winter campaign against the Young Marshal's anti-Communist drive in Northern Shensi. Marching in bare feet through deep snow, suffering from frost-bite, he and many of his comrades collapsed from exhaustion, few only were fortunate enough to survive.

Educational work among the ranks, as distinct from the officer training done at Kangta, was under a special department of the army headquarters. We met the head of that department later, Chairman Pan Tze-lin. Pan was thirty-seven, lean and intellectual, with a broad smile, thick-lensed spectacles repaired with adhesive tape. As a student he had never really completed his middle school training, but was carried away by student excitement into patriotic activity during 1924. He then enrolled in the Peking National University as an unregistered auditor with special intent to stir up student agitation against the reactionary government authorities. He did practically no study in college, and was eventually arrested by General Feng Yu-hsiang for disturbing the peace. At that time this so-called Christian General was pacification commissioner or some such token official of the Peiping area, and, in the usual tradition, did not bother to give his political prisoners any form of trial. However, shortly afterwards, General Feng was again defeated in civil war by his rival satrap, and during the confusion, while these gentlemen were exchanging seats, Pan eluded the prison guards and fled. He joined at once with Chiang Kai-shek's Revolutionary National Army, but after two months he in turn was disillusioned, decided his most urgent need was a better education. In the usual Chinese way Pan raised funds from among his friends and admirers, and was able to make the journey to Moscow, and enrolled in the China Labour College for the cultivation of Communism in the Orient.

He came back to China via Mongolia, taking four months to reach Sian where, however, he was shortly arrested for Communist sympathies, November 1928. He was given two years' educational treatment by the National authorities in an effort to counteract the influence of his Russian experience, but after his release he decided another trip to Europe would be good for his health. This time he studied in Paris for eighteen months, London for three months, and again in Russia for a year. Instead of returning to China directly from Russia, he came via Western Europe and India, and was therefore able to make his way through to the Reds in North Szechuan province while they were still on their long march towards Shensi.

The leaders of the " Communist " Army are an astonishing mixture of outcasts. They have seen life in the raw. In war, theirs is no arm-chair-and-cigar strategy, nor is it the result of hot-headed conspiracy in dark basements or dirty garrets. They have lived their lives for the most part among nature's noblest creations, great forests, immense mountains, grand rivers and wide steppes, and they have been born of a heroic peasant people. There is a clearness and crispness about them all that one seldom finds among the denizens of a giant metropolis, a forthrightness that feels almost Western by contrast with the usual temperament of the scheming merchants on the populous plains.

It is true that they almost all started out as bandits to disrupt the existing, and in a sense accepted order, of semi-feudalistic war-lord government. Their vision has, however, carried them far beyond mere rebellious insurrection. They have helped to turn some of the worst aspects of China's social scale upside down. The Chinese soldier used to be set below the common criminal as an illiterate parasitic brigand, his war-lord master a predatory tyrant. But through the cultural campaign of the Communists in North China the soldier has been transformed into a leader of a great social renascence. Their leaders have recognised, even in their battle with the Japanese, that the pen is mightier than the sword.

Chapter IX

PEASANT PATRIOTS

WE had walked among the cornfields, along the edges of the little irrigation channels, through the tiny village where the big persimmons grew, along the tiny footpath by the side of the buckwheat field terraced on the slopes of the hill, under the hedgerow of date shrubs. We had watched those exquisite insects hysterically sipping nectar from the blossom, breathed intoxicating perfumes from the flowers of date and buckwheat too. Then from the crest of the hill that looked like a giant toad, we had gazed in rapture at the valley below and the birds above, gliding gracefully in dynamic harmony ; the poetic rhythm of nature in full mastery of earth, beast and man. Golden corn was ripening on cottage roofs, gleaming in the sun.

There were not many opportunities for this day-dreaming. Next morning a Japanese plane came scouting along the valley and we ran out of the village for safety. Bombs were dropped on a village a few miles to the north, and on its return trip the plane came down to about fifty feet above our house and opened fire with its machine-gun on the cottage where our radio classes were usually held. Bullets entered the windows of the peasant's kitchen but no one was actually hurt. Two peasants were killed a few minutes later in a village to the south of us. We heard later that seventeen people were injured in another village where a large group of army boys were attending political examinations, and that another plane had simultaneously attacked still farther north, and that about sixty people had been injured in the village of the bath-house.

Apart from this kind of intrusion, the farmers' lives continued in the normal routine all year. Autumn harvest coincided with autumn planting of next spring's winter wheat crop, a double strain on the man-power of the countryside. By October 4th the first shoots of the winter wheat seedlings were coming up. It was October 18th that the whole landscape was green again with these gentle little shoots like fine grass ; and going to class that morning through the fields, we were enchanted by a scene like fairy land : each tiny frond capped by a dewdrop glistening in the rising sun. A perfect setting for poetic romance about the beauties of nature, but born from the sweat and toil of an energetic, realistic peasant people. Delicacy and idleness are no more typical of the Chinese people than of any other race on this hard-pressed earth.

On top of the natural hardships of a farmer's life war-time adds its own. Our village was perhaps typical, or rather average : there were many villages that suffered a great deal more, others escaped more lightly. A few families had abandoned the village, built themselves temporary cave houses further up in the small valleys. The majority remained and repaired their cottages after the Japanese had done their damage and retired. The last great campaign had been a few months before we arrived, starting in the middle of August and continuing through September 1941, timed, of course, to have the maximum disturbing effect upon the harvest. The enemy had rampaged through this village three times during the campaign, had once stayed several days systematically burning the place down.

Throughout the guerrilla areas the people suffered loss from deliberate and ruthless destruction of property, and pillage of anything removable ; but worst of all perhaps was the enforced exposure to the coming winter weather because their homes lay in ruins ; and not only the weather, but the autumn mosquito. Nearly every family throughout the region suffered from malaria before the Japanese mopping-up operations had run through two seasons.

And yet, in 1942, with one clear year without a major campaign, the peasants were able to pull right out of their depression and achieve a prosperity even greater than before the war. News of Stalingrad spread through the mountains, there were posters in every village explaining what that victory meant, and it was thrilling indeed to see them undertaking repairs and rebuilding their cottages in the expectation that never again would the enemy be able seriously to endanger their lives and property.

UNITED FRONT ARMY PEASANT LIAISON

From the very beginning of the Japanese invasion, co-operation between the peasants and the army had been an astounding success. Astounding because never before had any Chinese soldiery been regarded with anything but dread and loathing by the country people ; and the Japanese had not gone in at first to pillage and destroy ; they had gone in merely to govern and control. To the peasant and the landlord they had a very reasonable programme of organisation and stability.

To counteract this treacherous scheme of the enemy, liaison officers of the Eighth Route Army came to the villages with promise of resistance to the invaders and news of successes already achieved against the national enemy. Their welcome was wildly enthusiastic, exceeding the most optimistic hopes of the army leaders. As an example, during the first week in August 1937 the liaison office in what is now the third subdivisional headquarters received three thousand old rifles and one hundred thousand dollars in cash as presents from the villages of one county. The desire to resist Japan was already alive even among uneducated peasant folk ; all it lacked was leadership.

Leadership the nation as a whole indeed had, but it was leadership of the city dwellers, the educated merchant classes, the readers of newspapers ; it was inspired leadership, at that, and commanded the headlines of the world's press, but it was not a leadership that went down to the roots of China's own real strength. The farmers, still practically untouched by modernisation, still ignorant of nationalist ideologies and industrialisation in the New China, were nevertheless proud and independent as they had always been. They had been aroused to the dangers of exploitation, by the patriotic student campaign during the previous two years ; and had been quick to recognise Japanese plans of conquest and, as in the past, when they had rebelled against Mongolian, Manchurian, even Chinese tyrannies, so now they responded immediately to the first real mass leadership against the threatened evil.

The new "Communist" Army campaign started with a brilliant victory at the strategic pass, Ping Hsin Kuan, the propaganda value of which the army's liaison officers exploited to the full. In return for protection from the Japanese, the peasants volunteered to supply the army with uniforms and shoes, and showered the soldiers with gifts of meat and vegetables at every local victory. Since those exciting early days things have settled down to an organised efficiency. With army came party workers pledged to the building up of local self-government among the villagers with whose democratically constituted bodies the regular support of the local anti-Japanese war of resistance could safely be entrusted ; and now the whole organisation of the armed forces in North China is legally supported by the local governments of the border regions, the purpose of the army and of the peoples organisations being fused in one great vision of resistance to foreign aggression and of rebirth of the Chinese nation by the united efforts of the common people of all classes.

Under this United Front programme, the people of the liberated areas in North China, behind the enemy's front lines, co-operate directly in military operations against the enemy. For example, in the Hopei region alone, during 1941, 145,000 civilian men took part in the filling-in of Japanese blockade ditches, cutting roadways, damaging bridges, tearing down telephone wires, de-railing loco-motives and carrying away railway tracks. Every village main-tains a volunteer guerrilla unit in which nearly every able-bodied man plays his part. The county government supplies hand grenades and small land mines and ammunition for small arms. The village guerrilla units co-operate with the regular troops in raids upon Japanese-held towns, block-houses, stores, convoys. During major mopping-up campaigns they operate continuously around their own locality, providing perfect information services for the regular forces and government personnel. In order to maintain their hold against this continual pressure, the Japanese had to station three full divisions and six brigades as a permanent garrison force on the railways of this one province, which works out at about eighty men per mile of track.

All this specifically military activity is most significant. It goes to prove beyond doubt that, reasonable and philosophical though the Chinese may be, his enthusiasm and courage in a long-term programme of struggle and conflict in the face of almost hopeless odds is unexcelled ; and still more impressive is their organisation on the home front for total warfare against the Fascist invaders.

On the high tide of initial popular enthusiasm for the anti-Japanese war in 1937, young student volunteers from the schools and colleges of the cities, and party representatives from Yenan toured the countryside founding " National Salvation Resist Japan Mass Associations ", with special branches for youths, for women, for labourers and for peasants. Their purposes were two-fold : (a) to resist the Japanese invasion, and (b) to watch the class interest of their memberships. These mass associations were started off with democratic constitutions, and, with the emergence of the democratic regional government, their constitutions and fundamental purposes were legally ratified by the local government authority.

ANTI-JAPANESE YOUTH MOVEMENT

Our first contact with these bodies was with the Youth Mass Association at an international youth meet on September 7th, 1942, held in a Roman Catholic Mission Church about six miles down our valley. The mission had abandoned the place when the Japanese invasion had started, and had not felt like returning after the "Communists" had liberated the place. But the caretaker, suffering from malaria according to his own diagnosis, was still in residence, living off the rent he was still collecting on the lands the Church used to own in the village. The Roman Catholic Mission was one of the biggest land-owning interests in North China before the war, the only one that has been dispossessed by the Communists; and even this, the Communists claimed, was only because the Catholics did not care to return, due no doubt to their rather violent anti-Communist prejudices. All other land-owners in the areas liberated from the enemy have retained their land and joined in the United Front resistance movement against the enemy. To the general question of the freedom of religious belief and practice in the Communist areas we shall return later.

The youth meet was essentially a conference of youth workers and their representatives. Attending were eight representatives from the local Youth Mass Association, eight from the army youth clubs, eight from the local government civil service, two from the local Kuomintang Party office, and several visitors like ourselves. There were reports on the condition of youth in many parts of the world, specially in Japan, Korea, Manchuria, Peiping, and Chungking. The two Kuomintang representatives were taking copious notes. It was interesting to watch their blank expressionless faces as the corruption and poverty of educational affairs in Kuomintang China were being alleged by one delegate who claimed to have received letters from a relative in Chungking.

We had lunch with one of the Youth Mass Association representatives, who was the officer responsible for the building up of a local boy scout movement in the valley. He gave us the essential details about his scheme. The membership was strictly limited to ages between fifteen and twenty-three. At the fourth annual assembly on May 4th, 1942, it was reported that there were then 150,000 members of the association in the areas west of the Peiping-Hankow railway in Hopei Province. This number represented roughly 65 per cent. of all eligible youth in that area. Membership was of course purely voluntary. At first there had been considerable opposition to the association from older members of the community, because one of the avowed purposes was the liberation of youth from the ancient family tyranny, the assertion of the rights of the young man over against family authority, specially in matters relating to marriage and the choice of a career. But the old people were persuaded eventually to desist from active opposition to the movement : the anti-Japanese programme and activities of the association formed an acceptable sugar-coating over the otherwise bitter pill. By skilful handling of a very delicate situation, the leaders of the movement have now succeeded in democratising not only the political structure of the region, but the social and family life of the peasants as well.

In accordance with their legal constitutions, every member pledges himself to do whatever possible in co-operation with other anti-Japanese bodies. The local government can call upon youth members to assist in the collection of tax grain, a business that has to be carried out with the utmost despatch and secrecy to prevent Japanese raiders from descending upon the village during collection and carrying away the grain. Youth members are asked also to help in the teaching of letters at adult schools for illiterates. They carry out extension work for the Government Bureau of Agriculture, distributing new seeds, improved farm implements, supervising the improvement of old irrigation channels ; they act as messengers between army and local government officers, carry stores into hiding when Japanese raiding parties threaten any district, and act as guides for government or army groups evading large Japanese concentrations.

As part of the work of the Youth Mass Associations, Youth Pioneers and Children's Corps have been set up. The pioneers are military training groups for volunteers from among the mass association members. No less than 90 per cent. of the youth members became pioneers.

The Children's Corps, something like our boy scouts and

girl guides, were still in their experimental stages in Hopei. Of the 350,000 eligible children in the area west of the Peiping-Hankow railway, between the ages of eight and fifteen, some 200,000 had enrolled in these corps. Their special tasks were to help in times of emergency as guards, scouts, inspectors of passports and travel permits, in counter espionage, vigilance and the detection of traitors. The seeming innocence of small children, especially of Chinese children, makes them very useful in such work.

PEASANTS' AND LABOURERS' UNIONS

The mass associations for the peasants and labourers embraced almost the whole male population of the region, except for the small but important minority, landlords and merchants. Labourers, people who owned no land at all, for the most part consisted of farm hands, brickmakers, carpenters, a few factory workers and government employees, and were much less numerous than the peasants who either owned or hired sufficient land for their own food crops.

These different groups had natural class interests which sometimes came in conflict with each other, and these conflicts would be brought out in the open by the associations' delegates at the various democratic congresses in the regular government or parliamentary procedures. But to watch these particular interests was only one of the functions of the mass associations. Their first and most important constitutional objective was to support and promote anti-Japanese activity, to organise for home defence. In particular, all types of productive work in direct support of the regular armed forces and of the village guerrilla units was organised through these associations ; mutual help schemes for increasing the speed of harvest gathering, and storing away of grain crops were worked out by them ; labour gangs are recruited from among their membership to help the army in transport of supplies and ammunition, the repair of bridges and paths, carrying wounded to hospital. Officers of the mass associations act as liaison officers between army and people, explaining when need be the purposes and meaning of strategic operations, and to keep the army leaders well informed on particular needs or weaknesses of local populations. The officers are key-men in the maintenance of the people's fighting morale.

During major Japanese operations the army deploys selected

teams of its own officers to work alongside the mass association officers in this local liaison work and in the maintenance of popular morale. They help with the evacuation of women and children from threatened points, hide sick and infirm, maintain transport facilities and information services, and generally help prevent defeatism from spreading under what often become apparently hopeless local conditions. The army's very existence depends critically on the stubborn resistance and loyalty of the entire population during enemy offensives ; in spite of torture and death the people must not lose heart, or the whole resistance movement would collapse.

LIBERATED WOMANHOOD

Most spectacular has been the success of the Women's Mass Association. Before 1937 the social status of women in the country districts of North China, like the rest of the country, was controlled by patriarchal familism. The Nationalist Revolutionaries had pronounced many ancient evils illegal and had embarked upon a campaign for the liberation of women ; this movement had had marked success in the port cities and provincial capitals, but was spreading but slowly into the countryside. In the small villages where the great mass of the population lived, there had been almost no change. The average peasant woman lived in a world about three miles in diameter ; she had not even heard the word "Jihpen" for Japanese, and had not the slightest conception of national problems, let alone international ones.

It was the Japanese themselves who directly removed the bliss from their ignorance ; China's peasant women were shocked to the quick by unspeakable outrages committed by strutting little Japanese beasts. Zealous young girls from schools and colleges in Peiping and Tientsin, themselves awakened and liberated by the Nationalist movement in those cities, arrived in Hopei along with the Communist Party workers and the Eighth Route Army, with "marching orders" to spread the liberation movement among the peasant women, organise them for resistance to the invaders.

These organisers arrived at the correct psychological moment. The peasant women were boiling with indignation, ready for any drastic measures for revenge. Their conservative defences were broken down, and they were enthusiastically willing to embrace

PLATE VIII

An Eighth Route Army raiding party surveying a Japanese held coal mine which they sacked the next night.

the whole programme of liberation from family serfdom and mass organisation for home defence in social equality with their menfolk. After all, the social prestige of foot-binding was poor substitute for agility in evading those tormenting lustful beasts.

The liberation movement spread like a forest fire through the villages. To help conquer their illiteracy the women united in night schools, noon schools, baby-minding groups. With infectious enthusiasm, daughters of the wealthier landlords, who had already received a modicum of education, volunteered as teachers in a region-wide campaign. Within a few months the movement was psychologically secure, the eventual equality in social, political and economic status between men and women was guaranteed. In fact when democratic machinery for local government was introduced, men and women were enfranchised at one and the same time. It has been one of the most romantic of revolutions imaginable : the whole thing was achieved without the slightest sign of a struggle on the part of the women as against vested male interests.

The Women's Mass Association arranges for many agricultural activities. In the first rush of early enthusiasm many women went too far, and attempted tasks for which they were not physically equipped. There were even examples of pregnant women indulging in heavy work on the land. Now, however, they have settled down to a more reasonable interpretation of equality between the sexes, more on the lines of " from each according to his or her ability, to each according to his or her needs ".

In political life, women take a very active part. For example, during the 1939 elections in the Hopei area, five county magistrates elected were women, and 30 per cent. of the village heads were also women. Practically 100 per cent. polls by women were recorded throughout the area.

Through the mass association, women now play a very important part in guerrilla warfare. First aid and stretcher-bearing are the chief two occupations. There was a story we heard of one old woman who was taking care of eight wounded soldiers hidden in a cave some distance from her village ; they were hidden because the Japanese were on the rampage, and were in no condition to be moved about. She would make the trip back and forth from the village several times a day, bringing them food and water, and news. But when the Japanese took up their quarters in that very

village, she, with other old and infirm inhabitants who could no
hope to escape, were called in by the Japanese officer and cross
examined. Did she know anything regarding hidden food supplies
government or army personnel in the neighbourhood?

Refusing to reveal what she knew only too well, she was le
free on probation. She sneaked back to the cave with what she
told her men might be the last meal she could bring to them. She
was right. The Japanese noticed her absence, and on her return
tortured her to reveal her secret. Her lips were sealed in simple-
minded loyalty like many thousands of similar martyrs the world
over.

One of the most significant changes produced by the war and
the renascence among women in North China has been the breaking
down of the family-centred, self-interest that so largely controlled
individual behaviour in former times. Mutual co-operation cutting
across family boundaries for such obviously essential war services
has broken down hitherto impenetrable barriers. The village
works as a unit, and as a unit, its strength is indefatigable.

About twelve miles from the village where we had been
entertained by the third subdivisional headquarters, was the site
of the Border Region Memorial to twenty-five thousand martyrs
of the resist-Japan warfare. We made one day's easy walk on our
way down to General Nieh's headquarters, and stayed over night
at Tao Yuan just across the stream from the memorial—or what
was left of it. The memorial had been completed in August 1941,
just before the big Japanese mopping-up campaign. It was destroyed
on October 15th by enemy action.

We were the first Westerners to see the ruins. Before we had
actually seen them we had thought to ourselves how stupid it had
been to build an elaborate memorial on a site which was bound to
be threatened by the enemy before the war was through. Why
not wait until the thing was over? Then one could memorialise
the complete and final honours roll? But the Eighth Route Army,
by whose labour it was erected, had a well-developed sense of the
dramatic. By destroying the monument the Japanese had played
into the hands of its designers. A more impressive symbol of the
peoples' sacrifice, and of Japanese barbarity could scarcely be
imagined. One wonders at the mentality of the Japanese command
that permitted the destructive action. That monument will be

ebuilt. It will contain a monument to the first memorial, and
he story of its destruction. Not only will it establish the heroism
of the people it commemorates, but the full story of the eight,
or nine, or if necessary even ten years of murder, arson, rape, that
have debased the Japanese armies of occupation below even sub-
human levels. The peasant peoples of North China will never
forget.

Chapter X

BORDER PEOPLE'S GOVERNMENT

OUR first appreciation of these peasant people's system o
self-government began when we met Mr. Chang, the counties
supervisor, near Bethune College. He had been appointed by the
regional administration to supervise the conduct of local affairs
by the various elected county magistrates in his particular circuit
of five counties. Mr. Chang, far from being either a professional
politician or even a retired merchant, was a young chemistry
graduate who had completed his college course at the National
Peking University as late as 1936. During the year preceding the
outbreak of hostilities with the Japanese, he had taught physics,
chemistry and mathematics in a Ninghsia provincial middle school.
When the war started he tried to get into some kind of war work,
specially where his knowledge of chemistry might be useful. But
no matter which official agency he approached, he was met always
with the same polite evasiveness : there was nothing he could do.
To his dismay he found no national organisation for the recruiting
and employment of young scientists anxious to help their country ;
not even a national register upon which they could be enrolled
as available if and when their services could be used. In the end,
overcoming his political disinclination, he approached the Communist Party's army office in Sian, which had been advertising
their anti-Japanese programme for patriotic youths. He was
embarrassed by the warm reception he received there ; they assured
him that although there might not immediately be work of a technical character for him to do, his scientific training and his scientific
attitude of mind were things to be appreciated and to be applied
in other fields. They offered him service in civil administration
in areas liberated from the Japanese.

Although he had no training, or so far as he knew, aptitude
for this kind of work, their appeal moved him to accept ; and in
October of 1937 he took up office as a county magistrate appointed
by the then Provisional Regional Government. His tasks, apart
from routine civil administration, involved the setting up of democratic machinery within his county ; he was in fact one of the many

midwives in action during the birth of the people's new democracy. He recalled for us with much amusement his early efforts at chairing the county congress meetings and the various executive committee groups. Of the correct procedures he was quite ignorant, and in many cases relied upon his junior clerks to keep him from going astray.

Chang estimated that roughly 30 per cent. of the civil administration in the Border Region under that first Provincial Government had been carried on by men whose original training had been in technical science, without practical experience in political affairs. It warmed our hearts to hear him say that he felt that the border people had been given a more sincere administration and had won through to their own self-government more quickly and completely than would have been possible had the liberating army been able to secure a sufficient body of civil service personnel with a traditional political education. He reminded us that poorly paid teachers make the best revolutionary material, and that the great majority of men and women in the Provisional Government had, before the war, been poorly paid teachers either in natural science or the humanities.

Whatever one's opinions on such a controversial point may be, we could see for ourselves that here, behind the Japanese front lines in areas liberated and held by hard fighting from the enemy, they had succeeded in setting up a modern scientific democracy among thirty million people * that really worked, and that they had done this in less time than it takes to train one class of students in the red tape of the British civil service. We do not wish, by this remark, to create the impression that the tasks of the Border Region Government even begin to compare in complexity with those of any large industrial nation ; nor can we suppose that the success of the Border Government is due entirely to the lack of political astuteness and expert knowledge of its civil service officials. There are more valid reasons. But we do wish to emphasise the spectacular nature of their success.

In Chang's circuit was included the county of Ting, familiar to readers of rural reconstruction literature as Ting Hsien. This county was the field of operation of the great mass education and rural reconstruction project started by Dr. James Yen in the early

* This is the approximate population of all the border regions liberated north of the Yellow River ; adult population of the Hopei Border Region alone is about ten millions.

1930's. And Chang had good news for us of that experiment. When the Japanese came in and occupied the county, closing down the headquarters of the project, the locally appointed lower salaried clerks and workers, including a number of technicians and research men, escaped into the hills and joined up eventually with the new local government service under Chang.

Now, throughout the whole Border Region, the methods of Ting Hsien were in wide use, the results of the researches at Ting Hsien had been of immense value to the leaders of the administration. In Chang's own words :

" Whereas the men of the Ting Hsien project were formerly compelled to confine themselves with almost purely academic research, now they are able to get down to practical work in applying their findings to the actual operation of the border people' administration. The former regime prevented them from doing anything outside of the confines of their special model village or area ; here they function throughout the entire region and are making a fundamental contribution to the welfare of the liberated people at the express invitation of the people's elected representatives."

It was February 17th when we took our leave of Chang's district, and stopped off by the war memorial for the night. On the 18th we were again guests of a local government department. We had walked the eighteen miles from Tao Yuan to a little village in a winding glen in the Fairy Mountain range. The mountains were so named because, according to local folk-lore two monks with magical powers used to dwell among the precipices. Here was stationed the local office of the Border Government's Bureau of Mines and Industry, and here we were made welcome by the officers in charge—three former students of our own science college in Peiping, working miracles more marvellous than any of which those mythological monks had ever conceived.

While their cook was preparing a welcome meal, they showed us their exhibition of products of the bureau. Leather goods : holsters, saddles, riding coats, belts, breeches, boots. Hardware : cooking urns, agricultural tools, kitchen tools, small tools, nails and screws. Small arms : revolvers, bayonets, spear heads, rifles, hand grenades, land mines. Porcelain for both domestic and factory use ; soap, alcohol, lubricating oil, kerosene ; paper of different grades, ink. Every item was manufactured in their own guerrilla workshops scattered through the mountains.

In this particular village they had a small iron foundry with two miniature blast furnaces producing half a ton of iron goods a day. The foundry was operated as a self-contained unit with twelve workers, including general service and kitchen staff. There was also a large machine-shop unit turning out about five hundred pounds of goods a day, mostly hand grenades and farm spades. In this unit there were six carpenters and twelve bench workers ; they had a wood-turning lathe and were busy in their spare time constructing a metal lathe. It was a thrill to recognise the lathe bed as obviously a piece of railroad track taken from the Japanese-operated railway not many miles away.

Every such unit must be self-supporting so as to ensure mobility during enemy action. They have their own cook and service boy, their own kitchen equipment, transport animals, bedding, and so forth. During minor enemy raids, the unit simply packs up and moves temporarily to some other village, returning in a few days. During major operations, the greater part of their equipment is taken into hiding among the barren rocks and caves in the great mountain range ; the personnel as often as not being transformed into a propaganda unit for local work among the stricken people.

To one whose experience of machine-shops had been confined to the orderly and well laid out affairs attached to university research departments, this village set-up was a refreshing enterprise. To pass from the room where the workers slept to the various machine and work rooms, one had to dodge round donkeys turning peasants' grindstones, avoid slipping into several sunken pigsties, and take care of the rear ends of mules unloading coal for the iron foundry, pass through courts crowded with peasant families going about their ordinary business, admire the rich foliage of the old persimmon trees, take a deep breath of rich country air, and realise with a glance towards the heavens, that over all there brooded the grand mountain peaks bathed golden with the evening sun. These young scientists were right down in the thick of real peasant life, and thoroughly enjoying it ; and dirty and squalid though that life might be, there was something so intensely human, so solidly real about this unique mixture of old and new, that there was no escape from its thrilling fascination.

Their researches were perhaps not the type for which universities award degrees, and it is possible that their results will not be of great intrinsic value after the war, but they were of the utmost importance in breaking down the blockade of the area by the Japanese and providing material and equipment for their war effort and still more, these scientists were training themselves as leader in the future industrialisation of the province.

Three guerrilla-sized heavy industries had already been successfully established in the Border Region : sulphuric acid, coal mining, and iron smelting. The Border Government had early issued a call for the introduction of home industries with the idea that every family who could possibly afford it, should invest in at least one industry for themselves by the end of the year 1942. Mobile teaching groups were organised to tour the region, " selling " the guerrilla industry units, and training those interested in the simple techniques required. Model mobile factories were on show for the home production of paper, cloth, lamp oil, soap, leather, furs, wool. The local government's terms to private owners were highly attractive : government guarantee of raw material, and government guarantee of market, commission paid for all goods produced. Where labour was hired by the private capitalist, who purchased the unit, labour conditions were closely supervised, every worker being required to do two hours' study per day in literacy, technics and world events, the local government providing the teachers.

It was claimed that great success had already been achieved in this home industry project. To our expressions of surprise that a Communist-sponsored regime should be so enthusiastically developing private capitalism as a basis of industrialisation, the chief chemist replied :

" You must remember that this is not a Communist society, even though it may have been started by the Communists. We are a scientific democracy : a United Front anti-Japanese scientific democracy, and whatever economic methods may be required for the efficient carrying out of our fundamental objectives will unhesitatingly be adopted by our popular representatives. As a matter of fact the Chinese peasant will work far more efficiently for private profit than for any Communistic ideas, and under proper control, private capitalism is the best economic system for this Border Region at the present time. We are realists, not political idealists."

Next morning they called a meeting of all the scientific workers in the neighbourhood. Among the forty or fifty present were ten graduates from engineering colleges, six chemistry graduates from universities. The political commissar of the bureau presided at the meeting. There were addresses on the new phase of World War II with Britain and America allied with China in a common struggle against Japan, followed by a talk by Bill on the latest developments in technical science.

LOCAL GOVERNMENT LEADERS

From the Bureau of Mines we continued our journey south-west towards the Border Region Government headquarters. The route took us through Wentang hot springs where the Congress Auditorium was later erected, through the villages where we visited the various departments of Kangta. We finally arrived in the government headquarters on February 24th and were at once ushered into a programme of personal interviews with their leaders. But before we could get down to business we had to deal with the throng of village children that crowded the court to have a peep at us. The chief secretary of the government was a former biology student at Yenching University, and he acted as special officer in charge of our comforts. He arranged for the children to sing us one of their popular patriotic songs in return for which we responded in like manner with the national anthem, after which, in accordance with the bargain struck, they dispersed to their homes and left us in peace ; and so while supper was being prepared, the interviews began.

Sung Shao-wen, Chairman of the Provincial Government of the Border Region was thirty-three, and had just married a mathematics graduate from Tsing Hua University in Peiping. He was a native of Taiyuan, Shansi, had studied classics at an old-fashioned Confucian school—he could recite Mencius by rote. In middle school he had developed an interest in biology and mathematics. This cured him of all leanings towards Confucianism, and during his college life at the Peking National University, an interest in the evolution of society inspired his study of history for a couple of years. But history, he said, gave him only the skeleton of social change. Real living evolution he could discover only through Marxist economics. However, he did not join the Communist Party, and the Mukden Incident of 1931 aroused him from his theorising : China's salvation required an awakened national consciousness, no mere economic theories would suffice.

During the next two years, although at college, he did just about one-half a year's study. Instead he spent his time in active work with the patriotic student movement. By 1933 he was a marked man, and the day before he was to graduate from the University, he was arrested by the police. Almost a year later he was released, and his University graduated him just one year delayed. Those were the " good old days " of academic freedom China has not known since 1937.

After graduation Sung took up work in his native district with General Yen Hsi-shan, but when the Japanese began campaigning along the railway towards that city he was sent by Yen to help fill the administrative vacuum in the counties of Northern Shansi. Within three days of assuming his new office, Sung found himself completely surrounded by the enemy, along with Hu Jen-kwei. As sole representative of the National Government administration throughout no less than eighteen counties he was obliged to act simultaneously as magistrate for that whole area.

When the Eighth Route Army came through in their advance to the front in Hopei, Sung was invited by them to help in the United Front administration of liberated areas, and he was appointed, on January 15th, 1938, to his position as head of the Provisional Government for the Hopei Border Region.

In Sung's judgment more good had been done for the people of Hopei during the four years 1938-42 than throughout the whole twenty-seven years of administration by private war-lords nominally loyal to the Republic since the overthrow of the Ching Dynasty in 1911.

Chang Chen, head of the Bureau of Industry and Mines, was a quiet, keen-eyed chemist who had taken a leading part for two and a half years in active guerrilla warfare. At the head of a small army of fellow-student volunteers he had fought in twenty serious battles with the Japanese in one of which his personal body-guard had been wiped out, and in every one of which he had had a narrow escape. He had been a pre-medical student at our University for a year, then had transferred to the Catholic University in Peiping and graduated from there in Chemistry in 1932. He was on the Japanese black list for being editor of a patriotic journal called *Scientific Life* and in 1937 he escaped into the plains of Central Hopei when the Japanese took over the administration of the cities.

Within a month he had collected seven hundred fellow-students and teachers and was later joined by a brigadier-general with five hundred armed men from among the defeated provincial troops. Within two months this patriotic force was in control of ten large towns in the area, and had doubled the number of men from farmer volunteers. The Japanese had not taken them seriously until one day when they made a raid on a Japanese garrisoned city, captured the Japanese commander and the puppet magistrates, many munitions, and killed five hundred enemy. News of this victory spread through the country and brought in five thousand recruits ; also many troubles. There was no one with guerrilla experience or knowledge of how to organise such considerable numbers of fighting men. They were all innocent of scouting experience. Fortunately at about this time Eighth Route Army units penetrated as far as the plains and Chang's gang of bandits joined up with the larger group and were reorganised on efficient lines. Chang himself, being a scientist, was taken off purely combat duties and was placed in charge of demolition work.

Here is the story he gave us of one of his early successes in the days before the Japanese had established their hold on the main communication lines :

"It was a raid on the Jap road from Paoting to Kaoyang. The guerrilla base was only six miles south of Kaoyang. I selected forty men for ambush work, and within half-an-hour a dozen Jap motor trucks approached. Sixteen of the eighteen Jap guards were shot out of hand, the other two fled. Supplies of salt, fish, rice were seized. The two Japs who had fled were captured by farmers and drowned. But traitors must have reported the event. Two hundred Japs arrived to attack the guerrilla base so promptly that we were at first caught off our guard.

"However, the enemy had grossly under-estimated our strength, which was three hundred men with ten machine-guns, three trench mortars and innumerable hand grenades. Twenty of our men were on the roof-tops within a few seconds of the alarm being raised and discovered the enemy within fifty metres of the village. The first twenty Japs to enter the village lane were killed outright by hand grenades, and in the pause which followed, our machine-guns were rushed into strategic positions to cover the corpses. These the Japs attempted to recover, and in three waves they tried to rush through our cross-fire, losing more than a hundred men before they realised the futility of these efforts. We had meanwhile arranged to cut off the retreat of the remaining eighty men. They tried to extricate themselves by making a dash across a frozen pond, but the ice was too thin, and as they were splashing and struggling with the broken surface we eliminated the lot The whole village was out to see this final round. We captured seventeen machine-guns, a hundred and twenty rifles, two trench mortars and two horses.

"But our best fun was on the railways. In every town we controlled we had set up munitions factories ; we could still use electricity as power in those days, and we could detonate mines electrically. I was watching my chance to blow up one train, standing something like 200 metres from the line ; the locomotive rose in the air, just like a movie show ; but, listen to this, one huge driving wheel came back to earth just behind where I was standing. Unfortunately, it proved to have been only a decoy train loaded with stones to test the safety of the line. After that we changed to the bicycle strategy. We would have an agent at the railway station with a bicycle, watching the passengers on the trains. Our detonating party would take up positions near enough so that when the cyclist had picked up information of value, he could dash off and arrive at our position a few seconds before the train. In our first experiment with this strategy we blew up coaches containing eighty horses and forty Jap officers."

Chang was now busy in problems of reconstruction instead of demolition.

Referring again to the campaign for establishing home industries throughout the Border Region ; during the year 1942 greatest emphasis was laid upon wool spinning and woollen cloth weaving from rather coarse native wool from small mountain sheep. Apart from privately owned factories, the government bureau itself operated eleven small concerns where they produced army blankets, socks and vests. Besides this a number of paper factories had been set up sufficient to supply the administrative personnel with all essential requirements in the way of writing material and news sheet. There were ten paper factories west of the Peiping-Hankow railway, and forty on the plains of Central Hopei engaged in this work ; work which was regarded as an important part of the Region's economic warfare, permitting it to become independent of their former sources of supply now in Japanese hands. They were turning out three million sheets a month, which, considering that every one of the factories was working under threat of sudden raid by the enemy at any time, was no mean achievement.

Since 1942, the Border Government, in order to stimulate still more vigorously the industrialisation campaign, decided to exempt from all taxation any such enterprise embarked upon by peasant families, and to guarantee compensation for losses due to enemy action. There has in consequence been a great boom in oil presses, spinning jennies, water mills, etc., and a considerable influx of the wealthier peasants from Japanese garrisoned zones where enemy taxation and restrictions were growing daily more severe.

ECONOMIC WARFARE

The most important aspect of economic warfare would seem to have been the battle for cotton crops. Even before 1937 the Japanese had been intimidating local Chinese authorities in North China to increase the areas under cotton and opium poppy, so to provide the basic raw material required for the Japanese long-range programme for the subjugation and exploitation of the people and their country. After 1937 Chinese peasants were forced under pain of punishment by death to confine their attention almost entirely to these two crops, the produce of which was commandeered by the Japanese military authorities.

With their advance along the railways, the Japanese attempted to spread their control throughout the surrounding areas, to make North China a great cotton producing area for their military needs. The Border Region Government accepted the challenge, and in February 1938 prohibited opium growing entirely, and embarked upon a campaign for the limitation of cotton crops to the barest minimum needed for their own local consumption. This, of course, involved little enough struggle in areas distant from the Japanese, although even here it meant a serious campaign among the people who had been used to rely upon export for livelihood. But it did involve a furious struggle in all areas close to the occupied zones where the peasants, nominally subservient to the enemy, were nevertheless loyal to their own free government; a struggle in which methods of non-violent resistance alone could succeed. In Central Hopei, where the Japanese have the highest measure of control, it was reported in 1942 that only one-tenth of the area actually suitable for cotton was in fact producing that crop.

As an alternative to cotton, the farmers were encouraged by the Border Government to increase production of cereals. The area thus produced a great deal more food than required in normal times, and considerable hidden stores were rapidly accumulated. This in itself was a great economic advantage in a region where a whole season's crop might be ruined by a major Japanese campaign during seed-planting periods. It was perhaps the major factor on the economic front upon which successful resistance was built.

Even though the food production campaign in fertile areas like Central Hopei was successful it was still considered essential to increase production in normally unfertile areas among the mountainous districts where Chinese control was far more secure than on the plains. In 1938 there had been widespread pessimism among the peasants of the mountain villages because the Japanese invasion during the previous autumn had disrupted the sowing of winter wheat, and the spring crop of 1938 had been much below normal. Land had gone to waste, food was short, morale ebbed. With the setting up of the Border Government's Bureau of Agriculture, a re-cultivation drive was set afoot, accompanied by a ruling that all land remaining uncultivated for two seasons running shall be regarded as waste land open to anyone willing to work it, rent free. In nine counties affected by this drive more than 25,000 acres of waste land was put back into cultivation during 1938. Peasant confidence was re-established.

One of the most effective of North China's traditional ways of reclaiming land is to control the flooding of wide areas in the river beds. By a cunning arrangement of boulder dams, large flat areas of shingle can be covered with a layer of fine silt deposit from the stream during summer floods, a layer deep enough for the cultivation of rice. By 1939 the Border Region had reclaimed about 30,000 acres of such land, but the heavy floods of that summer —the same floods that inundated Tientsin—washed away no less than 25,000 acres of these river beds, and 100,000 tons of grain were destroyed by the floods.

In war-time this was a more serious loss even than the losses caused by a major Japanese campaign ; it was the worst calamity the people had experienced in a hundred years. Even in peace-time, under ordinary pre-war circumstances, at least ten years of misery would have followed before normal conditions could have been restored. But by prompt action the situation was saved within three months. The entire army and government personnel were mobilised, a million men spent all possible spare time assisting the peasants rebuild 23,000 acres of river bed. The government extended a loan of 170,000 lb. of grain seed, and by 1940 a normal crop was harvested.

At the same time on the plains of Central Hopei, there were serious floods due in part to excessive rainfall, in part to the fact that the Japanese broke down the dykes in critical areas to hinder Eighth Route Army operations. During 1940 the army joined with the peasants in dredging fifty-five miles of river, repairing sixty miles of damaged dykes, and building 143 miles of new dykes. This work had formerly been left to an international commission with both American and Chinese experts, its headquarters in Peiping, its funds raised abroad. The war had interfered with its work, the Japanese considered that such philanthropic agencies were "superfluous". But from the Border Region the Chinese were taking over the job themselves, without a cent from outside, without expert conservation engineers, without proper survey instruments, even doing the job under fire from the enemy.

In the Hopei mountain areas the rainfall is normally inadequate through eleven months of the year, and great importance is attached to the cultivation of special drought resistant varieties of seed. In the Border Region it was, however, found that greatest scope for improvement lay in the possibilities of increasing and improving the land under cultivation by an extension of irrigation systems. During the three years 1939 to 1942 a team of irrigation specialists toured the entire region, planned and supervised the repair of nearly three thousand old or disused channels irrigating 57,000 acres of land, constructed 2,000 new channels, opening up 70,000 acres of barren ground to irrigation. As a result of this campaign the peasants have become more conscious of the possibilities of irrigation, and 130,000 acres of land that was formerly under dry-farming crops like peanut, sunflower, castor-oil or other seed crops, were now under high-yield wheat or barley, corn or millet. It was claimed that these activities, and other measures of the Border Government had succeeded in raising the living standards of the mountain peasants even above their pre-war level in spite of the ravages of the enemy.

THE BORDER REGION CONGRESS

When we first met these local government people they regarded their authority as provisional ; they had, in fact, been
formally ratified as such by the National Government. From the
point of view of the National Government, the Border Government would remain provisional until the end of the war, or until
such time as the central authorities could send their own political
agents to take over control. But from the point of view of the
Communists who had sponsored the formation of the Provisional
Government, its authority was provisional only because the manner
of its appointment had not been completely democratic, and could
be remedied as soon as proper democratic machinery could be
set up for its ratification or re-call and re-election by the people
of the region themselves.

By 1940 democratic machinery was in operation at all the lower
levels of self-government, village, parish and county congresses
had been elected and had started functioning through 25,000 administrative villages and ninety-eight counties (hsien), and had
taken over responsibilities for all local administrative work from
the Provisional Government. There remained only the task of
setting up the regional congress, and during 1940 the 383 members
of the Border Region Congress were elected in a 90 per cent. poll
of the entire adult population of the region. For the purpose of
this poll the region was divided into electoral wards each containing roughly 30,000 adults, with the right to elect one congress member each ; the army, as such, appointed a few "tens" of members,
and the employees of each government department, each cultural
institution, and the mass associations appointed one member each.
This system was patterned after that used in Soviet Russia. The
physical difficulties to be overcome in conducting such an election
among the mountains where almost no convenient communications
exist, and where enemy raiders continually threaten large concentrations of people, were so great that the results were obtained
only after almost a whole year had passed. And in 1941 there was
no safe enough period in which to call a meeting of the newly
elected congress.

The year 1942 was spent in recovery from the 1941 enemy campaigns ; nobody was willing to take enough time off to attend a
congress meeting ; and since this meeting was to be a great historic
occasion, the inauguration of the first full democratic government

PLATE IX

Burned village in Ping Hsi guerrilla area.

he country had ever known in its long history, it was felt that no
hastily or ill-planned makeshift arrangements should be tolerated.

And so it came about that in the depth of winter, the last two
weeks in January 1943, we were permitted the privilege of being
the only Western observers of the first full democratic congress
of the Hopei Border Region.* Its formal opening was on January
15th, the fifth anniversary of the founding of the Provincial
Government.

Exact date and place of the congress meetings had been kept
as secret as possible, announcements to more distant members
had gone out giving only the county government at which they
would have to report during the first week in January. Our
invitation arrived on January 12th, and we spent the 13th and 14th
walking the forty odd miles from our village, spending the night
as guests at the government's offices near Chen Chuang market
town. The same boy who had looked after us on our first arrival
a year before, was there to welcome us again, but all the government leaders had already left for the congress meetings. The
second day's walk was more strenuous, involving climbing three
mountain passes and crossing on foot several frozen rivers that had
begun to thaw in the brilliant sunshine. Roger Liu, who was
guiding us, was suffering from an attack of malaria, rode a mule
all the way, but lost the track ; we spent about an hour detouring,
but eventually arrived late in the afternoon.

We came down a rocky defile over a range of hills to a point
half-way between the village of Wentang and the site of the new
auditorium, to discover the little glen transformed. Throngs of
people were passing to and fro, a large marquee had been erected
in which reception offices were located, and exhibitions on display.
Signing the register, we were quickly given a guide and taken to
our room, in a small new stone building on the hillside overlooking
the auditorium. We were more than well provided for as specially
privileged guests. The great majority of congress members themselves were billeted among the villages one, two or three miles
around. The other two rooms in our building were occupied by
members of the congress presidium. Just below us was General

* Gunther Stein in his *The Challenge of Red China* (Pilot Press, 1945), page 311,
quotes General Yen Lihsuan as claiming Professor William Band to have been a member
of the People's Political Council. Either Yen was exaggerating, or Stein has misinter-
preted the old gentleman. I had no political connections whatever, and was merely a
guest-observer without right either to vote or to take part in discussions.—W.B.

Nieh's personal headquarters, and on the other slope of the hi
a larger building with a dozen rooms for military representativ
and the officers in command of the special guard detailed to prote
the congress in case of enemy action. Another new buildin
housed members of the Provisional Government. All these builc
ings were of rocks, built at the time the auditorium itself was pt
up ; we visited the site one year before ; there had then been n
sign of any of the structures.

The kang was too hot for comfort and we had a poor nigh
and were aroused at three separate times by three enthusiasti
messengers between five and six in the morning to get up an
walk three miles before breakfast to see the review of the regiment;
guard in the broad sandy valley that runs down to the town c
Chen Nan Chuang to the north. Such a display of troops w;
considered unwise in broad daylight ; and in the dim light c
dawn, under the slender poplar trees, several thousand neatly uni
formed and well-equipped men passed in review before the whol
congress.

After breakfast we were called to the auditorium. Here wa
collected a most impressive variety of people dressed in all manne
of garments, speaking all the local dialects. It was at onc
obviously representative ; among the crowd one could pick ou
the wealthy landlords, the independent peasants, the hardy labourers
hooded priests, uniformed army representatives, the women
From East Hopei came four representatives ; they had taken ;
perilous journey lasting two months, crossing two Japanese railways and two highways, travelling all round the north of Peiping
There were forty people from the plains of Central Hopei whc
had been smuggled across the Peiping-Hankow railway. There
were even a number of representatives from occupied cities, bu
these had not been elected by popular vote, they had been invitec
upon recommendation of the army's underground workers ir
those cities, and had been smuggled out at the risk of their lives,
to join the reconstruction movement in the Border Region.

The thing that impressed us most was the fact that all these
people seemed perfectly at home and at their ease ; there was no
unnatural pomp or ritualism, these democratic processes of self-
government seemed to have been in their blood, as if they had
been born in them for generations.

Yet they could certainly not have been used to their immediate

rroundings, which were unique among the mountain villages.
he auditorium was a large building in imitation Western style,
t by electricity from a small generator, set up in a nearby cave.
ur large coal stoves prevented the hall from freezing up. Seating
rangements were clay benches with straw matting for upholstery.
edecking the hall were a hundred beautiful banners embroidered
ith congratulatory messages to the congress from as many different
roups and institutions through the Border Region. In the back-
round, overlooking the large stage, hung a portrait of Dr. Sun
at-sen, founder of China's Revolutionary Republic.

At the formal opening, welcome speeches were made by Sung
hao-wen on behalf of the Provisional Government, now resigning
ffice, and by General Nieh on behalf of the Chinese Communist
arty. Replies on behalf of the congress were made by a delegate
om the Kuomintang Party office, and by the representative of
1e Mohammedan minorities. The Kuomintang man expressed
is party's whole-hearted desire to co-operate in the United Front
esistance movement; the Mohammedan expressed his con-
tituency's deep appreciation of the fact that this was the first time
1 history that Mohammedans had been given fair representation
1 the governing councils of the country.

The first two days' business was to discuss the printed report
f the five years' work of the Provisional Government, following
n explanatory address by Sung Shao-wen. This address was a
natter-of-fact report, without the least attempt at electioneering
hetoric. The comments and criticisms from congress members
vere either highly complimentary or politely constructive; there
vas no argument of the kind one would get under party politics
vith an organised opposition. The Provisional Government had
one a really good piece of work and everyone knew it; mistakes,
f any, were mistakes of inexperience, not errors in policy; and
indly folk with local experience were ready to point out ways
nd means for correction on matters of detail.

After the discussion on the report there was a debate on the
ractical policy for the Border Region as proposed (and previously
ublished) by the Chinese Communist Party. It was accepted with
cclamation; the Kuomintang delegate pledging support in an
loquent address. After discussion it was voted to pay special
ttention to three points in this programme: (a) to ensure rigid
conomy and utmost efficiency in the army; (b) to strengthen

the economic war against the enemy ; (c) to extend local defence
and mass guerrilla warfare. All elections were by secret ballot
The results were a highly gratifying example of a true United Front

It was just before the voting began that General Nieh had made
a special announcement concerning the military situation. News
had just been received that only thirty miles away a concentration
of a thousand enemy troops had crossed the Sha River at a point
which seemed to indicate a possible attack upon the congress
It was, of course, hoped that no news of the meetings had leaked
out, and that the Japs were out on other business ; but nevertheless
congress members should hold themselves prepared for a possible
raid ; Eighth Route Army troops would be able to hold the
enemy long enough for all members to disperse should the necessity
arise.

The last day's discussion was when a real argument got started
Congress was asked to decide upon matters of importance to the
practical everyday affairs of the peasants and the landlords : usury
land rent, interest on investments, the single progressive tax system
The landlords here found themselves as a group having interests
at variance with the rest of congress, and they were quick to make
their voices heard. However, the first constructive modification
in the proposed regulations came from a young officer in the
Labourers' Mass Association ; all contributions to the discussion
seemed to be highly practical in character ; the problem was
discussed throughout in a friendly spirit of compromise on all
sides in the interests of the United Front. There was much fun
over local dialects when the Chairman sometimes failed to follow
a proposal, and the proposer disagreed with the translation volunteered by another member. It was a moving experience to watch
these hereditary enemies in China's old class struggle discussing
with each other in an open and friendly spirit on a basis of equality ;
that landlords and tenants, peasants and labourers could work
together harmoniously for their mutual welfare augured well for
the future of the country.

After the conclusion of that debate there was an announcement
that the Japanese on the Sha River had veered south, and appeared
to be preparing to build a new line of block-houses a few miles
further up the valleys ; they were evidently ignorant of the
meetings : proceedings could continue undisturbed.

There were then discussions of detailed proposals by private members in amplification of the general political programme agreed to earlier in the meetings. The more serious of these were voted on by congress, one hundred and fifty minor proposals were delegated to the continuing congress committee with power to act at a later date.

Before closing this account of the congress meetings we must at least mention the programme of entertainments put on by various drama clubs for the benefit of congress members during the evenings. Altogether four full nights were given over to as many different entertainment troupes. They presented four classical dramas, five modern plays written specially for the occasion, and two plays translated from the Russian. A museum was arranged to display the results of the various economic reconstruction enterprises sponsored by the Provisional Government departments, charts giving statistics of interest to the members, exhibits of cultural activities by the different mass associations, soldiers' hobby clubs, and so on. All these diversions were appreciated by all with great enthusiasm, especially by the new arrivals from Occupied cities to whom the whole thing seemed like a miraculous apparition.

And it was true that here, surrounded by a vile and ruthless Fascist enemy, a most significant experiment in social and political rehabilitation had been brought to a triumphant climax.

As the meeting rose to the tunes of China's national anthem, they wound up the proceedings shouting slogans :

" UNITY FOR THE WAR OF RESISTANCE AND NATIONAL RECONSTRUCTION ! "

" DOWN WITH JAPANESE IMPERIALISM ! "

" LONG LIVE THE LIBERTY OF CHINA ! "

A soft white mantle of snow had fallen over the countryside. In an inspiring and invigorating atmosphere members of the congress dispersed, taking with them messages of good courage and hope to all corners of the mountainous Border Region.

On our return, we had to pass within ten miles of the Japanese block-house building party, as we were entering the market town of Chen Chuang. Several families were evacuating the town as we entered, in fear lest the enemy might attack that night. One old man, alone, carrying a bundle of bedding on his back, stopped to ask us if we had any news. We had nothing special to report,

and we asked him what he was doing. Ashamed to admit h
nervousness, he replied :

" Oh ! Just taking a walk around ! "

Two or three miles beyond Chen Chuang we stopped for t
night at the government offices again. The place was still almo
deserted, the officials had not yet come back from the congre
Mr. Wang was still there to welcome us and make us comfortab
with a straw bed and a charcoal fire in the same little room in t
main court.

Outside large gentle flakes of snow were falling. The do
of the courtyard was open to the street. There were no guar
in sight anywhere. An atmosphere of calm confidence in a ju
cause that cannot fail.

Chapter XI

A LITTLE GOATHERD

т was a thrilling day for the Border Region on June 14th, 1942 ;
t was then that we heard that Mr. Churchill had concluded the
Anglo-Soviet military alliance, and pledged Britain to open second
front operations on the continent of Europe at the earliest possible
moment. We had just returned to our village after attending the
first Border Region Science Workers' Congress, and this seems
the appropriate place to describe the occasion.

GUERRILLA SCIENCE CONGRESS

The conferences were held at the Border Government village.
About a hundred scientists were present, and this created considerable strain on the facilities of the village. The special residential
quarters were at one end, the kitchen in the middle, and the conference and dining-room at the other. It was at the height of the
fly season and the heat was terrific.

The chief food was plain rice gruel, served piping hot ; bean
curd soup was almost the only other hot item. These were
paraded through the village street, supposedly covered from the
flies. In the dining-room we kept everything covered the whole
meal through. Anyone anxious for something to eat would
sing out :

" All get ready ! " A wave of the hand over the table and
' Bzzzzzz . . ." go the flies. Someone lifts a cover, we all take
a hasty chopstickful, and down drops the lid before the flies can get
inside. We did pay one visit to the special kitchen, but we could
hardly see across the room for flies ; we could not carry on conversation there, the buzzing was so fierce. One day some cold
vegetable was served to add a little variety to the diet ; two people
tried it ; they came down with dysentery next morning.

Some of the little children in that village were really appalling.
One family that lived next to the re-built ruin where we slept,
would leave their half-starved youngest child sleeping in the shade
on their door-step a few yards from where the mother was spending
her energy grinding peanut husks and tree-bark for their meals.

A hundred flies spent the day on the child's lips and eyelids. The squalor was depressing, and President Ch'eng Fang-wu's assurance notwithstanding, we felt that it was not all due to the Japanese offensive ; it seemed a condition to which the poor people were inured by long usage.

It was ironical to us that here was the seat of administration of the revolutionary democratic government, and that their programme of reform should misfire so sadly right under their own noses. But perhaps it was appropriate enough that the leading scientists of the region should come here to discuss among other things public health problems.

The conference room was a newly repaired schoolroom that had been wrecked the previous autumn by the Japanese. Long new planks resting on clay brick pillars served both as benches and desks for the conference members. We noticed that although these planks were freshly cut only a few days prior to the meetings, their white surfaces were already spotted all over with fly-mark. The bowls of hot drinking water that were served out from time to time to quench our scientific thirst, were at once accepted by the flies as convenient parking places during the discussions ; average count, twenty per bowl.

At the conference, the Association was in fact founded with five branches : agriculture, medicine, radio, engineering, and teaching ; all intensely practical in outlook. Yet at the first open meeting Bill was asked to read a paper on the properties of liquid helium at minus 271° C., and there was a keen discussion after it, too. But the main business of the conference was a discussion of a number of reports on the practical work done to date in the region by the scientific and technical workers employed by the Border Government. Iron-smelting, reports on the work we had seen the previous February ; cast-iron factories ; oil-cracking ; leather-tanning ; medical work ; grain storage ; extension work among the peasants by the Bureau of Agriculture. There was also an exhibition arranged by the Bureau of Agriculture : life histories of local plant diseases and insect pests ; samples of improved grain, local handicrafts and the products of home industries ; improved goats, sheep, pigs and chickens.

It was an amazing experience. Here we were in the roughest of possible environments, completely surrounded by Japanese and cut off from everywhere, attending a scientific conference, discussing

echnical papers as calmly and thoroughly as we would have done
n peace-time on any college campus. Here were young scientists
who had deliberately gone in behind the enemy's lines and built
up apparatus in this guerrilla area where facilities for technical
work simply did not previously exist in any shape or form. They
were pledged to take their part in total war on Japanese Fascism,
and although they had next to nothing with which to work, they
were obviously enthusiastic in their support of the Border Region
programme.

After living among these young people we came to feel that
China's intellectuals, specially her scientists, have in the past taken
too little real interest in the ordinary people of their own country.
Here we found Chinese intellectuals with no false pride or intellectual snobbery, with courage enough to face life with the peasants
even through the dangers of war-time. We felt proud to find so
many of the graduates and students from our modern universities
among them. They are planning to return to Peiping after the
war, but not to the old ways, the artificial academic life, isolated
from the real life of the country. They have learned an unforgettable lesson : their social responsibility for the welfare of the
peasant population who, in fact, form the backbone of China's
ancient culture, the fulfilment of which will be their main task.
They had suffered together with the peasants through nine, perhaps
ten years of warfare ; they will not forget. They will make sure,
also, that future generations of China's students learn the same
responsibility, learn that it is part of any true patriotism. The
New China will need all the scientists she can train, and she will
need them patriotic in the highest sense.

As we remarked at the beginning of this chapter, on returning
to our own village we learned of Mr. Churchill's announcement
regarding second front operations on the Continent. Always good
at imitation, the local Japanese also made an announcement : that they
would begin large scale offensive operations on our Border Region
on June 30th. But like the second front, nothing happened. On
August 8th the Japanese made a second announcement, that the
promised campaign would begin within one week. This would,
in fact, bring them to their usual autumn schedule.

By August 22nd the Chinese intelligence service brought news
that Japanese reinforcements were being concentrated in one
section, and shortly afterwards a Japanese force moved out of their

defences on a block-house building expedition : " long and careful preparation ". A month later there was a series of air raids, and a sudden infantry raid through Fuping town a week after that. But there never was a major campaign that autumn. Instead, there were reports that seasoned Japanese troops were being moved into Manchuria, to be replaced by new recruits from Japan.

We knew that the fate of Stalingrad hung in the balance, and with it the fate of Russia and of the world. Cut off from everywhere except for the briefest of news summaries via the Chinese Communist Party headquarters in Yenan, we found it difficult to understand why there was no second front materialising from Mr. Churchill's promise. We got the impression that there was some kind of "monkey business" going on. Our anxiety was most grievous ; but we did not care to face up to the possibilities of defeat ; for us, isolated as we were, they were too terrific.

The victory of Stalingrad was a real VE day as far as we were concerned. And through all that winter with the Germans in continuous retreat, morale among our mountains ran full tide high. The Border Region Congress had been held on the crest of that optimistic wave.

We were all laughing at the Japanese and their " silkworm-eating-leaf" strategy. But it was no laughing matter. In December 1942 the nearest block-house had been about thirty miles from us. The line of forts the Japanese started while Congress was in session was only twenty miles east of our valley, and it was completed in about two months. Japanese plans had already been captured which indicated that this line of forts would later be extended in a south-westerly direction as far as the Hutou River near Gosu market town at the mouth of our valley. On February 2nd our wireless school unit was moved up into a small glen in the rear of the headquarters departments and a unit of fighting men took our place ; preparations for battle were pushed ahead.

LUNAR NEW YEAR, 1943

We shall call it Goatherd Glen. A clear stream flows all the year round. About half a mile from its mouth a tributary valley joins it from the north, and in the angle between the two streams is sufficient ground for the village hamlets and their cultivated terraces of winter wheat. To reach the row of cottage rooms reconditioned for our unit we had to climb a footpath following the tributary and out on to a wide terrace overlooking the main village. The tributary was dry except during summer floods. Our terrace was irrigated from the main stream some distance farther up, and by following the channel we could rejoin the footpath above the village. Behind us, one terrace higher, was a goat-house, and behind that a great rocky mountain face.

The opposite side of the main stream was a massive range of mountains, cut by gullies terraced every ten feet almost to the top. In one typical gully we counted more than a hundred ten-foot terraces built one above the other to catch and control the summer rains, grow corn and millet. Every gully, every terrace, was periodically fertilised and cultivated, manure from village pigsties and goatpens carried laboriously up precipitous slopes hundreds, even thousands of feet. The top few hundred feet along the ridge of the range on either side of the valley was sheer cliffs with here and there a rugged pass cleft in the beetling rocks.

In the stream and near its edge were beautiful spruce, juniper and cedar shrubs, walnut, persimmon and apricot trees ; huge green rocks of jade. Among the branches sported a flock of azure-blue jays with black-barred tails and vermilion beaks.

Ours was an end room facing south. We arranged loose rocks of calcite, feldspar and quartz under our window for a rockery, shaded by a large apricot tree. At the foot of the apricot a small shrine brooded over the terrace of winter wheat. There was a shrine for every major group of terraces near the village, each with its miniature image of Buddha, in good repair ; we were evidently among a pious community.

It happened that the day after we arrived was New Year on the old lunar calendar, and the valley community celebrated the occasion with considerable relish. We had noticed the men having their heads shaved the afternoon we arrived, and on the same evening a neatly dressed old peasant woman had come and placed an oil lamp in the shrine under our apricot tree. All the larger shrines around the village were illuminated throughout the night. In the morning our old lady came with some pieces of mantou (steamed bread) to leave at Buddha's feet in token offering.

According to custom on New Year's Day, everyone calls on everyone else, and our presence in the village added point to the formality : we were included in their calls. In fact we were greeted with an almost embarrassing enthusiasm.

Goatherd Glen is about five miles in length, and the five little village hamlets in the glen form a single administrative village unit. On New Year's Day the whole population of the valley visited our room. There was a continuous stream of people calling on us throughout the day. A dozen lively young women would come inside at a time, and in a few moments one of them would find some pretext for peeping beyond the screen to the sleeping section of the room ; then at her exclamation, they would all troop within to admire our portable wooden bedstead with its straw-filled mattress. They were thrilled with it, just as we had been when first installed at the headquarters the year before.

They were all so courteous and so warm-hearted that we could only respond accordingly. It was impossible to stop them from sitting on the bed to feel how soft it was compared with the standard kang. They could hardly believe that only two of us slept there, it was wide enough for four on their standards. All our visitors were spotlessly clean, but we had qualms about how superficial that might be, and accounted ourselves fortunate that, after they had all retired to their own homes, we could find only one stray memento on our bedding.

The very next day the village was entertained by a most frightful row. From our terrace we could see an old woman on one of the flat roof-tops going at it full steam, the noise of it echoing back and forth between the mountains. It would have been hysterical had it not been so deliberate and systematic ; she seemed to have had it all worked out in advance, and the flow of tirades was interminable, her energy inexhaustible ; she kept it up for at least two hours without pausing, and returned to the attack periodically for the rest of the day. We never quite found out what it was all about, but someone seems to have borrowed one of the old lady's kitchen utensils and failed to return it before the New Year. It was a trivial matter, and the rest of the village seemed no more than mildly amused at the affair ; the roof-top was the accepted place for letting off steam in public.

A few nights later our sleep was rudely disturbed by a man bellowing with mighty lungs from the doors of the goatpen one terrace behind our room. He sounded as though he was giving alarm about a Japanese raiding party ; but after we had fully awakened we realised what he was doing :

" Eldest son ! Eldest son !

" Starting to rain !   Starting to rain !
" Clear the roof !   Clear the roof ! "

That went on for more than five minutes before he was sure that his son had come out of his sleep, and then followed a rapid fire of instructions rattling over our roof ; then peace again, except for the dogs barking.

THE LITTLE GOATHERD

On our daily walks up the valley and round the narrow trails that skirted the mountain slopes we began to make the acquaintance of several little goatherds. Every evening just before dark several herd of black mountain goats would converge upon the village from different directions, and go noisily into their respective pens. One of the youngsters was particularly attractive ; he was not more than twelve, thoroughly business-like in his job and as thoroughly mischievous and boyish in his general outlook on life.

We tried to imitate him, calling to his goats ; it made him laugh.

" They won't listen to you ! They won't listen to anyone but me ! "

There were two herds coming in at the same time ; they threatened to get mixed up, and he was holding back his animals while the other herd went by. It was not easy, and every now and then he had to throw a small stone at one unruly animal, shout at another ; his eyes were continually alert. Meanwhile he was carrying on a conversation with us :

" Do you have goats in England ? "

" What kind of fruit do you have there ? "

" What ! You don't have persimmons ? " and then a most winning and mischievous wink as he offered :

" Just come down to my place some time and I'll give you some good big persimmons ! "

" Thank you ", we replied, " you come and call on us some time, too ! "

To our surprise he did, a few days later, after he had put his goats to sleep. Bill was using a typewriter and this intrigued the youngster tremendously. He started counting the keys, and Bill gave him a test in mental arithmetic which he passed with flying colours.

" Where did you go to school ? " we asked.

" Haven't been to school ! "

" Then where did you learn to add numbers ? "

" Oh ! That's easy ; we have to count the goats every day ; and now is the kidding season ; we're always adding numbers ! "

He kept dropping in every other evening after that, and several times came during our English conversation class with the wireless officers. The first time he found the big fellows sitting in our room he beat a hasty retreat, but he was just too late. One of the boys jumped up and caught him by the arm ; and we all coaxed him to overcome his shyness. In he came, bashful, but ready for any fun, with that fascinating mischievous twinkle in his eyes.

" Oh ! But your face is awfully dirty, you ought to wash it before you make calls ! " teased one of the officers.

" That's what you don't understand ! " replied the little chap quite unhurt ; " I don't get back from the mountain until nearly dark, and then when I have the goats all inside I've got to go and collect some weeds for them, and by that time the family is all waiting for me to join in the evening meal ; and it's nearly dark and I can't see to wash myself."

" You smell of goats, too ! " complained another boy.

" So would you ", retorted the youngster. " I sleep with them all night, and stay with them all day."

" You sleep with them ? My goodness, doesn't your employer give you a proper kang to sleep on ? "

" Yes, of course, but the kang is inside the goatpen."

" Good grandmother ? Whatever for ? "

" Well, someone has to be with the goats all night. They have to be disturbed three times between sundown and sunrise, or they'll get sick."

One of the officers confirmed that this custom was universal among goatherds in North China ; they say that if the animals are allowed to sleep through the night without being awakened and moved around two or three times they get sick and die.

This conversation had kept the youngster much longer than he had planned to stay out, and as he was going he found himself stepping out into a black night—the moon had already set. So we lit him a straw torch, and off he went in great glee.

Next time he came he had remembered : his face was washed, leaving a deep " tide-mark " round his neck. And he brought a collection of straw torches of his own to reserve in our room for future use.

The officers began teasing him again.

"Do you believe in devils?"

"Yes, of course!"

"For example?"

"Well, there's the mountain devil!"

"What does he do?"

"He tells the foxes and wolves to attack my goats; that's why I have to stay with them all day and bring them home at night."

"But suppose the mountain devil told the wolves to come down to the goatpen at night! Wouldn't you be afraid?"

"No! I'm not afraid of wolves!"

"But suppose the mountain devil told the wolves to open the door and come inside the pen?"

"But the wolf couldn't do it, even if the mountain devil told him to; and, besides, the mountain devil doesn't know how to open the door, I've a good lock on it!"

So the mountain devil had his limitations.

Then they complimented him on his clean face; but his clothes still reeked.

"You didn't change your clothes!"

"How could I? This is the only suit I have for this time of the year. I have one summer suit, and one winter suit, that's all."

"Do you have to buy your own clothes?"

"Yes, but my boss makes an allowance for them."

"Does he treat you well?"

"Yes, very well indeed. I am like one of their family; in fact he is my uncle. They always await their evening meal until I have finished putting the goats away, and we eat together all the same food. I have been working for them for two years now, my pay increases every year, and they give me a new clothing allowance every year."

"Wouldn't you rather go to school than look after goats?"

That puzzled him rather. Even after explanations he didn't seem to be sure whether the question was meant seriously or whether they were still teasing him. In the end he never admitted a preference for study. His attitude was thoroughly realist, what was the use of entertaining a preference for the impossible? He seemed somewhat embarrassed, and to relieve his little soul we asked him who was his employer, this uncle that treated him so well?

"Don't you know? You ought to! His is that family jus
down the glen where you have a dry daughter!"

That fairly started a howl of delight.

"What! Does Mrs. Band have a dry daughter in th
village?"

"Yes, of course, you should know that!"

"But it's the first time we've heard of it!"

"Yes, you know! The little girl for whom you made tha
nice red necklace!"

Then it dawned upon us.

OUR DRY DAUGHTER

A week ago we had been complimenting the old lady whc
tended the shrine by our window upon the cleanliness of hei
youngest granddaughter, and she had asked Claire to make hei
a necklace. This Claire had gladly done. The child was particularly attractive, and the old lady was a delight. We had not
realised at the time, but the wireless boys now explained that the
transaction was accepted in polite Chinese society as signifying
willingness on the part of both families concerned to enter into a
"dry" relationship. This corresponds somewhat with our ideas
of adopting "godparents", but there is more lightheartedness
attached to the Chinese custom. The actual ceremony of adoption
should involve much teasing of the mother by the dry father, and
of the father by the dry mother.

The old grandmother had certainly tricked us into something
interesting.

A few days after the little goat boy had revealed the fact of
our dry engagement, a message came for us from grandmother
asking if we would accept an invitation to lunch for the adoption
ceremony. She was sorry they had nothing wonderful to offer
for the meal—just "chiao-tse" (boiled pie), but it would be very
polite of us if we would give them the honour. We wondered
if we ought to accept, but Roger Liu assured us that they would
really like us to do so. Roger refused to come with us, we must
face the situation ourselves without the help of an interpreter :
this occasion was a personal one between the families, and no
outsider should be present.

So on April 11th we had lunch at the Tsui's home. Their living
room had been specially cleaned, and we were asked to take our

PLATE X

Mass meeting to appoint first Border Government in Hopei.

General Nieh Jung-chen, Commander of the Communist forces in Hopei guerrilla area.

Mr. Sung Shao-wen, Chairman of the People's Government in the Hopei guerrilla area.

seats on the edge of the kang where they had laid out some skins. Our gingerly hesitation passed for real Chinese courtesy; and while their backs were turned Bill flipped one little thing off one of the rugs on to the floor. But really the place was beautifully done, and we felt like being polite. The pie was excellent, but we had a big courtesy battle to make the family eat at the same time as us; we became still more courteous when they brought in a dish of some mysterious looking meat. Small disc-shaped things which the young father, our dry brother, explained with a grin were " hou yang tan ", or, literally, " living goat eggs ". This was a special treat, with some symbolic meaning attached to it appropriate to the dry relationship. The young men sucked the pieces from their chopsticks with noisy relish and delighted laughter, and with a twinkling eye urged us on :

" Come along, you take some more ! "

The only moment when our Chinese had proved inadequate was when the young brother had explained about the sweet-breads. We couldn't make out what living goat eggs could mean, and this amused the family immensely. The young brother demonstrated graphically the part of the goat's anatomy where the things came from, and was highly delighted at our stupidity.

For the ceremonial climax the child herself was marched in and asked to " ko-tou " to Claire.

" Touch your head on the floor three times to your new dry mother ! "

" No ! "

" Come on ! Be a good girl ! "

" No ! I don't want to ! "

" All right ! "

And with that the old grandmother took firm hold of the child's little head, made her kneel on the floor, and forcibly performed the required movements. At the third touch the little girl burst into tears of protest, picked herself up and dashed from the room amidst shouts of merriment from the adults.

THE VILLAGE HEAD

It was in this glen that we caught some intimate glimpses of local self-government in action, and the difficulties to be faced.

Early in the morning of March 5th we noticed a sedan chair, bedecked in red, parked just outside the village with a crowd of children round it. Evidently a bride had arrived. But the sedan chair was still there an hour later. Rumours came through that there had been a hitch. During the afternoon the red decorations were removed and the sedan chair, with its occupant, were taken away. In the evening we had the full story from the service boy.

The elected head of the village was known to be an enthusiastic administrator of the new marriage laws. But one of the leading families wished to add a daughter-in-law to their family, and did not wish to wait until their son had reached the new legal marrying age : eighteen. They knew that if they followed the rule and made application for the marriage licence, it would be refused. So as one would expect, they arranged the betrothal with another family in a nearby village, and planned to bring the bride to Goatherd Glen on the appointed wedding-day and present the village head with a *fait-accompli*. What could he do about it then ? It would be age-old custom of conservative folk matched against new-fangled and artificial rules agreed to by upstarts.

But the old people miscalculated the speed of the grape-vine system. A young goatherd had no doubt seen the sedan coming into the valley and warned his pals down in the village that something interesting was afoot. Before the bride had even come inside the village, the head had heard about it and at once guessed what was planned. He called on the family, forced a confession and issued his ban. The argument continued through the morning while the bride cooled off in the chair outside the village. A third family took her in for a meal while the chair was being undressed, and she was carried home without even seeing her intended husband, and leaving behind the fine silks in which she herself had been arrayed. On our walk that evening we met one of the villagers carrying the wedding trousseau back to the place from which it had been borrowed ; he was proud to display it to us, right there on the little mountain footpath.

With this success, the village head swelled visibly. But his pride came near to pitching him into serious trouble, strangely enough in connection with ourselves. The story is worth giving in some detail because it illustrates well enough the pitfalls which a young democracy will have to face throughout China no matter how much tutelage may have been provided before its inception.

A short while after we had been installed in Goatherd Glen our old serving boy was promoted to become messenger at the central headquarters, and a younger boy named Chang Chin-tsai took his place. This little fellow, in his early teens, was a gentlemanly, quiet, dreamy type, very unlike the robust peasant; his family had been well-to-do farmers on the Central Hopei plains, and at the Japanese occupation he had run away from home against his parents' wishes. Our cook, a forthright business-like rascal of the old school, quite uninfluenced by Communistic ideas of the army he was in, very quickly got exasperated by this new youngster, regarded him as a good-for-nothing lazy child.

Before many weeks had passed, the boy Chin-tsai was giving back cheek to the cook, as boys will, especially as he had succeeded more or less in pleasing us. Cook, being hot-tempered, at last lost control one morning, let fly with his fist and struck the boy. The boy reported this knowing full well that the discipline rules of the Eighth Route Army could be applied to punish the cook for bullying. The discipline officers at headquarters in fact decided to recall the cook for a period, leaving the boy to be disciplined by Roger Liu.

Now it happened that this incident occurred on April 1st, and the cook had not made out the full statement of accounts for March. Eventually these were secured from him and Roger Liu checked them over with the substitute cook, who had already been coolie and assistant cook for several months. This man was a simple-minded peasant lad who had evidently not been taken into the confidence of the cook. The amount of flour put down as having been received from the village head did not agree with the facts as recalled by the assistant cook. There was apparently 60 lb. of grain still at the head's house waiting to be ground, which the cook seemed to be claiming had already been delivered to us.

The village head at first agreed with the cook's statement; there was nothing owing to us. But later he realised that the cook might be trapped into admission, and protected himself by saying that perhaps his wife had not got around to delivering the flour; could he have time in which to make inquiries?

The cook was then called back from headquarters and brought on the mat. After much argument and cross-examination by Roger Liu in the next room to ours, he finally confessed that he had intrigued with the village head to squeeze that much flour. He was, in fact, laying up a private store of grain, making hay while the sun shone, blaming the large consumption of cereal on the

Westerners' big appetites ! The thing had apparently been going on for a long time, and this was just one instalment that had been discovered. After the war he was going to resign from the army and open a small cafe of his own. He was fed up with life under the Communist system !

Roger Liu then brought the cook and the village head together. The village head was too clever for the cook ; he swore on oath that there was not a word of truth in the confession ; as far as he was concerned he was merely holding the flour until we asked for it. What our cook was expecting to do was no concern of his. Unfortunately for our faith in his veracity, he had contradicted himself, or rather shifted his ground twice during the progress of the discussions. To avoid scandal the charge of corruption was not pressed against him. He got off lightly.

But the cook himself got the scare of his life. Maximum penalty for proven corruption in the Eighth Route Army is death. He pleaded with Liu not to report his confession to headquarters, to pretend that he had not been found guilty. Finally he broke down in tears ; he would not believe that the headquarters would satisfy themselves with educational discipline in view of his having confessed his guilt before he had been formally charged with it. In the end he was persuaded to leave for headquarters with another company of men who happened to be going that way. But he disappeared for three days, hiding with a friend in a village not far away ; but was eventually persuaded to give himself up. There are no police, civil or military, in the Border Region for this kind of thing, by the way.

Next time we saw the cook, he was as perky as ever, working as an assistant cook to General Nieh at the central headquarters.

If we may point an obvious moral here, we would like to remark that, strict though the village head had been in the application of the new marriage laws, he did not appear to be above the playing of the old tricks when it suited himself. Even though their democracy is young, the people are old with cunning, and no political system can afford to ignore that for long.

Chapter XII

JAPANESE OFFENSIVE

On March 11th, 1943, a party of a thousand Japanese and three thousand conscript Chinese labourers came out on a block-house building campaign less than twenty miles away, and as a precaution we were told to pack up and hide away everything not essential to immediate work. The village head put the stuff in the local dug-out under one of the cultivated terraces across the glen some quarter mile from the village. The new line of forts tallied well with the plans that had recently been captured, and indicated that later, the enemy would attempt a more serious penetration in the direction of Gosu market.

The Chinese were concentrating upon harrying tactics, but the Japanese were pressing on with their plans regardless of heavy losses : if a thousand labourers escaped into the hills another thousand would be conscripted and pressed into service ; the loss of fifty to a hundred Japanese men they apparently thought not too high a price to pay for the erection of each block-house ; from their point of view, they felt that each block-house was another nail in the coffin of the guerrilla organisation.

The success of the enemy in setting up these block-houses, while not of major importance, did indeed force an intensification of warfare throughout the guerrilla areas ; and, of immediate concern to ourselves, it meant that our headquarters district became more liable to sudden raids by the enemy. We were advised that the whole headquarters were preparing a new location to which we must expect to move before long.

It was glorious spring weather ; the apricot tree by our window was in full bloom. We watched many a great V of wild geese flying optimistically north. But V or no V, we were astounded at the news we were brought on March 17th : this is what Roger Liu exclaimed as he came in that afternoon after a visit with the General :

" Eden and Hull have decided to prolong the war ! "

" What the —— ! Explain yourself, please ! "

" That's all it says : Anthony Eden and Cordell Hull have decided to prolong the war ! "

Apparently these Chinese guerrillas could not conceive of two such leaders of the great Powers taking a passive observer's attitude towards the probable length of the war, and an agreement between them that the war would be prolonged was taken to mean literally an agreement between them to make it last longer! That was how the news was disseminated in the local version as we received it.

By the end of March the Japanese had field guns in action within ten miles of our place, and on the 27th the various headquarters departments began moving farther north to a new group of villages around the Congress auditorium. In a few days only two departments were left in our district : the pictorial printing unit and our wireless unit. The pictorial was finishing the printing of their next issue and wanted to get it off the press before packing up ; we were waiting for orders. Headquarters explained that they were preparing a specially nice cottage for the Westerners, and the wireless unit might as well stay with us until our place was ready. We retorted as politely as we could that we preferred safety to fastidiousness ; and we did not like the idea of being blamed for holding back the whole party until the last minute.

We sent Roger Liu up to the new headquarters to see for himself about the state of affairs, and to present our claims for an early removal. The morning after he had gone our whole village was aroused in alarm by artillery fire that seemed to be exploding just over the hill at the market of Huikou. It was much too close for comfort. The wireless boys got on the 'phone to the local military headquarters and overheard their report to the central headquarters at Wentang : a Japanese party had come out and captured Gosu market, and another party, the one with the field gun, was within a few miles of Huikou. The local troops had the situation well in hand.

We were advised to be prepared for evacuation any minute. It was not a very happy morning. As so often seems to happen, rain accompanied the bad news. The roof repairs to our cottage were revealed : the place dripped mud all over us. After noon the rain turned to sleet, and then snow. To evacuate suddenly in such weather would be decidedly uncomfortable.

Roger Liu returned in haste next day ; but he brought a message from the General to say that we were in the best place ; the earliest we would need to move would be four or five days later.

Refugees were already pouring through the valley, villagers

escaping from the areas likely to be overrun by the new Japanese block-house zone. Chinese military equipment and stores were being taken south towards Gosu. The enemy had retired from that market the same day, and their raid was interpreted by the Chinese as a probe to test the Chinese defences. Having found nothing the enemy were expected to return in some force within a few days, and commence their next line of forts. We were told that the Chinese were preparing strong fortifications in Gosu somewhat on the lines of those used in the battles in Central Hopei plains ; in fact it was the regular troops from Central Hopei who were being detailed for this work. They were hoping to give the Japanese an unpleasant surprise at Gosu.

Finally—it was the day after the dry-adoption ceremony at the Tsui family home—five mules that had been carrying military equipment near Gosu were diverted to our place on their return trip. The furniture and equipment of the whole unit was loaded on these animals, and our whole party trekked up north.

Somehow we felt it would be a long time before we saw that warm-hearted little community again ; and that they would have to suffer much more before final victory. It was with sad steps that we climbed the hill overlooking the village ; but once over the top, descending again upon Huikou, the stimulating spring air got the better of us. It was with our usual gay spirits that we greeted some old friends, including our old landlord, at the market at Huikou. The peasants were going on with their normal peaceful life, and if the Japanese came on the morrow, let the morrow take care for itself ; theirs was very much the art of living in the present.

We ambled leisurely over the pass down into the valley of Chenchuang. The terraces were green with the winter's wheat ; white wagtails flitted among the rocks in the little stream ; swallow-tailed butterflies, black, yellow and red, floated on the gentle breeze that rustled the young leaves of the tall poplar trees.

Shortly after noon we arrived at the seat of the Border Government, entered Chairman Sung's office and announced our wish to stay in the village overnight. Bill needed a haircut, and the government's barber was brought in off the basket-ball ground to perform in the Chairman's office. In half an hour we were sharing afternoon tea with Chairman Sung and President Ch'eng Fang-wu. With a small group of government officials we were then taken out to see a big land-reclamation project in full swing. The wide river bed had been washed out in a flood as long ago as 1921 ; now the local government had reclaimed 80,000 square yards by building a great boulder dyke, and marking out the area in three hundred square sections by lines of boulders to check the flow of the flood waters. The team of several hundred men, peasants and civil servant personnel together, were putting the finishing touches to the big dyke ; they were expecting to secure a first layer of about four inches of soil from the summer rains this season, in which rice and later, winter wheat could be planted.

We were invited to stay a second night so that we could have a long conference with the members of the Continuing Congress Committee. Between conferences we took a pleasant stroll around the valley. Here we explored an ancient temple with a large pagoda. The temple had been erected about A.D. 400, repaired by the Mongols about eight centuries later, destroyed by the Japanese in 1941. Fortunately the pagoda was scarcely touched, and three great marble Buddhas within the base of the pagoda preserved the exquisite art of fifteen centuries past. To think that when those were being created by master sculptors, our ancestors may have been hairy cannibals ! Our hosts retorted : " Think rather that while you have progressed so far, our own civilisation has hardly changed through all that long time ! " But now, during the past few years, these old Buddhas were, at least in a poetical sense, presiding at the re-birth of their country, for here in this little village was a brain-cell of the new democracy.

The following morning after a delightful farewell feast we continued on our way rejoicing. Rejoicing in these people's remarkable social rejuvenation ; rejoicing in the exhilarating spring atmosphere ; rejoicing with every other living creature in that lovely country : hoopoes, starlings, magpies, heron ; through a long winding valley whose sides were covered with apricot shrubs in blossom ; through the solid little picturesque village called Dragon Hall, protected by a sturdy temple snuggling among ancient persimmon trees and immense moss-grown rocks ; by long terraces of luscious wheat, irrigation channels lined with the rich green foliage of edible golden lilies ; in reverie we longed for times of peace, when we would choose just such a spot for an ideal holiday.

At one of the hamlets in this apricot valley our hostler had bought a live chicken and tied it by its feet to his saddle. Just before we reached the top of the last pass, this chicken laid an egg, or more literally dropped an egg. The egg, no doubt subconsciously aware of the thousands of hard boulders that made up our narrow path, landed skilfully on a tiny patch of soft sand, so the hostler, with immediate returns on his outlay, also went on his way rejoicing.

Our destination, the village of Middle Poplar, was one of three villages known collectively as Poplar Valley. We were within two miles of the Congress Auditorium where the military headquarters had established themselves, and about twelve miles from Fuping town. Almost every village within a radius of five miles was full up with different departments of the headquarters organisation.

The cottage, to await the preparation of which our journey had been so long delayed, was indeed a pleasure to behold. Outside had been painted white to look like an old English thatched cottage ; inside they had arranged our collapsible furniture. There were two rooms under the one porchway, one for us and one for the L.'s who were expected in a few days : L. had been farther north for some months on technical work with the various subdivisional field headquarters.

There was little if any impressive scenery around Poplar Valley, the hills were more barren than those of Lingshou county, the soil more sandy ; Fuping county is the poorest of all the mountain districts in Hopei. The villagers were noticeably more ragged and less healthy than those of Goatherd Glen. Waiting for the wheat harvest, last year's corn and millet being exhausted, many families were reduced to peanut husks and elm leaves ; children were bundles of skin and bone, pot-bellied with the bulk of indigestible material with which they were trying to fight their hunger ; what nourishment might have been in the stuff was being absorbed by ascaris, an almost universal parasite.

And yet these poor folk were happy and confident. Better times were coming ; they felt themselves to be masters of their own fate ; they were struggling through hard times, but they were no harder than they had suffered for generations past. When their harvest comes it will be their own ; they know how to hide it from the Japanese, and the Japanese were soon going to be beaten ; before long peace and prosperity would be theirs the like of which their forbears had not known. They were facing the troubles of the last years of the war with a courage fortified by the new-found self-respect of a liberated people. They had need of every ounce of courage for the years of bitter struggle that remained ahead of them.

On April 19th, just one week after we had left Goatherd Glen, five days after we had left the Chenchuang valley, the Japanese suddenly pounced upon Gosu and Chenchuang in two separate concentrations. A third concentration struck from the rear at Huikou market. If the headquarters had not moved out three weeks in advance of them, the Japanese would have succeeded in surrounding the Chinese, and us; but as usual, Japanese surprise tactics succeeded only in producing surprises for the Japanese.

This time it had been quite a near miss for us. We had moved when we did only after much urging on our own part; had we listened to the headquarters reassurances we might still have been in Goatherd Glen at the last minute, and been forced to make a sudden get-away of the kind that means one loses most of one's encumbrances that go by the polite name of furniture and amenities at ordinary times.

As it was there were a couple of unpublicised accidents. The pictorial department had still not moved when the Japanese party started out to encircle Huikou. Somewhere about one in the morning the printing department received warning that an enemy party was headed in their direction; hectic preparations were accordingly set going for the dismantling and hiding of the heavy equipment; some of the people escaped, but the Japanese were already passing through the village before everything was ready. One photographer was just making his departure as the Japanese were entering the village, and noticing his haste they shot him down. But the enemy was in such a hurry to get to Huikou before dawn that they passed right through the village without stopping to investigate, the printing equipment was still being packed up inside, many officers were still in the village and did not know the danger they had been in until after the enemy had passed through. No equipment or pictorials were lost.

The enemy unit that attacked Chenchuang did more damage. A unit of the headquarters education department was doing local work in Chenchuang market town, received due warning of the approaching enemy, and estimated that they would have at least an hour to get away. They sent special scouts to the outskirts of the town to give the last urgent signal, and proceeded with their preparations. Most of the people got away within the hour, a few of the higher officers remained behind for the final warning. But it never came. The Japanese had experienced these tactics before; their force veered north and cut right round Chenchuang without giving the scouts a chance to issue warning, came in from the rear and captured the party.

The force that raided Gosu were, according to our previous information, supposed to have received a warm welcome from the Central Hopei forces who had been preparing special defensive fortifications. We heard nothing definite about the battle, but it seems that the Japanese came in such great strength that the battle was never fought; finding themselves overwhelmed at the outset, the guerrillas had withdrawn to await a more auspicious opportunity.

The Japanese occupied the group of valleys where we had had so many happy times: from Gosu up through Huikou and over the pass to Chenchuang; they stayed for a whole week, and appeared to be making ready to build a series of big fortresses to allow their permanent occupation of the area. Meanwhile, assuming this to be the enemy's object, the Chinese began concentrating a large force among the hills on the north side of Chenchuang valley; should the Japanese attempt to dig themselves in, the Chinese would join in pitched battle; otherwise they would just wait until the Japanese were worn out by the usual harrying tactics.

Several Chinese regiments were brought down from the third and first subdivisional areas in preparation for the big battle; they even mustered their few pieces of field artillery—we saw them being proudly marched through our valley on the way to the front. But exactly one week after their first pounce the Japanese withdrew as suddenly as they had come in; and simultaneously a large concentration of Japanese pounced upon the third and first subdivisional headquarters, about the same distance to the north of us as their first pounce had been to the south. This thrust caught the Chinese badly by surprise; their highest officers were all down with the troops getting ready to fight for Chenchuang. It was in this mess that Jack Shih lost his life.

The whole affair considerably shook our confidence in the guerrilla organisation. Why had we been advised to stay in the danger zone so long? Perhaps our suspicions were ungenerous, but we felt that we were deliberately left down there as a decoy. Wherever the headquarters moves, the peasants soon know it;

and when the peasants know it, the Japanese espionage system will get to know it in due course, although the course may be a matter of weeks. Where we moved would be even more conspicuous, and if we didn't move it would be an indication that the headquarters had not moved either. The Japanese, according to some captured individuals, would find out where we were approximately within a week of any move we made. Since we were still in the neighbourhood of Huikou until April 11th, it was clear that the Japanese would not have verified the fact that headquarters had moved out of the Huikou area before that big raid was made. Two days after they had withdrawn from Huikou, they had already ascertained where we had gone to, for an observation plane came circling over the Congress Auditorium, probably the first time they had noticed the place.

After the Japanese had withdrawn from Huikou, Gosu and Chenchuang, a news reporter was sent to visit the valleys ; he found the whole area strewn with the skeleton remains of animals ; the peasants had suffered loss of almost all their livestock ; many herd of goats had been captured, the goatherds forced to drive them away to enemy occupied districts. Our Tsui family had suffered loss of their whole grain stock. The equipment that had been left in hiding by the wireless unit was still safe. The unit accordingly sent a messenger and a mule down to Goatherd Glen, who returned with their books, duplicating machine, and a basket-load of young spinach that they had been cultivating. With the spinach the man brought back some atrocity stories of which this is typical :

Three old people alone remained in the village, one man and two women, when the Japanese arrived. The raiders demanded that they lead them to the village cache ; but they pleaded ignorance and infirmity. The old people were badly beaten up for their unco-operative spirit. As soon as the Japanese had left them, the old man, forgetting that he had claimed to be too infirm to help the Japanese in their search, climbed down the gully to the stream and collected a drink of water to help revive the two old women. The Japs spotted him on his errand of mercy, dashed out his brains with a rock.

The day the observation plane circled the auditorium, headquarters sent us a warning that the enemy had sixteen planes in combined operations with the ground offensive ; we must be ready for bombing raids, preferably keep well out of the village for most of the daylight. The Chinese had scouts posted within sight of the airfield being used by the enemy, and headquarters could receive warnings about five minutes before the planes arrived, but that did not give enough time to notify everyone else. We must therefore expect to look after ourselves, the sound of the plane approaching would be the first warning to us to keep out from any possible target area.

To Japanese planes operating over guerrilla areas, without air opposition of any kind, any village might become a target, and specially a village out of which a large crowd of uniformed people might be seen scattering. So the only wise course was to eat breakfast as early as possible and get out into the valley away from the village before the planes came over. This we did for a couple of days before we were rewarded on May 1st with the sight of six bombers coming directly from the east. They reached a point directly over the auditorium, broke formation and circled round machine-gunning and bombing for an hour on end. Their circle took them right over our heads at every turn, as we were lying in a little gully on the hillside.

We held the regular physics and mathematics classes out in the gully with a portable blackboard immediately after the raid was over; and in the afternoon we walked over to the auditorium to take a look at the damage.

The planes had dropped one bomb on the auditorium, successfully knocked the flimsy structure out, and then scattered large numbers of small bombs among the hills all round. The official version was that the Japanese had been aiming all the time at the building; but our own private explanation was that the raiders had been instructed to blow up the building first, expecting to surprise a mass meeting in celebration of May Day, scatter the hillsides with bombs and machine-gun bullets to do as much damage to the audience as possible. Fortunately there was no meeting in progress at the time, and therefore no one had been injured.

Expecting further raids in the immediate future, the headquarters people set up eight heavy machine-guns on the hills around the auditorium, to act as anti-aircraft battery, in hopes of doing some slight damage to the raiders on their next visit. The guns were kept on the hills for a week and nothing happened. But the day after the guns were taken down the planes came again. There must have been some smart espionage work going on, or else it was a most unfortunate coincidence. This time the planes came at five minutes to six in the morning ; it caught us at our morning ablutions ; Claire was quite undressed when we heard the sound of the planes and had to dash out. We changed our habits after that : wash-time was after dark in the evenings in future ! Bombing that morning continued for an hour, and at seven we came back for breakfast. At nine the planes came again and bombed for another hour ; they machine-gunned some mules in our village this time, too, just for fun.

Official explanations could not this time cover up the Japanese good marksmanship. The six o'clock raid scored direct hits on every one of the subsidiary buildings round the auditorium ; fortunately the bombs were quite small and the buildings, most of them of solid stone, were only slightly damaged. The early hour had also caught the headquarters people napping, most of them had been making a dash for the shelters as the planes came in sight.

The second raid, after breakfast, made a concentrated attack on the entrances to a few of the shelters. Fortunately they were fairly long U-shaped tunnels in the mountain face, and safe enough against anything the Japanese usually carried ; but the blast was terrific. The chief leaders of many of the Hopei Army units were trapped inside one of these tunnels while the Japanese were blasting away at its entrance with everything they had. General Nieh himself with his feet apart and his mouth gaping open, was mentally counting the explosions : one, two, three . . . ten . . . twenty . . . thirty . . . still no serious damage to the shelter ; well it should stand the entire load of all six planes ; and it did, but only just. Seventy-five bombs, none under 100 lb. weight, were exploded near or within the entrance to his cave. He moved his headquarters to another village that night.

The thing we had been afraid of was that while the Japanese planes kept the headquarters underground, and presumably disorganised, a land party might start out to make a sudden raid and capture us all. We had in fact been warned to be ready for just such an emergency, for a thousand enemy soldiers had been observed at a point not more than twenty miles away in such a position as to be able to attack the auditorium district. Lying in the gully watching the planes over our heads, these were by no means reassuring speculations. In fact we learned later that the Japanese had started out with exactly such intentions.

We discovered, right after the raid, that the headquarters people had all the telephone sets with them in the shelters throughout the raids; they knew the whole time just where every Japanese soldier was, and where every plane was operating; there never was a moment when they could not have given us at least an hour's warning—ample time to keep a safe distance from the enemy.

Small service boys attached to the headquarters collected no less than 1000 lb. of scrap metal for the guerrilla hand-grenade machine shops, after that series of raids on the auditorium.

The day following the big raid we were warned at six in the morning by telephone that planes were out again. We dashed for the gully, but the planes did not come over us, instead we could hear them bombing in the directions of the Chenchuang and Huikou valleys. They had apparently expected the headquarters to move back. To return to an area just mopped-up by the enemy was an old trick of the guerrillas, and the Japs knew it, but this time the Chinese had not gone back and the enemy were wasting their bombs.

At supper-time the next day, which was May 11th, we were told that the Japanese column previously mentioned were getting close; their efforts at a surprise land raid combined with the air raid had been frustrated by land mines. But we must now prepare for an emergency. At nine p.m. we were told that the enemy were now progressing rapidly towards Fuping city along the Sha River, which would take them within an uncomfortable distance of our place; moreover, they might easily be making for the auditorium village, so we must now be ready at a moment's notice. Orders to prepare for immediate departure were received at eleven-thirty p.m. It took about an hour for the unit to hide everything. Final orders for departure reached us at one a.m.

It was a pitch black night, and we had moved only a little more than eight miles before dawn at five a.m. when we took cover in a small village on a direct line towards Chenchuang. A very dishevelled party we looked. We had all been splashing into irrigation ditches and tripping over rocks in the darkness, our clothes were muddy, our knees and shins were bruised and cut. But first thing we had to find a convenient gully a few hundred yards from the village to hide in case of air raids. Then we returned to the room assigned to us by the manager, stretched ourselves out on a wooden board and slept like logs.

While we had been exploring the gullies, the cook had unloade
the kitchen mule and by eight a.m. he aroused us to an excellen
hot breakfast. And at 4 p.m. he repeated the miracle.

The Japanese occupied Fuping city during that day, but di
not attack the auditorium village. Late in the afternoon we a
got on the move again, and before dark were well into the are
devastated by the enemy in their invasion of Chenchuang. Th
village that had been mapped out for the wireless unit was dis
covered to have been too badly knocked about; most of th
villagers were huddling among the debris beneath ruined wall
there was not a roof left in the whole place. After about an hou
and a half wandering round in the rain another village was found tha
came up to the standards of the unit's manager; about two hundre
men and boys crowded into two or three rooms; and a small kan
was made available for ourselves and a service boy—Chin-tsai.

In the morning we got chatting to the peasants who had bee
pushed out for our benefit: the mother had brought her son int
the room and started to shave his head. She told us that they ra
into trouble in the night when the army manager pushed them int
their neighbour's cottage:

" The neighbours have now gone to relatives in another villag
and locked up their room, so we can't go and share their kan
to-night. You see ", she came nearer and said in a confidentia
whisper, " I've lost several children, all due to eye disease, and th
neighbours say it's contagious ! "

She probably hoped we would be as nervous about the con
tagion as her neighbours were supposed to be. But she had les
cause to worry than she thought; we did not stay in the villag
another night.

During the day, classes continued in a little glen covered wit
trees, making an excellent screen from the air. Japanese plane
were over several times, bombing Wentang and Fuping, but b
early afternoon we heard that the enemy had continued west an
withdrawn across to the other side of the Border Region. Ou
victorious return to Middle Poplar took us four hours betwee
three-thirty and dusk. We had just time to recover the bedstead
and other bits of furniture scattered around the hillside before dark
By nine we were ready for sleep on our straw mattresses, prime
with the good news from headquarters that the Allied campaig
in Africa had been brought to a victorious conclusion.

PLATE XI

Top   Continuing Congress Committee in Hopei guerrilla area. Front row—left to right : Mr. An from Wutai ; General Yen Li-hsuan, wealthy landlord ; and Professor Ch'eng Fang-wu, President of the " Guerrilla Lienta University."

Bottom   The authors in conversation outside the congress hall, January 15th, 1943.

Chapter XIII

THROUGH ENEMY FRONT LINES

ALL through June 1943 we were still waiting for the second front in Europe ; we found it quite impossible to imagine the immense preparations that were said to be proceeding in North Africa. By July 9th we knew that the German offensive in Russia had already been smashed, and on the 12th we rejoiced in the news of Allied landings on Sicily.

But drought was threatening our little Poplar Valley, and the peasants were praying for rain. There was a ceremonial procession, beating a gong, visiting the shrines in the valley ; and they announced a bargain with the Dragon King. If rain came before the next Wednesday, they would slaughter a goat in the Dragon's honour. It worked like a charm. On Tuesday the rain started at about tea-time, and the peasants selected the oldest billy-goat in the valley, one that should have been disposed of long ago, and every family paid the owner of the goat for a share of its meat. Out of mischief we approached the crowd that had collected round the butcher as he was skinning the animal, and enquired whether we could buy some of the meat.

" Sorry ! But all this has been assigned in advance to those taking part in the ceremony ! "

And then we heard on July 26th that Mussolini had resigned ; at last things were beginning to move in the right direction. Throughout the spring and early summer the war had gone very slowly for us ; there was nothing sufficiently hopeful to keep our spirits up in those isolated surroundings. As the heat of early summer began in April and May, we used to spend long hours sitting on the hillside overlooking Middle Poplar. The village was surrounded by a lozenge-shaped area of cultivated ground in the broad river bed, a pleasant enough oasis in a barren rock-strewn terrain. Our own cottage immediately below us, opened on to a rather large threshing floor and beyond the threshing floor, to the north, terraces dropped off a few levels into a tributary of the main valley coming into it from the west. The villagers also cultivated a considerable length of this small tributary, long narrow

terraces of millet and corn shaded here and there by apricot tree
and date bushes. Beyond the mouth of the tributary on the side
of the main valley was another intensely cultivated area surroundin
a second large threshing space overlooking which was a larg
cave.

But the villagers were more interesting than their village. Th
courtyard immediately behind our cottage was the home of
comparatively small family ; they owned the cottage we wer
living in. The father, a man of about forty, took his siesta on ou
porch every afternoon, laying himself out on a goat-skin mat acro
our door-step after a hard morning's work among the terrace
He also stored his plough and a supply of brushwood fuel und
our shelter from spring showers. His wife was a pleasant enoug
young woman, and they had three children ; the eldest son wa
exceptionally well-behaved, one felt compelled to describe him a
a refined type even in those surroundings. With this family live
a sister-in-law, and she was a "holy terror". In her contente
moods she reminded us of an illustration of H. G. Well's "M
Parham" who "saw it through" ; and we nick-named her Mr
Parham. When she had anything on her mind the whole worl
soon knew about it ; the threshing floor was hardly wide enougl
the valley resounded with her flow of expletive ejaculations. Eve
her whispered confidences to her neighbours were loud enougl
to awake us from sleep.

There was a public grindstone just outside our room, by th
side of the threshing floor, and Mrs. Parham had a habit of risin
at about four a.m. and grinding the breakfast for her household
Early risers the world over seem inordinately proud of the ac
complishment, and instead of keeping specially quiet, make mor
noise than usual just to let the neighbours know. If anyone cam
out in sight of the grindstone while Mrs. Parham was busy ther
she would hail them in great glee. There was no doubt she set
high standard in joviality before breakfast—she had the villag
cockerel quite eclipsed.

Perhaps the most miserable of all members of the communit
was an old mother who had lost her husband and was keeping
body and soul more or less together with the help of two worthles
sons. One was a simple-minded cripple with a mental age abou
three years, still inarticulate, but willing enough to stagger roun
the grindstone while his mother brushed and spread the grain

he other was a physically strong but dangerously intelligent half-wit ; he spent most of his time lying among the rocks outside the village, and was always missing when his mother had work to do.

"Winston" was the most impressive old woman in the whole community. In her face she was the image of our respected Prime Minister, hence her nick-name. She was the family head in a home just below the threshing floor. She was at least seventy, and so determined a spirit did she have, that we have seen her, bound feet and all, climb single-handed up a rough ladder to her cottage roof, carrying in her other hand a huge basket of corn-cobs. She had a large family of strapping daughters, any one of whom would have been glad to do the job for her. One of these days she will break her neck.

Then there was the former occupant of our room. She was, if possible, even poorer than the mother of the two idiots. She was always dressed in rags, seldom bothered to repair the buttons on her torn jacket. She had a wild drawn face, quite unlike a Chinese, and a reckless unconcern for her own nakedness ; we called her "south-sea islander" ; her one child had advanced tuberculosis. We wondered how many millions of the germs were still mixed up in the loose soil which formed the floor of the room.

Even from our perch on the hillside where we could watch these poor folk going about their daily affairs from a reasonable distance, the scene was almost always depressing. It was better to be down among them, helping them in their work. So between classes we would sit with the women cutting off the wheat ears. At harvest time we spent some days up the valley carrying sheaves of wheat. We turned the grindstone, helped to flail the barley, and learned to make fans from the stems of the wheat.

The refined eldest son used to drive his father's two cows, drawing a small roller, over the ears of barley to crack open the husks on the threshing floor. We would follow him, turning over the mass on the floor to make sure the whole thing got uniformly crushed. Now and then the youngster would have to stop and humour the cow's personal idiosyncracies. Once he had started work without his special gourd-bowl, and all of a sudden we were startled to hear him shout at the top of his voice for someone to fetch the bowl, holding the cow's tail down as hard as he could.

INTERNAL CRISIS

In March at Goatherd Glen we had talked with Roger Liu about the advisability of our proceeding through to Yenan and Chungking. We had come out of Peiping with the idea that the Pacific war would last no more than about eight months after the Japanese came up against the American Navy. We had hardly expected to live with the guerrillas for several years. But we had made no formal request, and Roger had encouraged us to think of staying on until some definite arrangement could be fixed up to have us stay in Yenan University. We were not inclined to consider such a possibility, but it would be soon enough to refuse if and when an invitation materialised.

But in Middle Poplar, sitting there on our little hill, we made up our minds to get a move on. The life was telling on us a little too much. In principle one could easily adjust oneself to it if one was mentally decided to do so, but we were not. In fact we congratulated ourselves at times upon our having already been so long with the guerrillas without once having been down with sickness. Every other Western visitor they had had seemed to have been through a bout of dysentery at the very least, usually malaria, typhoid and typhus thrown in as well. Physically we seemed better able to endure it than most. But, to tell the truth, we had had enough of uncertainty, and too long a time from home ; the mental strain was more serious than the physical. We were not adventurous by profession ; and while any journalist of spirit would have given almost his skin to have been where we were, he would have been welcome to take our place.

The deciding factor was our strong suspicion that we were becoming more of an embarrassment to the military headquarters, and that our usefulness to them was beginning to wear out. We no longer felt content to accept their generous hospitality in return for so little in direct help to their battle against poverty and the Japanese.

And so, early in May, we sent a definite request to General Nieh that we be sent across the Japanese lines as early as it could possibly be arranged. The reply was what we had feared. The General was sorry that there was no chance to go across the lines at that time of the year ; crops were too low, and no convoy could be arranged. In any case they hoped we would stay permanently ; the courses in physics and mathematics were of great value to their wireless people, and they were hoping to expand their educational work as time went on. If we insisted upon going, would we please try to complete the present courses ? The earliest time for safe crossing would be during August when the corn would be high. Could we finish the courses by that time ?

We worked it out in detail and replied that all the courses could be completed by the first week in August, and that we would plan to be ready for the journey on or after August 8th.

From then on, through three months of heat, Bill was lecturing four hours a day, which was as much as the boys could spare from their more definitely military duties. Some of the more advanced men came for special tutorials, preparing them to take over teaching after we had left.

In July the internal crisis flared up. We were told that the Kuomintang were concentrating a large force around the Shensi-Kansu-Ninghsia Border Region, and seemed to be planning a " blitz " on the Communist headquarters at Yenan. An airfield was under construction and planes were ready to take part in the offensive. The Chinese Communist Party representative in Chung-king, Mr. Chou En-lai, had been sent back to Yenan, and an attempt had been made to " bump him off " at a deserted spot in no-man's land. Evading the gangsters, Chou had slipped through the blockade, seen truck-loads of artillery shells on their way to the outposts overlooking Communist areas.

Of the background to these troubles we shall speak later. In Middle Poplar it struck us first in the form of an invitation to attend and address an anti-civil-war meeting at the local head-quarters. The Communists were embarking upon a big publicity campaign, ostensibly against civil war, but, we suspected, in fact against the Kuomintang. We had no wish to be drawn into any such dispute, even under such a plausible slogan. We refused the invitation, and they sent some journalists around to interview us on our views concerning the threat of civil war. We tried our best to let them understand that in any internal problem we had no wish to interfere in any way whatever. While they had a United Front, we would wholeheartedly support their anti-Japanese programme ; but if they started arguing about internal political problems they must please leave us out of it. They obviously did not like this ; they felt that no one can be neutral these days. Perhaps they were right. The situation was not a little delicate for us, because our plans for going through to Chung king were supposed to be kept most secret in order to facilitat the arrangement of safe convoy across the Japanese lines. Bu to gain sympathy from our questioners we had to hint that som time we were hoping to go through to Kuomintang areas, an could not therefore afford to qualify for their black lists.

The tension was eased for us, personally at least, by the arriva in the Border Region of one of our scientific colleagues from Peiping : a Chinese biologist who had just managed to escap from the Japanese in that city. He was wildly excited about al the social progress and political reconstruction going on in th Border Region, surpassing anything conceivable in occupied areas. He was so overjoyed at gaining his freedom, and finding so much useful work waiting for him to do in connection with the army's medical programme, and celebrated his escape so heartily in date wine that on several occasions he was thrown (that was how he put it) from his mule, and suffered minor injuries. He brough us much detailed news of our friends in Peiping and we stayed up all night talking. Particularly exciting was the fact that several of our best friends had escaped and were already in Chengtu, Szechuan. It would not be long now before we could meet them again, like the good old times.

FAREWELL TO FUPING

On August 4th we sent a special message to General Nieh, reminding him that we had promised to be ready by August 8th, and assuring him that the courses were now complete ; we were awaiting his command. Next day the reply came : the General had just received telegraphic instructions from Yenan to transfer certain troops to the Yellow River ; we could safely travel with them ; we must be ready for the journey on August 8th.

Of all the miracles ! It seemed more like booking a passage on a peace-time steamer than waiting for a guerrilla escort behind Japanese lines. As a rule these things are never less than two or three weeks later than expected ; more often one had to wait half a year from any date suggested. Here we were being offered a first-class escort on the very earliest date upon which we had expected to be ready, and it had happened entirely because of events over which nobody directly concerned had any control. It was obviously the threat of civil war that had stimulated the troop movements; we were going to travel on a four hundred miles forced march with the headquarters of what from the most obvious point of view could be regarded as an insurrectionary army.

On the evening of August 7th reports had come in that the Japanese were pressing a peace offensive on the Central Government. Chiang Kai-shek was said to be wavering, and there was grave danger that Kuomintang China would go over to the Axis. Roger Liu was talking excitedly with the L.'s, and L. was indulging in what to Bill seemed silly speculations about what would happen if the Chungking crowd did go over to the Japanese. No doubt the Communists were almost hoping that that would happen; it would prove that they were the only really anti-Japanese organisation in the country. This chop-licking was audible far into the night. In the end it annoyed Bill so much that he exclaimed:

" Don't talk such a lot of rot! You know as well as I do that Chiang is not such a damned fool as to go over to the Axis at this stage of the war!"

For some reason that deflated the discussion, and we were able to get some sleep, although the civil war threat still worried us: it might mean that we would have trouble getting out of Yenan.

On the morrow we said good-bye to the wireless school at Middle Poplar.

There were special rooms prepared for us at General Nieh's village that night, and a farewell party was planned for the next morning. A strong contingent of officers included General Lü, commander-in-chief of the Central Hopei regiments, General Nieh, several commissars and Chiefs of Staff.

General Nieh presented us with a Japanese officer's armorial sword as a memento of our stay in the Border Region. We accepted it as a very valuable trophy. It had been captured from a Japanese general in the previous spring campaign. We took it with us on our two months' march to Yenan, the army boys vying with each other for the privilege of carrying it. We found it a fatal embarrassment on the way into Sian, and left it with missionaries in that city. We heard later that it was taken out of the country by the local American Consul, and presumably it is now somewhere in the United States. We hope that whoever has it now will appreciate what it actually represents.

During that night at General Nieh's, a heavy cloud-burst brought up the floods on the Sha River to such a height that we could not proceed, as planned, to the north bank, where we had expected to make contact with the escort. Instead we played dominoes with General Nieh and General Lü, on the verandah of a tiny chalet under the spruce and juniper trees that overlooked the headquarters village. The weather showed unmistakable signs of coming autumn; it augured well for our journey across the province. Nothing worried us so much as the oppressive heat of the first week in August.

We were told to be ready for an alternative route early next morning. So on August 10th we were up at about five-thirty, with the army boys, and ready for the road in about an hour, except that there were still no signs of breakfast. By seven the guide was waiting for us, but still no breakfast. Eventually we got over the meal, but at nine there was a more serious hitch. The Sha River flood had prevented the arrival of the youth who had been selected for our personal bodyguard and service boy on the trip. Our own little Chang Chin-tsai volunteered instead, but all his worldly possessions were back in Middle Poplar. A 'phone message was therefore sent to the cook there, and we were hoping that he would turn up with Chin-tsai's things in time. But the serious hitch was an absence of pack animals.

There had been a slip up somewhere. The man in charge of the animals had not been warned to have any ready for us, and all the road-worthy creatures had been sent out to collect fodder earlier in the morning. The General also wanted to lend us two animals to ride. But all they could find was a couple of decrepit mules, more dead than alive, and on one of these they piled our baggage, the other they reserved for riding. And then at the last minute, which was almost ten o'clock, the hostler appeared with a beautiful white pony which they offered to Bill on loan until we made contact with the regimental headquarters with whom we were going to cross the enemy lines. It was not until late that night that we understood why they had been so anxious to provide us each with an animal to ride. They had told us the journey would be no more than twenty miles, and we felt equal to walking that; but in fact it was well over thirty miles, the last ten exceedingly hard going, and of course they must have known this well enough.

Roger Liu was made responsible for us until we caught up with he regiment; our party for the first two days was therefore: hostler, guide, service boy, Roger Liu and the two of us. There were four animals including Roger's.

It was an exceedingly hot afternoon and we rode the whole time with our animals going at a steady walk. We struck the trail from Fuping city to the west about ten miles west of the city; t was the same route as that taken by the Japanese on their last offensive. We found ourselves amidst tremendous scenery on he Hopei-Shansi provincial boundary, among the foothills of the Heng and Wutai mountain ranges, towering up into summer thunderstorms.

As darkness came on, we were climbing over the second pass north of the Fuping to Lungchuan Pass trail, still a good ten miles from our destination on a path that only the guide knew. Down the other side we came up against a raging torrent up which the guide said we had to make our way. Although we had lunched from the generous supply of little dry biscuits our cook had made for us, and drank hot water from one of the hamlets on the way, we were pretty well tired out by the time this barrier appeared; not so much from exercise as from exposure to the sunshine and the fact that we had been up since five that morning, about fourteen hours already.

It was obviously impossible to retrace our steps, and there was no alternative route. We simply must make contact with the regiment, or we should miss the chance perhaps for another year. So if the flood has to be crossed, crossed it will be. Getting up on our steeds again—we had been walking down from the last pass— we followed the guide as he plunged waist deep into the rushing waters. The animals behaved excellently, and we heaved a sigh of relief as we climbed safely up the opposite bank and turned upstream. So that was that! But it was not! Another crossing back again higher up; and this time the animals began stumbling on the rough boulders in the river bed, nearly upset us amid stream; and another, and yet another crossing; each time either the flood was actually worse, or the animals were growing tired, but we seemed to get across with just a shade less margin of safety. Then on the sixth crossing we felt we had reached the limit.

Here the approaches were so steep that each animal had first to be coaxed to jump into the water from the top of a great rock, then be pulled back against the rock so that its rider could slide on to its back. In midstream the animals scarcely had foothold. On the opposite bank we had to climb off the animals while they were still in the depth, perch on another huge rock and coax the animals to make a leap out on to the rock beside us. Bill followed these instructions carefully, managed satisfactorily. Roger, following, thought he could leap the mule without dismounting. He slipped off his saddle, fell into the stream and was dragged to safety by the guide, minus one shoe. His mule, too, fell back into the flood, lost its nerve and went pounding back to the other side to the confusion of the rest of the party. Chang Chin-tsai, wading almost up to his arm-pits, heroically held on the nose of Claire's animal and she got across safely. Liu was badly shaken by his narrow escape. It took about ten minutes to calm down the animals.

"When we first came to the river, you said there were only a very few crossings," we complained to the guide ; "now we have done six, surely we are through with it now ? "

"Yes, almost over now ! " he replied. "Only ten more crossings ! "

Faith, hope and charity ; and the greatest of these ? Yes, it is still charity.

The next fording was near the foot of a tremendous waterfall, roaring ominously in the pitch darkness. The guide couldn't seem to make out where the correct point was. Up to then he had been uncannily accurate. The flood must surely have obliterated every sign, and yet each time we reached the other side we would come exactly upon the faint traces of a footpath that had been quite invisible as we had plunged into the flood.

"Excuse me a moment, while I first go across to check up whether this is the right place to cross," he said, this time. Accompanied by the thunder of the cataract, he disappeared into the darkness over the waters. In a few minutes there came back a faint hail from the far side :

"All right ! Come along, this way ! "

So in we plunged again into the fluid darkness. And after breath-taking suspense, arrived on the opposite bank to find the guide standing on a perfectly clear trail that took us abruptly up the face of the ravine above the top of the falls.

After that the crossings became a little easier, and after the sixteenth we saw a light ahead. The valley had become narrow and steep. It was shortly after midnight, and we came upon a tiny village in perfect preservation ; it seemed impossible that it should be real. Roger told us that this village was so difficult of access that the Japanese had never yet been there. We could well believe it. It was used as a base during serious enemy operations, and at present it was occupied by a military training camp for youths. The way we had come up to it was the only way to get there unless one was prepared to climb an exceedingly high and easily defended pass.

The officer in charge prepared us some boiled rice, and between one and two a.m. we enjoyed a few bowls of this gruel sweetened with honey that we had brought with us from Middle Poplar. Then a sound sleep on a hard kang until seven next morning. After breakfast we heard that the regiment we were after were also delayed one day by the flood ; we could take a rest, proceed later. So we washed and sunned the dirty uniforms, socks and cloth shoes, lolled luxuriously on the kang, hoping to heaven that there would be no more nights like that one had been.

Continuing on August 12th we climbed higher round the slopes of the Wutai range, over a tremendous pass, resting every few minutes to recover our breath in the rare air and brilliant sunshine. Wild flowers were gorgeous here ; there was nothing barren about these mountains ; asters, scabias, roses, wallflowers, wild snapdragons, rhubarb, oats, scrub oak, and all manner of shrubs and plants that it would take an expert botanist to identify ; absolutely heavenly country.

But the two mules were completely done up. The baggage animal collapsed half-way, and we transferred his pack to the animal that had been for Claire to ride. Even then the first animal was almost dead by the time we reached our destination. The fine white Mongolian pony was fresh enough ; which was fortunate ; Roger informed us that it was in fact General Hsiao Ke's private animal that had been loaned to Bill. The General was not in the habit of letting others ride it, nor did he usually take it on such strenuous journeys as we had just done. It came as a shock to Bill to realise that he had been riding what was probably the most precious animal in the whole guerrilla base, and come very near to losing it in the floods. The General could not have done more to help us on that first journey, and perhaps it was better that they had not warned us of it at the start. After all,

actions speak louder than words, and we shall be everlasting
grateful for the care they actually took for our safety.

The horizontal equivalent of the distance we did that secon
day was only about ten miles, but we do not know how man
thousands of feet we climbed ; however, it was fairly early in th
afternoon that we arrived at the village where the regiment ha
halted. The officers in command were not there. We were tol
that they were calling for us, and we had been expected to arriv
in their company. After half an hour they arrived ; we had misse
them, and beaten them to their own headquarters. Much merr
ment accompanied introductions. Colonel Ma, Commissar Chiang
Chief of Staff Yang, Political Director Mah. The Colonel wa
the oldest, and must have been about forty ; Chiang, the commissa
was only twenty-seven, he had been an engineering student at th
Communications College, Tangshan near Tientsin, before the war
he could still speak some English, and was anxious to brush up hi
differential calculus with Bill. All four of them impressed us a
being very much alive ; we promised ourselves a good trip in thei
company, and our expectations were fully realised.

There was a drama group in the village. The girls of the grou
vacated their special room for our benefit, but warned us that th
kang was full of bed-bugs. So we took precautions : spread ou
an oiled cloth sheet, unrolled our bedding upon it, slung ou
mosquito nets and tucked them between the oilcloth and th
bedding, then smeared the outer perimeter of the oilcloth with
kerosene. It was substitute kerosene that our friend Chang th
chemist had cracked from tung oil, but it worked excellently
the bugs did not know the difference. Although we had mastered
the bed-bug problem, we still failed to get any real sleep ; with
about two thousand men sprawled in every available corner, men
coming in late, others going out early, and the regimental managers
taking accounts with the village Government officers for the grain
supplies that the army was taking with them, there was hardly a
moment of quiet all night. And at four in the morning we were
aroused, served breakfast of steamed potatoes as a special treat
with millet gruel and some beans fried in crude castor oil—also a
special treat, but we did not know the nature of the oil until later.

The whole regiment had been fed and was assembled in the
river bed, and listened to a harangue from the Colonel, and we
were off on the trail before seven. It was good-bye to Roger Liu

nd the white pony, good-bye to Hopei Province and the " Chin
Cha Chi Border Region ".   Later in the afternoon we entered
hansi Province, climbing along the slopes of the Wutai range,
vithin two miles of the boundary of Wutai county, into the land
f oats and potatoes.   We logged a total of about ten miles and
ome very steep climbing.

Forced March through Enemy Territory

Through Saturday the regiment rested, preparing for a dash
f more than thirty miles across the Hutou River and a Japanese
motor road.   The boys washed their uniforms in the river, decked
he village walls with khaki cotton, but the fine drizzle prevented
heir clothes from drying.   The Colonel borrowed a young mule
o replace the white pony for Bill to ride, and that night we re-
acked our bedding so as to distribute the load as evenly as possible
ver three animals, hoping thereby to ease the strain on the decrepit
nimals.

Our reputation with the officers was established after Bill suc-
eeded in putting right a new model portable trans-ceiver radio set
hat had gone out of order, and we all had a lively chat in Chinese
nd English after the evening meal.   Chiang started to keep a
iary in English, and we fixed up a daily schedule of one hour's
alculus lessons for him, planning to cover the whole college course
etween there and the Yellow River.   The excitement of his
nticipation was a joy to see ; a touching reminder of how much
hese patriots had given up in their country's cause.

The big day was Sunday, August 15th.   We rose at four,
reakfasted before five with the officers, and after waiting for about
n hour to make sure that the drizzle was not going to develop
nto a downpour, the regiment, damp but happy, was off in single
ile by seven.

Feature of the morning's trip was the slimy summit of the
ass.   Several hundred men were ahead of us in the column, and
y the time the footpath came under our tread, it was absolutely
mpassable.   The regiment had to scatter out over the mountain
ace to avoid each other's tracks ; hostlers in charge of mules
nd ponies had great trouble keeping the animals on all fours.
On the down slope, which we reached around noon, it was all we
ould do to keep from proceeding per posterior.   We arrived at
he village selected for the day's second meal at about three p.m.,

but the regiment, and the baggage animals, were dribbling in for another three hours or more. During that time we did our best to relax on a warm kang, and succeeded at least in drying out, and in getting a good meal inside of us—good in a relative sense.

There were some pretty nasturtiums in the little courtyard with their stimulating scent. The women, the first real Shansi natives we had seen, amused us by their style in waistcoats : a more or less square piece of material covering their backs, tied in front of their stomachs from the two lower corners of the square, and from the upper corners, two ties crossing in front between the breasts, which were left deliberately exposed.

After dark, about seven, the regiment started out on an all-night forced march to cross the danger zone.

We had been warned to expect a dangerous river crossing ; normally at this time of the year its current would be so strong that, wading up to one's neck, each passenger has to be supported on either side by a peasant. All animals have to swim, their baggage being carried on the heads of local villagers specially experienced in the crossing. Indeed these flood troubles were worse than the Japanese ; we had had a foretaste, and were apprehensive.

After much halting in the darkness on sandy river beds and under precipitous rocks, waiting for the return of advance scouts, the regiment at last filed out into the low hills fringing the Hutou valley, and by midnight we had entered a large village. Here the men assembled in companies in the stony bed of a tributary of the Hutou, the officers and we were conducted into a temple building, served hot tea, and waited for final details from the local intelligence agents of the local defence guerrillas.

It was apparent that this village was what the Japanese regarded as within their control ; the temple was acting as an Eighth Route Army contact station only during the night. We were then in fact only about three miles from the motor road that cut right up the valley from Ningwu on the Shansi railway.

In about an hour we were off across the broad valley, over rolling plains planted with millet. The whole country seemed parched by drought, very different from the wet we had experienced on the southern slopes the previous few days. It had developed into a brilliant moonlight night, and from our point of view this made the crossing rather dangerous. Some time before we reached the roadway there was a moment of near panic for us.

Claire's foot had slipped from the stirrup, and the boy Chin-tsai had helped her to get it right again ; but in the moments of hesitation we had lost sight of the men in front, and a few yards further on, the path forked. Which way had they gone ? The animals wanted to veer right, but we had a feeling that we ought to be going straight ahead. To call out was dangerous, but there was nothing else to do. In reply to our third shout a clap of hands came back, and we knew that the animals had chosen the right path.

Why had we been unable to see ahead better than that in such broad moonlight ? Glancing up at the moon we suddenly realised that an eclipse was pending. The moon was already more than three parts covered. As we approached the roadway we could see the great telegraph poles silhouetted against the sky, and as we stepped on to the metalled surface, the Guerrilla Army boys, local villagers, were crouched and standing in three tiers on either side of us, right athwart the roadway. Over their heads hung a thin crescent of the moon at maximum eclipse. It was an uncanny coincidence. So uncanny that we forgot about the Hutou River until we were well over the other side of the valley.

" But, say ! What about the Hutou River ? " we asked Commissar Chiang, after we were safely out of range of the road.

" Oh ! Didn't you notice that patch of dried mud about halfway between the motor road and the last village we just came through ? That was the Hutou River. It was dry ! "

A double miracle in one night was almost too much for us ; and stories they had told us about the Hutou floods seemed exaggerated. Two or three days after, to anticipate a little, it started to rain, and we were up on the mountains looking down on the valley we had crossed. There was the Hutou River winding like a dragon along the middle of the plain, in full flood. We felt something like the children of Israel after they had crossed the Red Sea. It was intriguing—to anticipate at still greater range— to look up the Nautical Almanac after we arrived in Chungking and discover the following paragraph :

" Eclipse of the moon, totality 0.876 : 1 visible on August 15th."

For our position, which was approximately 113.4° E. and 39° N., the maximum should occur at 19.30 G.M.T., which would put it at about 3 a.m. local time, agreeing with our rough estimate of time as being in the small hours of the morning of August 16th.

About half an hour after crossing the road, the whole regiment took a rest, and, to a man, including the Colonel, they collapsed on the footpath and fell fast asleep. Somehow we could not bring ourselves to lie down on the earth, tired though we were. It was too cold for one thing, and for another we were too excited to relax. In about ten minutes a couple of peasant soldiers came running along and accosted us.

" Where is Colonel Ma ? " one of them asked.

" Who are you ? " asked Bill.

" Local Defence volunteers. We want to welcome the regiment to this district."

" All right ! That's Colonel Ma ! " said Bill, pointing at his recumbent form a couple of strides away on the footpath.

They held a hurried consultation between them, seemingly hesitating to awaken the Colonel. Finally, plucking up courage they called his name softly in his ear. The Colonel awoke.

" Please will Colonel Ma kindly come back a mile to our village ? We had prepared a special welcome celebration for your regiment, expecting you to come through that path. Now you have gone another way, won't you please come back ? We will not delay you more than half an hour ! "

We were worried lest Colonel Ma consent to this request, but we had under-estimated his powers of diplomacy. It took about ten minutes of politeness, and in the end the two emissaries went away, apparently satisfied. Colonel Ma then aroused the men and we continued on our way.

We were still marching at seven that morning, twenty-seven hours since our last sleep, twelve hours since our last meal, forty miles on the log. We were approaching some pleasant village dwellings, but had hardly strength left to cover the last half mile. Since about four we had tried all kinds of tricks to keep awake. First we thought it would be less tiring to sit on the animals, but soon discovered it was too dangerous—we would suddenly wake up and find ourselves falling off. Then we decided to stay walking, and staggered along like drunks, dozing off and coming up with a start as we stumbled into a rut. At last the regiment halted outside the village, and we all collapsed among the rocks while the Chief of Staff and his managers went in to arrange with the village government for hospitality.

Oh ! The luxury of sleep ! Breakfast was nine a.m., and

PLATE XII

[*Photo by Michael Lindsay*

The village of Middle Poplar where the authors lived during the summer, 1943.

then more sleep. They had found us a beautiful clean room in an old Manchu Government official's home, with glass windows and painted walls ; it was like a dream. More sleep. They awoke us again shortly after noon, the local commander wished to entertain us at a welcome party for the regimental officers. Would we please get up immediately and ride over to another village about a mile and a half away ?

Oh ! Hell ! The annoyance did more to get us awake than the invitation. And in the end we did get up and we did ride over there, and even succeeded in being polite ; and our Manchu court was real—we had not been dreaming.

At the tea party we met two more colonels, whose regiments were marching on routes parallel to our own. We were evidently a part of a considerable movement of troops. In fact rumour had it that General Lü himself was coming over with his entire division, the larger part being on a more southerly trail. We may have been acting as a kind of northern flank to the expedition. We had noticed in fact that General Lü had been very concerned about his Hongkong foot the day of our farewell breakfast, and he had remarked that he always had had trouble with his feet whenever anything really important was expected of him.

DODGING THE ENEMY

Speculation apart, our unit kept in continual radio contact with General Nieh's headquarters in Hopei, and on the following afternoon, after making everything ready for immediate departure a message came through that the Japanese had concentrated a thousand men and a few airplanes at a point some sixty miles south of us ; we should stay where we were for a day or two and await developments. So we continued in our efforts to catch up on sleep.

All night long, however, messengers kept coming in and out of our courtyard, where the regimental headquarters had been set up. The Colonel had been keeping in contact with the local intelligence units for miles around. He knew how many Japanese there were in every strong point within striking distance of our unit, and what they had been doing up to a very few hours ago. He was taking no chances of being caught by surprise. He was particularly anxious to know whether the Japanese had received any information of the passage of several thousand men across their motor road the other night. He estimated that it would take them at least three days to find out about it, and he was hoping to be able to get away first.

On the 18th some three hundred Japanese were reported out on a foraging raid twelve miles north-east of us. Did that mean anything? Our route, however, lay due west, so the three hundred did not worry us. It was the 19th before we received orders to proceed. The large concentration of Japanese to the south had moved farther south, and we were not in danger from them so much as from staying too long in one spot near the motor road.

At four-thirty p.m. the journey was resumed; but we had not been gone one hour before right ahead of us loomed a huge rainstorm. The western sky was black and yellow; it was coming straight at us. We were marching in a dry river bed. Ahead of us was a herd of cattle, and the cowherd was already hurrying his animals towards the steep banks. There was a small temple some quarter mile ahead, and we made a dash for its shelter. About two companies managed to reach the temple before the deluge began, a couple more came in wet to the skin; and the rest of the regiment were trapped in the centre of the river, marooned on an island in the midst of a raging torrent that swept everything before it.

Our little temple was perched on a precipice that dropped sheer down into the roaring waters, and from its door-steps bugle messages were sent out to the stranded men below. After an hour the storm abated, a messenger tried to ride through the floods, but failed. A few minutes later Chief of Staff Yang, the best rider of the regiment, himself plunged into the waters. We watched with bated breath. A false move, and he would be gone. Several times his white horse was carried out of its depth; several times we thought he was giving up. But he emerged safely on the barren island and held consultations with the captains there. It was decided that the men wait there until the flood waters had subsided sufficiently to allow them to make the opposite bank, from which they were separated by a less treacherous channel than on our side. They would then proceed to our next destination by another route.

From the temple we then threaded our way along to the hamlet of mud cottages that spread out along a narrow path on the steep clay sides of the valley. Most of the men slept in the temple, the enior officers found a peasant willing to put them up, and they gave us a corner on a piece of board in a small barn. The perch eemed precarious in the extreme; the roaring river shook the whole hillside, and at any moment we felt a landslide might obliterate us all. But the ground held, and at three in the morning we were aroused to join the senior officers at a rice gruel breakfast, sitting by the meagre light of a little oil lamp in the middle of a snug haystack where they had been sleeping. By five, with the first dim streaks of dawn in the cloudy sky, we were away and climbing up into the mountains.

It was early that morning that we looked down upon the Hutou River valley, saw the flooded river that had been so miraculously dry for our crossing; we had escaped the flood by a matter of a few days.

Another cloud burst drove us into yet another temple refuge at half-past ten that morning; but this time we were not caught in a river bed. Instead, we were literally in hell. The temple was a very well appointed institution, with giant images of Buddha, and a gruesomely realistic materialisation of Buddhist hades. There is a famous temple to hell in the eastern suburbs of Peiping; this one was far superior, and in excellent state of repair; it deserves exploration after the war. For ourselves, we were less interested in archaeological relics than in the chance to get another feed. While all around us, life-sized images of men were being tortured by fantastic representations in gaudy colours of the most hideous of evil demons—disembowelled, hacked to pieces, mangled, burned, bastinadoed, stretched, lacerated, and otherwise rendered penitent for the sins of this world, we set to and ate with relish the hot millet porridge served for lunch, assisted by the temple acolytes.

After this meal, most of the men nonchalantly slept among those monstrous forms. After the horrors of the Japanese war, these horrors of hell meant even less to them than they did to us; we found a pleasanter position and relaxed at the feet of Buddha in another court.

Before we continued for the remainder of the scheduled fifteen miles hard climbing, we were informed that the Manchu village we rested in after crossing the highway had been raided the day after we had left. Two hundred Japanese had attacked it from the north, and a dozen motor trucks of men had come along the motor road in the south. Evidently they had at last heard something about large troop movements across the valley. However, the cloudbursts had served us well, would wash away our tracks and keep the enemy fairly well immobilised. It was just as well. We had come only about seven miles from the danger point.

During the afternoon we had a grand view of the Wutai mountain range, around the peaks of which still hovered the remains of yesterday's storm clouds. The Hutou River valley stretched between us and Wutai, lying there deceptively peaceful, rich crops waiting for the enemy to harvest.

Up next morning at two, breakfasted in the dark and off again by four, we left ten sick men behind to be hidden in the village and tended by the local government until well enough to follow on their own, or to be returned to the nearest local garrison. Two local guides walked ahead of the regiment throughout the day; at first it was lovely country, the hillsides covered with wild flowers, delphiniums, larkspur and wild snapdragon. We climbed up right on top of a narrow fish-backed range of mountains between two plains; and plains mean Japanese. We would have been in sight of the enemy on both sides all day long had it not been for the mist and the rain that cut us off. We two were following close on the heels of the two local guides, but very often lost sight of them in the fog. For miles we went on and on, up and down, in the driving wet, our cotton-padded winter uniform coats heavy with water. Then in the midst of all this invisible wilderness we were called suddenly to a halt. Following the direction of the voice, we came upon a tiny cluster of cottages; we had almost passed them without seeing them. We were ushered inside, and threw ourselves down on a luxuriously hot kang.

A jolly peasant woman bustled around preparing oatmeal for the officers; we helped press out the dough with a heavy wooden noodle-press; steamed oatmeal was all we had to eat, but the sauce of our hunger made it taste like a first-class feast. We stayed there long enough to get thoroughly dried out, and when we started off again, more soldiers dropped off with malaria or dysentery, and were left with a couple of male nurses to arrange for their care by the peasants. We almost lost Chang Chin-tsai here, too. When we started off, he complained of sickness, dizziness and feverish feelings. He thought he was coming down with malaria and was getting alarmed. We had noticed him sitting almost on top of the kitchen fire in the peasant's room, and guessed he had been poisoned by the fumes in his efforts to get dried out. With a little encouragement he pulled through all right.

By about six-thirty p.m. we had tramped thirty miles of mountain trail since morning. The village we came to was completely deserted. We just went in and chose our own lodgings for the night. Before long the peasants came home in twos and threes. At the approach of our regiment an alarm had been raised ; our men were all in khaki uniforms, the same colour as the Japanese ; local Eighth Route Army troops wore grey ; we were therefore mistaken for the enemy, and, like the enemy, had been given a cold welcome. When the error was discovered, no one could have been more anxious to rectify it ; we were very quickly made snug and comfortable.

Next day, August 22nd, the regiment had been on the march for a whole month, having come directly from Ping Hsi, where they had been fighting for a month or more before that. The command was worried over the sick list. There were upwards of thirty men in the regiment down with some more or less serious complaint, including their chief powder-maker ; and we were now approaching the crossing of the railway where things might begin popping. In an effort to give the invalids a chance to regain a little strength, we waited until late in the afternoon before continuing the march, but on arrival at the next village during the night it was found that all the local government food stocks had been supplied to one of the other regiments moving with us. The short supply probably undid what the good day's rest had done ; the whole regiment had to be satisfied with the " iron rations " that they carried with them for emergency. We made a good meal from porridge made from mixing toasted wheat flour with boiling water : the wheat we carried with us in long tube-shaped canvas bags specially for emergencies.

ANOTHER MOTOR ROAD

We had been warned that Monday, August 23rd, would be a hard day, and during the night a crossing of another motor highway was to be expected, the highway from Tai Hsien to Yen Men Kuan for Tatung. The journey started after noon. Our mules were more dead than alive ; we had long ago given up trying to ride them, except where we could avoid wading through rivers by doing so. By evening we had come out into clear weather, and were in full view of Japanese units on the plains below. Through the Colonel's binoculars we had a good look at the garrison town of Tai-hsien, could see several block-houses and the highway which we should cross later that night. Had the enemy been keeping a look-out on the sky-line they would have seen more than three thousand armed men on the march in single file—we had been joined by one of the other regiments and were planning to make the crossing together.

Throughout the evening local scouts were bringing in information from all round our intended point of penetration. Seven miles away there was a small party of thirty Japanese patrolling the road; but never mind, the local defence volunteers would see to them if they got any closer. At about ten p.m. we filed across the highway, goggled again at the mass of telephone and telegraph wires that followed its metalled ribbon from one garrison to the next. How long would it be before we should experience the thrill of driving along a road like that again?

Shortly after we had moved safely over, the company of local guerrillas who had been guarding the way came running past us at full speed, nearly knocking us over on the narrow footpath. "What on earth is the matter now?" we wondered. "Is there a scare on?" In a few minutes we understood; there was a subsidiary road, and the boys were again lined up across it for our protection. Considering that our own regiments of three thousand men were fully armed, this enthusiastic protection by a company of local guerrillas seemed just a little like a pantomime; but it made a good show, and we all felt the warmth of welcome that it was meant to convey to the weary travellers.

It was four in the morning before we had completed the task, roughly thirty-five miles in fifteen hours without a meal or a wink of sleep between. We were marching on our physiological reserves with a vengeance.

But we were now in the thick of enemy occupied territory and must be prepared for anything. We found three potatoes to help out for breakfast, and managed to get in two hours' relaxation, though hardly sleep, before starting off again on the same morning at ten. To help us keep up speed, we were told that there was a rumour going round among the local peasants that down in Tai-hsien the Japanese had concentrated a thousand men and were planning to chase after us. Later in the day more accurate information was secured through the regular channels : the Japanese were only holding an inspection of transport facilities available in the county, and had collected a thousand donkeys in the town. Well, the Japanese, we all agreed, may be donkeys, but donkeys are not Japanese, so our march continued in high spirits.

According to the rough maps available in this district our journey for this day was estimated as only fifteen miles ; and we had started in ample time to get to the end of it before dark ; and as darkness came on, everyone was expecting the village any minute ; those ahead were hurrying on as fast as they could go, hoping to make it before dark. The result was that when darkness did fall—and it was pitch dark that night—the regiment was split up into quite disconnected sections following blindly along the footpath without clear guidance of any other kind. For night marching it is most important to keep close contact throughout the long file. We got ourselves horribly lost, and the distance we had gone had already stretched itself out to at least twenty-seven miles since morning.

Fortunately the boy Chin-tsai and our baggage mule and two or three army boys were still with us. The senior officers, all the other animals, and practically the whole regiment had disappeared into the night. We seemed to be miles from anywhere, and no one seemed to know whether we were following the right path or not.

Suddenly a peasant called us by name. He told us we were almost there. He took us down off the path into a deep gorge. We could hardly see a yard ahead of us. Then the trail disappeared completely in a wash-out, and our baggage mule, with Chin-tsai, just could not go any further ; we were skidding on a steep slant of rock. The boy was thoroughly alarmed, but told us to go ahead while he went back to the main path with the animal to try and find another way round alone. Alone with this peasant in the pitch black night, away from the path, we had a moment of doubt ; had we been kidnapped ? After all, this was Japanese held territory, and anything might happen.

But in a few moments we were climbing up a steep stony path into a large village, where, in the tiny gleam of a few oil lamps we could just make out the recumbent forms of army boys, and here at the top of the hill was Colonel Ma himself, who had sent the peasant to collect us. About half the regiment had got in before us, and had been waiting more than half an hour already. Stragglers kept coming in after us for another hour or more, and Chin-tsai turned up along with them. It was eleven p.m. before we were able to get a meal. The other baggage mule, by the way, had had to be abandoned during that day ; one of the climbs had been too much for it. The total distance we had done since morning was estimated at thirty miles.

UNDER FIRE OVER THE RAILWAY

Our next jump was going to be across the railway, and it was decided to rest one day in this village to make sure we could do the job without breaking down half-way. Messengers and scouts were coming in all day long, and every precaution was taken to prevent information leaking out about our presence in the village. Fortunately it was misty and drizzling and not very healthy weather for small enemy patrol units. The village was normally under Japanese control ; the Eighth Route Army organisation was underground ; only the presence of a whole regiment permitted it to come out into the open for the present. Around the hillsides were broad terraces under opium poppy, the first we had seen since leaving Peiping : there was trading with the enemy going on here in the railway zone.

Our second baggage mule was abandoned at this stage : it was too unreliable to take across the line. The baggage was split up into small bits and carried by several messengers. We still had a red pony with us that the regiment had borrowed—an animal that had been captured from the Japanese—but it proved more trouble than it was worth ; a plains animal, it shied at going down anything steeper than a one-in-ten gradient, and on the narrowest of paths insisted on straying out of line, its nose against the steep hillside, or its rear projecting perilously over the outer precipice.

Starting at eight in the morning, we were up on the mountain ridge in the rain all day, got lunch in a small village at one of the " gates " through the Great Wall. Here there was another party of people from Kangta waiting for convoy across the railway ; it was amusing to see our Colonel passing the buck to the other regiment, complaining that in we two Western friends, his regiment had sufficient responsibility.

Two of the Kangta party were Captain Chang Wen and his wife, the couple who had escorted us part of our trip in Ping Hsi a year and a half earlier : they had been fighting continuously ever since that time, and were now on their way to Yenan for rest and recuperation. A few weeks before, they had been surprised by an enemy raid on the village they were in, escaped with their lives, but lost almost everything they were bringing with them. Here they had just what they stood up in, a donkey borrowed from the peasants, and about two pieces of bedding. They had been hiding in this dangerous place ever since, hoping against hope for just such a convoy as had now materialised.

That afternoon Colonel Ma assembled his men and gave them a pep talk about crossing the line. He reminded them that they had crossed every Japanese railway line in North China in the last few months, and that every one of those lines had been more heavily guarded than this one. To-night's crossing would be the easiest crossing they had ever made. There was only one simple pre- caution necessary : because the peasants in this area had not yet been very well organised against the Japanese, they were not very reliable ; therefore it was important not to talk to the peasants, nor to let them get any idea of what we were doing or of where we were going, otherwise the enemy would get to know of our plans. It was desirable to keep our crossing secret at least until after we had got safely across.

It had been pretty tough going for the men, and it had been very hard on the sick ones. Colonel Ma was trying to keep up their courage for this supreme and final danger. Once across the line, the way would be clear for a pleasant picnic party, and all would be well. But considering how easy it seemed for these boys to take things haphazardly, the Colonel's belittling of the dangers of the night's job seemed to us a trifle risky, to say the least. Our anxiety proved correct.

Starting at about five p.m. the march began. Company by company in strict order, they swung into line ; we took our appointed place with the officers about the middle, coming up behind the men of the headquarter's unit carrying their huge water-boiling cauldrons on their backs.

As darkness fell we were slithering down a steep shoulder of red mud and sandstone into a wet gully that evidently ran down towards the main valley and the railway line. It was very difficult keeping contact with the men in front. The night grew very black, and the speed of our progress was most irregular. Half-way down the glen there were some local guerrillas squatting at various points, and as we passed them they shouted at us in back-stage whispers to keep on hurrying because it was not safe to loiter there. They were anything but reassuring.

Then after we had snaked out fairly into the centre of the main valley, within view of the line itself, there was a hold-up ahead. Something was wrong, and the officers went ahead at a gallop to discover the trouble. A few minutes later they came back and disappeared towards the rear. A captain brought us an explanation :

"Don't worry ! A company has got lost behind somewhere, didn't keep contact and got left behind in the dark. We shall have to wait a while for them ! "

By this time the whole regiment had fallen fast asleep on the path. There was no sign of the senior officers. A bitter wind was blowing across the broad fields in the valley. We two huddled together in an army oilskin cape trying to keep each other warm ; the ground was wet with rain, and we preferred to stand, tired out though we were.

To our right was a Japanese block-house on the railway line, not a mile distant. They had a searchlight in action. To our left was the dim form of a village—one of the Japanese garrisoned ones.

After at least an hour of this agonising suspense we noticed a lantern coming out of the village, slowly and steadily coming towards the path along which the regiment was soundly sleeping.

"Look at that ! It must be the Japanese ! " exclaimed Claire in a startled whisper.

"No ! It must be the Colonel looking for the lost company ! " replied Bill, trying to allay Claire's alarm.

"Don't be silly ! They wouldn't be shining a light round here ! Better try to find the officers and warn them ! "

But there was no sign of the officers anywhere. The night was as still as a graveyard. The lantern crept nearer and nearer, reached a point right ahead on the track of the footpath, swung its beam in our direction for a brief moment, paused, and continued on its way towards the Japanese block-house, in the vicinity of which it finally disappeared.

Not a soul but ourselves had seen that light. And there was no mistaking its meaning. The presence of the regiment had been discovered and reported to the Japanese guards on the railway which we still had to cross. Following Colonel Ma's optimism, nobody had taken the precaution of keeping a look-out while the men slept, it seemed.

But before we had a chance to report to the officers there was a signal passed down the line arousing the men, and we all started forward at a run, blindly following whoever it was in front leading the way. Through the village where all the doors were bolted and the dogs indoors, and along a sunken cart-track we discovered Commissar Chiang waiting for us :

" It's all right, we'll be across in a moment ! " came his cheery voice. " Stay right by me, you'll be O.K. ! "

There was no opportunity for conversation. The words were hardly out of his mouth when heavy gunfire broke out from the direction of the fort, bullets smacking stone somewhere in the direction of the village on our left. There was an answering rattle of machine-guns from another point on our right.

" The shells are going over our heads ; its quite safe, never mind ! " whispered Chiang. And we followed his example, running in a crouched position.

By the time we had come to the track and clambered over the embankment, the gun-battle was going strong between the block-house and the Chinese machine-gun unit that had been specially placed for just such an emergency. We were told later that one of our men had been slightly injured in the shoulder ; otherwise there were no casualties. The shooting had failed to break up the line of men. But shortly after the railway we came to a fairly wide river. The officers decided they would wait for their animals and ride across ; but we dashed on into the water, waded through with the men. Regaining the opposite bank, we looked back, found to our dismay that there was not a man in sight ; we seemed to have broken line completely, and with us in front only seemed to be about half a dozen youngsters. The last one of these we recognised in the darkness as one of the captains.

Hailing him, we said :

" Where is the Colonel ? " to which he gaily replied :

" Oh ! They're all lost behind now ! "

We began to get panicky.

" Please go back and find out what's happened to them ; maybe we are on the wrong path ? "

Apparently he thought that was a point to be considered, and dropped behind. But the other men in front were evidently not interested, they just kept right on, and we almost lost them too, until we realised that if we don't keep up with them we'd be just two wandering isolated idiots waiting for the Japanese patrols to arrest us in the morning.

Shortly after that piece of excitement along trotted Colonel Ma, Commissar Chiang, and the others with a long continuous line of men.

" Well, here you are ! All safely through now ! " they called out cheerfully, just as if nothing had been amiss. It was only then that we began to realise that animals can see in the dark far better than we can ; it was another good reason for riding across rivers at night.

After about half an hour's march across cornfields there was a call for a rest. The regiment again collapsed on the clay banks and went to sleep. This we felt was taking things just a bit too easily ; if we could go on, why couldn't these youngsters ? After all, we were still no more than a mile and a half from the railway line, and the Japanese knew we were there.

While the men were dozing, we heard the rumble of an approaching train, and saw its headlights coming slowly along the line from the direction of Ningwu. It stopped at just about the point we had crossed. This time we felt like taking command of the marching operations ourselves, walked up to Colonel Ma and pleaded with him to get a move on—for all we knew the train was bringing a strong force of Japanese to run us down. Reluctantly he roused his men, and reluctantly the march was resumed. They apparently felt that now they were across the easiest of all railway lines to cross they had earned a real rest from their weary months of forced marching ; we made very bad progress that night, and were only just out of sight of the Japanese before dawn.

Before six in the morning we had climbed a stiff pass, and at seven we were within sight of the village where the regiment was expecting to have several days' rest. We had been on the go since the previous morning twenty-four hours ago with only one meal half-way, and had walked a good thirty miles in that time. We were joyfully anticipating celebrations when a violent machine-gun battle broke out just over the other side of the hill to our south.

The officers all broke into a run, shouting orders for certain units to rush to strategic points on the hills round the village.

"We must get the village defended before we are attacked", explained Chiang. "But it means we shall not be able to rest here; we must go on as soon as possible!"

Racing each other to the village, we discovered it quite deserted; they had again taken us for Japanese troops. Breakfast was, however, eventually prepared, and messengers brought word that one of our other regiments had run into a party of Japanese by accident; six of the Chinese had suffered wounds, and the Japanese had retired to the railway after the battle which we had heard. When his regiment had crossed the line they had captured several puppet soldiers, two of them had escaped since and carried information to the enemy. The Japanese would be on the alert all round now. We had disturbed a real hornets' nest.

The officers were consulting maps and talking with local guides all morning, and we tried our best to get a little sleep. But the regiment was called out to be ready from about half-past ten in case of emergency, and we spent two hours or more sitting on a tree stump in the village lane.

We marched another fifteen miles before tea-time, and after another meal another fifteen miles hard slogging over two high loess mountains in the dark. Great pits in the loess earth yawned on either side of us, steep inclines took our breath away. Everyone was dog-tired. Waiting for those ahead to negotiate a difficult stretch, some of the men would fall asleep literally standing up, fail to see when the column started moving ahead of them. Time and again we poked one chap awake in front of us with a stick, or we should have broken the line and lost our way. We were on the move like this, slowly struggling along all through the night, too tired to walk fast enough to keep warm, and never a wink of sleep.

Daylight at last, and again hopes for breakfast in peace at the next village. As we approached, a rifle shot rang out, and the villagers evacuated in a hurry; again we were mistaken for the Japanese; and again the local information was such that the Colonel decided not to wait longer than was absolutely necessary. We were well into Western Shansi now, but the Japanese were still on our trail.

We did ten more miles that afternoon, August 28th, and the

country was broadening out into undulating plateau, with the main Great Wall visible in the distance. The villages were all caves, or built in the style of caves on the hillsides, the roof of one home being the playground for the home one terrace higher up.

Twelve miles more next day, and the villages were getting so small that the regiment had to split into three or four groups to obtain billets in as many adjacent hamlets. That night we had the first sound sleep since ten days before, when we had collapsed in the dream-like Manchu court after crossing the first motor road. In those ten days we had walked a good 180 miles, mostly by night, and been under danger of enemy encounters the whole time. We had each burned up almost all our natural fat, having lost something like twenty pounds in weight. But we were through at last.

SAFETY AT LAST

Just one more move to get completely out of reach of the Japanese, and we were promised a good holiday ; so on August 30th the regiment marched another seven miles. Half-way the Colonel called a halt to give them a lecture on the lessons of the crossing. We preferred not to wait ; we had drawn our own lessons, and were more anxious to get accommodation in good time. We went ahead with a local guide. In the absence of the regiment, however, we found considerable difficulty in securing an acceptable room.

The first cottage into which the officer ushered us was openly hostile. The entire family crowded in ahead of us, the old folks spread themselves on the kang and produced the most heart-rending moans and groans imaginable, and ended up with churchyard coughing calculated to scare away anyone in the least bit concerned to avoid tubercular infection. There were about half a dozen children and infants crawling over the place, and a young woman, nude from the waist up, lolling voluptuously on the edge of the family bed. We backed out precipitously.

Eventually our little boy Chang Chin-tsai found us a cave. It was not being used by any of the villagers except as a storage place. When we retired for the night a couple of cockerels tried to roost in our mosquito net, and there were indications of other and smaller live stock about the place, but we fared well enough. We had altogether four days' rest there, sleeping, feasting on chicken and goat-meat, and water-melons, and giving Chiang his calculus lessons ; and watching the weird ways of the local peasants. There was one young mother, dressed like all the others in the Shansi waistcoat for her unweaned infant's convenience, who, before feeding her infant, squeezed some of her own milk on to the end of her finger to bathe a bad eye.

The group of " little devils ", one service boy to each of the four senior officers, and our Chang Chin-tsai, had a strenuous time washing clothes in muddy water. Water was so scarce, and the hills up which it had to be carried so steep, that washing was an unknown ceremony among the villagers. Drinking water looked like some cheap brand of coffee. But the villagers were none the less generous for all that. They gave eight goats as welcome gifts to the regiment. They had heard a rumour that foreign troops had come to the province, troops that wore khaki like the Japanese, but were not Japanese because they did not murder the peasants or steal their things. And they had a Western officer in command. General Band, we presume ! Well ! Well !

There was one goat-meat feast at which the colonels of all three regiments joined with us. There was another feast at which we devoured donkey's flesh ; and on the last day of the holidays we had a grand time making a stew of carrots, potatoes and pork. Commissar Chiang was a tremendous eater. When everyone else had satisfied themselves, he would always take another bowlful. We teased him, he was so thin with all his appetite, that he must be suffering from ascaris parasite. This amused him immensely, and whenever we had meals together, and it came to the last left-overs, he would suddenly jump up with his bowl, reach over to the bucket of gruel and sing out in English :

" One more for the worms ! "

He was a great lad ; and his mathematical ability was of no mean order either ; he galloped through our calculus course without a hitch, producing " home-work " exercises every day throughout the whole march that somehow he had found time to work out while the others were trying to snatch a few moments of sleep. We had brought with us from Fuping a complete set of outline notes of the mathematics and physics courses as they had been given to the wireless school. When we said good-bye to Chiang at the Yellow River, we left these notes with him to encourage his further study and to express in some way more substantial than mere words, how grateful we felt for his safe convoy through enemy territory.

Chapter XIV

YELLOW RIVER GUERRILLA BASE

WE resumed our joyful journey on September 3rd. It wa glorious autumn weather. There were grasshoppers dancing in the sunshine on the grass-grown sandhills : zzip, zzip, zzip as they flitted here and there. The army boys clapped their hands in time with the rhythm ; a happy, carefree frolic.

Half-way on the day's fifteen-mile trip we struck a clay-surfaced motor road that had been built by the Japanese a year or two before on one of their big campaigns. The red pony pricked up its ears and snorted with delight—the road was home for him. Bill jumped on the saddle, and away it trotted racing past everything else the regiment could produce.

It was a much more prosperous village we stayed in that night, and there was a temple and an ancient ruined walled city to explore. But the peasants still had quaint habits. Our hostess let her pony drink from the family water-tub, the one from which they made tea for the officers, and for us.

Next day we reached the end of the telephone line from Paoteh, and the officers sent a message ahead announcing the regiment's arrival. The village we came to was memorable for its complete innocence of private toilet facilities. We hunted all round the place, and not the slightest sign of privacy could we discover. Finally we asked the hostess where her own arrangements were, and she just didn't know what we were talking about. There were no words for things that did not exist.

And the room we were given for the night was marvellous. It had been recently decorated. When our boy Chin-tsai asked the peasants how they managed a new coat of paint in war-time, he was informed that an old woman had been lying in her coffin in the room for some months, had been taken for burial only a few days previously. We tried to open the windows on hearing that, but the hostess came running in :

" Please do not open them ! It would be disrespectful to the departed ! " We left the door open instead ; she had no objections to that ; neither had the farm's dog and poultry.

PLATE XIII

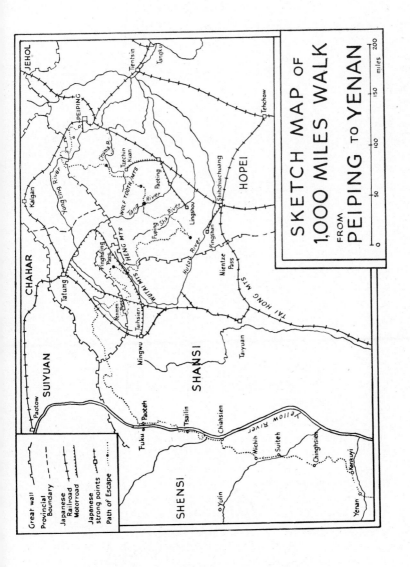

SKETCH MAP of
1,000 MILES WALK
FROM
PEIPING to YENAN

On Sunday, September 5th, we had our first view of the Yellow River basin ; it was a real thrill to see so vast an area of free country ; a relief to realise that at last we were practically beyond reach of the Japanese. In this area the small streams we had to cross were edged with quicksands, and crossings had to be made with care. One officer tried riding through until his animal sank almost up to its belly in the slime. After that everyone paddled across, it was like walking on pale chocolate blanc-mange.

On the 6th the regiments all rested, cleaned their uniforms, expecting to arrive at the Paoteh headquarters next afternoon, from whom a letter of welcome had already been received. We had a chicken supper with the four senior officers of our regiment as a farewell party ; they were about to reach their destination ; from Paoteh we should be going on without them.

We, too, with Chang Chin-tsai and a local guide, were off on the last leg of the journey to Paoteh at six next morning, leaving the regiment to its own devices, and by noon we were down on the banks of the Yellow River. The first big river we had seen since 1937, there was a deep thrill of romance about that magnificent expanse of calmly flowing water ; an atmosphere of peaceful industry about the scenes of civilisation by its banks.

And what a royal welcome we received from General Hsii at the local army headquarters ! Their offices and reception rooms were in a wonderful old courtyard, with ornamental eaves, stone-paved paths, painted pillars, carved lattices and grand doorways, in the true Peiping style. What luxury to sip green tea, taste grapes, water-melon and small red apples ; and to have nicely polished furniture about the place ; and the feast that followed made us gasp with astonishment : with excellent crockery, perfectly served in full Norwegian style. They had in their service the former Chinese cook from the local Norwegian Church Mission at Paoteh.

Later in the afternoon we were taken by the General and his staff officers to a private court in the next village, another suburb of Paoteh, where they invited us to stay a week or more to re-cuperate from the journey before going on. A private kitchen and a full-time cook were placed at our disposal, with authority to purchase whatever food we fancied. Our own boy Chin-tsai was to stay with us in the same courtyard. Their hospitality was quite overwhelming.

During the week we were in Paoteh we feasted on the fat of

the land, both in our own room, and when we were out at parties
In addition, we were presented with memorable gifts : two pound
of white sugar, two tubes of tooth-paste, a small shaving mirror
a pocket knife, and a bar of Sunlight soap. And they kept our
room stocked with trays full of apples, grapes and water-melon
we were so hungry for fruit that we must have devoured about two
hundred apples between us during that week : our celebrations of
the British landings in Italy and that country's capitulation were
teetotal, but by no means temperate.

On the 10th was held a formal welcome meeting for the regiments with whom we had come across from Hopei. Out on the
large playground they had erected an open-air stage, decorated
with larger-than-life pictures of Mao Tse-tung, Chu Teh and
Joseph Stalin. Chiang Kai-shek was conspicuous by his absence
in this gallery, a new feature in our two years' experience of United
Front meetings in guerrilla areas. The regiments were squatting
in neat columns on the ground, peasant army local volunteers were
standing with their long spears all round the square ; the regiments'
heavy machine-guns were conspicuously mounted near the stage,
and up on the stage we took our places with the local general and
his staff, the three colonels and their commissars.

A great peasant procession was in progress, bringing welcome
gifts for the troops : animals for meat, mules laden with baskets
full of vegetables and fruit, herds of goats and swine, literally
hundreds of creatures coming in from miles around to demonstrate how cordially these boys were being received by the local
inhabitants. Commissar Chiang had given us hints enough to
guess the explanation of all this. The regular garrison troops from
North-West Shansi had recently been withdrawn across the Yellow
River in reply to the threat of civil war, leaving their home province
denuded of defence against the Japanese. We had noticed that
nowhere through Shansi, west of the railway, had there been any
regular Eighth Route Army garrison troops. The peasants had
been getting thoroughly alarmed at the consequent probability
of a Japanese come-back during the autumn, and the timely
arrival of these boys from Hopei was a guarantee that the area was
not being abandoned to the enemy.

Still, we got quite a shock when the local general opened the
proceedings with a violent speech denouncing Generalissimo
Chiang Kai-shek and the Kuomintang for their treacherous

preparation for civil war at a time when the war with Japan was at such a crisis. The sins of the Kuomintang, selling their country to the enemy, collaborating with the Wang Ching-wei traitors, blackmailing America for immense loans by threatening to capitulate, squandering the Government's money on air-passages for wedding parties and pet puppies, all this and more, decorated with vivid epithets which we must omit, were poured out in a great stream of eloquence ; Chiang Kai-shek was charged with piling up Lend-Lease arms from America for his anti-Communist blockade lines, and with negotiating a secret pact with Japan to leave the Kuomintang free for an anti-Communist blitz.

A more damning picture of the Nationalists could not have been imagined. Something must certainly have happened to upset the Communists ; never in our two years had we heard a word against Chiang Kai-shek until that moment. If nothing worse, a violent propaganda battle was in progress on the civil war front, and it boded ill for our hopes of an easy passage from Yenan through Sian to Chungking. In fact we were told during the meeting that fighting had already broken out in several isolated incidents on the blockade line. The Communists claimed that at one point a whole battalion of Nationalist Party troops had marched into Communist territory, but had fled in disorder when one company of the Eighth Route Army had fired on them. There was a great show of fists and shouting of slogans at this, and at all other dramatic points throughout the proceedings :

" Protect the Shaankanning Border Region ! "
" Defend the people's democratic government ! "
" Down with the Kuomintang traitors ! "
" Down with Chiang Kai-shek ! Long live Mao Tse-tung ! "

It seemed to us that they were getting a lot of things off their chests that had been bursting to come out for a long time ; the United Front seemed to have involved quite a strain on their self-restraint, and they were now thoroughly enjoying themselves for a change.

During our week there we had several interviews and receptions. Particularly memorable was the one with the local government counties supervisor at which we heard his account of the structure and history of the North West Shansi Border Region. It contains a certain degree of debatable material, and of course we have had only his side of the story ; but we shall give it here for what it is worth.

In 1937 autumn, the Japanese had defeated the local mercenaries of General Yen Hsi-shan, the progressive Shansi war-lord representative of the Kuomintang, and the enemy occupied the whole of Northern Shansi. The Communist General Ho Lung recaptured it from the Japanese, and handed over the administration of the north-west of the province to General Yen's government officials who had proved themselves honestly willing to cooperate in a United Front against the Japanese. As we have mentioned before, Chairman Sung of the Hopei Border Region was one of the leading men in Yen's administration.

Unfortunately, according to the Communists, the Yen Hsi-shan regime failed to maintain itself against the Japanese, and the area again fell into enemy control during 1939. This presented a serious threat to the rear communications of the Eighth Route Army in Hopei, so that during 1940 the Communists launched another all-out campaign in Northern Shansi, and this time it was decided to maintain the region as an independent Border Region of a type similar with that in Hopei. The Communists could not afford to have such a strategic region unreliable in anti-Japanese activity.

In the two and a half years since the Border Region had been established, the conditions there had improved by leaps and bounds. The cultivation and use of opium was being gradually eliminated. In 1943 the harvest of grain was the best they had seen in twenty years, the peasants no longer needed to eat leaves and the bark of trees between harvests as had been traditionally the case.

After re-establishing order, and persuading refugees to return from occupied areas, the tasks of the local government through 1941 had been democratic reconstruction starting at the village level; stimulating the planting of edible crops; social reconstruction, specially regarding the legal status of women. During 1942 and 1943 efforts were concentrated on economic reconstruction. They succeeded in raising the livelihood of the peasants beyond their pre-war standards, and they had already stored enough grain in government caches for the needs of the army and government personnel to last through half of 1944. This economic programme would be continued through 1944, with emphasis on the extension of home industries, such as cloth weaving and on the encouragement of village co-operatives and the growing of cotton.

During 1943 democratic reconstruction had jumped from the village level, and the full Border Region Congress had been elected, but the counties' supervisors were still army or Communist Party appointees ; the final step of putting these officers under control of the representative Congress was scheduled to take place in 1944, after which the region would be completely self-governing.

Educationally the progress of the region had been phenomenal. Before 1940 no modern schools had existed. Now there were over 200 primary schools run by the county governments, 9000 pupils enrolled in them out of a population of about 300,000 in the Paoteh supervisory area alone.

We paid a visit to the Paoteh Middle School. Opened in 1941 with 30 pupils, the school now had 230 pupils and sixteen teachers. They were housed within the precincts of an ancient and beautiful temple standing on a precipice overlooking the Yellow River. Students were making their own maps and clay relief models of all areas involved in World War II. There was no narrow parochialism about their geography lessons. They were strong in mathematics and general science too ; the teachers of these subjects were university graduates from Peiping. Their study of history was on a similar scale : they started off by studying the fossil remains of a tree that stood just outside the temple gateway ; they were learning to value their past heritage and looking forward to a great future. Revolutionary enthusiasm tempered by a thoroughly Chinese respect for tradition was the dominant note for these builders of the New China.

Old Paoteh city stands on a hill dominating the river crossing, at the other end of which stands the twin city of Fuku, in Kuomintang territory. Paoteh had been razed to the ground by the Japanese ; Fuku stood unspoiled. The people of Paoteh lived in temporary dwellings on the north side of the old city ; busy trading in the old market was in full swing every day of the week. Fuku seemed to be little more than a garrison town, and we watched the Nationalist troops drilling on the sandbanks across the river. There was a ferry service between Paoteh and Fuku ; it was conducted by the military, and all passengers were searched, at both sides of the river, in both directions. Parties of Nationalist soldiers would come over to shop in Paoteh market. The pocket-knife that General Hsu gave Bill had been bought in Fuku ; woollen goods from the north-west, Lanchow and Yulin, were imported

from Fuku. " Likin " duties were said to be imposed by th
Kuomintang officers on all goods crossing the river. The rive
was regarded by the Nationalists as a defence line against th
Japanese, but the Communists regarded it as a Nationalist blockad
line against the Communists. The Japanese came to Paoteh o
an average twice a year, but they had never been across the river
This circumstance did not help to improve feelings between th
two parties, especially as the army on the safe side of the rive
were supplied with arms by the central government whereas thos
defending the exposed area were denied them.

Our bedroom in Paoteh was a pleasant room. The kang wa
surfaced with polished grey tiles. But in the cracks between th
tiles were the permanent inhabitants. While Claire was keeping
up a one-sided war with the bugs, Bill was turning over in his mind
the possibilities of civil war in China and our chances of getting
through without too much embarrassment.

The Red Bogey had reared its ugly head in China during 1927.
The Chinese Communist Party had been founded in 1921 as a
Left Wing section of the Alliance " Tung Meng " Party of Dr.
Sun Yat-sen, later re-named the Kuomintang. The revolu-
tionaries were still united under the banner of the " Three Peoples
Principles " at Canton in 1926 and in the historical Northern
Expedition's advance upon the Yangtse valley, and still united in
the revolutionary government under Wang Ching-wei at Hankow.

It was Shanghai that caused the split. The united revolutionary
parties had, under Russian guidance, instigated workers' uprisings
in Shanghai, but these had been suppressed by the local authorities.
The third uprising was, however, successful in overpowering the
police and seizing control of the Chinese city, forming a revolutionary local government. This body sent a delegate to the
Hankow (Wuhan) national revolutionaries inviting them to come
in and take over control of the city.

Meanwhile representatives of the Western Powers in the
International Settlement, thoroughly alarmed at the violent anti-
foreign activities of the revolutionaries, in co-operation with
certain wealthy Chinese capitalists with interests in the factories
of the Chinese city and in the millions to be reaped from Shanghai's
underworld, arranged a coup with the Right-wing elements of the
Wang group at Hankow, of whom Chiang Kai-shek was the military
leader.

Details of this affair have never been made clear ; they have naturally been hushed up. It is certain that something had been arranged beforehand, because the entry into Shanghai of the Nationalist forces was a signal for the sudden anti-Communist drive by Chiang Kai-shek's forces. According to the Communists, and their story sounds most plausible, one of the kings of the Shanghai underworld arranged for hooligans to shoot at the forces of the Nationalists as they were marching proudly through the welcoming crowds of labourers ; immediately, officers who had been primed beforehand, ordered the shooting up of the labourers, starting a bloody fracas, and providing sufficient excuse for the disarming of the workers and clamping down of a white terror throughout the city.

April 12th is well remembered throughout North China as Martyr's Day, when thousands of students and other Left-wing agents who had been doing dangerous work in Shanghai, preparing for the triumphant entry of the Revolutionary Nationalists, were massacred in cold blood by the very army they were welcoming.

And whether the Communist version of this is true or not, the fact that they believe it to be true—and we can guarantee that they do believe it to be true—should be remembered by anyone who seeks to understand why negotiations between Nationalists and Communists in recent times have so often seemed to fail. Fundamental difficulty is the re-establishment of mutual trust after a long history of mutual suspicion, it is not so much a question of whether this side or that side can put forward a reasonable programme or formula of co-operation.

Following the successful coup in Shanghai, and the new alliance between the Nationalist forces and the Shanghai capitalists, an anti-Communist Government was set up in Nanking, in open opposition to the united Revolutionary Government in Wuhan. With its new financial backing, the Nanking Government was in a strong enough position to clamp down an economic blockade against Wuhan. This put the Revolutionaries in a hopeless position. Wang Ching-wei was himself the first to resign and come over to the Nanking group, and shortly afterwards the Hankow group dissolved itself. The Nationalists thereupon declared war upon the Communists, and in June 1927 formally expelled all members of the Communist Party from their membership of the Kuomintang with very few exceptions. On August 1st, those units of the Revolutionary forces that had been under the influence of the Left Wing members of the former united party mutinied against the reactionary policy forced upon them by this new turn of events and the attempts to eliminate the Communists resulted directly in civil war.

In reaction to the white terror the Communists swung ever more violently to the Left. The early history of the Red terror through Kwangtung, Fukien, Hunan, Kiangsi is well enough known. The Reds established themselves in a strong soviet state in Kiangsi against which the Nationalists threw their whole strength in five successive major campaigns, the last of which continued a whole year, finally ousted the Communists from their stronghold, but failed to defeat them.

Through eight thousand miles of bloody fighting the contest burned on, devastating the countryside through eight provinces ; what the Communists did not do by their butchering of landlords and middle-class people, the Nationalist troops completed by extortionate plundering of the poor. It was a shocking climax of a most deplorable attack of political hysteria. In polite circles it was not talked about. Even the Shanghai millionaires seem to have grown worried about the situation. It was quite clear that they were losing money on it, and the Japanese were licking their greedy chops with imperial anticipation.

By 1936 the Communists succeeded in entrenching themselves in Shensi Province, far more strongly than they had ever been able to do in Kiangsi. The entire strength of the Kuomintang was massed around Sian for a final drive against them. The brunt of the fighting was to be borne by the troops of Marshal Chang Hsueh-liang of Manchuria. But Chang's men were anti-Japanese in spirit ; they wanted to fight back to their homes in the north-eastern provinces ; they were not interested in the civil war, and they were exposed to energetic propaganda from the Communists against civil war ; Chang Hsueh-liang was obliged to do something about preventing disaffection among his men or face mutiny. He flew to Yenan without orders from the Generalissimo, and proposed to the Communists to intervene in favour of a settlement in the interests of the United Front against Japan such as the Communists had already been demanding. His offers were accepted, and he returned to interview the Generalissimo.

Finding the Generalissimo unwilling to negotiate, Chang, in desperation, engineered his spectacular kidnap of the Generalissimo and his entire staff. The Sian Incident has already gone down in history as the turning-point of China's fight against Japan. But it was more than that. Chiang Kai-shek was at the mercy of the Communists in a very real sense. It was a crisis where the wiles of diplomacy were stripped away as two great spiritual forces clashed to discover each other absolutely sincere.

Although Chiang Kai-shek's release was finally said to be unconditional, the civil war was called off; Chang Hsueh-liang succeeded in his mission but gave himself up to his prisoner to demonstrate his apologies for his mistaken tactics. A thoroughly Chinese solution to the problem : everyone comes out of it a hero.

During the two weeks of negotiations, while the fate of China was in the balance, pro-Japanese factions of the Kuomintang were feverishly active. They cabled to Wang Ching-wei, then on tour in Fascist Europe, to come back to China, allegedly to help release Chiang Kai-shek, but more probably to replace him in a New Order Alliance with the Japanese. The Peiping Pacification Commission, dominated by these same pro-Japanese factions, sent bombing planes over Sian during the crisis to help stir up mistrust between the two parties and so delay the settlement.

For two years these factions were kept in check by the progressive sections of the Kuomintang and the United Front was faithfully maintained. Trouble, however, began in 1939, first on the propaganda front. In the Chungking Press appeared accusations that the Communists were neglecting their share of the anti-Japanese warfare, preparing instead an invasion of the Nationalist territory in order to start a land revolution. Stories were also printed of boys and girls in nude dances at Yenan ; childish nonsense invented by petty officers in the Kuomintang cliques and secret service corps seeking promotion from anti-Communist superior officers. The Nationalist military political bulletin even published a story that Mao Tse-tung had just returned from Sinkiang bringing with him an army of Russian advisers and experts, and a supply of military equipment, including planes, in preparation for a campaign against the National Government, with the object of setting up a Chinese Moscow at Lanchow.

To this Mao Tse-tung publicly replied :

" Why does Chungking reprint Japanese propaganda ? It

would be a grand idea to try to usurp power from the Nationalist at the present time ; but the facts are the reverse. It is the Chung king Party that is usurping territory by means of artillery and planes ; they have already occupied three counties of the Border Region in preparation for an attack on Yenan. The Communist Party is operating only in twenty-three counties of Shensi ; our area is insignificant compared with that overrun by the Japanese why is Chungking wasting its efforts here instead of fighting the Japanese ? "

All very pretty. Nice material for the Japanese to use in their international derogatory propaganda about China.

Military incidents also began in 1939, in Central Hopei, first. The Nationalists despatched certain troops to help defend that area against the Japanese in co-operation with the Communists. The Communists complain that these National troops spent their time only in disruptive activities directed against the local demo-cratic regimes and the Eighth Route Army organisations, making raids at night on garrison posts and recruiting offices. People disappeared mysteriously, others were slaughtered crudely in their sleep. Repeated formal protests were sent to Chungking about these incidents, but they brought only polite promises to in-vestigate. Between March and May of that year the Eighth Route Army claims to have lost a thousand men at the hands of these subversive agents. They welcomed the Japanese offensive in the area during that summer, in the face of which the National forces fled, leaving the Eighth Route Army to defeat the enemy and settle down again to their constructive work.

More serious was the so-called New Fourth Army incident. This army was a Communist force recruited from among the population around Shanghai, Nanking, Hangchow, and operating in those areas as anti-Japanese guerrillas, under the command of Chu Teh at Yenan. This army was not recognised by the National Government even after the United Front policy had won official recognition for the Eighth Route Army in the north. And in October 1939, when the eyes of the world were turned elsewhere, Chungking sent peremptory orders to the Communists to remove the New Fourth Army forces from around Shanghai to north of the Yellow River.

Negotiations proving futile, the Communists were preparing to comply in order to avoid an open clash with the government forces, even though the move required a crossing of Japanese communication lines. Secret agents of the Kuomintang posted in areas around there, observed these preparations, notified their headquarters where the news was immediately published. In the Chungking Press appeared an announcement that the New Fourth Army was about to move north. This gave away a most important military secret to the enemy, the Japanese, who immediately sent strong forces to prevent the move. Simultaneously the Nationalists sent four divisions to the attack : not, according to the Communists, to attack the Japanese, but the New Fourth Army. Ten thousand men were thus trapped between two forces ; their local commander, General Yeh Ting, was captured before the Nationalist forces were withdrawn. His fate is still not known in Yenan. On January 17th it was announced in Chungking that the New Fourth Army had mutinied against the National authority, had been eliminated in resulting hostilities. The Communists cancelled plans for moving the remaining forces, rebuilt the army, and it has continued to do valuable anti-Japanese work ever since, in spite of its legal non-existence.

The Japanese made great propaganda capital out of this incident. The Communists likewise did their best to balance the account ; they broadcast the following demands :

1. Withdraw the Communist repression army from Central China.
2. Remove the blockade from North-West Shensi.
3. Release all patriotic political prisoners in Free China.
4. Abolish the dictatorship of the country by one party, and immediately introduce democratic self-government.
5. Obey the last will and testament of Dr. Sun Yat-sen, the Three People's Principles of 1924.
6. Arrest all pro-Japanese clique leaders in Free China, and submit them to public trial on charges of treason.

When these demands became known they aroused considerable sympathy throughout the country. No reply was received from Chungking.

It was only too true that the reactionary Chungking cliques had acquired their wealth and their power through corrupt practices ; and that there was no effective democratic check to their predatory propensities. So far as these gentlemen were concerned, the talk of political tutelage for the masses was all " eye-wash "

It had been amply proven by the Communists in North China tha the peasants were more than able to govern themselves withou guidance from bloated absentee landowners and corrupt million aires. The struggle was then, and still is, fundamentally a conflic between progress and reaction caused partly by the fact that China progressive capitalists were allied with her feudal landlords instea of with the Left-wing reformers.

The situation would have deteriorated into an out and ou class war if on the one hand the progressive sections of the Kuomin tang had not remained loyal to their ideals, and kept their reactionar colleagues in check ; and if on the other hand, under Mao Tse-tung leadership, the Communist Party had not undergone a marke change in policy since 1936. To the Communists Mao Tse-tun; successfully preached that it was not necessary to fight the capitalists with a democratic system in which ninety per cent. of the electorat would be peasants, there would be no difficulty in keeping capitalist under decent control. To the capitalists he called for a break awa from the feudal war-lords and landlords who were acting only a parasitic drags on the construction of a modern industrialise nation, for a United Front between the capitalists and the peasant to combat the inroads of predatory invaders.

As their part of the United Front the Communists promise to abandon their former insurrectionary movements against the Nationalist authorities, dissolve their soviet governments in favou of coalition democracies, and to move all their troops into the anti-Japanese war zones.

On July 7th, 1942, the Communists issued the following manifesto :

" For five years the Chinese Communist Party has not only adhered to its promises, but has realised their purposes. The Eighth Route Army and the New Fourth Route Army have been fearless in their war of resistance against the Japanese ; we have faithfully co-operated with the Kuomintang and other anti-Japanese parties ; our decisions regarding political programmes, land policies, labour legislation, cultural programmes and systems of popular representation, have all been adapted to the actual conditions in the military bases we have built up behind the enemy's lines ; every one of these policies, programmes and systems has been based squarely on the spirit and the fundamental meaning of our promises. Now we wish to emphasise once more that that pirit, those principles, programmes, policies and systems are not only adapted to the carrying on of the war behind the enemy's ines, they are also suitable for the period of reconstruction after he war. The Communist Party therefore is struggling whole-heartedly for their full realisation throughout the country on a permanent basis.

"Selfish interests have generated the rumour that the Communist Party sabotages the war of resistance, or is hoping to dominate China after the war. As the war enters its final phases, all Chinese people should have a common policy, not only for achieving the final victory, but also for reconstruction after the war. We should establish mutual trust, extinguish suspicion in order to fight together for final victory for the New China ; an independent, peaceful, united democracy prosperous with the co-operation of all political parties."

This appeal was not entirely fruitless. In December of that year the Kuomintang sent a message to the Communists to the effect that the government would grant personal rights and party freedom to members of the Communist Party (they had previously been outlawed) provided the latter would not set up separatist governments or operate a private army after the war. To this gesture the Communists replied that since 1937 their areas had been governed only by locally elected democratic congresses just as loyal to the national cause as any other government could possibly be, and that their armies were purely anti-Japanese forces. Because the Kuomintang had refused to recognise these governments, that party should accept full responsibility for any separatist tendencies that may still exist. Superficially, we may say, the outlook was hopeful.

Unfortunately pro-Japanese cliques were still in a dominating position within the Kuomintang. Their generals were capitulating to the enemy : up to September 1943 no less than fifty-eight of them had gone over. The process continued through the big campaigns of 1944 when the Japanese captured the big American air base at Kweilin and succeeded in driving a land route through from Hankow and North China to Hanoi and Indo-China. Politically still worse was the fact that nearly thirty members of the central executive committee of the Kuomintang had become puppets to the Japanese, and yet had never been struck off the party lists, nominally they were still members of its executive ; and yet

the Communists had been removed from the executive years before
Most notorious was the case of one Wu Kai-hsin. After being
placed by Wang Ching-wei in his puppet regime at Nanking
this man was flown to Chungking in a Japanese plane, welcome
officially on May 7th, 1943, and was still at large doing pro-Japanese
work in the war-time capital of Free China for the rest of that year

While this kind of thing was going on in Chungking there
was little enough hope that any real mutual trust between the two
parties could be achieved. In fact there was almost no way in
which those people in Chungking who wished to see such
rapprochement could bring any influence to bear upon the situation
The pro-Japanese and Fascist cliques had so saturated the whole
political community with their secret espionage gestapo system that
no one who valued his life dared to come out openly in favour of
a deal with the Communists.

Nevertheless the eventual defeat of Fascism and Nazism in
Europe became obvious even to the reactionaries in Chungking
Mussolini had been silenced, and although the Burma come-back
had been delayed by malaria, the balance of power had been
changed; pro-Fascist cliques in Chungking began to think furiously
of their own future. They were wedded to an orientally twisted
Fascist policy of exploitation for personal profit, and their capitalist
feudal-war-lord gang must defeat the Communists and get control
over their progressive colleagues before the European phase of
the world war was ended or they may be too late. Suppose they
gave the war another two years : it would mean they had just
two years during which China must " solve the internal Communist problem " while there was no chance of outside interference

In May 1943 it was publicly announced by the Kuomintang
Plenary Session that it had been decided to start at once upon
solving the Communist problem, by political means. But in secret
it was decided, if one can judge by events which followed the
announcement almost immediately, to fight down Yenan in a sudden
blitz, and so present the world with a fait accompli, the details of
which could easily be hushed up.

Almost immediately the normal blockade forces around Yenan
were greatly increased (the Communists claimed that the normal
thirteen divisions were increased to twenty, the new units including
one artillery brigade), and work was commenced hurriedly upon
an airfield within striking distance of Yenan. Special Kuomintang

sabotage agents flooded into the Border Region to prepare surprise diversions during the blitz.

For several reasons the blitz did not materialise. First, the sabotage plans of the Kuomintang agents were discovered by the Communists and the whole gang was rounded up. Secondly, the men in the Kuomintang armies were not anxious to fight the Communists, and in spite of enthusiastic leadership were completely routed at the first trial border clashes. Thirdly, a series of peasant uprisings through Kansu, Hunan, and other provinces mysteriously flared up at the critical moment to divert attention of the Kuomintang forces. Fourthly, the Kuomintang censorship was over-enthusiastic in suddenly clamping down upon one of the regular publications of the Communists a 100 per cent. veto on some perfectly harmless material, causing some " sticky " international questions in the capital.

And of course Yenan has its own broadcasting station to which all Western agencies interested in Chinese affairs regularly listen : efforts of these censorship gentlemen in Chungking appear to all informed Westerners in that city just about as fantastic as a Gilbert and Sullivan opera.

Here is General Chu Teh's communique in reaction to the new crisis, which the Nationalist authorities in Chungking pretended that no one would hear :

" In the past the Eighth Route Army has retreated at each attack made by General Hu Tsung-nan's blockading armies, in order to avoid clashes that might lead to civil war. After June 18th of this year, however, when the Kuomintang military leaders held a secret meeting to decide upon anti-Communist plans, all National defence forces were moved west of the Yellow River area. A state of war therefore exists around the Border Region, and responsibility for this rests entirely with the Kuomintang.

" Our Eighth Route Army troops in Shensi are but few in number ; they have been busy only in the maintenance of public order, in productive peaceful occupations, and in educational activity. Staff officers of the Nationalist forces have visited Yenan on friendly terms, and they know this is absolutely true. Now these same officers are helping the Kuomintang prepare for civil war against us. The Japanese alone will profit by this policy."

There was no reply from Chungking.

It was then that the Communists let fly with all their propaganda guns, some of which we had heard in Paoteh, others we had avoide in Fuping ; and it was obvious enough that the troop movement that had escorted us safely out of the guerrilla areas had been con nected with this threat of civil war. Nor could we write th whole thing off as a scare deliberately invented by the Communist to stir up trouble with the Kuomintang ; they had far more t lose than gain by any such antics, and the deliberate removal o forces from the front where they were sadly needed to defend thei areas against the Japanese was not a thing to be lightly undertaken Their accusations against the Kuomintang must have been wel founded, even if exaggerated. There was certainly a first-clas crisis brewing. Our prospects for a peaceful journey were non too bright. Having escaped the Japanese frying-pan, we seemed to be jumping into the fire of civil strife.

PLATE XIV

A Taoist monk is giving information about Japanese troop movements to a guerrilla scout.

Chapter XV

ONE–TIME CHINESE SOVIET

FIRST stage of our journey to Yenan from Paoteh was a four days' walk along the banks of the Yellow River to Tsailin on the opposite bank. This was General Ho Lung's temporary head-quarters and rear base for the North-West Shansi Border Region. We were not expecting to cross the river until reaching the ferry at Tsailin, but at midday on our second day out of Paoteh the guide received a message from farther south warning us to cross to the west bank at the first available crossing that same afternoon. We were a little puzzled by this order, and the guide was equally in the dark, though he said it sounded to him as though there must be news of Japanese movements in the vicinity.

By two p.m. we were down on a wide stretch of sand out in the middle of the river basin, waiting for a ferry barge. About twenty mules had got there just before us, and their loads of winter clothing for the army boys were perched in odd clusters along the edge of the stream. The headquarters supply department was moving over to the other side too, the mule-men told us, but whether it was to avoid a Japanese campaign or just returning to their regular site after the threat of civil war had died down was anybody's guess. We hoped very much it was the latter, but a rifle shot from up in the temple overlooking the crossing from the east was not very reassuring.

There was no sign of the barge for nearly two hours. At long last we espied a team of men hauling a rope from the foot-path on the face of the opposite cliffs about a mile down stream, and on the water we could just make out the form of the barge. In half an hour they had reached a point some distance above us, and a crowd of passengers had scrambled down the rocks on board ; in almost no time the barge swept down stream by the current and propelled by a few oarsmen standing in the stern, had reached the sandbank a few hundred yards below us ; the passengers jumped out and were hurrying across the beach for the date groves and the village we had left.

In another fifteen minutes the boatmen had drawn the barge to the spot where the mules and we were waiting and the process of loading up began. The loads of bedding were handed carefully over the sides of the boat and deposited in the fore-quarters. Our baggage animal was unloaded and our bedding rolls tossed into the stern, and we ourselves followed as best we could. Then the animals started leaping in after us. Some of them seemed to enjoy this, but most of them had to be coaxed or whipped into making the jump over the foot or more of water from the top of the sand-bank into the hold two or three feet below. Many of them made false starts, got stuck with their rears on the sand-bank and their middles bumping clumsily over the side of the barge. By the time half the animals had got into the middle section of the hold, they were all over-excited, milling around, kicking and biting each other in fright. Then they got into a jam, and two animals leapt into the stern along with the passengers, which did not help to reduce the general atmosphere of excitement. However, we eventually made the crossing without mishap, and made a quick get-away on the opposite bank.

That night we had a clean cave room to sleep in, and between us and any possible Japanese surprises, the strong silent Yellow River.

The walk down the Yellow River was not just pleasant foot-path strolling. The river is for ever changing, and where the path normally keeps as near the water's edge as possible, there is risk of running into blind ends that have been washed away beneath great overhanging cliffs. At one point we had cheerfully made a bee-line along a broad trail that crossed a bank of earth, planted with corn and millet and dotted with date trees ; in the bend of the river, helping ourselves to the rich brown fruit as we passed along beneath the shrubs, only to find that at the far end the path had disappeared overnight. We had to retrace our steps a weary mile, climb up a stiff incline for nearly a thousand feet, wind for more than two miles among terraces on the plateau before dropping down again to the village that had been just around the corner where the river-side trail had disappeared.

At other places the trail, a mere mark on the face of a pre-cipitous wall overhanging the rushing water, was so narrow that the mule could not proceed without being first unloaded ; we had to carry its saddle-load endways ourselves over these dangerous points and lead the animal gingerly by the nose. Even on the safest parts, there always seemed a great risk that the animal would spill its burden over the side ; we had our hearts in our mouths many a time picturing our stuff rolling helplessly down the steep slope into the river. But it never did, in spite of much provocation.

Just after noon on September 17th we reached Tsailin, and enjoyed the luxury of a beautifully clean courtyard decorated with flowers and a sundial. Here we were told that three days previously seven hundred Japanese had raided the military headquarters of the North-West Shansi Border Region, due east from there, and simultaneously had bombed from the air the ferry crossing here at Tsailin. This explained our hurried ferry crossing ; we had had another narrow escape without at the time knowing. Our convoy friends from Hopei would have their rest period upset if the Japanese were beginning an offensive : their arrival had been nicely timed.

On the morning of the 18th, anniversary of the Mukden Incident, while we were waiting for new guides to be arranged for the next stage of the journey, General Ho Lung sent us a great basketful of fruit as a welcome, and followed it up by calling on us in person. We had been told that his name was a name that struck fear into the hearts of all reactionary war-lords ; " lung " is the word for dragon, and " Ho " is an alliteration of the word for fiery : General Ho Lung had indeed been a fiery dragon in the Chinese Revolution. We asked him about the civil crisis then still at its height, and he gave us the following statement :

" Even if the Kuomintang does start a civil war against us, never mind ! We can fight them! Both by direct military action and through popular uprisings we can defeat their aims.

" The Kuomintang cannot prevent the realisation of democracy in China after this world war. The Communist policy towards the big feudal landlords is merely to introduce democracy ; in an agrarian democracy it will be impossible for a few wealthy individuals to oppose the will of the masses.

" The United Front policy is still being practised in all areas not controlled by Fascist elements of the Kuomintang. Chiang Kai-shek and Wang Ching-wei have now identical ideologies ; the only difference between them is that Chiang is betting that the Japanese will be beaten, while Wang has backed the wrong horse.

" Through eight provinces there have recently been peasant

uprisings demanding democracy from the Kuomintang rulers Chungking has been using British and American arms with which to suppress them."

Ho Lung's remarks about the alleged similarity between Chiang Kai-shek and Wang Ching-wei were a reference to the book *China's Destiny*, which had recently appeared over the Generalissimo's signature. An Oriental version of *Mein Kampf*, this book represented the climax of success on the part of the Fascists in China ; while it is certain that the Generalissimo never wrote a word of it, it is probable that his signature was secured by the usual combination of forgery and blackmail on the part of the Fascists that has characterised the behaviour of those despicable gentlemen the world over.

In the evening twilight we sat watching the Yellow River. There was one great group of " standing waves " through which the sandy current rushed with steady speed. Every few minutes the waves would reach a critical amplitude, break at the crest with a rippling noise that echoed through the surrounding hills, die down to repeat the process over again. In a few hours the whole group of waves had shifted slowly up stream. A symbol of China's immense strength, ever changing yet essentially ever the same, always through the laws of her own being, able to maintain her essential form through the most turbulent currents of history.

Five days' march to Suiteh was the next schedule, starting on September 20th, two young army boys with rifles to act as guides and guards, and one hostler. First morning we had to ferry across a tributary estuary while the animals waded over the quicksands. Second morning there was another estuary, but no ferry. Everyone waded through, hoping to strike a safe crossing. It had started to rain, and we were all anxious to get over before the stream rose too high. One of the guides, leading the mule, stepped into a deep channel, slipped, and got a thorough ducking ; otherwise the party crossed without trouble. But there was heavy rain that afternoon and through the night, and we were held up next day because the paths were too slippery. The local garrison, however, made us more than welcome, gave us chicken feasts both at breakfast and at supper, and we played chess with the guides all morning.

On the 23rd it was still misty and threatening more rain, and it was much against the guides' wishes, but we insisted on continuing the journey. We got started by seven-thirty a.m., only about half an hour later than usual. Just before reaching Chiahsien, a walled city set on a high peak overlooking the Yellow River, we struck inland away from the river, crossed another treacherous tributary with the rain beginning to come down in a good steady drizzle. The boys wanted to call it a day and stop at the garrison camp on the edge of the tributary, but we urged them on. The path climbed steeply over loess hills, and with every minute it became more slippery. By the time we had struggled to the summit there was a heavy downpour, and our further progress reduced itself to an undignified skidding expedition. The mule was sitting it out bravely with the bedding trailing in the mud on either side. The guides were chivalrously helping Claire keep her balance after her first skid had covered her clothes in mud. Bill had given up trying to control his own motion, slithered down ahead of everything, coming to grief only at the bottom. It was impossible to go further.

Luckily there was a cave village just round the corner, and although there was no army rest-house there, we persuaded some peasants to lend us a couple of rooms for the night. The two guides were quite unhappy about staying in such a deserted place, warned us that there might be raids from " Kuomintang bandits " during the night. If we heard any noises outside we were to keep quiet ; they would be responsible for our safety. Before retiring one of them visited the village head and requested that special care be taken to have night watchmen round the village. There was a building in our courtyard that had recently been burned down, and the peasants said it used to be a handiwork shop run by the Eighth Route Army, and that it had been burned by soldiers from the Kuomintang unit encamped about twenty miles to the west.

These peasants had two huge dogs with clipped ears. Several times during the night we were awakened by furious barking. Following instructions, we kept quiet, but we were up early in the morning, before the boys. Bill peeped in at them in their cave room two doors away, and saw them sleeping peacefully : but they had barricaded their door, and they had their rifles placed on the kang in such a position as to cover the windows ready for self-defence. We had laughed at their tales the night before ; we laughed still more heartily (although privately) this morning at such signs of valour. They evidently believed in the danger to themselves, at least.

They were more than eager to continue, and the weather had cleared up nicely. We reached Wulungpu market town that afternoon and had our first taste of astronomical prices. A box of matches that would have cost no more than twenty cents in Paoteh here cost seven dollars; and five dollars for a " bing " (fried bun). Everything was about fifty times the price on the east side of the Yellow River.

The army rest-house at Wulungpu was about the dirtiest in all North China, with bedbug spoor on every square inch of wall. The kangs were horribly infested. Inspecting the doors in hopes of being able to unhinge one for sleeping on, we discovered every one of them similarly infested. Worse still, it started heavy rain again just before dawn, and we had to spend a whole day and a second sleepless night there. It was hard work the following morning getting the guides on the move, even though it had stopped raining : the bedbugs evidently made them feel at home.

But once started, we made excellent speed because the sky was continually threatening, and the boys did not wish to be trapped half-way again. So anxious were they to reach the next garrison that we managed to keep them going at top speed through the whole twenty-five miles without a single break, and by two p.m. we had entered Michih city, a very fine little place with stone-paved streets and smooth parapets, buildings in Peiping style, prosperous-looking people in long gowns, but still mediaeval as regards its toilet facilities.

After the meal we visited a soldiers' co-operative where the local garrison were producing socks, jerseys and gloves from local self-spun wool for public sale.

From Michih we were on a motor road right through to Yenan. A few years before there was a regular bus service on this road, and we had been hoping that perhaps there were still occasional trucks running, upon which we could get a lift. At Michih we were disillusioned on this ; we would have to walk or ride the whole distance, although of course the road, with its gentler gradients and even surface would make the going much easier.

Suiteh Visit

As we left Michih we were coming into the heart of the Shaankanning Border Region ; tall corn was growing all along the broad valley, caravans of mules laden with goods kept passing at frequent intervals ; life began to feel much more stable ; coming within sight of the built-up hillside that was Suiteh, the road swept round in a great curve to cross the broad Wuting River over a graceful nineteen-arch stone bridge. Suiteh seemed a romantic old city. We had to climb right to its summit to report at the brigade headquarters.

Handing in our introductions to the guards, we were ushered into the office of the Chief of Staff, and in a few minutes that Officer, a General Chia-Tao, entered and welcomed us in perfect English. He had been brought up as a Christian by British missionaries in Mukden and was more than delighted to entertain us. He was sorry that there were important meetings in progress at the headquarters, which meant that there was no spare bedroom available for us. Instead they got some bed-boards arranged in one of the soldiers' classrooms, and we spent two very enjoyable days and three not so enjoyable nights there while a new convoy was being arranged.

The soldiers' classroom was memorable chiefly for the rats and the fleas. Even in broad daylight, a couple of rats would frequently come and play with each other on the floor ; at night they were never absent. The fleas were the largest and most voracious we had ever seen. Coupled with these pleasantries, the whole court-yard was crowded with military personnel, spinning wool and discussing politics well into the small hours of the morning. There was not much sleep in Suiteh.

On the first morning Chang Chin-tsai helped us launder our underwear and uniforms, and hung our private washing-line across the tomato beds in the courtyard. In the afternoon host General Chia-Tao took us a walk around the town, visiting the Normal School with 220 boys and 70 girls studying in Peking-style school buildings, the public library, book-shops, and a well-stocked market with all the usual local manufactures and agricultural pro-ducts for sale at astronomical prices. There was plenty of business being done in Suiteh.

Second day General Chia-Tao took us to see a company of deserters from the Nationalist blockade forces. A hundred and fifty ruffians who had, during the previous two months escaped from the 86th division of the 22nd National Army, were being drilled as new recruits in a special Eighth Route Army company. It was the civil war crisis that gave the Suiteh command the excuse

for accepting these men instead of returning them to their origina
unit. Four of the men were called upon to answer our questions
as to how and why they had deserted. Maltreatment and cruelty
from superior officers seemed to be the chief excuses ; rumours of
better treatment with the Communists another. They had all
risked their lives, they believed, in coming across the blockade ;
deserters who had been recaptured were said to have been publicly
tortured or done to death. In the Nationalist forces, they had
received only anti-Communist propaganda, no anti-Japanese
training. Here they felt there was more meaning in their routine ;
but what seems to have impressed them most was the easy educative
discipline and the better rations for the common soldier in the
Eighth Route Army, as compared with their particular unit of the
Nationalist forces. Perhaps they had been garrisoned for some
considerable time in some forgotten out-of-the-way section of the
blockade front ; they must have been having a lean time of it, to
say the least.

The third morning we began the last leg of our journey to
Yenan. Three cavalry men had been assigned to act as our convoy,
their steeds being placed at our disposal should we feel at any time
like riding instead of walking. Unfortunately one of these animals
gave Bill a nasty kick on the knee-cap as its saddle was being tight-
ened up, and although we spent an hour or more while they found
some embrocation to rub on it, Bill had to keep walking most of
the next six days to prevent the knee from stiffening up.

In spite of this little accident, we carried away pleasant memories
of Suiteh and the hospitable Christian Communist General, and of
the civilised meals he had provided for us, and of the enthusiastic
army boys too busy in productive work to notice their rats and
their fleas.

We made excellent speed with the cavalry boys, specially when
they rode and we walked. The highway was thronged all day
with caravans of mules and donkeys, officers and civilians, pedlars
and merchants galloping or ambling along in the invigorating sunshine. Our first night was spent at an army hostel where the cook
was proud to tell us of his experiences in France during World
War I. The second night at the army rest-house just outside the
north gate of Chinghsien city, whose high embattled walls stretched
far up over the steep loess mountain at the foot of which the city
nestled. There was cotton growing on the hillsides, just south of

Chinghsien, the whole countryside was rich with a wealth of crops.

An atmosphere of peace and plenty pervaded everything, and even the peasants seemed more easy-going. Enquiring our way from one of them, our guide asked him what was the name of the next village; he received the reply:

" Is it not Yangchiehkota ? " as if the peasant himself did not wish to make too definite a statement about the name even of his own native place. With a hearty laugh, the guide shouted back:

" Of course ! It is Yangchiehkota ! "

And it was; the army rest-house there being our third stop after Suiteh.

Next day we made a short cut over an exceedingly steep loess mountain and arrived at noon at the little market town of Yuchu where we bought fruit and eggs, and were impressed by the unusual laziness of the garrison staff. We had been told that the next day's trip to Kankuyi would be at least twenty-five miles—they were seventy " long " li, and the normal garrison breakfast would not be served until ten a.m. Moreover, Kankuyi was a busy town, next stop before Yenan and would be thronged with travellers in both directions, so we had better get there early in the day to secure good accommodation. Our cavalry escort had told us this in the evening, and the kitchen had promised to get us a meal before seven next morning. But when we got up we found the garrison still half asleep, and it took some ten minutes of persuasive but vigorous argument to get the kitchen busy with breakfast.

Fortunately the seventy " long " li turned out to be no more than seventeen miles, judging by the time we took to walk it, and we were in the guest-house courtyard at Kankuyi by two p.m. with almost the whole place to choose from. An army hospital had been set up in the large Catholic Church at Kankuyi, but we did not have time to visit it. We tried to buy some eggs, but discovered that the whole supply from this district was regularly transported to Yenan where prices were higher, and nobody ever got any eggs in Kankuyi except party or government and army officials.

ARRIVAL IN YENAN

We were now about to start on the last lap of the journey to the Border Region capital; it was therefore still more important to start early in order to be able to complete all arrival formalities at our destination in good time before the evening meal. So at five a.m. we aroused our convoy and got out on the road by five-thirty without waiting for breakfast. There was a convenient town about ten miles out from Kankuyi where we could have breakfast at about eight, and after that we could make a non-stop dash for Yenan.

At that early hour in the morning the air was so crisp and cold that we both felt like giving the boys a demonstration of our walking prowess. There were several long mule caravans and party officers on the road before us, but we startled everyone by slogging past the lot at full speed. The cavalry could hardly keep up with us, had to keep urging their animals into a trot, and before eight we were all seated on a bench munching mantou at a roadside restaurant long before the mule caravans came rolling by.

The mules with their great harness head-gear decorated with red tassels and tinkling bells, the first animal in each train carrying a large flag displaying the name and business of its owner, the peasants and merchants with their great coarse goat-skin coats and breeches, the soldiers galloping past ; primitive and crude though so much of the scene was, still it held for us a fascination and old-world charm that is unforgettable ; the lusty shouts and joyful laughter, good-natured invective, a zest for life that bespoke prosperous stability.

As we approached Yenan the traffic became still heavier ; convoys of high-wheeled carts drawn by four or more mules carrying high loads ; long trains of donkeys carrying salt ; a caravan consisting of several Nationalist Army officers and a family litter tied to four mules, two in front and two behind ; and—but what was that noise ? A Japanese plane ? We started thinking quickly about A.R.P. but before we could do anything about it, round the next turn of the hills came a motor truck. It was the first automobile we had seen in almost two years. The donkey trains broke formation, careered uncontrollably across the cornfields, the mules in their carts strained and snorted, some of them succeeded in overturning a cart, we grabbed our animals by the nose and rushed them off the road as fast as we could go ; and the truck continued, negotiating the cart ruts in the dry clay road in its noisy bottom gear.

For the last six or seven miles into Yenan the road was anything from four to eight lanes wide, a great ugly clay abrasion running down the middle of a broad valley. On either side of the valley the loess cliffs were riddled with long lines of caves, each hillside allotted to some particular party or government department. By the edge of the road itself a ribbon development was springing up. New shacks and sheds were being built. Co-operative shops and private enterprise, roadside restaurants and market stalls, were appropriating conspicuous sites by the artery to cater for the needs of passers-by. The whole place looked far more like a frontier town in a gold-rush than the metropolis of a planned Socialist economy.

As advised at Tsailin on the Yellow River, we made directly for the Government Guest House near the New Market outside the south gate of the old city. The staff here at once fixed us up with a room in one of their new buildings (not a cave) and refreshed us with some hot tea to drink and some good hot water for a wash.

We were given just one week to settle down before starting official visits, and on October 11th came a telephone message calling on us to be ready within half an hour to be taken by special truck to the military headquarters for an interview with General Yeh, Chief of Staff to General Chu Teh, to whom General Nieh's letter of introduction had been addressed. We found that General Yeh could speak a little English, but he had with him Huang Hua from Yenching as official interpreter. We had a pleasant meal with them. They promised to have a full-time guide and interpreter specially assigned to us for our stay in Yenan if we would prefer such an arrangement, and forthwith telephoned to the Yenan Daily News office instructing them to send one of their staff, named Wang, at once to the Government Guest House to be at our service.

One of the first pieces of information that Wang brought to us was of the fate of two Westerners who had left Yenan only about four months previously; they had been arrested at the blockade border on charges of espionage. They had passed through at the height of the civil war crisis without waiting for proper permits from the Kuomintang side, and may have seen more than the Nationalists wished to have known by foreigners. Even a year before, other Western nationals had been subject to much indignity and even danger at the hands of local Kuomintang officials. Wang said he entertained much anxiety about our own possible journey through Sian and strongly advised us to wait for some time until the civil war situation cooled off. At the moment everything was still very tense ; the whole of the Yenan Region was mobilised and practically under martial law in readiness for any emergency ; should we attempt to go south at this juncture, we should undoubtedly run straight into trouble. We only half believed his stories at the time, but he was the only source of information, and so far as the local authorities were concerned he was their official representative. There was nothing to do but accept his statement, and settle down to wait for more auspicious times.

So began an exceedingly enjoyable three months of interviews, entertainments and visits. In a variety of ways, formal and informal, we were able to learn a good deal about the history, present achievements and future plans of the Chinese Communist Party and their Border Region around Yenan.

LOCAL HISTORY

China's ancient civilisation is generally believed to have originated in this geographical region. The earliest recorded civilisation was centred around Sian and the Yellow River basin about 1000 B.C. The country's first Emperor, Shih Huang Ti, was buried, about 200 B.C., only a hundred miles south of Yenan, at Ch'iao Lin. And Yenan itself was always of strategic importance for the defence of these early civilisations.

Up to a hundred years ago, Yenan had been fairly prosperous, but at the time of the Taipings, robber bands laid waste to the whole region. Ancient towns still lay in ruins—we had seen many of them on our journey already. The country became semi-desert, because semi-nomadic bandits had destroyed the trees : bandits against whom the few remaining larger towns organised their several systems of self-defence. During the Ching (Manchu) Dynasty there had been no pretence at rehabilitation of the area, and the Republican Revolution never really reached these remote areas in anything but nominal form.

In 1919 the local garrison of troops under a petty war-lord nominally loyal to the new Republic assumed administrative control of the surrounding twenty-three counties in the name of the Pei Yang clique of politicians in Peiping. In practice there remained complete local autonomy on the same old feudal lines as had previously existed. The only self-government that existed in the region was the traditional local self-defence volunteer organisation for bandit suppression.

During the ten years preceding 1931 the provincial authorities conscripted from the population of the Yenan area enough men to fill five divisions of soldiery. This, combined with two years of famine in 1928 and 1929, taxed the endurance of the peasants beyond the limit they were likely to regard as reasonable. General Feng Yu-hsiang had once been in the area, and his Leftist doctrines helped to sow the seeds of rebellion. In 1931 a former officer named Kao Kang, in the local garrison at Yenan, organised a mutiny against the feudal authorities and founded the Shensi People's Red Army. Civil war against the so-called Republican Government continued for some years, but Kao eventually set up a soviet government at Yenan, alienating the local gentry who had fled to Yulin. It was Kao's soviet that welcomed the Communists from their "Long March" in 1935, and it was under Mao Tse-tung's persuasion that the Shensi soviet was dissolved in favour of a United Front democracy. The first full democratic congress was held in 1938, but the local gentry remained lukewarm until the second congress in 1941, when the three-thirds policy seems to have won for itself the enthusiastic support of all sections of the population.

Chapter XVI

YENAN DIARY

WHEN we first arrived in Yenan we spent at least a week keeping our eyes open for friends and acquaintances whom we knew had left for Yenan from the Hopei area some months or weeks before we had. One of these was Mrs. Kotnis, Chinese widow of the Indian doctor, and her child, a beautiful little boy. They had set out disguised as peasants, but they had not yet arrived in Yenan. When they did get through, they had been four months on the trip with many sufferings on the way.

At the Government Guest House itself we were greeted by one of the service staff; and we recognised him as the boy who had come over as private body-guard to the one American who had escaped from Peiping; and from him we heard his story of their crossing the railway and the Hutou River under more desperate circumstances than ours.

We were also surprised at the guest house by the presence of about twenty Japanese, some of whom we recognised as among the prisoners we had seen in Hopei. They left by truck in the direction of Sian a day or two after our arrival. We were told that the National authorities required the Eighth Route Army to hand over to them all Japanese prisoners captured in North China.

Then a few days later we met on the market road old Feng who had cooked that unforgettable welcome meal for us at General Nieh's headquarters, and who had for some time been manager of the staff at our International Peace Hotel in Fuping.

From various sources we heard rumours about conditions in Hopei. The Japanese were said to be launching simultaneous offensives on Hopei and Shansi, using something like twenty or thirty thousand men on each region. We wondered how the L.'s were getting on, and Roger Liu, and whether General Nieh and his wife were still in the same little village where they had said good-bye to us just two months before. Two months that seemed like a year.

These questions were answered in a most surprising way eight days after we had come to Yenan. We had just finished the morning meal when someone knocked gently at the door of our room,

nd there came in upon us, with his hands outstretched and his
mouth wide open in a great smile of astonishment, none other than
General Nieh himself.

General Nieh and his wife had accompanied General Lü and
his wife and child ; they had all come across from Hopei with the
Central Hopei forces by a route different from ours. The Niehs
were wanted in Yenan for important conferences ; they had arrived
two days ago, and were anxious to know how we had fared on our
journey. He told us that general conditions over in Hopei were
still essentially the same as when we had left ; the offensive was
no worse than usual.

CHAIRMAN LIN TSU-HAN

The day after General Nieh had surprised us, we were invited
to call on Lin Tsu-han, Chairman of the Yenan Border Region
Congress. We found him in his cave room a few terraces above
the congress hall. A most attractive and genial old white-haired
man with an enthusiastic light in his keen eyes. We sipped green
tea while he chatted with us about the history of the district. He
assured us that while we were in Yenan we should be guests of
the Border Government at his special invitation ; we were to
feel free to stay as long as we liked.

Lin had been a co-worker with Dr. Sun Yat-sen even before
the beginning of the revolution of 1911, at the failure of which he
had been very distressed. He could think of no way in which
China's problems could be solved until he chanced to read the works
of Karl Marx. These works, he claimed, brought him great
illumination, through which he was able to see his way clearly to
a solution of China's chief problems. He was with Dr. Sun Yat-sen
in his northern expedition against Yuan Shih-kai, and with Dr.
Sun at the latter's death in Peking, 1925. Lin was again political
commissar of one of the four armies in the northern expedition
from Canton in 1926 to 1927, and joined the Communist Party
only when, according to the Communists, the Kuomintang be-
trayed Dr. Sun's principles by their reactionary alliance with the
Shanghai underworld in 1927.

Lin helped to organise the Nanchang peasants' uprisings with
General Ho Lung in August 1927. Later he joined the Kiangsi
soviet and was with the Red Army on its Long March. After the
formation of the United Front in 1937, Lin was invited to act as

provisional President of the Congress at Yenan, to which office he was later elected by the democratic authority. His sixtieth birthday was February 1943.

VICE-CHAIRMAN LI TSUNG-MING

Vice-chairman of the Yenan Congress was one of the local gentry, Mr. Li Tsung-ming, and on October 27th we were invited to call upon him at his cave not far from the congress hall. On the clay terrace outside his cave we were met by his two sons decked out in new woollen suits made by the Yenan Government tailor from army-spun wool and army-woven cloth. The old man was similarly dressed, looked very snug ; the cave was heated from the floor ; he was sipping tea from the spout of a little teapot boiled over a private little kerosene flame stove in the good old classical style. Aged sixty-four he seemed much less robust than Lin.

A native of Michih, Li had been a classical scholar in a Ching dynasty school ; had become headmaster of the Yulin middle school during the Red uprisings around Yenan, with which movement he had been very much out of sympathy. After the Sian Incident he had consented to return to Suiteh to co-operate with the United Front movement in his native district, and became exceedingly popular as a mediator in private disputes between local families—settling things out of court.

He said that the Kuomintang at Yulin had put him on its black list for returning to Suiteh, but the Kuomintang members in his own district paid him great respect. The first congress in 1938 elected him as the vice-president, and at the second congress he was elected Vice-Chairman of the Government. He represented the wealthier classes among the peasants and landowners of Suiteh and Michih, was locally famous for his exploits in his youth as a leader of ten thousand local defence volunteers for protection against bandits. Although we could sense the easy sing-song flow of his smoothly-running intonation, similar in quality to that of all classical Chinese scholars, his dialect was completely un-intelligible to us.

THE GOVERNMENT OFFICES

When we arrived in Yenan, construction work was already started on a new set of government offices. These were not the

PLATE XV

An Eighth Route Army regiment on the march across an enemy-held plain.

usual caves built in the loess mountains, but cave-shaped rooms formed like the arches of a long bridge the top of which served as a flat roof. The whole building was of hewn rocks, almost fire-proof, and safe against all the small bombs that the Japanese had ever brought that far inland. By the beginning of November the buildings were complete, and the offices installed. On November 9th we were taken on an inspection visit by Miss Tang Liang, Chairman Lin's private secretary, and another Yenching graduate.

First we saw their library of books and magazines, a fair selection of which were Western publications. For the first time we saw a copy of that American Communist propaganda magazine called *China To-day*; it was a solitary volume for 1934-35 in the days of violent excitements following Agnes Smedley's early " revelations " about the Chinese Reds. We were both startled and amused to see in this volume some reference to our Yenching University as being a stronghold of reaction and American capitalist imperialism in the Orient. Yenching can well afford to leave it to history to judge whether or not our educational work in China was or was not for China's own benefit as a progressive and independent nation. For the Communists to have dubbed us as reactionaries must have done their own interests more harm than good.

There was a meeting going on in one of the offices; the clerks and secretarial staff of a number of departments were discussing the week's news as part of their required educational activities.

In the office of the Finance Department, Miss Tang introduced us to Mrs. Nan, a most charming and artistic lady dressed in civilian clothes—cloth blouse and slacks—instead of the padded uniforms that were generally worn by the women workers. Her room was delicately decorated and tastefully furnished. She offered us some excellent red tea that she had secured from Chungking through some banking friends : her husband was the Finance Commissioner.

Mrs. Nan was knitting socks. We asked her for whom the socks were intended. She replied :

" For my youngest child."

" How many children have you ? " we asked.

" Only twelve! " she answered with a mischievous twinkle in her eye. " Yes, they are all my own! "

She looked about thirty-five, but must have been older. Her

children were being educated at the Communist Party boardi
school which we later visited. She was busy part-time with gover
ment office work, but was looking after her youngest child herse

GENERAL CHU TEH

Huang Hua was again interpreter when General Chu T
first called us over for a meal with him at the military headquarte
on October 24th. He struck us as a " rough old bean ", to p
it in slang. He was dressed, like Lin and Li had been, in a ne
woollen uniform of their own army's manufacture, and to us l
certainly looked equal to the part of a hard-boiled old bandi
This was probably in part due to his pock-marked complexio
and bull-dog figure ; but that was as far as the bandit appearan
went ; in his table manners and his conversation he was as gentl
manly as anyone could wish.

In reply to our questions about the current civil crisis he ga
us a lengthy statement, a brief translation of which follows :

" Mountbatten's recent visit to Chungking has definitel
reduced the threat of civil war. The Allied generals are no
planning the defeat of Japan, and must therefore be interested i
our army as one of the main anti-Japanese forces in China.

" All the same Chiang Kai-shek would still blockade eve
conducted supplies of war material to this region. The Allie
have repeatedly urged the Kuomintang to reorganise the countr
on democratic lines in order to secure national unity, but they hav
so far been deaf to these arguments. However, the problem
will gradually become less acute with time. It is now practicall
impossible for the Kuomintang to realise their civil war aims befor
the world war is over. And after the Japanese have been defeate
China's problems can be easily solved : we can solve them ou
selves without outside help. It is only the old reactionaries i
China who are pro-Japanese.

" If the Allies wish to conquer Japan, they must have a lan
force, and if the Soviet is not in the war at first, the United State
and Britain must use China as a base for operations. Landing
operations are exceedingly difficult : look at the time required fo
preparing the landings on Europe even from bases only a few mile
distant. To co-operate fully with these land operations China mus
become more democratic so that the whole people can be mobilised

" Since October 1st, Chiang Kai-shek has assumed the offic

f Chairman as well as Supreme Commander ; he has also received
five hundred million dollar loan from the United States. All
hese circumstances influence the National Government away from
a pro-Japanese and a civil war policy. Japan's invitation to a separate
peace for anti-Communist purposes have failed against contrary
pressure from Allied diplomats.

" This means that Japan will shortly renew her military pressure
against Chungking, and this will bring about a more co-operative
atmosphere between Chungking and ourselves. If Chiang Kai-shek
wished to defeat us he would have to use Japanese help ; but to
defeat the Japanese he needs ours.

" Formerly, when the Allies were too weak to help Chiang
Kai-shek against the Japanese, Chiang was afraid of us, and sought
by underground methods to secure Japanese co-operation without
committing himself openly : he schemed thus to divert the power
of Japan away from himself. Now that he has better hopes for
final victory against the Japanese his own self-interest will swing
him more into line again with the United Front which we have
been advocating since even before 1936.

" Chiang Kai-shek is a practical man. If circumstances prove
it expedient, he will swing right round towards the Chinese
Communist Party. We will accept him as the nation's military
leader provided only that he supports our democratic policy for
the political reconstruction of the country.

" Because Japan's defeat is coming nearer, the pro-Japanese
clique in the Kuomintang is losing some of its present great
influence. Pressure from within as well as from outside the
country will compel a change in policy. Chiang Kai-shek must
organise the people for the final offensive. Otherwise the country
could not afford the cost : it would suffer from starvation and
famine. Already we can see the failure of the Kuomintang landlord-
tradesman's policy of suppressing peasant uprisings ; they are now
sitting on a live volcano, and the longer the suppression is maintained, the more dangerous will become their position."

His prediction of renewed Japanese military action against the
National forces was fulfilled within a few months and his prediction
of an attempted *rapprochement* between the two factions in China
came true shortly afterwards. From our later observations in
Chungking, we now feel that Chu Teh's analysis of the situation
was substantially accurate.

Chu Teh looks about forty-five, but was reported to be fifty-seven. As early as Christmas 1915, Chu was a brigadier-general in the first Yunnan Army in action with the Revolutionary forces against Yuan Shih-kai. During the confused civil wars between then and the 1930's he stayed in Germany studying military science. He had studied Marxism in Europe, and on returning to his own country renounced his former class privileges and joined the Communist movement, became the founder of the Red Army.

Though at first independent of Mao Tse-tung, he had been thinking along similar lines; in particular he was not satisfied with the way in which their early Russian advisers had been forcing their party to extremes too violent to be practical in China, the land of compromise. When he and Mao met, they formed a sufficiently strong combination to carry the party with them against the Russians in favour of their present moderate programme of agrarian reform. It is a pity that they have never seen fit to change the name of their party; for their actual programme, since the defeat of the Russian influence during the Long March, has never been Communism as it is understood anywhere else in the world.

General Ho Lung

It was on December 20th that we received an invitation to visit General Ho Lung again, this time at his headquarters in Yenan. Since our first rather meagre interview at Tsailin on our way down we had gathered some biographical details about him from Wang. In his youth he had been a cowherd in Hunan. His uncle was done to death by the local magistrate as a punishment for tax defaults. Ho Lung had avenged the death of his uncle by murdering the magistrate, so became an outlaw. Since the age of twenty he had lived a kind of Robin Hood life, leader of a gang of outlaws, robbing the tyrannical rich but protecting the poor against the power of the feudal landlords. Here we were talking with Robin Hood himself, a survival from the Middle Ages, dark times that still hung like a cloud over vast areas of China only a few years ago. A handsome chivalrous knight, who, to the Nationalist authorities, was still something of a dangerous bandit.

During the 1911 Revolution Ho Lung joined up with the new armies and was with them right up until the 1927 split, when he stayed with the Communists. When his Nanchang uprisings had been defeated by the Nationalist forces, he escaped in disguise to the coast, sought refuge with Chou En-lai and Lin Tsu-han in Hongkong. Returning inland later via Shanghai, he reached his native province and started peasant organisations in Hunan, raiding pawn shops to get funds and arms. He linked up with the Red Army on their Long March and came with them to Shensi. At that time he was still illiterate, but was now catching up on his studies.

GENERAL KAO KANG

Two days before Christmas, when we were already preparing to continue our journey, General Kao Kang invited us to his headquarters, south of the same hillside where the guest house was built. Interpreter this time was a Mr. Yu who had been an engineering student in Ann Arbor, Michigan, but had actually spent ten years in New York's China Town between 1929 and 1939 doing Communist Party work there. Through Yu's fluent interpretation General Kao gave us a thrilling picture of his revolutionary career in Shensi.

According to Kao, the previous government of Shensi Province had been by independent bandit warlords only nominally under the control of the National Government. There was no consideration for the welfare of the people, who were exploited to the utmost in taxation and forced labour for the private profit of the rulers. The peasants were so poor that very often the farmers' daughters could not afford sufficient clothing to cover their nakedness, and would perforce have to stay indoors all winter for lack of a pair of trousers. Kao's own father was murdered by the government for tax defaults.

The Shensi rebellions began when young students, native to the district, came back from Peking and Tientsin with national revolutionary ideas in 1919 and 1920. These boys set up what they called the "People's Great Alliance of Northern Shensi" in the four middle schools of Fushih (otherwise Yenan), Suiteh, Michih and Yulin, where they had become young teachers on the staff. In reaction to this dangerous activity, the provincial authorities condemned a number of the teachers to death, banished the others, and closed all schools for a whole year. After that a new set of classics teachers were imported and the schools re-opened to teach only a reactionary Confucian type of scholasticism.

During the famines of 1928 and 1929, Kao and a fellow

conspirator successfully organised a mutiny among the provinci: troops, who, conscripted from the local population, were badl treated and dissatisfied. But the mutiny got them nowher Repeated attempts merely brought added misery to the poo people. Learning by these mistakes, Kao realised that his failur with purely military insurrection was because he had not estab lished liaison with the peasants whose welfare he was trying t assist.

So, collecting a number of progressive students who had bee associated indirectly with the former revolutionary movement in the schools, he organised them into a Robin Hood gang, hiding among the forests, working with the peasants, leaving the loca feudal authorities at first well alone, until goodwill with the oppressed peasants had been thoroughly established. Upon thi more solid basis, a really significant uprising could be built.

Peasant uprisings in China have always occurred when oppres sion by autocratic governments has become unbearable ; Kao'; uprising was one of these, but it was different in that it had a definite political programme for the assumption of political powei after the oppressing regime had been overthrown. Three points preached to the peasants were :

(1) Redistribution of the feudal landlords' excessive land.
(2) Abolishment of onerous taxation.
(3) Local self-government by the masses.

Almost exactly the same programme of liberation preached by the National Revolutionaries under Dr. Sun Yat-sen, it was in fact the national revolution coming to Shensi under another name.

The local feudal authorities, smugly satisfied with their ancient methods of exploitation and their lip-service to the national revolutionary programme of the Republic, remained ignorant of the popular movement, regarded its early manifestation as just local disturbances requiring firm local action to suppress. They miscalculated. Starting with no more than three rifles in all, Kao's gang developed a strategy of attacking local bases of the feudal authority one by one, thus acquiring arms and gaining confidence and experience, without raising undue alarm on the part of the authorities, until the revolutionaries were ready for the big coup.

After their successful seizure of local power in North Shensi, Kao changed the name of the army from " Red Revolutionary

Army " to " Anti-Japanese Revolutionary Army ". This was in
September 1931. But they continued to have to fight for their
existence against neighbouring Nationalist forces that were sent
time and again to eliminate them and seize again the old feudal
power for exploitation of the local peasant population in the name
of the National Government.

First, Yen Hsi-shan from Shansi sent an army to wipe out the
revolutionaries in Shensi, and Kao eliminated two brigades of
Yen's men before the latter withdrew. Again a whole division
of troops under the Nationalist General Kao Kwei-tse were
defeated in another attempt to oust the Reds from Shensi. General
Kao Kwei-tse was reported to be now in command of the 33rd
Army of the Kuomintang blockade forces in the north-west of
Shensi. All of Kao Kang's arms and equipment had been secured
in battle with the forces of the established authorities.

Kao continued :

" In 1936, after welcoming Mao and Chu to this area, we
changed our policy, and planned to get into immediate action against
the Japanese, and so avoid all further civil conflict. In fact in the
autumn of 1936 we actually started an expedition towards the east
with the object of preparing an anti-Japanese front. Perhaps in
support of their appeasement policy at that time, the Nationalists
ordered an attack upon the rear of this anti-Japanese expedition.
We therefore retraced our steps, dealt the menacing army a de-
cisive blow. We had thirty thousand men involved, and General
Hu Tsung-nan had fifty thousand men in the field against us at
San Chengpu, with another fifty thousand in reserve. Our men
eliminated a whole division of Hu's forces, and routed the remainder. It was this battle, more than anything else, that decided
Marshal Chang Hsueh-liang to attempt to call a halt to the civil
war, and to kidnap the Generalissimo at Sian.

" The United Front policy that arose from the Sian Incident
was extracted from Chiang Kai-shek against his will. Chiang
was still trying to trap the Communists by underhand comparadore-
like trickery learned from the examples of Japan, Italy and Germany.
The economic blockade, and the secret understanding with Japan
for joint anti-Communist military campaigns, were their methods
for trying to destroy us. But the blockade has done us good ;
it has taught us self-reliance ; and the civil war has strengthened
us—we have grown strong through struggle. The Kuomintang

wish to destroy us because by our good example we expose their rottenness. We laugh at their foolish efforts; they can never destroy the truth!"

Kao Kang was perhaps the most indiscreet of all the Communists whom we interviewed.

PARTY ELDER HSU

Perhaps our most enjoyable series of meetings was with Elder Hsu, an old party member honoured among his comrades for his private middle school at which he used to give free schooling to poor children in Hunan Province, and for the fact that one of his pupils had been Mao Tse-tung. Hsu used to be a philosophical deist, but converted himself through the study of natural science to dialectical materialism. At the age of forty-two he went to France with some of his own students for further study. He was now sixty-seven, was living in retirement at the party headquarters in Yenan. A hardy old nut, he still indulged in swimming in the river, never wore an overcoat even in the depth of winter, and was a semi-vegetarian. He came to lunch with us many times while we were at the guest house, and he never ate more than about a quarter of what either of us would take. He explained his continued good health to his having hardened himself, and continuing to harden himself even in old age.

Elder Hsu was exceedingly bitter about China's political problems. Many of his own students, simply because they had been his students and so labelled as dangerous thinkers, had been massacred in the anti-Communist terror during 1927. He exclaimed at one of our meetings:

"The Chinese Fascists are not actually fighting against democracy in this world war, so they will come out of the war fairly strong. While an Allied victory will help our own democratic movement, nevertheless China's Fascism will be the last to disappear from the world."

CHAIRMAN MAO TSE-TUNG

Elder Hsu was proud of his best student, Mao Tse-tung, and eager to give us his analysis of Mao's career. Here is a resume of what Elder Hsu had to say about Mao.

"Democratic revolutionary ideas were permeating school life during World War I while Mao Tse-tung was at school. Mao made a special study of the failure of the 1911 Revolution, and concluded that it was caused by the isolation of the Chinese intelligentsia from the common people. It was imperative that the intellectual leaders of any successful revolution must be in close touch with the peasant masses of the country. It was for this reason that Mao refused to come with me when I invited him to go to France just after the last war was ended. He preferred instead to increase his knowledge of China. He refused the usual clerical job awaiting middle school graduates, and took up soldiering from the beginning.

" Mao's experience of the mercenary soldier in military training camps taught him the futility of depending on such material for revolutionary purposes : it was too difficult to educate them politically. Mao realised that to build up a successful agrarian reform movement and break the power of the ancient feudal war-lords and bandit governing authorities, it would be necessary to arm the peasants themselves.

" In order to side-step the feudal authorities' opposition to peasant armies Mao planned to organise them in guerrilla groups, trained to produce their own requirements, among the forests and desert areas remote from the great tax-producing populations in which alone the war-lords and landlords were really interested.

" Mao's most original contribution to revolutionary strategy is in his use of regular armies only as a means of securing power, while the maintenance of power is not based upon the regular armies, but upon an immediate arming of the peasants themselves. In this way alone could the young agrarian democracy guarantee itself against betrayal to ancient feudal authorities in surrounding districts.

" Mao did not wish to have to wage an aggressive civil war before being able to set up these new democratic peasant governments. But the Japanese occupation of North China offered him exactly the required opportunity. The enemy had smashed the authority of all war-lord governments throughout occupied areas, and had put, or were putting in their places, a system of puppet control that had no popular support whatever. Here, deep in the rear of the Japanese, were exactly the conditions best adapted to Mao's new revolutionary tactics.

" Mao had worked out these ideas in great detail before they were accepted by the party ; since then they have been carried out with brilliant success. While Chiang Kai-shek has been scheming to let the Japanese crush our movement, Mao has successfully used the Japanese Occupation as a stimulus to the Revolution. In this the reactionaries have been completely outwitted.

"From a middle class peasant family, Mao could not afford a modern university training, but through experience he has learned to mix with all classes. After his early military training, he came to Peking and spent half-time working for a living at the National Library, and half-time studying in college. He acquired a clear understanding of the mentality of China's wealthy classes, and of the militarists and the politicians. He knows all strata of Chinese society better than any other leading figure in the country.

"The fundamental points in Mao's policy for China are based upon the fact that, due to poverty and weakness as a nation, the Chinese must learn to live together as peacefully as possible, the old Chinese attitude of 'live and let live' must include even traditional class enemies. We must go to all lengths to convert exploiting classes before resorting to civil war, even landlords can be converted to our progressive policy when they see clearly the need for national unity in the face of Fascist imperialism. To expropriate landlords is to create a strong counter-revolutionary enemy at home, as if the Japanese imperialists were not already more than enough for us to cope with.

"When at school Mao showed no special talent for leadership. He had a humble spirit, was good at making friends, and was always alert for the reception of new ideas. Seventeen years ago he was already publishing the germs of the party's present policy; if they had been acted upon at that time, China would have been saved much civil conflict, conflict which greatly assisted Japan in her aggressive actions. Mao had gone on record, even before the 1927 split, as against the excesses of the United National Revolutionary Party and their Russian advisers.

"Now, under Mao's inspiring leadership, the whole of North China had been organised on democratic United Front lines as a war base against the Japanese. Contrast this success with the abject failures of the Kuomintang in Chungking, begging for American and British financial support in order to prevent collapse to the enemy! Here we are organising prosperity and waging a vigorous war even behind the enemy's rear without a farthing of help from outside in any form."

Mao Tse-tung's criticisms of the Russians' policy in China

proved so obviously correct that Moscow eventually withdrew their representatives and formally appointed Mao as official agent of the Third International in China. When that International was dissolved, Mao was elected Chairman by the Chinese Communist Party, but he is said always to prefer to use the committee system in arriving at important decisions. There are supposed to be no dictatorial methods within the party. The strict party discipline to which every member submits himself is democratically determined by the party members as a whole. Their idea seems to be that political leadership demands a nucleus of what we would call spiritually exalted devotees—almost a political priesthood. Their objection to existing national leadership would seem to be that the shaping of national practical political policies was being mishandled by people whose only qualification was either inherited class privilege, or the possession of power through financial exploitation of the common people.

Mao had been exceedingly busy all autumn. Not until our preparations for departure for Chungking were practically complete, were we informed that we might expect to see Mao within a few days. Had we any questions we would like to ask him? Because if so he would prefer to receive notice beforehand. So we wrote out some leading questions, and prepared some deeper ones to keep the discussion going. Mao's public appearances were very few. He was a prolific writer, but apparently not addicted to the glamour of public speaking. Working until the small hours every morning, chain smoking to help concentration, he managed to get through an amount of administrative work and literary creation at least double the capacity of more average men. We had been told that the usual procedure for an interview with Mao was to await a telephone call from his secretary, and then to make a dash to Mao's headquarters. Mao made a practice of never going out to call upon others, but maintained the dignity of his office by holding receptions on his own ground. Exceptions were made only when he called upon party members senior to himself, or Kuomintang officials of higher military rank than his own who might be visiting the region.

Imagine our surprise therefore when on January 4th, 1944, Chang Chin-tsai—who had become attached to the staff of the guest house permanently—came into our room, his boyish face gleaming with excitement :

" Chairman Mao is here! He is going to have tea with you in our dining-room! "

" Already here ? " we asked in astonishment.

" Yes! He is talking to Manager Chin at the office. He will be ready in a few minutes."

Huang Hua had come with him too, as official interpreter.

In about half an hour tea was served. We thanked Mao for giving us the honour of calling on us in this way, when he was such a busy man. He replied that he had included us in his New Year round of calls which included the Elders of the Party, like Chairman Lin and Vice-Chairman Li. He was sorry that we had been in Yenan for just three months before he had had time to meet us. He was also sorry that he had had no time to prepare answers to our questions ; he preferred to have just a tea-time chat. He made us talk—in Chinese most of the time—instead of talking himself ; about our journey, about teaching the radio boys in Hopei, and about our pre-war life in Peiping, about England, about China's future. He gave practically nothing away himself.

We were sorry to note that in appearance Mao seemed an effeminate type. He seemed over-tired, too, and kept stroking his half-bald head with one hand as if he was suffering from insomnia. He had, however, a winning, kindly smile, a keen sense of humour, and would gaze at one during conversation, with steady, thoughtful eyes. He gave us the impression of absolute sincerity, and a deep feeling of responsibility for his position in a critical period of his country's history. There was no blustering cock-sureness in his make-up ; hot-headed revolutionary fanaticism was completely absent.

He took his leave of us after tea, departing in a closed van, on the outside of which were painted the words :

" GIFT OF THE CHINESE LAUNDRYMEN'S NATIONAL SALVATION ASSOCIATION, NEW YORK."

About a dozen young soldiers formed his private bodyguard. As an after-thought, as he climbed into the van, Mao turned round and requested that we would publish nothing of what he had said. He had already taken good care to say nothing!

In this chapter we have described so far our interviews with the Yenan leaders. Now we narrate a different strand of experiences—how we were " shown the works " of the Yenan Border Region Government.

OCTOBER 14TH, 1943. THE YENAN SCIENCE COLLEGE

This college was accommodated in several terraces of caves in the loess mountains to the south of Yenan. Professor Chen, the Dean, received us in his cave office, described to us the organisation and achievements of the college. He said their chemical equipment and stock of supplies had been brought in over the Burma Road and transported through Sian while the United Front was still in action, before the New Fourth Army Incident. Their physics equipment was next on the list for purchasing abroad, but the Burma Road had been closed before it could be imported.

Their best successes had been, said Dr. Chen, in biology : experiments in dairy farming, crop improvement, medicinal herbs, forestry work, had all been stimulated by the need for self-sufficiency in the Border Region, and had all contributed materially to the region's success.

A middle school attached to the college had enrolled 160 students. But so far there was only one year's course in the science college, because of lack of both adequate equipment and reliable staff. Fifty students had been enrolled in this year course. The staff and student body all lived in cave dormitories in the same hillside, boarded at the institution's expense. When we inspected the place, the staff were busy packing away their chemical supplies ready for moving to a new site, where the college was going to a better set of caves nearer to the other colleges of Yenan University.

The college ran a fairly well-equipped machine shop, which we discovered busy on outside orders from soldiers' co-operatives for large numbers of spoons, buttons, belt-buckles, and boiler-vats for a soap factory. They had been melting down an old bronze Buddha for metal, that had been removed from an abandoned temple. Their stock included large quantities of their own former products : clamp stands, tweezers, small tools, storage batteries and dry cells.

Dr. Chen's own special interest was in geology : he was acting in an advisory capacity in connection with the government's oil refineries and salt fields. He showed us samples of kerosene and alcohol obtained by distillation, leaving pitch as residue from the natural oil found in the region.

OCTOBER 16TH. OVERSEAS WOOLLEN FACTORY

This was " overseas " because its initial capital had been subscribed entirely by overseas Chinese. Three sets of machines, that had been manufactured at the science college machine shop, were powered each by one mule. After shaking and combing by these machines, the wool was farmed out to private individuals for home-spinning through a home-spinners' co-operative. Four grades of product were accepted. The factory then combined the homespun strands into knitting wool, or wove it into material on their hand-operated looms. In the past the factory had been turning out large numbers of rugs and carpets, but those lines had been discontinued in favour of a big programme of re-clothing the entire army and government personnel for the winter.

On a war-time programme, the workers were doing ten hours a day, including two hours' study. All food, clothes and medical supplies were provided plus between four and five thousand local dollars a month for pocket money.

The raw wool came from Inner Mongolia, under Prince Teh Wang, with whom the Communists maintained close diplomatic relations to prevent his going over to the Japanese.

OCTOBER 19TH. A CHEMICAL SOAP FACTORY

This was the co-operative soap factory that had been started by Rewi Alley as part of the Chinese Industrial Co-operatives. After the New Fourth Army Incident, all connection with the parent organisation had had to cease.

The factory was turning out two grades of soap, for toilet use and laundry purposes ; also an alkaline tooth-powder and purified table salt. For the soap they were using ox fat ; the free samples they gave us proved quite good for Bill's bi-weekly shave.

OCTOBER 19TH. THE LÜ HSÜN ACADEMY OF ARTS

This arts academy was in the same village as the soap factory, but no visible connection with it : our impression was that a closer liaison with the soap factory would have benefited the arts.

President Chou Yang, one of Lü Hsün's most brilliant pupils —according to his colleagues' statement—entertained us with a most lavish lunch. The President did not impress us with his artistic personality ; the emphasis seemed to be Bohemian in the extreme, and we have a prejudice against that extreme : maybe we misjudged him.

After the meal we were shown around the caves where the college academicians were living : the advanced students were all out on their terrace spinning wool. One of them interrupted his work (spare-time) to show us a full-sized portrait of Mao Tse-tung that he was getting ready for an exhibition. It was an excellent likeness, no doubt, but in the nature of what we would call a " potboiler ". Down below the hillside were some regular buildings, and in one of the courtyards a mothers' group was knitting baby garments. In another were a number of girls cutting out and sewing winter clothes for themselves, and a team of boys, also arts students, were doing coolie work nearby on the foundations of a new building that was going to be their dining-hall. We were told that the majority of boys were out on the hillside gathering the autumn harvests. The academy had succeeded in making itself almost self-sufficient both in food and clothing, required practically no assistance from the tax-payer, and no fees from the students, of whom there were one thousand, including two hundred girls.

We had to take for granted the high quality of the creative artistic work of the academy, for we had seen the excellent dramatic production of its graduates. But we wondered how much time for real study the students were now getting, apart from their labours for self-sufficiency ; and it was not reassuring to find their big outside convenience the most disgustingly dirty in all Yenan. We do not imagine that " contact with the masses " as pictured by Lü Hsün in Shanghai need involve such slovenliness in personal habits.

OCTOBER 21ST. CENTRAL PRINTING PRESS AND LIBERATION NEWS

Stock-room of the Central Press was in a huge rock cavern overlooking the ruins of Yenan city ; its walls were one great mass of tiny carved Buddhas. The site had once been a " Ten Thousand Buddhas Temple " ; we approached it from the river valley by a long winding paved staircase cut from the solid cliff face. It was amusing to realise that here was one of the most powerful of revolutionary forces in the Orient at work in the very arms of Buddha.

Among the stone tablets and memorial murals in another cave, a Peking Union Medical College nurse was supervising the workers' clinic, where three hundred employees of the Press received free treatment and medical care.

In another cave we were introduced to the manager of the printing shop. He had been an employee of the Commercial Press in

Shanghai, and had taken part in the workers' uprisings in that cit to welcome the National Revolutionary Army under Chian Kai-shek, but was lucky enough to have made his escape from th white terror that had ensued. Most of his friends in Shangha had been shot.

The *Yenan Daily*, published by this Press, was a heavily sub sidised sheet. The paper alone cost four times the subscription Paper shortage forced them to limit the circulation to seven thousan copies, distributed only to important organisations and local govern ment offices throughout the region. It was the only newspape published in the region, and while there was no law against, fo example, an opposition paper, there was no other press, and n more paper available, so that in practice any opposition would fin it troublesome to start one.

We saw their listening stations, with special receivers tuned tc intercept all the better-known international news services, including Reuters, Tass and Domei. Their own broadcast news service under the call-sign CSR, was also operated from here, and al inter-regional news systems for the front areas in North China We were particularly thrilled to see a schedule in progress with the offices of the *Hopei Daily News* ; evidently things were stil proceeding normally over there in spite of the Japanese offensive.

OCTOBER 23RD. CENTRAL HOSPITAL AND CHILDREN'S HOME

This was one of our most enjoyable days. Lunch with the staff was like old times in Peiping. Head of the pediatrics ward was a former girl student of ours at Yenching who had completed her medical degree work at the Peking Union Medical College and the Shanghai Medical College. All the staff lived in caves in the same mountain as the hospital wards.

It was called colloquially the "Ten Storeys Hospital" because it occupies a whole loess mountain face with ten terraces of caves. Founded in September 1939, this hospital had been staffed with experts from outside, and gradually extended until it now included medical, surgical, pharmaceutical, "E.N.T.", "OBS.", "GYN." and "PED." departments, isolation and "T.B." wards, a dental clinic and an "O.P.D.", altogether there were 150 beds.

Medical services were entirely without cost to the patients, and there were no class distinctions, each patient theoretically receiving the best possible treatment for his particular disease. Regular

PLATE XVI

Top left
General Mao Tse-tung, Leader of the Chinese Communist Party.

Top right
General Chou En-lai, Deputy Leader of the Chinese Communist Party.

Bottom left
General Chu Teh, Commander of the Chinese Communist Armies.

Bottom right
General Ho Lung, smoking pipe given to him by Major Carlson.

ill, soft and liquid, diets included milk, eggs, and sugar, all difficult
to obtain in the region. There was a babies' playground near
the summit of the mountain, and a babies' room in two caves
where we saw twenty-one infants all born at the hospital during
the previous two weeks—they had an average delivery rate of
fifty a month.

But the hospital's troubles were not all little ones. Several
truck-loads of medical equipment and supplies that had been sent
to them from abroad were, they said, being held up in Sian, on
some pretext or other by the blockade authorities : these included
indispensable laboratory equipment and X-ray replacements.
Nothing had been received from outside the Border Region for
over a year. They were functioning under very difficult conditions and were in desperate need of supplies. The dental clinic
in particular, at which Bill had several nerves removed to save three
teeth, they were running short of dental cement and amalgam,
and their drills were almost all worn blunt. Except in special cases,
all the dentist could do was to make extractions ; even so he was
attending to something like fifty patients a week in addition to
training a class of dental students. Trained in Singapore, the
dentist could easily have made a comfortable living in any of the
port cities under the Japanese regime.

We discovered later that medical supplies in general, and dental
supplies in particular, were in exceeding short supply everywhere
—reserved for armed forces all over the world—and to blame the
Yenan shortage on the blockade would be, to say the least, exceedingly controversial. Nevertheless stuff had been sent to them,
according to the people in the know at Chungking ; and according
to the intended recipients, they had not been received, and they
were feeling bitter about it. We trust that transport conditions
have since improved sufficiently to allow this little cause of friction
to have been smoothed out.

The children's home was on the next mountain beyond the
Ten Storey Hospital. Neat rows of stone-faced caves and clean-
swept playground terraces thronged with happy, laughing children
welcome the visitor. Founded by Madame Chiang Kai-shek,
whose portrait hung in various conspicuous places about the home,
this institution was, said the matron, unique throughout the Border
Region in that it was not entirely cut off from the rear by the blockade. They were still receiving something like 10 per cent. of the

cash needed for running expenses from Madame Chiang, in son
what irregular and unpredictable amounts.

In the home were 260 children, between the ages of one a
six. There were forty teachers, several cooks and laundrym
Children were from busy parents all over North China, many
war duties at the front. Modern psychological methods of d
cipline by kindness were being practised ; the teachers eviden
were in love with their work and the children. In line with t
campaign for self-sufficiency the teachers were creating for the
selves the toys and equipment needed for their classes : dolls, pictu
books, illustrated stories, building blocks, mechanical plaything
were all being made in the teachers' spare time. Lack of ma
power among the staff was overcome, for example, by means
a co-operative transport system with the local farmers, in whi
the school provided the mules and the required capital for the farme
to enter transport business, in return for which the farmers engag
to transport free of charge all the fuel and food needed for t
school.

The children were given an excellent diet that included eg
and milk ; two resident physicians cared for mild attacks of norm
children's ailments ; the staff managed their own dairy farm ar
fruit orchards. Director and spiritual mother of the children
home, Lin Sha, had been trained in child education at Moscov
and was obviously completely absorbed in her work.

We watched the children playing games and singing nurser
rhymes ; there were one or two new arrivals, and it was enter
taining to see how awkward they were in joining these grou
activities. But there was no effort to force conformity ; it wa
left to the natural imitative instincts of the child to bring it graduall
into harmony with the group. The whole community was on
happy family in the atmosphere of which no sensitive child coul
fail to respond.

We had a ten mile walk to get back to the guest house befor
dark ; on the way we could not help thinking that up there in thos
caves was something significant for China's future as a peace-loving
nation.

NOVEMBER 7TH TO 30TH. YENAN FAIR

The annual fair was staged on the wide open flats in the river
bed just below the foot of the guest house hill ; our terrace was

ke a grand-stand for the whole show. Over two hundred stalls
ere arranged in two lanes, and on the far side, facing towards us,
as an open-air stage for mass meetings and entertainments.

To this "Lo-ma-ta-hui", literally "Mule-horse-big-meet",
me merchants from all over the Border Region, and long caravans
om Mongolia selling ponies, wool and furs. In the three weeks
f the fair over 150 million local dollars worth of business was
one in local manufactures, home crafts, live-stock, food, grain,
lt, and a sprinkling of goods smuggled through the blockade
o the south.

The formal opening of the fair was held in celebration of the
uccess of the Three Powers Conference, and of the October
evolution. And after that there was drama practically every
ight : local classical drama by a Yenan amateur team, folk dances
y students of the Lü Hsün Academy, Peking drama by a profes-
onal troupe. The folk dances were specially interesting and
ntertaining : original compositions depicting the conversion of
n idler, the adventures of a refugee from Honan, and the detection
f a Kuomintang sabotage agent, village scenes and family life—
oming to the fair, and so on, in which the arts boys and girls suc-
eeded in expressing to their audience some modern progressive
deas through a popular traditional medium of public amusement.

The various leaders of the region, including Mao, Chu, Lin
Tsu-han, Chou En-lai, and others, paid informal visits to the fair
grounds, mingling with the crowds in a casual way, accompanied
by the most meagre of body-guards and an entire absence of
ceremony. One afternoon we were taking a stroll down the lane
of stalls and accidentally ran into General Chu Teh and Chief of
Staff Yeh ; from a distance we had not been able to tell anyone
unusual was at the fair. General Yen Hsi-shan of Shansi had sent
a special representative, partly to the fair, partly for more important
business, and this officer was accommodated in the guest house for
wo weeks. In his flashy uniform he was the only conspicuous
military figure in the Border Region at the time.

NOVEMBER 15TH AND 16TH. PARTY SYSTEM EXHIBITION

In a specially erected pavilion, some few miles north-west of
Yenan, the Chinese Communist Party headquarters held an ex-
hibition of hobbies and produce of their self-sufficiency drive.
The walls were bedecked with statistical charts and propaganda

pictures. Their shelves were laden with exhibits of great interes
Here was a display of the monthly supplies given to each part
worker, compared with previous years ; they showed great increase
Present monthly totals were $37\frac{1}{2}$ lb. of vegetables, $33\frac{1}{4}$ lb. of mille
$1\frac{1}{2}$ lb. of pork, 15 oz. of cooking fats. Self-production supplemente
this basis, which was still very short on meat.

Some modern style furniture was being made by party worke
in their spare time ; it seemed most incongruous out there amon
the loess caves, but its spirit was certainly one of buoyant optimisr
and its artistic quality was very high.

According to the wall displays, their breeding of cattle, pig
and sheep, had netted the headquarters a year's profit of nine millio
local dollars ; other projects altogether yielding ten million dollar:
Nearly half of this had been spent on clothing for the workers, th
rest invested in local enterprises.

NOVEMBER 16TH AND 17TH. MILITARY SYSTEM EXHIBITION

This was in the same valley as the exhibition of the party system
and we proceeded to an introductory inspection after completing
our second tour of the party exhibition.

According to their statistics, the military headquarters at Yena
had made four times as much profit from their self-supporting
drive as claimed by the party headquarters. One-third of the
amount had been spent on extra food.

Their displays were similar in general, with those of the party
but their artistic styles were quite distinct. Of special interes
was their exhibit of small tools that they had made themselves,
fire-arms, footwear, refractory products, drugs (including morphine
and novococaine). Nowhere else in the world could an army
claim so little economic dependence upon the civilian population
for its daily wants.

NOVEMBER 19TH. YENAN LOCAL CIVIL SERVICE EXHIBITION

A brand new set of caves hewn out of solid rock in the base of
the hills facing Yenan from the east, intended later as a permanent
site for a museum of local history, were formally opened for the
Civil Service Exhibition ; and under this head our host institution,
the Government Guest House, was included.

The total profits for the year's self-production campaign were
only four millions, made chiefly out of growing cabbages. One

epartment was more than 100 per cent. self-supporting, six touched
00 per cent., three were over 85 per cent., seven over 50 per cent.
nd three less than 50 per cent. The guest house was bottom :
ll the staff were too busy looking after the guests, and the guests
vere not producing at all—we were all idlers within the meaning
f the act !

The staff of the Yenan University had an excellent record :
43 people spun 503 lb. of wool and knitted 1139 lb. of woollen
arments. The children's home exhibition was a great attraction.
All manner of toys, dolls, baby clothes, and a child's dress made
rom material sent by Madame Chiang as part of a gift to China
rom Mrs. Roosevelt.

NOVEMBER 26TH. WELCOME MEET FOR LABOUR HEROES

This was held on the open-air stage at the fair. Over two
hundred champions (literally heroes) elected from all over the
Border Region for excelling in all kinds of productive labour.
Planting, ploughing, spinning, weaving, bringing up a family, men
and women peasants, rough folk with great characters and simple
minds, in whom the dignity of labour was inspiringly personified.

These labour heroes, elected by their fellow villagers, had come
to Yenan as guests of the government, were now being invited to
attend a series of conferences with the government leaders in which
plans were to be drawn up for the further increase in agricultural
production during the following year.

NOVEMBER 27TH AND 28TH. GENERAL BORDER REGION EXHIBITION

Here were exhibits showing the work of the labour champions
throughout the Border Region. Pictures and charts showed the
daily lives and achievements of the farmers. Interesting salt samples
from the lake deposits ; fine cloth ; cotton, raw and spun ; paper
products ; silk-worm cocoons ; and fine silk materials ; woollen
goods, including rugs, blankets, carpets ; leather goods ; iron and
silver ores ; oils and waxes and pitch, coal and charcoal ; prize
vegetables, corn and millet, sugar beet that was just beginning to
come on the market.

According to the wall-paper statistics the Border Region was
already 70 per cent. self-sufficient in cloth, 84 per cent. in paper,
100 per cent. in oil, coal, iron, wood, and food except for sugar.
Two million sheep were being reared in the region.

DECEMBER 3RD. EXHIBIT OF THE NANYIWAN BRIGADE

This brigade of the Eighth Route Army, formerly garrison
at Suiteh, had, two years before, been assigned a stretch of virg
land sufficient for a self-supporting community, and plans we
drawn up for the brigade to become completely independent
outside support. Here we saw the story of their success. The
had gone in and cleared away the brushwood, built themselv
cave quarters, farm buildings and factories. They were now pr
ducing everything for their own needs; clothing, footwear, foo
soap, medicines, machinery and tools, arms and equipment, tobacc
coal (from their own mine), bred animals for farm labour, foo
and transport. With the profit from the sale of surplus produc
they were able to buy such materials as were not available in the
own grounds such as salt and oil, and iron ore.

OCTOBER 28TH. TASS AGENT

A few days ago we were offered a new room on a higher terrac
with a more southerly aspect. We were waiting only for th
expected departure of its present occupants, and yesterday they lef
We were up there this morning, had just arranged the bed-boar
and were standing on the terrace admiring the view when a hug
twin-engined plane zoomed low over our heads skimming the top
of the hills and dropped down into the valley just beyond Yenar
About half the guests panicked, rushed for the caves thinking
was a Japanese attack; the others recognised the plane as Russian
It landed on the airfield north-west of the old city; and an hou
later we were given notice to make our change of room at once
two or three officers of the National Army who had come in th
plane were to be accommodated in our former room for the night
This naturally started a lot of interesting speculation. Ha
the Russians been doing something to help smooth out the troubl
between the Communists and the Nationalists? Had they brough
representatives to start negotiations? In any case the fact tha
the Nationalist authorities had permitted a Russian plane to come t
Yenan, whether via Lanchow or Chungking, it was a sign that th
crisis was definitely easing. These speculations were somewha
chilled by the official information that the plane had brought onl
a new Tass agent, and would take away the previous representative
the Kuomintang officers were merely coming as security inspector
to keep an eye on the plane and the travellers.

But the mention of Tass News agents made us ask Wang how they got their news out. He said :

" By the Post Office telegraph system to Chungking, most probably."

" What! Can we send ordinary telegrams to Chungking from here ? "

" Yes, of course! But you must remember that the Post Office here is run by the Kuomintang secret service agents ; nothing you send will be private once it gets into their hands."

We wondered how much more private anything was in the hands of the Communists, for that matter. The Chinese Post Office was an institution in which we had the most profound trust, and for which no praise can be too high for the way it has handled its business in war-time. But of course war-time censorship in any country would involve the inspection of letters written by foreign nationals, and no doubt Wang was correct in his statement though unfair in his implication.

Somehow that airplane, coming in out of the blue, and flashing away again next morning, made us feel homesick for Western civilisation. Let's get going! We might almost have made an urgent appeal for a " lift " with the Tass man, but we had not in fact been told that such a man existed in Yenan until that moment ; and after all there was a lot to be done before we could safely proceed, even if a plane passage were available : the people in Chungking did not even know yet that we had arrived in Yenan.

OCTOBER 29TH.   TELEGRAMS TO CHUNGKING

We got Wang to send two telegrams for us to the Post Office ; one for the British Embassy in Chungking and one to Yenching University in Chengtu, announcing our safe arrival in Yenan and our intention eventually to proceed to Szechuan and Chungking.

NOVEMBER 4TH

Those telegrams were the first definite move we had made in preparation for the journey south, and our hosts were quick to recognise our intentions. To-day we had a call from Chou En-lai. He brought us news that the two Westerners who had gone through to Sian that summer had been placed under arrest in that city. He strongly advised us to wait at least for a definite invitation from either our University or from the Embassy, so that we could be sure that formal permission might be received from the Kuomintang for our journey to be unmolested by the authorities in Sian. Chou En-lai also promised to get in touch with the Chungking people through his party office in that city, via the Eighth Route Army radio. He thought we should plan to stay in Yenan at least until the end of November to make sure the crisis had blown over and our journey be perfectly safe.

NOVEMBER 26TH. MORE TELEGRAMS

To-day we received a letter from Chou En-lai stating that from his wireless station in Chungking he had received a message to the effect that the people in Chengtu regretted being unable to invite Bill to teach there at the present time because his name had become too Red. Negotiations were, however, proceeding through the Embassy with the National authorities, and it was confidently hoped that a *modus vivendi* would soon be worked out.

We thought this might be a hint from Chengtu that political conditions there were such that our presence would embarrass them; we had heard all the Communists' tales of corruption and Fascist tendencies in Chungking, but had written them off as so much anti-Kuomintang propaganda, but this seemed to lend colour to those stories. Anyhow, whether the message had been doctored up by the Communists to keep us quiet, or whether it was a genuine indicator of conditions in the south-west, it was clear that there was nothing we could do about it but await developments and sort out the facts when we got through.

DECEMBER 8TH

On this second anniversary of our escape from Peiping, we received another letter from Chou En-lai stating that his wireless had received a message from the British Embassy to the effect that permission had been received from the National authorities for us to travel through to Chungking, and that details of the journey were now being arranged. Meanwhile we were encouraged not to worry.

Good work! We wonder how long it will take for the details to be worked out, whatever they could be, and whether the Embassy will send us a direct Post Office telegram in confirmation.

DECEMBER 15TH

Good news! A Post Office telegram was brought to us signed by Ralph Lapwood, Acting Dean of the Science College at

Chengtu : " WELCOME TO FREE CHINA. TRAVEL FUNDS AWAIT YOU AT THE ——— MISSION SIAN. ADVISE PROCEED CHUNGKING FIRST ".

But we were still concerned over the fact that we had nothing tangible of this kind from the Embassy that we could show to the inspectors at the boundary of the Kuomintang areas. So we asked Chou En-lai to try and send a message through his wireless asking the Embassy to send us a Post Office telegram confirming the former message, and Chou agreed to do so.

DECEMBER 21ST.   CELEBRATIONS

We were growing more and more impatient. To-day we had a visit from Chou En-lai and General Nieh to chat about the coming journey. They suggested that we could hope to proceed in about a week, by which time the desired message from the Embassy should have arrived. They would arrange for a truck to take us as far as the border. But in any case they urged, we should celebrate Christmas and New Year with them at Yenan!

DECEMBER 25TH

Still no further word from Chungking. But we had a marvellous Christmas party at the guest house, followed by a special showing of their movie of the Nanyiwan Self-sufficient Brigade in the guest house reception room. We were at this time informed that Mao Tse-tung was arranging to see us after the New Year, so we must stay at least another week and pass the New Year with them.

JANUARY 1ST

Still no more word. A whole week of impatience. There was a light fall of snow which, coming on New Year's Day, was considered locally as a good omen for the spring crop. There was a great feast in the reception room of the guest house for the residents, and a special drama at the congress auditorium in the evening.

JANUARY 6TH.   FAREWELL TO YENAN

We finally got so impatient that we decided not to wait a moment longer ; we would proceed as soon as possible even though there was no further message from the Embassy. We

realised, of course, that we must wait long enough for the Kuomintang officers on our route to receive instructions from headquarters
concerning our safe passage, but this time we felt had now passed.
Everyone on the line must surely be waiting for us ; if we waited
any longer they would think we had been up to some tricks in
Yenan. So we sent a message to Chou En-lai to-day, asking that
arrangements be made at once for our departure at the earliest
possible moment.

JANUARY 7TH

The effect of our message yesterday was electrical. Reply
came early this morning that we must visit the Army Peace Hospital,
founded by Dr. Bethune—this same morning, and that there would
be a farewell party for us this evening. Then all we would have
to do would be to wait a day or two for a truck to be making a
trip towards the boundary.

A special truck took us out to the Peace Hospital. It began to
snow just after we had started out. We found the hospital very
much like the Ten Storey Hospital, though there were only five
departments : medical, surgical, isolation, obstetrics and gynæ-
cology, and outpatients' departments. There were 160 beds in
the caves, a good baby room (cave) in which an average of seventy-
five infants were delivered a year. They had a brick building for
an operating theatre. Five Western-trained doctors headed the
departments. Four tons of supplies addressed to them were said
to have been held up by the Sian authorities ; nothing had come
through to them since 1941.

On our return trip to Yenan the snow was wonderfully beautiful,
but we could see that if the fall continued much longer, the road
south would be impassable. What the failure of the telegram could
not do, the weather could ; we should be held up again much against
our will.

That evening the snow lay five inches thick on the ground
when General Chou En-lai, General Nieh, Chief of Staff Yeh,
Miss Tang and Huang Hua and the guest house manager, Mr. Chin,
welcomed us at the reception room for the evening meal. We
shall never forget that last repast.

Outside there was a good old-fashioned Christmas atmosphere
that had relaxed for a moment our nervous tension. But this was
a farewell ; we were taking another step into the unknown. If

we could make the critical stage of the journey at the "blockade", we should be through to Chungking, and then home for England! But we hardly dared to think that far ahead. One step at a time. Whatever happens we shall somehow find the right way to go. But the uncertainties were exciting.

Chou En-lai was nervously talkative throughout the meal; he tried to make us drink a special brand of pear wine, drank plenty himself. General Nieh was morose and thoughtful. We got a feeling that both men were genuinely apprehensive for our safety and reacting in opposite ways.

As they were preparing to leave, Chou En-lai became almost too talkative; yet he avoided all mention of our journey, neither did he discuss the telegram that had not come from Chungking. General Nieh, on the other hand, seemed really upset. In Hopei when he said good-bye to us it had been a happy farewell: he had known, of course, that we would be meeting him again. This time he seemed to think it would be for ever. Even our most hearty "See you again in Peiping!" failed to raise a smile. Grasping our hands in both of his he exclaimed with deep emotion: "Good-bye! And God bless you!"

Chapter XVII

NATIONALISTS' WELCOME

ALTHOUGH the farewell party had been on January 7th, we did not actually leave Yenan until January 11th; traffic was held up by the snow. While we were waiting, Chairman Lin Tsu-han sent over to us as gifts four pounds of knitting wool, two woollen blankets, an exhibition corn-cob about a foot in length, samples of woollen material, a set of photographs, a bundle of roots which were some kind of precious medicinal herb, and $5000 national currency to cover our travel expenses to Sian. We still have the excellent woollen blankets as a memento of Yenan's home products. Chairman Lin's hospitality was overwhelming, and we cannot adequately express our indebtedness to him.

On Monday the truck for which we had been waiting was able to come into Yenan from the outpost where it had been held up by the snow, and we were told to be ready for the road on Tuesday. We sent telegrams to the British Embassy and to the University at Chengtu, not so much to inform the addressees, as to make sure that the inspectors on the road would not be caught unprepared : if they had anything they preferred us not to see, we definitely preferred not to embarrass them by coming unexpectedly. We were all for taking no chances of offending the " gestapo " even though we felt that the Communists had painted an exaggerated picture of the situation. Also we felt that by thus advertising even so flimsy a connection with the Embassy, we stood a better chance of being unmolested on the road.

The Communists had warned us that should we carry any written or printed material from their area, we should run a risk of having it confiscated by the Nationalist authorities either on the blockade line or in Sian. We might even be detained indefinitely in that city, and there were possibilities of mysterious disappearances in the deserted tract of country between the Communists and Nationalists, if, at the blockade line, we were discovered to have any information derogatory to the Nationalist plans for dominating the country. We discounted all this, but when it came to the

point, discretion seemed the better part of valour ; neither of us
was looking for unnecessary adventure.

However, we had collected much valuable information that
could not very easily be stored in one's memory. There was
our five years' diary, the collection of photographs, the story of
our adventures up to date, and a number of unique mementoes
and publications produced by the guerrillas behind the Japanese
front fighting lines ; it was all historical material ; not a word
of it was anti-Kuomintang. Moreover, we had our " Okay "
from the Chinese authorities, unofficially ; and our " contact "
with our own Embassy ; we could hardly disappear mysteriously
when our journey had been so well announced. Nor could the
" gestapo ", if it existed in fact, really do us any serious harm ;
there was nothing legally wrong about any of the stuff we had ;
it was only that petty local officials might become over-suspicious
and cause serious delays and tiresome inconvenience.

So we packed all the literature in the big mule hold-all, padding
it well with all the woollen goods that Chairman Lin had presented
to us. The bundle was horribly heavy, but so soft to the touch
that no superficial inspection could possibly reveal the nature of
its contents. The diary, the most precious of all, was lost in the
recesses of Bill's heavy over-coat pocket, on the principle dear to
mystery novelists that the more obvious the hiding-place the safer
from detection by professional spies.

In normal weather the truck should have taken us to the last
outpost in the Communist area in one day. But, while the road
had already dried out in the sunshine on the southern slopes, the
northern slopes uphill were still frozen during the morning, thawing
out each afternoon into an unclimbable slime. As it was, we had
to stop and attach chains to both back wheels before noon in order
to reach a convenient stopping place before the roads gave out.
The young man who had been sent with us from the guest house
managed the whole business of installing us at the wayside hostelry
and providing us with special fare for supper.

Next morning we were breakfasted at six, and out in the court
at seven watching the truck-driver and his mechanic thawing out
the motor with glowing charcoal. We were on the frozen road
by eight, and had reached our destination early in the morning—
last frontier village between the Communists and the Nationalists,
scene of any border incident that might break out.

This gave our manager plenty of time to arrange for a farmer and a donkey to carry our baggage across the blockade line into Kuomintang territory three miles further south. Even so he seemed to have a lot of trouble finding anyone willing to do the job. The villagers, he said, were talking about a recent incident in which the Nationalists had arrested five hundred coolies engaged in transport across the blockade, and buried them alive.

There was an army unit of about fifty men drilling in this village. The end of the lane running out of the village on to the plateau to the south, was blocked with a brick wall and a sentry box. There was a tense atmosphere about the place, but otherwise no abnormal signs. The usual strings of transport mules were passing through the village in both directions, and if there were any blockade, it did not seem to have interfered with normal farm traffic.

CROSSING THE BORDER

It was a lonely little procession that emerged from the village next morning on to the snow-covered table-land. We walked ahead, alone ; behind us came two donkeys and their owners ; that was all.

About half a mile out we passed a temple, and on the lane was an Eighth Route Army sentry who stopped us. We presented our special travel permit that had been made out for us by the military headquarters at Yenan, complete with terrific red seals and official signatures stating that we were travelling to Sian via Lochuan, and giving other personal details about our having come from Peiping. The sentry asked us to wait while he arranged for an armed escort to take us a little further on, to make sure that nothing happened to us before we came in sight of the Kuomintang sentry on the other side of the line.

In about fifteen minutes, six uniformed men with rifles came marching out of the temple, and asked us to follow them at good speed. The lane from here on was a well-worn trail cutting fairly deep into the ground. We could see nothing of the surrounding country until in about half an hour the escort called a halt, scattered along two sides and took up positions overlooking the fields to the south. We continued in some trepidation. The donkey men seemed very nervous. A few yards further on we came to a turn in the lane, and immediately came out of the cutting on to open land, and there, not a hundred yards ahead was the Kuomintang outpost.

A briar hedge stretched away on either side of the lane, and across the lane itself a barbed-wire barricade, a barbed gate overlooked by a well-built pill-box, slits for machine-guns grinning at us. The sentry was on the alert and ready for us. We wondered whether he could see the six rifle nozzles and the six pairs of eyes watching him from behind corn-stubble about fifty yards behind us. We wondered whether the man in front would shoot us and blame the Communists—or for that matter, vice versa! If either side were planning to discredit the other in the eyes of the world, here was their golden opportunity. Happy thought! We brushed it aside as preposterous.

Putting our best legs forward, we gaily hailed the sentry :

" We are English! " and as cheerfully he replied :

" Good! Pass down the lane! "

A steep clay bank on the right, clay brick wall on the left, we marched down for perhaps two hundred yards when from over the top of the wall another sentry cried " Halt! " There was a side road coming in from the left round a blind corner, on the right was a little rest-house in the clay bank. In a moment an officer and half a dozen unarmed men emerged round the corner, the soldiers shuffling hastily into the rest-house. The officer saluted us politely and we presented him our travel permit and our British passports. He politely withdrew to show the documents to his superior officer. The soldiers started talking together in hushed whispers, taking shy looks at us—specially Claire. They would not talk to us, and we were amused at the difference in attitude between these lads and the Communists, whose very first action had been to greet us personally in a friendly way. Here was more respect ; we could hardly object!

" Yes! They are English."

" How old do you think they are ? "

" Who knows ? "

" Wonder how they have travelled so far! "

" They must have had a very hard trip! "

and other things we could not quite overhear.

After about ten minutes the officer returned, gave us back all the documents with a courteous bow, and told the donkey men where to go for the baggage inspection. He used a local dialect, and we did not catch the instructions ourselves ; the officer sent no one with us, and we had to rely on the donkey men. We had not gone very far before it was apparent that they too were not at all sure of their instructions. They had been too nervous to take them in properly.

Coming to a crossing, the place widened out into a kind of village square ; there were large numbers of soldiers about, and it was obvious that what had once been a village had been turned into a very considerable army base. There did not seem to be a peasant in residence ; all the buildings had been rebuilt and fortified. Our donkey men were quite bewildered, and after discussing for a few moments, decided to take the left turn, and started looking around for the inspection station. We were all gaping in at the entrance of one of the buildings when suddenly an officer inside shouted at the top of his voice :

" You must not look in here! "

We hurriedly turned the other way, and were met with angry glares from another doorway on the opposite side of the street. This seemed to be getting unhealthy, and we urged the donkey men to make some polite inquiries instead of trying to recall their original instructions. At last we got set in the opposite direction, and soon came out of the fortified lane into an open stretch of fields, and there ahead of us we espied what seemed like a very considerable fortress complete with moat and drawbridge, outside of which were assembled a large cluster of donkeys and a group of donkey men and their loads, being inspected by several army officers. Over the fort was flying the Nationalist flag. Perhaps this was the concentration camp ? Would they open our baggage ? If so, what next ?

As we approached the edge of the crowd, the officers ceased their inspection, and approached us with friendly smiles :

" So you've come! We've been expecting you! "

" Please come inside ; you can leave your stuff out here, and we will arrange fresh animals for you to continue the journey."

We were taken into their own private rooms. As we entered the courtyard of the fortress we were astonished to see about a hundred peasants drilling, with long spears, just exactly as we had seen them drilling in Yenan. We rubbed our eyes, and looked again. Yes ! There was no mistake. The spears even had similar little red tassles tied round the neck of the blade ; and the men were running around in the court, training ; training, no doubt, for the war against Japan, same as they had been in Yenan.

Were these some of the five hundred who had been " buried alive " ?

In the officers' rooms we were refreshed with tea, and made warm with charcoal fires, and entertained by polite inquiries about our escape from Peiping, and the dangers of our journey through the Japanese lines.

We had been asked by the guest house manager to make a special request of the Kuomintang to give a return travel permit to the donkey men ; otherwise they feared they might be held. This we did, and received assurances from the officers that the return travel would certainly be without hitch. After all the stories we had heard, it was hard to let it go with these verbal assurances, but what else could we do ? We were, or at least hoped to be, welcomed as allied nationals, escaping from the Japanese, and we had thrown ourselves upon these people, uninvited ; a couple of donkeys were an inadequate reason for getting on a high horse at this stage ; nor were we going to risk the making of trouble by relaying to our new hosts the stories of atrocities that the peasants had been relating on the other side.

As these thoughts were passing through our minds the peasant army drill class broke up, and a crowd of peasant lads came tumbling in with their instructor to have a look at us ; with a polite " If you have no objection ? " from the officers. Human nature was evidently the same under both political banners.

After about half an hour the new animals were reported ready, so out we all went across the drawbridge and through the crowd of still waiting travellers. The baggage had been packed on another pair of donkeys, and there was a jolly farmer and a young boy ready to guide us on our way. It was clear that nothing had been opened for inspection. As we were saying good-bye the two coolies who had brought us across the boundary came running up beckoning with their arms, asking us if we had arranged for their return permit.

" Yes ! Yes ! It will be quite all right ! " insisted the officers.

" Please give us the permit now ! "

" Yes ! Yes ! Don't worry ! "

" Shall we wait and write out a formal request ? " asked Bill, his thoughts returning to those five hundred.

" No ! No ! That will be quite unnecessary. They had no need to be so nervous ! "

So, a little hesitatingly, we took our leave. Whether t
fellows got safely home we shall probably never know, but v
believe they did ; there would have been no sense in detainir
them.

From here on, the lane was a regular cart track, cutting throug
the high spots in the plateau, dropping zigzag down immen
canyons in the loess earth, climbing breathless slants again towar
the sky. Snow lay thinly everywhere. By three in the afternoc
we had reached the first village, five times having been held up l
roadside inspection stations through which we were passed up
showing our Yenan permit form.

Entering the village, which was leading a normal life, tl
donkey man complained of hunger, and suggested that we wou
have to get a change of animals from here.

" Why don't you buy some food here ? " we asked in reply.

" Oh! We poor civilians cannot get money! " he answered.

" Good heavens ", we thought, " how different from tl
Yenan farmers, rolling in money at this very moment ! " Bi
we refrained from audible comment. Even now we were su
picious of agents provocateur, trapping us into Communi
propaganda.

He took us to the garrison headquarters, where a soldier tol
us that the higher officer in charge was not in ; therefore he wa
sorry that a junior officer would have to be called to welcome u
It all sounded very impressive. The officer duly arrived an
started throwing his weight about to get some boiling water fc
tea.

" You know, the army makes this charcoal for itself ! " he tol
us proudly, as he tickled the fire. Then he shouted to someon
in the street :

" Comrade! Hurry here with the packet of tea! Thes
Western comrades are tired and thirsty! "

We dared make no comment on this use of the expression
we had thought a monopoly of the Communists. What was hi
little game ? And why had he called us " Western comrades "

When we were sipping tea, the fellow started conversatio
something on these lines :

" Did you see Chairman Mao Tse-tung ? "

" Yes ", we replied in as offhand way as possible.

" And Commander-in-Chief Chu Teh ? "

" Yes."

" Well, how about them ? "

" They were all very polite to us ! "

" Good men, aren't they ? " he suggested.

To that we made no comment, but smiled non-committally. was now obvious, from his use of the formal titles used only mong the Communists, that he had been instructed to create a omradely impression, to counteract or contrast with the atmophere on the north side of the border. Unfortunately for him, his fforts were a bit overdone. He found difficulty in keeping it up vithout encouragement from us, and presently busied himself bout our further transport, shouting for comrade this or comrade hat to arrange for animals for our remaining ten-mile journey.

When we left the village, we found ourselves with a long rain of mules returning empty to Lochuan, after having delivered harcoal to the garrison. Two of them had been allocated to our se. The men were in good spirits, but the going was nevertheless lower than our normal walking speed, and it was a good six o'clock efore we arrived outside the town, and it was getting quite dark.

We were afraid the city gates might be closed. And as we eached the walls, the mule men informed us that their train would ot enter the gates, but be looked after by their usual hostelry vhich was not far away. In fact the road took us right p to the gates, and the whole party was going blithely by, arrying our baggage with it. They took no notice of our urgent eminder that they were supposed to deliver us safely with the ounty magistrate, and in the end Bill took matters into his own ands, grabbed the rope leads from both animals and forcibly removed them from the train, and marched them in through the city ates. No one stopped us, although there were armed guards in lenty. We asked them the way to the county magistrate's offices, nd received courteous instructions. Whether the mule men ollowed or not we did not care, but we found the seat of authority nd presented our Yenan permit to the guard at the gates, asking, s we had been advised in Yenan, for the Counties' Supervisor, ne Mr. Yü.

LOCHUAN TO YAOHSIEN

The seat of the county government was a typical courtyard urrounded by ornamental buildings with deep overhanging eaves, shaded by great conifers, paved with huge slabs of stone, neatly laid out with pebble walks. The main building facing the formal entrance structure was tastefully furnished and beautifully decorated and we were ushered into an entertaining room that evidently served also as an office. A highly polished lacquer-topped desk stood in the centre of one end of the room, and hard-wood chairs arranged around it in a business-like manner. The atmosphere reminded us of our old Peiping days; and when Mr. Yü came in, with his warmly solicitous welcome, we felt that at last the hazards of the border crossing were now bad dreams of the past.

We had a pleasant chat for about half an hour with Mr. Yü although conversation was on a restricted scale due to language limitations. Then, evidently in response to a special message, two inspectors arrived, one in the usual long grey gown of the Chinese civilian, the other in a Sun Yat-sen uniform as worn in schools. The latter proved to be an interpreter. The four of us had supper together, served in the office, Mr. Yü excusing himself on matters of personal business—he had already eaten before we arrived.

After examining our passports and the Yenan travel permit, the two inspectors subjected us to a long string of questions about our escape, what we had been doing and why we had spent so long a time in the guerrilla areas, whether we had been entertained by the Communist leaders, what were our impressions of everything and everybody, how things compared up there with what we saw here, and so on and so forth. It was all done most courteously, and in so friendly a way that it was, of course, easy to imagine that there was no ulterior motive in their minds. Yet we knew well enough that they were trying us out on what were in fact to them red-hot political issues. We had to be exceedingly careful in our answers to stick to the truth, because, of course, they knew all the essential facts as well as we did, and at the same time not to appear in the least bit interested in politics; and above all to appear happily unconcerned and innocent over the whole process.

By about ten p.m. they seemed to be satisfied, said good night, and left instructions for a board bed to be made up for us at the other end of the same room. "Thought examination" notwithstanding, we had a good night's sleep. Next morning the two inspectors had breakfast with us, and while we were waiting for transport to be arranged, we were invited to give an address

o the boys of the local middle school, at which school the interpreter was a teacher of English. This was surely a sign that we had
passed our examination ; topic of the address was about Japanese-
occupied Peiping, not about guerrilla warfare.

Mr. Yü had arranged for a rubber-tyred cart to take us on the
next three days' trip. Each night we were to stop at a county
town, and he gave us a letter of introduction to each of the county
magistrates. This brought us to the edge of his supervisory district,
and the last magistrate would pass us on to the next district. There
were to be no charges : we were guests of the government.

The interpreter accompanied us to the south gate of the town,
and told us a little of his own personal story. He had been converted to Christianity in Peiping, and had worked with British
missionaries in country districts in Hopei. We asked him if he
could tell us where in Sian we could make contact with British
missionaries, and he gave us the address of the Mission.

The next three days were most enjoyable. The cart with its
old bus-wheels made a good four miles an hour, and was a most
comfortable means of transport. We arranged our bedding rolls
in such a way that we could recline at a luxurious angle and watch
the snow-decked rolling country slide smoothly by. There were
two carts ; they belonged to a private transport company—
consisting of our carter and his three mules. There was a hired
man to watch the second cart. The company was doing a regular
transport business between Yaohsien and Lochuan, carrying grain
to the troops garrisoned at Lochuan.

We did thirty miles a day, spending ten hours each day on the
road, jumping off for a walk whenever we felt so inclined ; thrilled
with the stimulating sunshine and bracing air, and the great expanse
of undulating plateau gleaming white in gentle snow.

Each night we were entertained right royally by the magistrate,
were cross-examined by another inspector in an equally polite
but rather less thorough manner. Our carter was hugely impressed by our reception after the first day's journey. The second
morning conversation started as soon as we got out of town :

" I heard you were entertained by the magistrate last night !
Am I right ? " he asked us.

" Yes. He was very good to us ", we replied.

" How fine ! You must have had a real feast, with plenty of
meat dishes ? "

"That's right! We had meat, vegetables, mantou and ric and soup. It was a delicious meal!"

"How about the morning meal?"

"It was almost the same. What about you?"

"Oh! Just a few bing—you know, the usual; ordinary fol cannot eat like the county magistrate!"

As we passed through the next village, the carter hailed an ol crony of his at a roadside stall:

"These people were entertained by the hsien magistrate la night! I've an important commission this trip! They're goin to the hsien magistrate at Lichun to-night, and he'll have a mea feast ready for them!"

"Ah! Yah! Curse his mother! How much are you makin on the commission?"

But the carrier was not being trapped into giving away trad secrets; with a gay laugh he cracked his whip and jumped u again on his seat at the base of the shaft.

At noon we treated the two men to lunch, and it made them a happy as larks. It was the first time we had been able to offe gratuities in two years; and in a way we felt more at home i this old world atmosphere of class distinctions and private enter prise; although we seemed to have landed "butter side up" o either ground.

Every village and town through which our route took us wa thoroughly fortified; most of them surrounded by trenches anc block-houses. The whole plateau was dotted with stone fortresses and while these were undoubtedly relics of the earlier civil war and mostly seemed to have been abandoned, the village fortification were kept in excellent order. There were occasional gangs o raggedly dressed troops on transport or trench-digging operations and all along the road dozens of well-dressed officers in fur cap and padded greatcoats. There must have been a corresponding host of "other ranks", but they were not in evidence on the main road.

In striking contrast with the character of the Border Region' preparations for guerrilla warfare, these garrisons were holding strategic strong points over a wide zone some hundred miles in depth; it was the same strategy as that used by the Japanese in defence against the guerrillas in Hopei, a strategy which the Japanese had claimed was the most reliable foundation for successful

ffensive action against the Communists. This obvious com-
arison between the Kuomintang and the Japanese was most dis-
essing to us.

The main road along which we were travelling was practically
eady for motor traffic ; only about two bridges were incomplete.
lready long trains of heavily loaded mule carts were trundling
orth, carrying grain to feed the troops, which were evidently
ather more numerous than could be supported on the locally grown
orn. We met at least thirty cart-loads each day, four, five or six
nules per cart, representing a daily delivery of some twenty tons
f flour, enough food for forty thousand men. That was small
n comparison with the million men claimed by the Communists
o be stationed in the blockade zone, but how many were being
ocally supplied is anybody's guess.

On the steeper gradients there were some free-lance muleteers
loing a ferry business ; hitching their teams on ahead of the
egular animals to help draw the overloaded vehicles to the top.
t the foot of the hill, awaiting the extra help, was a congestion
f traffic, a peaceful smoking of pipes, stamping of hoofs, and an
ccasional wheezy, long drawn-out bray. On the up gradient,
he violent cursing of the drivers, sharp cracking of whips. Coming
lown towards us, the piercing shrieks from wooden brake-blocks.
t one bend, a carcass of a mule had been cut up, the greater part
f its flesh carried off for meat.

Our own carter was independent of the ferry business. He
vas carrying no load besides us and our tiny bundles, and his
hird mule was hitched first to one and then to the other cart, hauling
hem one at a time up the steeper stretches of the road. This third
nimal was a pitiable creature. It had a comic limp in one hind
eg, and was skeleton thin. After hauling the first cart to the top,
it would come trotting down all alone, trailing the ropes in the
dust behind it, nose in the air, and teeth snarling. At times it
seemed so enthusiastic that the fat mule in the shafts appeared to
be half asleep by contrast. But when the job was done, the halt
animal would collapse on the road, roll over on its back and refuse
to budge.

Once or twice the men succeeded in catching the mule before
the collapse, and held it up until the fit had passed. But once it
remained practically unconscious for so long that special treatment
was considered necessary. From among some dirty rags in the

back of the cart the men produced a long needle. With this they punctured the skin of the prostrate animal in a number of places: the ears, end of its tongue, just above the hoofs, and the tip of it tail. After a few moments during which a little thick blood oozed from the various punctures, the poor creature jerked into activity struggled to its feet and was off at the pull for all it was worth.

Our third day was spent winding down off the plateau, in a beautiful narrow valley. Where this widened out on to the rolling plains north of Sian we came to a small coal town called Tungkuan. The name is easily confused with that of the great strategic centre at the bend of the Yellow River to the east of Sian ; this town is slightly west of a line directly north from Sian. A standard guage railway connects Tungkuan with Yaohsien, thirty miles nearer Sian ; and although the carter was continuing next day to Yaohsien, we had been advised to secure a ticket for the guard's van on the daily coal train. The line had been built too recently to be marked on any of the latest maps. One of the Communists had hinted darkly to us that the railway's real purpose was military ; that the coal at Tungkuan was not worth a railway. Our observations do not bear out these suspicions. There were immense stacks of fuel all round the station, gravity operated narrow-guage haulage systems were bringing it in continuously. The train that we saw coming up from Yaohsien was crowded with civilian passengers. The train we went down in was loaded with coal, and third-class passengers were sitting on top.

We had said good-bye to the carters the previous evening. The magistrate had offered to telephone to Yaohsien to make sure the magistrate there would be ready to receive us, but we had requested rather that a letter of introduction be written for us to carry : an addressed envelope is a handy thing to have in a strange town. Armed with this we presented ourselves at the Tungkuan station-master's office early in the morning, the magistrate first having telephoned there to make sure that passage would be available.

The station-master was disinclined to sell us tickets, and anyway he could give no definite time for the train ; it was not nearly loaded up yet ; in fact there was no guarantee that a train would leave at all that day. By this time, of course, our jolly carter had already left, so we had nothing to do but sit on the baggage in the sunshine and watch the world go by—or perhaps it would be better to say that we were watched by the world standing around. It was three in the afternoon before we got on board, and even then we had had to wait for our tickets until the station-master had ushered some special friends of his into the guard's van. We were lucky to be able to squeeze in at all. The actual trip took only two hours. At the station outside the walls of Yaohsien we were able to hire a wooden barrow to carry the baggage, and as we struggled through the crowds on the main street through the city gates, we had not gone more than about two hundred yards before we met the carter himself—he had beaten the coal train by about half an hour, and we could have had a much pleasanter trip had we been content to stay with him instead of rushing for the train.

As we had left the station we had been accosted by a couple of young louts in long gowns and soft slouch hats, living images of the caricatures of secret service agents presented by the Lü Hsün academicians in their Yenan folk dances. With an unpleasant leer they had demanded of us :

" Foreigners ! What are you doing here ? "

" We are going to the hsien magistrate."

" What are you, missionaries, business people ? "

" It's not your business! " replied Bill, and we had pushed on. Official examination we could not prevent ; after all there was a war on! But at all costs we intended to avoid being bullied by casual adventurers of that unhealthy type. With an uneasy laugh they had slouched away.

The magistrate's staff at Tungkuan had been happily efficient in caring for us the night before, and at the same time exceedingly busy with their office work. There was an air of progressive activity about the place quite different from the dignified pomposity at the two previous yamen ; and there had been no trace of a " thought examination " ; the industrial revolution had caught Tungkuan and its leaders had more important things to think about than the puerile nonsense of the political cliques.

RAILWAY PANTOMIME

At Yaohsien the magistrate was not available ; his secretary was distressfully flustered by our unexpected arrival. He was very sorry, he said, that we had not arranged for a telephone message from Tungkuan. However, he had an excellent meal ready for us in less than half an hour, and shortly after that we were asleep ; there was no one to examine us here either—until morning.

It was then that we realised why the secretary had been so annoyed that he had not been warned by telephone.

We had to be down at the station before breakfast, and when we got there, found the train still locked up. While we were waiting on the platform a smart young man in military uniform came bouncing up to us :

" Good morning, Mrs. Band! Good morning, Professor! "

" Good morning! How do you do ? " we answered ; we did not recognise him, but it pays to be courteous.

" I hope you had a good sleep last night! " he asked, gushingly.

" Yes, thank you! "

" Very sorry, but we called on you yesterday evening and found you were already in bed," he said.

" Oh! We were very tired from the journey and slept early."

" Last year, when the American banker came through from Peiping, we talked with him all night long ! "

" Well, it is too bad we missed it! " said we, untruthfully, secretly glad that the lack of a telephone warning had relieved us of a night's mental strain.

About this time, a guard came along and opened the doors of the coach. We had pictured ourselves having a compartment alone, but as we entered there was a young woman who had been sleeping there, rolling up her bedding. Our baggage was placed on the racks, and the big padded hold-all with the " dangerous " literature was thrown in one corner of the seat by the door.

The young woman went out, and presently returned with a train inspector in uniform and dark glasses. He kept the glasses on even though it was so dark that we had to light a candle to see properly inside the coach in the dim light of early dawn. They all started pleasant conversation with us.

" How about your journey ? "

" Your hsien magistrates have been treating us much too courteously! " we countered.

" Not at all! Not at all! We must give you a good welcome after your long journey. You must have suffered much bitterness on the way ? "

" It was certainly a very hard journey," we replied.

" Now, tell us, you are a scientist, what are the real facts about conditions in the areas through which you passed since coming out of Peiping ? "

" Well, conditions vary a great deal. In some places we were given very good food, in others we had nothing to eat but millet gruel. But always we were treated most courteously—you Chinese are always too polite! "

" Not at all! Not at all! We know you are not used to the poor conditions in our country. We must do what we can to help you. Did the guerrillas look after you properly ? "

" Yes, indeed! Of course the most dangerous part of our journey was when we first escaped from Peiping . . .", and with that we were able to launch into a detailed description of the escape which effectively kept them quiet for some time.

Presently there were signs that the train was about to pull out. A crowd of excited schoolgirls were outside, and the officer in military uniform opened the carriage window and beckoned to the girls to come up and try out their English on us.

" These are schoolgirls from the Yaohsien Middle School, and they want to welcome you! Please will you say something to them, Mrs. Band ? They are learning English."

" Good morning! " prompted Claire.

" Good morning! How do you do ? Tee-hee-hee-hee! " replied one of the bolder spirits, bursting into laughter and turning her back upon us immediately.

" Is it going to be fine to-day ? "

" Yes, the weather is fine to-day! " came another response with a chorus of giggles.

" Does this remind you of Peiping ? " asked the officer.

" You are all very happy, aren't you ? " we replied, non-committally.

There was scarcely time for further pleasantries before there were whistles blown and flags waved to warn the world that the daily express for Sian was about to depart, and the girls started to skip away, waving and shouting " Good-bye! "

" They are travelling third class ", said the officer ; " they are going home for the Lunar New Year holidays ".

Before the train started, the military officer took his leave, and introduced to us instead a young dandy all dressed up in a new American style suit of fierce purple hue ; he was their interpreter, and would travel with us a short distance.

As the train started to move, the inspector got up off the seat opposite us and asked :

" Would you let me see your tickets, please!

" Thank you!

" And I'm sorry, but this is my duty ; would you mind showing me your passports, too ? "

" Certainly! It is no trouble at all! "

He took his seat beside the girl and made himself at home studying the passports. His command of English was exceedingly small—his conversation was all in Chinese—and we doubt whether he could make much sense out of the hand-written endorsements, but at least he could see the Lion and the Unicorn in gilt on the cover, and read the Japanese residential certificates for occupied Peiping. And the girl seemed to help him out, although she had claimed to be quite ignorant of English.

The dandy interpreter now took a hand in our entertainment in English.

" I studied in Peiping University. I teach mathematics in the Middle School at Yaohsien ", said he, introducing himself, as it were.

" What kind of mathematics do you teach ? " we asked, brightening up, visibly.

" I beg your pardon ? "

" What kind of mathematics do you teach ? "

" Oh! Yes! Er . . . well . . . I teach algebra and trig-trig, excuse me, trigmometry! "

" Very interesting subjects! Do you teach in English or in Chinese ? "

" Er . . . yes! Er . . . I beg your pardon ? "

" Quite all right ! I asked you if you teach in the English or the Chinese language ? "

" No! I teach algebra and trigmometry! "

" Oh! I see! Yes, trigonometry is a useful subject ! "

" I am so sorry! Yes, I teach trigonometry. Ah! Yes, that is right, thank you ! "

" Do you use English in your lessons ? "

" Yes, we have English textbooks and Chinese texts ; we teach sometimes in English and sometimes in Chinese."

But at this point the others were getting anxious to know how much information the fellow had got out of us, and he was called outside. By this time there was an intimate family party in our coach compartment. The train inspector introduced the girl to us as his wife, and a young boy had come in who was the young brother of the military officer who had stayed behind at Yaohsien, and one of the schoolgirls had looked in from along the corridor —a sister of one of the others, and a rough looking fellow with a slouch hat and working man's clothes was standing unobtrusively in the doorway. It made quite a crowd, and it was clear that our hold-all on the seat was being regarded with disfavour.

"Innocence is best", thought Bill, and, with his tongue in his cheek and a picture of all the "communist literature" in the bag in his mind's eye, approached the inspector with a polite :

"Can't you find some other place for this thing? Isn't there a baggage room or something?"

The inspector lifted the bag and pretended to look outside for space; he dropped it back on to the seat with a ponderous thud.

"Phew!" he must have thought, "there's something much heavier than clothes inside that!"

Young brother was then advised to sit on top of the hold-all in lieu of better seating space; he kept pressing it with his thumbs, but we knew it was well padded; and the inspector was watching us through those dark glasses, pretending to be interested in something else.

Presently the rough fellow in the door edged inside and took the corner seat opposite to us. He was ignored by the rest of the party, so introduced himself to us :

"I am on the train specially for your protection!"

"Really! How good of you!" we replied, trying not to sound sarcastic.

"You know this train is sometimes attacked by bandits. There are sometimes bandits on board—disguised. My job is to take special care of first-class passengers. In the old days before the war I used to carry a revolver, but now with the war, that makes too much noise. Instead I use this kind of thing."

He pulled out of his breast pocket a sharp dagger, the blade of which was well vaselined and wrapped in a strip of oiled paper to prevent the point from piercing the lining of his pocket. He slipped it back out of sight with a grin, and continued :

"You see I sit here by the door. Then if some bandit comes suddenly in to attack you, I am in the best place to stab him in the back. Or if he just pushes open the door and threatens you with a gun I can slash his wrist. It's a very sharp knife!"

"Do you really have such things happening here?" we asked, somewhat incredulously.

"Oh! Rather. Why, I remember once when . . .". But the inspector interrupted; there was much more on his mind to ask us, and the thug was told to keep quiet. The inspector's wife took the thug outside for a private warning, perhaps, to be more discreet.

"Now, Mr. Band, you escaped from Peiping into Hopei on December 8th, 1941; when did you leave the guerrilla areas?"

"We started from Hopei on August 10th, 1943."

"Why did you stay there so long? That is nearly two years!"

"Because at first we expected the war to be over in about six months—the American Navy would be able to beat the Japanese easily! Then by the end of 1942 we gave up hope, and asked the guerrillas to convoy us through the Japanese lines. But they informed us that such a journey would be impossible in the winter; we had to wait until August for the crops to be high enough for us to hide while crossing the country."

"August 1943. It is now January 1944. Why did you take so long to come through here?"

"We were two months walking from Hopei to Yenan, and we rested three months in Yenan before completing arrangements to come through this way."

"Three months in Yenan! How did you like it there?"

"They treated us very kindly and courteously!"

"Did they give you clay furniture and a cave, or did you have wooden furniture in a room?"

"Wooden furniture," we replied, as innocently as possible.

They all started to giggle.

"Yes! They did treat you courteously!"

They knew, of course, that the Communists made a point of treating non-Communists most politely; their own "comrades" were given more ordinary accommodation. But they were still not quite sure of our status with the Communists, and continued:

"You said you were two months walking to Yenan! Didn't the guerrillas provide you with riding animals?"

"Oh! Yes! We had animals, but we cannot ride; we really preferred to walk."

"What about the time you spent in Hopei? What did you do all that time?"

" Giving lectures in physics and mathematics to some university boys part of the time."

" How about that sword ? " asked one of them, pointing to the Japanese memento that General Nieh had given us.

" They gave us that as a memento when we said good-bye! "

" When you left Yenan to come here, did you walk too ? "

" No! They sent us in a motor truck."

With that there were still more giggles and they exclaimed :

" They certainly were courteous to you! "

All these exchanges were in a mixture of English and Chinese. The dandy quickly discovered that his English was inadequate, and the others felt they got more out of it by using Chinese. The language difficulty was most convenient for us. Our knowledge of Chinese deteriorated rapidly as the questions proceeded : our answers became less consequential.

" You were three months in Yenan. Now, did you meet General Chu Teh and Chairman Mao Tse-tung ? "

" Yes, we met everybody."

" What do you think of them ? "

" We saw Mao only for about an hour at tea-time. They were all very polite to us."

The family were all concentrating on our answers now, sitting on the edge of the seat and leaning towards us. " After you talked with Chairman Mao did you feel any changes ? " And both the inspector and the dandy put their forefingers to their heads and traced circles above their ears. The word " changes " in Chinese was " pienhua ", but for the life of us we could not understand it. The subject was too deep for the dandy's English, too. They tried another phrase, but we were still dumber. In the end they gave it up ; if we were so dumb as all that it evidently did not matter much about whether our minds had been changed by Mao Tse-tung or not.

In general, besides the particular exchanges recorded here, our questioners asked all kinds of questions about conditions in the Communist areas, pretending sympathy with the Communists in an effort to make us talk politics. In our replies we were careful to refer only to our own private adventures, comfort and welfare, pretending to a light-hearted indifference to everything else.

By about noon they had grown tired of the game ; or perhaps it would be more accurate to say that they had completed Act I of the pantomime. Act II commenced forthwith.

At a small station early in the morning, one of the party went out and brought in a set of pot bowls for cooking rice, made at a local pottery. At another station a bolt of woollen suiting material was handed in through the window, and they started planning what gowns they would make from it in Sian. We imagined that, had we been at pains to describe the work of the people in Yenan, these examples of local products would have been made object lessons for comparison. As it was their painstaking preparations went for nothing, for we showed not the slightest interest. But the biggest joke was their midday meal.

About noon they were getting hungry, and at the next station they were served a special feast of meat and vegetables of the same general type as those served by the hsien magistrates on the way down. We refused their invitation to join in, for we had had a late breakfast on the train, and did not wish to be obligated to them. Instead, we placed our heavy mule hold-all under the window table to make more seating space and left them to it.

They were trying hard to pretend that there was nothing unusual about the meal, but one could tell by the relish with which they fell upon it that it was not often they had been treated to such a sumptuous repast.

The most amusing part of the meal arose from the fact that they were all seated around the window table under which was our heavy bag containing all the literature from the Communist area. They all used it as a foot-rest. And between mouthfuls would press into the bag with their toes trying to feel what was inside it. Every now and then two of them would excuse themselves, go out into the passage and compare notes before returning to take each other's places at the table. Towards the end of the meal the dark-spectacled inspector was getting so desperate because no one had felt anything, that he stood up to lean out of the window, pretending to look down the line, with his feet standing the whole of his weight on a corner of the bag. The others were almost bursting with laughter as they watched him do this; while we kept pretending to be fast asleep in the far corner.

After the lunch they began questioning us about the old days in Peiping, the people we knew, and the kind of life we had lived. This made us feel much more at home, and they seemed to enjoy talking about the good old carefree times before the war. But it was still, we felt, part of our cross examination, and we had to be careful to mention the right people, and still pretend the whole thing was what they wanted us to think it to be, a pleasant casual travelling conversation.

As we were approaching Sian late in the afternoon, they began wondering where we would stay in that city, and recommended the Sian Guest House, where we knew their spy organisation would have free access to all our baggage. In fact they were very persistent in this recommendation, while we were equally insistent that we would go first to the missionaries where funds would be at our disposal for our further travel.

" Are you Christians ? " asked the inspector's wife.

" Yes ", we admitted.

" Well, I think heaven is protecting you! " she said.

" Oh! Why is that ? " we asked, in surprise.

" Because the train is making such good time! "

But we felt that she was hinting that we had passed their examination satisfactorily. We fell to guessing when the train would reach the terminus, joyfully anticipating our arrival in the first real city we had seen for more than two years.

" What will you do in Sian ? " they asked.

" Probably we shall stay there for two or three days and buy some respectable clothes to wear when we reach Chungking."

" Yes, you can buy anything in Sian! " they answered, apparently flattered.

" And what will you do with the Lunar New Year ? " we countered.

" May we come and call on you some time ? " they replied.

" Most certainly, you will be welcome ", we said, " and if you don't see us again here, please come and see us in Peiping after the war is over! "

MELODRAMA IN SIAN

It was nearly dark when the train pulled to a stop in Sian's big modern terminus, and the whole family disappeared so rapidly that we felt sure they were carrying a special message to the city police inspectors to have our baggage searched before we were allowed into the city.

We discovered an inspection platform at the end of the station, and Bill respectfully approached the officer :

"Look! Over there is our baggage, do you want to open i for inspection ?"

"Sorry, the clearance labels have not come in yet, so I canno do anything about it!"

This looked like delaying tactics, but Bill continued hopefully "You mean we can carry on then ?"

"All right! Go ahead!" replied the officer.

So without waiting for him to change his mind, we crowde through the barrier and hailed rickshas, got our stuff on one, an dashed off out of the station.

In a moment we came to the city gates, and the rickshas auto matically jerked to a standstill, almost tossing us out into the stree at the feet of a passport examiner. He seemed surprised to b presented with our two passports before they were asked for, an he forgot to look at the baggage ; before we realised that we ha hustled through we were off again inside the city. Phew! Wha a break!

At one point in the main street one of the pullers had to sto to adjust the tie round his ankle, and an officious policeman steppe off the side-walk, whipped the coolie over the back, angrily cursin him for holding up traffic.

"Where you want to go ?" the ricksha pullers had asked us.

"The British Mission," we had replied, in our best Chinese.

"Don't understand !" they had replied, merrily.

"You know ! Where foreigners preach!" we urged, hope fully.

"Don't understand! You go Sian Guest House ?" they asked

"No! No! No!" we replied anxiously, wondering whethe they were all part of the secret organisation. Then we remembere the address we had been given and asked for that.

"We go Main West Street, No. six", or something like tha the exact name has slipped our memory.

"Yes! Now we understand. All right!"

"That is the Mission!" we said again.

"Don't understand! But you say street and number, that i quite clear. We go Main West Street, Number Six. Is that right?

"Yes, go ahead, and go as quickly as you can!"

But it seemed an hour before we got there, and in the en they let us down outside a pawnshop. We examined the plac incredulously ; yes, there was the number over its door, just a

ve had asked, and the shopkeeper agreed that it was the street we
had asked for.

Well, of all the . . ., did that fellow play us a dirty trick like
hat ? Here we were stranded in what we now began to feel was
a hotbed of Fascism with " dangerous literature " in our baggage,
directed to a pawnshop for the night. Perhaps the shopkeeper
was a special agent, too. Visions of concentration camps, maybe
torture. . . .

It was obvious that the ricksha coolies were quite useless ; in
fact they seemed to enjoy our plight. But the shopkeeper looked
intelligent, and if he is the sinister gestapo we fear, at least let us
find out the truth at once. So with a brave front we explained
as casually as we could :

" Excuse us ! But we are looking for the Mission, and we were
told to come to No. six. Evidently there was some little error in
our instructions. Could you please be so kind as to let us know
how to get to the Mission ? "

Without a word, the old fellow stepped out on to the pavement
and pointed down the street. In the darkness we could just make
out a church tower and long Gothic windows on the opposite
side of the road. With a gasp of relief we thanked him, jumped
back into the rickshas and urged them on again at full speed.

The Mission compound—for indeed it was the Mission church
that we had seen—was walled about, and its main doorway was
bolted fast as though in siege. We banged lustily upon it, and
after a few minutes it was opened by an old Chinese caretaker.

" Yes, the pastor is in. He is at a meeting. But please come
inside and wait a while."

We paid the rickshas off, dragged the baggage over the foot-
board of the entrance, closed and bolted those heavy doors on that
evil world. Peace of mind at last.

We seemed to have stepped into a different universe. The
warmth of welcome at their quiet hearth, the peaceful atmosphere,
genteel manners, soft upholstered furniture, water-colours of
British scenery on the walls, silverware on polished mahogany
sideboard, shelves of classical and devotional literature. It was
incredible. We seemed to be a rude intrusion upon the even tenor
of their cultured lives.

Indeed, we created a major sensation. They had received our
telegram from Lochuan, signed " Claire and William Band ", and

had assumed that we were two American journalists. So they
had made arrangements for another (American) mission to put us
up although they had not really believed we would get through
to Sian. Every other Western traveller from the north had been
detained on one pretext or another, two of them were at that very
moment under martial arrest in Sian. The good folk were astounded at Claire having made the journey from Peiping, and
plainly believed that our safety thus far had been a special dis-
pensation of providence.

Not aspiring to such sublime faith, we did not find this point
of view very consoling : our special needs for the next few days
promised a greater demand upon providence than we had any
claim to. During supper, it came out how we had been delivered
at the pawnshop.

" But didn't our servant bring you here ? " they exclaimed,
in astonishment. "We sent him down to meet the train in case you
arrived as your telegram had predicted."

" No, there was no one looking for us there, although certainly
we rushed through customs rather quickly! "

A few minutes later the mystery deepened as the servant returned
to report that there were no foreigners on the train. He was considerably taken aback to find us already taking a meal with his employers.

Had the servant been " primed " ? Had we somehow evaded
a plot to force us into the " Guest House " ? Why had the clearance labels not come through to the customs officer ? Had someone miscalculated the customs attendant's loyalty to duty : they
had not expected our bluff to work. If they had wanted to detain
us, why had they not done so openly ? Someone quoted in
meaningful tones :

" In ways that are crooked and dark . . ."

" Oh, yes! This is still the Orient. You will be lucky if you
get out of this place, now! "

" Good Lord! But it doesn't make sense. Here we are escaping
from the Japanese, walking over a thousand miles through dangerous
territory, coming at last into Free China, and being treated more
like spies than welcomed as allies! "

" No! It isn't reasonable ", someone agreed, " but that is
what we have been up against here for some years now."

There were important mission conferences on, and their rooms
were full up. So under guidance of the same servant who had

failed to meet us at the station, we set out after supper, and arrived at the other Mission just as the missionaries were going to bed.

Among the two or three who were still up, we created another sensation ; and, if anything, they were more alarmed for our safety than the British missionaries had been.

We were warned that it would be better for us to clear out of Sian immediately and on to Paoki before the Sian gestapo had time to renew the attack upon us. But unfortunately the night train would have already left and we should have to wait until the following evening. During the morrow anything might happen. If we had the least scrap of literature from up north we should destroy it right away ; if anything was found of that nature, no matter how harmless in itself, our lives would be in danger. Even though all the material was anti-Japanese United Front literature, never mind, it should all be burnt.

During the morning before we had arrived, there had already been a mysterious telephone call inquiring whether we had arrived or not. Mysterious first, because the caller would give no in-dication of his identity, and secondly, because no one knew we were supposed to be coming there except the British group. There had been no telephone conversation between the Missions, the correspondence about us having been by private letter delivered specially by the Mission servants. The spy system evidently had them all "fixed". The gestapo did not bother to inquire at the British Mission where we ourselves had telegraphed, because they evidently already knew we were not going to stay there.

In the room they gave us for the night was a large iron coal-stove not in use, and in it we built a fire of papers. The fifty or so copies of an English bulletin describing the work of the army in Hopei, a two-hundred page (Chinese) report on the proceedings of the Hopei Border Region Congress, several copies of the Con-gressional Correspondence—a bi-monthly magazine for congress members in Hopei, a series of wall posters in colour used in patriotic mass education in guerrilla areas, a host of other miscellaneous pamphlets, propaganda sheets, and the like, all of which was in-tensely interesting material and far better seen than just talked about. Last of all we placed section by section on the pyre, the manuscript and crayon sketches we had drawn and written while we had been in Hopei—our first attempt at bringing this book into being— and it all went up into smoke.

What about the precious day-log ? It was well past midnight. We were hot and tired. Are we going to be allowed nothing but our memories of the two years with the guerrillas ? Just because a lot of cursed little rats want to suppress the truth ? Good Lord, no! The day-log nestled snugly in the depths of Bill's overcoat pocket. We said nothing about it to anyone there. To the rest of the world we continued to present an innocent, even vacuous exterior.

Next day at breakfast were about sixteen huge and stalwart Americans all anxious to help. Over a luxurious meal—it seemed to our unaccustomed appetites—plans were laid for our "escape"; as if we had not already made enough escapes without having to continue in the roll of fugitives.

We were advised to remain secreted indoors all day, while they would arrange to have our railway tickets purchased for us at the station. At the appointed time we would be safe-convoyed to the train, and after our departure a telegram would be sent forward in guarded terms to make sure that the people at the other end would know we were on the way. At Paoki, the end of the line, we were to call upon their representative for help in arranging the bus trip on to Chungking. Once out of Sian they felt our safety would be assured.

On the train the previous day the inspector had told us that baggage on the bus trip would be as limited as by plane, and that we would certainly have to lighten the stuff considerably either in Sian or in Paoki. The missionaries confirmed this. The fire had already worked wonders in this direction, but we still felt the need for unburdening ourselves of some of the woollen goods and padded clothes we had been given in Yenan. Also that Japanese sword, so continually a topic of remark by fellow-passengers would be better out of sight. So we left the precious memento behind in Sian.

One of the missionaries gave Bill a much-needed hair-cut; and we both had baths. We felt much more respectable, but not very much eased in mind as we set out for the station after supper.

The two men detailed to convoy us secretly, left by bicycle a few minutes earlier, to hang around for our rickshas at the next turning. The man who saw us off at the gates was on the alert for any monkey business nearer home, and, just in the shadow of the wall he noticed a Chinese lurking, indicating to us that fact by a slight inclination of the head.

As our two rickshas drew away, a third ricksha came from the opposite side of the road, stopped a moment behind us for the shadowy gentleman, followed us at good speed almost all the way to the station, disappeared again just before we alighted.

We took our places in the orderly queue that was forming outside the barrier to the platform. The station was certainly a beautiful modern structure. Over in the far corner were the two huge Americans. Nothing could very well happen to us, but would the gestapo let us on the train?

In a few minutes the ticket inspector arrived and the queue began moving through the gates. There was no hitch for us either, and, dragging our own baggage over the platform, we made a bee-line for the sleeper coach. We had been warned not to speak to anyone on the train, to sleep if possible all the way to Paoki, and sleep we intended to do at any cost.

As we staggered up into the coach whom should we run into, coming along the corridor, none other than our friend the dagger-man who had been so interested to protect us from bandits the day before. Had he been the fellow to shadow us from the house to the station?

He feigned surprise.

" You are leaving early aren't you? What is the hurry?"

" We must get to Chungking as quickly as possible."

" But this is not the right coach. Come with me."

Ho! Ho! What is his game? we thought, but said:

" Well, please help us with this baggage, will you?"

" Certainly! Come on, this way, please."

Instead of taking us, as we had fully expected, back into the station-master's room, or some other place off the train, he took us along the platform to the dining car. He found us a private table in the corner and placed our baggage neatly around. The car was already partly full, and the dagger-man took a seat at the table opposite ours with the remark:

" I'll sit here, eh? And make sure you are all right!"

It was then that we noticed a long mirror in the wall between our seats, and another in the end of the coach just behind where Bill was sitting in the corner. We were plainly visible to anyone in the coach from all angles. And at the far end was another inspector with dark glasses; at second glance he looked remarkably like the chap who had come with us from Yaohsien yesterday morning. He had his cap off now, and he had washed his hair and combed it differently, but we'll swear it was the same fellow trying to look like someone else. Bill stared at him steadily for a long time through half-closed eyelids; and after a while the fellow seemed to realise he was being examined, started pushing his hand through his hair to make it even more deranged: it had been neatly greased the previous day.

The daggerstapo was on friendly terms with the other passengers at his table, and in an undertone not intended for our ears, informed them that we had lightened our baggage, and that Bill had changed his clothes.

Just before the train was due to pull out one of the Americans took a casual stroll through the carriage, and as he passed us said, also in an undertone not intended for the gestapo's ear:

"Good night, and good luck!"

"Thank you! Thank you!" we replied with gratitude. We knew now that our departure from Sian would be properly reported ahead, and that should anything happen on the train, it would not go undetected.

Shortly after the train got moving, fatigue overcame Bill completely and he fell sound asleep. Meanwhile Claire's nerves were too much on edge to let her relax; and while she still pretended—indeed tried hard—to sleep, conversation in the coach took a turn that began to make her thoroughly alarmed.

She could not follow it all in detail, but it was about bandits, and about foreigners who helped the bandits, and how certain foreigners had got themselves into serious trouble that way, and how easy it was for foreigners to disappear while they were travelling. Claire felt that they were talking for our special benefit, because after an hour or so they suddenly noticed that Bill had started to snore; they broke off into peals of laughter:

"Ha! Ha! The foreigner has gone to sleep!"

and after that they shut up and went to sleep themselves.

PAOKI

It was still dark, at six in the morning, when we came into Paoki station, and Claire had imparted to Bill her apprehensions that something was certainly going to happen to us before we got out of the station.

To forestall this, we rushed excitedly through the barrier out into the deserted street, only to realise that it was still too early in the morning to expect the missionaries to be up; and, moreover, in the dark we could not see our way in a strange town, and any tricks that might be planned for us could easily happen at such an hour. We suddenly decided that it would be better to throw ourselves upon the railway officials' hospitality and await the coming of daylight in the station-master's office. The ticket collector was politeness personified. The station-master was a bit grumpy, but let us sit on our baggage inside his office, and we hoped against hope for the dawn.

After about half an hour we plucked up courage and asked a friendly-looking official whether they could arrange for porters to carry our stuff out and find us a ricksha to take it to the Mission with us. He replied that before seven the train would return to Sian, and all the porters were still busy; if we would wait, he would later attend to our needs. We told him that we had been called to the British Embassy in Chungking where Bill was going to do war work. That seemed to impress him favourably.

As the train steamed out, dead on time, we walked out on to the platform and reminded the young official of his promise to help us. Another unpleasant looking young scoundrel came dashing up to him as we were speaking and said in an urgent undertone:

" Don't let them go! "

" Who says so ? " asked the friendly one.

" I say so! " retorted the other, with emphasis.

" You! Ha! Ha! " our friend replied, with scorn. It seemed there were two factions, and we had approached the helpful one most providentially. In any case he found us a porter, and our stuff was loaded into the only ricksha visible in the street, and off we sauntered through the east suburb of Paoki.

The ricksha boy was a slight youngster, and he did not know anything about the Mission. But we had been given general directions, and had to rely on our own instinct. We passed crowds of troops marching up and down the street, and felt anxious all the time lest some of them would suddenly stop and arrest us. At last we came to a city gate. It was closed. On our right was an official looking place with men in dark blue uniforms standing about. Was that a police station? We asked one of them for the Mission, and received the disconcerting reply that there was no such place hereabouts.

We turned to a small ragged urchin on the footpath and asked him.

" Sure! " he replied. " Come with me! "

He skipped down a back alley under the city wall, and took us to what looked like the doorway to a peasant's cottage, and on the door was a card. What we read there told us that in fact this was our refuge.

" You stay right here! " the missionary had replied after he had heard our story. In Sian, they had told us that this family would most probably be unable to accommodate us, but that they would know where to go, and could arrange for bus tickets to Chungking. We did not wish to embarrass them further than that, but he insisted :

" You stay right here, and we'll look after everything for you ; and until I have the tickets, do not on any account show yourselves outside this court ! "

Three days of anxious waiting followed. At nights, over supper, we noticed that the old woman servant seemed deliberately to leave the curtains open, and the dog outside would often bark. During the day, soldiers would stroll casually along the top of the old city wall and stare down into the house. One evening, just before we went to bed, Bill had his " dangerous " day-log out, making entries up to date, when suddenly we heard a bell ring ; surely that must be the front door ? Was it some inspector coming to check us up ? What shall we do with the day-log ? No one went to answer the door. Perhaps they know who is there, and are pretending to be out ? After about five minutes of breathless waiting, Bill tiptoed out to the study to find out what was happening, and discovered the missionary repairing an alarm clock ! Our nerves were over-wrought, and we were seeing dangers where none existed !

Once we got our bus tickets we felt we would be through the dangers of the gestapo. If they wanted to prevent us from going on there were all kinds of tricks by means of which our departure could be delayed. But in fact we got away in record time.

It was Sunday afternoon, January 23rd, when we took our baggage to the bus office to be weighed in, ready for departure early next morning. Bill had to make a personal appearance then, to collect the tickets. On the way back, the two men were striding along at full speed down the centre of the street when suddenly from the crowded pavement there stepped a respectably dressed young fellow whom Bill at once recognised as one of his physics students from Peiping.

We had been warned that probably we would be watched whenever we went outside, and that if perchance we were seen talking to any Chinese acquaintance, suspicion would be cast upon the latter's political connections. There was a continuous series of unexplained disappearances from among the Chinese student population in the Sian and Paoki areas ; a wave of prosecutions had occurred only a few weeks before which had still not completely subsided. It was for this reason that we refrained from calling on the C.I.C. at Paoki.

Now the young boy from Peiping had evidently escaped through the Japanese lines in Honan, the usual route that avoided the Communist guerrilla areas, a route which, by the way, was obviously impossible to us after December 7th, 1941, because it involved a journey of some hours in a Japanese railway from Peiping towards Hankow. Should, therefore, this student be seen talking with Bill, it was exceedingly dangerous. So when he rushed up to Bill and exclaimed with great excitement :

" Well! Well! Mr. Band! How are you ? And how did you get here ? "

Bill replied in an undertone :

" Very well, thank you, but please do not ask too many questions."

The change in the boy's expression was instantaneous. From the sparkling enthusiasm of a normal Chinese welcome, his face became a mask. He raised his hat politely, and took his leave with a muttered :

" Good-bye! See you some other time ! "

" Good-bye! Best of luck."

There is one other point about our three days in Paoki which we must mention, and that is the unselfish hospitality of the missionaries. Our presence with them was not merely embarrassing, it was a real danger. To us it was an invaluable privilege. The unassuming spirit of kindliness in their simple home, the warm friendliness of their two small children, and the natural way in which we were accepted as part of the family for the time we were with them, was a very deep inspiration to us at that time.

On the Monday morning we had to get to the bus station by

about six, and we were up correspondingly early. As we emerged on the high street an armed guard inside the city gate called us to halt. He said it was only about two in the morning and we had no right to be on the street at that early hour. There was some kind of curfew, and he would not accept our statement that it was almost six. Finally, he agreed to accompany us a few hundred yards down the street where his barracks officer would give him the correct time. We won the argument, but the guard gained face by making us explain our business to the officer.

When we had finally been packed like sardines into the old bus, we felt that at last nothing the gestapo could produce would stop us getting to Chungking. We had more faith in the bus than any of the other passengers, perhaps. There were three military observers in the bus, but otherwise the passenger list consisted almost entirely of refugees from Shanghai, Tsinan, and other Japanese Occupied cities. Five of them were young college students coming to Chungking to continue their studies in Free China. The military observers kept a close watch on all of us, in a very unobtrusive and courteous way, and did nothing to dampen the high spirits of the party.

PAOKI TO CHUNGKING BY BUS

From Paoki to Chungking was a memorable ten days' journey. For our unaccustomed selves, the speed of travel was in itself sheer joy. Although we made only an average hundred miles a day. The first day we climbed up into high mountains, and rested for the night at a lovely old temple whose shaded courts had been rented and equipped by the China Travel Service as a special hostel.

On the Tuesday we noticed a change of scenery, palms and bamboo growing in profusion ; the road climbed among great forest-clad peaks, and the gradient was so severe that the old engine needed water every twenty minutes.

On Wednesday it began to snow, and the driver pronounced the road ahead impassable, played mah-jongg all day, gambling with his cronies in the garage.

On Thursday the snow showed no signs of abating, and the passengers were getting anxious—staying even at the wretchedly dirty inn was expensive, and the longer we stayed, the less chance there would be of getting out of the place inside of a week. One little fat man from Shanghai with a gift for persuasive argument was delegated to get into action on the driver. He explained matters to the fellow from the passengers' point of view, and listened to the driver's case. After about an hour's cross fire of statements and explanations, pleadings and counter arguments, things seemed to stand pretty much where they had been at the start. One thing was clear, however, the real motive of the driver was nothing to do with the weather, it was his interest in gambling at mah-jongg.

So the passengers' representative started a flank attack on the foreman of the garage, and after about another hour's heavy barrage, resistance was finally crushed, and the driver agreed to continue.

That afternoon, in spite of a still heavier fall of snow, we climbed the highest and most dangerous part of the whole road, the pass between Shensi and Szechuan Provinces. Coming down on the Szechuan side the road made uncounted hairpin bends at a stiff gradient ; there was nothing between us and destruction a thousand feet below, and the surface of the road was slippery with snow and ice. It was a miracle the bus did not skid. Many a time the tail end seemed to be swinging out over empty space.

Eventually we got down into the large town of Kuang Yuan before dark, and there was no snow down there. Surely we should be able to continue to Chungking now without a hitch ?

At Kuang Yuan there is another excellent hostel run by the efficient China Travel Service, but it was full up. The only inn we could get into was a stinking hole. The rooms were arranged in groups around dirty drains which the men would use as latrines during the night. It was infested with rats, fleas and lice, far worse than anything we had ever experienced all through the guerrilla areas ; and the bus company calmly informed us next morning that there was no bus, and might be none for several days. We had to sleep in that Stygian hostelry, there was no chance of a place anywhere else.

There were about four buses in the big well-designed garage compound, and all of them were out of order, including the one we had just come in on. There were no spare parts available, and we should have to wait until the next bus came in from Paoki before we could continue ; and the snow up on the pass had probably been getting worse, by now it would be impassable.

However, on Saturday evening the bus actually arrived. It was a new " Bank of China " bus with a relatively new Dodge engine. The passengers took our places in the inns, and we took theirs in the bus. Its body was, if anything, a little smaller than the old thing we had come in, but we all squeezed in on Sunday morning, rejoicing in the prospects of a fast trip to Chungking ; and to us it was real travel luxury, even though we were packed in so tight that we could not even move our feet for hours on end.

The driver and his mechanic were well-paid and responsible officers, they took great care of their machine, and, what was even more impressive, they succeeded in keeping out irregular passengers. If anything they were too careful of their machine.

On Monday we had run into rice country, and everywhere was thoroughly wet. It had been raining as usual, and in the evening the driver told us that if it rained again in the night, he would be unable to continue in the morning because the road would be too muddy. It sounded like more mah-jongg business, and on Tuesday morning, when we turned out into the street in the pouring rain, it looked still more like mah-jongg business : the mechanic was still asleep inside the bus, with the doors locked and the window shutters all down.

It took some minutes to awaken the mechanic, and half an hour for him to go and fetch the driver, and another two hours' persuasive argument before he would consent to proceed. His excuse was that with the thick red clay on the new road turned into muddy slime by the rain, it would use more fuel than he was allowed for the journey, and the fuel ration was very strict. The passengers retorted that if he waited longer the mud would get worse ; at this time of the year rain could continue almost indefinitely, there is seldom, if ever, enough sunshine to dry off the surface. In the end the rain decided to stop, and the ticket-holders got so persistent that the driver gave in, and about eleven a.m. resumed the journey.

We had, in fact, at that place been only one day's bus drive from Chungking, but because of the argument we had to stop about sixty miles out for Wednesday night and continue next morning. Meanwhile we were learning about the rat population of Szechuan. The night before we had bought some Chinese buns for early breakfast, because we generally got started so early in the morning that breakfast was out of the question. Following a hint from our fellow-passengers we put these buns in a small haversack and hung it from the mosquito frame above the bed ;

there was no other convenient place in the room. If left on the table or a chair the rats would get them too easily.

During the night we were awakened by the usual rat fight—we were getting used to it by then, but we at once thought of the buns, and Bill reached out with a walking stick which we kept handy for such an emergency, and waved it in the direction of the haversack. There was a hair-raising scuffle as one rat jumped off on to the floor, and a scream from Claire as another fell full on to her feet at the foot of the bed. In the morning we discovered a large hole in the haversack where the buns had been—" had been " is correct.

And we saw water buffalo for the first time, ploughing ponderously in the flooded rice-paddies. What a rich country it seemed ! The valleys were completely cut up into terraces, the flow of the streams diverted into controlled irrigation channels distributed throughout the width of the drainage area. Here and there an isolated cottage, or an ornate farmstead with high walls and a great curving roof, surrounded by ancient pines and dense clusters of bamboo. Except for the one long distance motor highway which looked strange and out of place, there were no communications except narrow footpaths paved with long-shaped stepping stones laid transversely, twisting between the dwellings and their surrounding lands. There were no villages, only the large market towns at intervals of ten or twenty miles along the main highway. Geographically and sociologically we were in an entirely different country from North China.

Compared with North China, this seemed almost prehistoric. One felt a lethargy of decay creeping into one's bones. The water-buffalo seemed like dwarf dinosaurs, the people, running like wild things from the passing automobile, survivors from some primeval age.

At one town there was a line of young farm lads tied together with rope, being marched off by a couple of armed soldiers, pressed into the army under the national conscription act.

And at last Chungking, like a malignant growth of excitement, conspicuously incongruous on the nose of that ancient green-faced province.

Chapter XVIII

CHUNGKING, 1944

THE only time our baggage was actually opened for examination was at the bus terminus in Chungking. Here the inspector peeped inside Bill's razor box, and very carefully read through some advanced mathematics notes which he held upside down.

The Chungking ricksha boys are the most independent in the world : it took us about a quarter of an hour to tempt one of them to quote for hire to the British Embassy, but eventually we did succeed in spending two hundred dollars for a lift.

It was a great relief when at last we came to a stop in a little lane called Consulate Alley, outside an arched gateway over which, in English, were the two words, BRITISH EMBASSY.

At last! We descended the garden staircase under the mulberry bushes and the climbing roses, admired the lawn and the view of the Yangtze River. In these gardens at least we were safe from espionage.

While talking with the Chinese call-boys at the inquiries desk, who seemed at a loss to advise us as to the correct procedure for new arrivals, a large Englishman bustled into the room to give some letters to a messenger. Claire nudged Bill :

" Go on! Ask him for advice."

So Bill got out the one precious calling-card we had saved from Peiping and handed it across with a request :

" Would you please advise us what to do next ? "

He glanced at the card and exclaimed :

" Oh! Yes! I know all about you! I know all about you! " And with a quick look and a merry laugh, added : " You'll be all right now. Needham's my name."

" You don't mean it's Dr. Needham of the British Scientific Mission ? I thought you had returned to Cambridge a long time ago ? "

" Oh! No! We are still very much around here! Look! You must come to my office at once. Well, no! You had better come and see the First Secretary and be properly introduced."

So just as we were, with the dust and the dirt from our ten

PLATE XVII

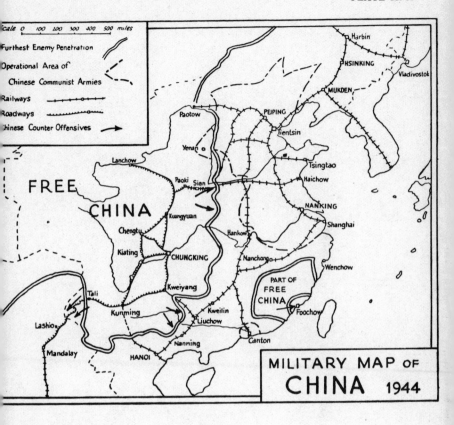

Scale 0 100 200 300 400 500 miles

Furthest Enemy Penetration

Operational Area of
  Chinese Communist Armies

Railways

Roadways

Chinese Counter Offensives

Harbin

HSINKING

Vladivostok

MUKDEN

Paotow

PEIPING

Tientsin

Yenan

Lanchow

Tsingtao

Paoki Sian

Haichow

FREE

CHINA

NANKING

Kuangyuan

Shanghai

Chengtu

Hankow

Kiating

CHUNGKING

Nanchang

Wenchow

Kweiyang

PART OF
FREE
CHINA

Tali

Kunming

Kweilin

Foochow

Lashio

Liuchow

Canton

Mandalay

Nanning

HANOI

MILITARY MAP OF
CHINA   1944

days in the bus, dressed in Chinese Communist clothes, we were presented to H.M. Ambassador, Sir Horace and Lady Seymour, the Counsellors and Secretaries. They were all amazed that we had come through from Yenan in such good time.

Conflicting opinions were expressed as to whether it would be better for us to get out of the country as rapidly as possible, or stay in Chungking long enough to let the Chinese authorities satisfy themselves that we were not Communists. Bill expressed his willingness to follow any course they recommended, so long as he could be useful in some way connected with the war effort. Finally, it was decided that we stay in Chungking to work with Dr. Needham on the Scientific Mission, as on loan from our University, the appointment being tentative for the first three months in order to make sure that the Chinese authorities would not object to our association with this semi-official body.

DECONTAMINATION

And so began our "decontamination process". We were warned that we must not breathe a word in public about any of our experiences if we wished to be acceptable to the Chinese authorities. It was certainly difficult to avoid answering the persistent questions of everyone we met, and yet for the sake of the constructive work we were able to do with the Mission, and for the insight we gained into conditions in Free China at that time, the price was well worth paying. We had some trouble with the Press. Our natural sympathies were with them. We knew what they wanted to know, and we knew that our story would have given them a valuable " scoop "; and we knew that publicity about the censorship and blockade of the Communist problem was one of the best ways of breaking the power of the Fascist elements in the Kuomintang. We had enjoyed fooling the Chinese gestapo at Sian, but when the New York Press representatives asked us questions, we felt more than mean refusing to give straight answers.

" Tell me, are the Chinese Communists on the level ? "

" They are doing their best ! "

" Are they really fighting the Japanese ? "

" Obviously they must in order to exist behind the Japanese lines."

" How is the food situation there ? "

" They gave us preferential treatment."

" Do they have any taxes ? "

" We didn't pay any! "

and at the end we said :

" Please do not publish anything of this."

" You haven't told us anything worth publishing! "

In Chungking we were not actually followed around by special agents, but we had special callers to question us. Naturally we had to register with the police and the Foreign Office within the first few days. After that, one of the officials at the registration bureau paid a personal friendly visit to see how we were getting along. He said he was a former student at the Tientsin Anglo-Chinese College. He was a very pleasant young man, claimed acquaintance with several British missionaries known personally to us in North China, and altogether we had an enjoyable evening's chat with him. But it seemed to us he had been sent specially to test us out ; he kept asking about the Communists in a way suggesting sympathy with them. Secretly this may have been a genuine interest on his part, but in his official capacity it was clear he was required to relay to his superiors the line of our conversation.

Less pleasant were the attentions of an elderly Chinese pastor named Wang, who was one-time private pastor to the Christian General Feng Yu-hsiang. He came specially for information about the Communist areas, but we refused to give him any. We had private information to the effect that he was in fact an espionage agent operating specially among Westerners, and had been attached to old General Feng in a similar capacity. He became so persistent with Bill that it was difficult not to be rude to him. Repeatedly Bill had to say quite plainly that we were unwilling to make any statement whatever concerning the Communists and the Communist problem, it was China's own domestic affair ; moreover, as a pure scientist, Bill was not interested in political questions.

Another regrettable aspect of the decontamination process was the necessity of avoiding all contact with the Chinese Communist party representatives in Chungking. We were warned by several reliable authorities that if we did make contact with them we should immediately engender suspicion : for the party members were under continual surveillance, and we should ourselves come in for undesirable attention.

We even felt obliged to avoid acceptance of an invitation to take tea with Madame Sun Yat-sen whose sympathies with the Communists were so well known that she, too, was hedged about in almost the same way as the Communists themselves. When in later months, Lin Tsu-han came down from Yenan for negoti-ations, we had to resist a great temptation to call on him.

Liberal opinion certainly existed in Chungking, but it was preserved as much as possible under a glass case specially as a show-piece for foreign consumption. In China's own affairs they could take no essential part so long as the Fascist cliques remained in the ascendancy.

There were other incidents connected with our decontamination, but the above must suffice. In the end it became known around the capital that " the Bands are not talking! " And after three months an official letter was received from the Chinese authorities to the effect that the semi-official appointment was formally approved.

ACRIMONIOUS ATMOSPHERE

In Yenan we had been provided with a fair amount of in-formation concerning the corruption and inefficiency of the Chung-king regime, but we had discounted it as party propaganda. A certain degree of corruption and inefficiency, surviving from the past, would of course be inevitable, but we felt sure that the Nationalists had moved forward a great deal more than the Com-munists were admitting. The Communists, we had to agree, had made great strides towards the elimination of these ancient curses, and we were looking forward to discovering for ourselves the progress in a similar direction under the banner of the Nationalists.

To our dismay we found among Western residents of Chung-king a cynical disillusion concerning the ability of the Nationalist leaders even to carry the country through to victory. The Com-munists' assertions seemed more than true. The Kuomintang had lost the confidence of educated classes throughout Free China, and the time was said to be ripe for a revolutionary change in the structure of the National Government. How such a change could come about no one seemed able to foretell, short of civil war, which would lead to defeat by the Japanese.

The Chinese authorities were irritably criticising foreigners with failing to understand the nature of China's problems, and

the Westerners were for their part openly and bitterly denouncing
the Chinese authorities for clamping down such unreasonable and
ridiculous censorships upon all information going out of the country
on the one hand, and coming from the Communist areas in the north
on the other. It was the latter that irked most at that particular
time, because even the foreign correspondents themselves were
prevented from receiving information; it was not merely that
dispatches abroad were being held up.

Our arrival in Chungking at the height of these mutual re-
criminations seems to have acted as a bombshell. Up to then
the authorities had refused permission for pressmen to visit Yenan
on the grounds that the place or the journey was unsafe. Here
we had arrived perfectly safe and well—and one of us a woman
into the bargain. Moreover, we were refusing to talk, and by
implication there was much that we could have said that would
have been politically explosive in nature. The foreign Press representatives in Chungking became wild with anxiety to go and see
for themselves, and struck hard while the iron was hot. A deputa-
tion called upon the Generalissimo in person, and secured his verbal
promise that a special inspection party would be sent to Yenan,
in which the foreign Pressmen would be invited to join.

In about four months, after innumerable delays, the party
actually went, via the special area under General Yen Hsi-shan,
not via the blockade zone through which we had passed. There
were specially selected Chinese Press reporters in the party, and a
number of " guides " for the benefit of the foreign Pressmen, all
of whom were well enough versed in Chinese to have found their
own way round. On their return three months later the Chinese
Press in Chungking carried reams of notes by the Chinese representatives, mostly coloured by special interpretations which, while
transparent enough in themselves and therefore harmless, were
nevertheless disappointing evidence that there was no very earnest
intention of working towards a *rapprochement;* and the dispatches
abroad offered to the Chinese censorship by the foreign representatives were hacked out of recognition. Nothing of publicity
value was obtained from the Yenan visit until the Pressmen themselves could get out of the country to publish their impressions in
India. And because of the atmosphere of conflict with the National
authorities, it is not surprising that these reports were strongly
biassed in favour of the opposition.

INDUSTRIAL RECONSTRUCTION

Meanwhile we continued to gather up the threads of information about the progress in national reconstruction in Free China, news of which we had found it difficult to get ever since 1937 had shut off Peiping from the rest of the country. There is both inspiration and exasperation to be derived from the story, and we must spend some time upon it.

Late in February we visited an exhibition of the National Resources Commission * in Chungking, and this gave us a good idea of the progress of industrial reconstruction since the capital had been established in this city. The Commission's laboratories, under the direction of first-rate Chinese electrical engineers were turning out sponge iron, cast iron, steel alloys, 99.95 per cent. pure tin for export, aluminium castings, modern radio valves, voice scramblers for radio-telephony, dolomite fire-bricks, high-voltage transmission-line transformers, electrical meters, and all conceivable paraphernalia of modern electrical industry. The Commission's oil fields in Kansu under a special Petroleum Administration, supplied high quality liquid fuel in large quantities ; a number of refineries were cracking vegetable oils and producing substitute gasoline. Alcohol plants, sugar refineries, coal mines, scientific instrument factories, ordnances, airplane factories, under their appropriate government commissions, were all in operation.

Under the National Resources Commission alone, four hundred Western-trained scientists and engineers, and five thousand Chinese-trained technicians had been mobilised for productive work. They had made outstanding technological achievements. Starting from nothing, with the local guilds and traditional industry of the province actively hostile to them, these young men and women had succeeded in creating at least the structure of a first class modern industrial technology. In brains, skill, initiative and resources, Free China is rich indeed. In this, tremendous progress had been made in spite of the disasters of the war. Compared with it, the Yenan show was mere child's play.

The pity of it was that this industrial reconstruction was not all being used. There was little if any demand for the results of their industry, their products remained chiefly museum pieces, in ones and twos instead of being produced in thousands.

* Under the Ministry of Economic Affairs, headed by Dr. Wong Wen-hao, China's foremost geologist.

Undoubtedly the country needed the goods, but there was no money to buy them; economically the public were not in a position to afford the kind of luxuries which the industry offered.

There was a marked contrast here with the reconstructive work going on in the Communist areas. There every improvement, although simple and elementary, was directly related to the needs and demands of the population, and was at once turned into wide-scale operation. Here in Chungking, which the Communists thought of as a reactionary centre, the industrial revolution was so revolutionary that it was above the heads of the common people. The material upheaval in their way of life that was being promised by industry in Free China was so great that in fact the country was not quite prepared to accept it. Their industrial exhibits were fantastically remote from anything that the average Szechuan resident had ever dreamed of seeing, let alone of using in his everyday life. In a sense the scientists of Chungking were far more revolutionary than the Communists, their promise for the future more vast and visionary; but their actual influence upon the real progress of the country as a whole was disappointingly small.

To turn all this industrial skill and promise into positive use for the war effort was the problem of the moment, a problem which seemed to have baffled the national leaders. In a very real sense the Nationalists had their hands tied. Exigencies of war had prevented any wide development of communications in the interior, even though any large-scale development of industry obviously needed them; and, what was worse, many of China's individual capitalists had lost faith in the industrial revolution at the very beginning of Sino-Japanese hostilities: instead of investing their wealth in native industry, it went out of the country to securities in Italy, Germany, Britain and America. The financial roots of the Kuomintang were in the West, not in China at all.

In spite of these drawbacks, progressive individuals both within the Kuomintang and not connected with any political party, have gone ahead quietly in constructive work as and when they found opportunity, never despairing even when their results have been exasperatingly thwarted by obstructive action on the part of reactionary gentry, or starved for lack of real financial support from their own wealthy compatriots. The struggle for progress goes on, and, contrary to the conceited opinions of politicians in both camps, not necessarily under the leadership of either party.

If there is any lesson to be learned from all this, it is that to industrialise a nation by deliberate planning will be a gigantic undertaking. The Chinese are trying to do it without the bloodshed the Russians caused in their country's revolution. The Chinese have a genius for compromise ; perhaps they will succeed. But in any case, China cannot break into industrialisation piecemeal. The revolution must come in well-designed stages, each one an actual economic possibility. The Kuomintang did have such plans, but the Japanese war upset their full co-ordination, and gave their own reactionary associates full opportunity to obstruct the programme.

RURAL RECONSTRUCTION

Conflict between the progressive and reactionary elements within the Kuomintang held up the country's war potential not only by frustrating the development of modern industry, but in other ways as well.

While the progressive supreme command would supply to the best of their ability, equipment and medical supplies to their armies, local corrupt officials diverted a proportion of these lease-lend materials on to the black market for personal profit. So long as the Central Government remained dependent upon reactionary local war-lords for defence of territory threatened by the enemy, there was no assurance that supplies sent to the front would not eventually find their way over to the enemy, either by smuggling, or even by direct military surrender.

Within the Central Government group itself reactionary cliques contrived to sieze control of the distribution of essential supplies, hoarded stocks of precious drugs and arms in order to ensure their own future power over their political opponents.

In rural reconstruction, especially, the Nationalists were far behind in comparison with their competitors up north. This was almost inevitable so long as the Nationalists relied for their strength upon the co-operation of rich landlords whose chief interest was in holding on to the solid sources of their own wealth. Local government does not appear anywhere in Szechuan to have succeeded in overcoming the iron rule of hereditary landowners, except in the immediate environs of the large cities ; and although excellent schemes of rural reconstruction have been worked out on paper, and even put partly into execution, obstruction is still fierce, and will remain fierce until the progressive forces in the Kuomintang become powerful enough to swing the landowners into line.

As a typical example of this frustration, we shall cite the new farmers' associations, reorganised by decree of the Central Government in 1939. The objectives of these associations are limited to the working out of improvements in agriculture and rural life in accordance with the wishes of the members themselves. But in order to prevent anything irregular arising out of such a beautifully democratic activity, no less than seven different political organisations and government departments have been vested with the right to supervise or check the workings of the associations.

(1) The Ministry of Social Affairs to make sure that nothing anti-social is being plotted.

(2) The Ministry of Agriculture and Forestry to make sure that expert advice is followed on technical points.

(3) The Kuomintang to make sure that the fundamental three people's principles are not violated.

(4) The Hsien Government Reconstruction Bureau, because these are locally concerned with all development plans.

(5) The Hsien Government Bureau for Co-operative Developments to watch over the interests of co-operatives.

(6) The Secretaries of the Co-operative Farms of the Central Ministry of Agriculture and Forestry to watch that their projects are carried out.

(7) The extension services of the Hsien Government, which by rights should be the only channel for liaison between the farmers and the Ministry.

What should theoretically become an excellent medium through which peasant life and culture might energetically be stimulated for the benefit of the nation, has been almost completely frustrated by the Kuomintang clique's insistent demand to keep all possible checks and controls in operation to prevent the movement from getting out of hand. Only in this way could the party gain approval from its reactionary supporters for such a revolutionary scheme. In practice the officers of the farmers' associations have to spend their time in dealing with busybodies and jealous petty officials from this or that party or government organisation, including others not listed above. Intelligent patriotic leadership such as has achieved such remarkable results in the " mass associations " in the guerrilla areas, has here been squandered in futile dealings with bureaucracy.

POLITICAL CRISIS

In spite of all these inner conflicts, the year 1944 was, from a political point of view, a hopeful year in Chungking.

Early summer the Japanese launched a military offensive up the Yellow River in Honan, threatening the strategic gateway into Shensi and Sian at Tungkuan. Its immediate effect was to re-open negotiations between the Kuomintang and the Communists, because the troops of General Hu Tsung-nan had to be withdrawn from their normal blockade duties and diverted to the region east of Sian. Chairman Lin Tsu-han and General Chou En-lai both came by invitation to Chungking for consultation with the Nationalist authorities.

Whether the troops of Hu Tsung-nan really scored the victory that the Chinese Ministry of Information claimed for them, or whether the Japanese move had from the beginning been only a feint, or whether the threat of union between the Communists and Nationalists was sufficient cause for the Japanese, always sensitive to the necessity of keeping China divided against herself, to withdraw the threat to Sian, we do not profess to know. Anyway the fact remains that the Japanese failed to take Tungkuan, and as soon as this military crisis had passed, the negotiations between Chungking and the Communists petered out.

Later in the summer we learned of the main Japanese drive through Changsha which soon captured the American airfields at Kweilin. By the autumn, effective communication between Chungking and territories in Fukien and Kiangsi had been cut off. The Japanese had succeeded in driving through Kwangsi to link up a direct land route to Indo-China via Kweilin and Hanoi. Early in November the Japanese started a thrust from this line direct into the mountains of Kweichow Province to threaten the main communication line between Chungking and Kunming at the provincial capital of Kweiyang. At the same time there were . signs of Japanese movements towards Tungkuan and Sian again in the north, thus seeming to provide the northern arm of a huge pincer operation upon Szechuan Province.

Negotiations with the Communists were now reopened in earnest. It was rumoured even that an agreement had been signed, and that some of General Hu Tsung-nan's well-equipped forces had been moved down to the Kweiyang front.

On November 20th certain changes in the government personnel were announced, and it became publicly known that, among others, H. H. Kung had been dropped from the Ministry of Finance in favour of a lesser-known member of his staff, General Ho Yin-ching had been removed from the Ministry of War although he still remained as Chief of Staff to the Generalissimo, and Dr. Chen Li-fu was removed from the Ministry of Education and shifted on to a purely party appointment as Minister of Organisation.

The three ministers involved were in fact the chief anti-Communist influences in the government; we knew that the Communists would lay down as a primary condition of co-operation the removal of all three from their positions; and while the announced changes would probably not meet with full approval of all the government's critics, yet they were an excellent gesture in the right direction.

The new Minister of Education, Dr. Chu Chia-hua, while by no means a sympathiser with the Communists, was at least a first-rate scholar, and, unlike Chen Li-Fu, would regard his post as a scholastic and cultural leadership rather than as an engine for political purposes.

The new Minister of War, General Chen Cheng, was welcomed with warmth from all sections of the public as a realist who would not let prejudices and sectional interests of this or that clique stand in the way of effective military action against the Japanese.

The new Minister of Finance started under an unexpected handicap. A day or two before he assumed office the Ministry's building, which, like most buildings in Chungking, was of lath-and-plaster with bamboo frames, caught fire and burned to the ground with, presumably, total loss of all records. Dr. Kung was not there at the time.

Two other stalwarts of the progressive section of the Kuomintang were also taken back into the government: Dr. T. V. Soong, as State Counsellor, and Dr. Wang Shih-chieh who, before the war, used to be Minister of Education, as the new Minister of Information.

Again we shall never know why the Japanese did not actually enter Kweiyang. Whether it was due to Chinese resistance, as claimed by the Ministry of Information, whether because the move was only a feint on the part of the Japanese who were in fact not prepared to go so far into the ice and snow of the Kweiyang mountains, or whether the Japanese feared again to stimulate Chinese unity, or whether a combination of all factors was the cause.

Unfortunately for the Ministry of Information there were too many Western observers all along the line of the enemy's advance, from Changsha through Kweilin to Liuchow and from Liuchow up to Tuyun, almost as far as Kweiyang. From their observations it became only too clear that the Chinese had nothing with which to stop the enemy. With their excellent rail communications and industrial bases in their rear, their complete mechanisation and excellent intelligence service, the Japanese could go wherever strategy required. Chinese resistance, depending almost entirely upon local troops without mechanised equipment, without adequate transport with the rear, without even the assurance of full support from formerly appeasing cliques in the government, was crushed unit by unit. When the enemy struck, Chinese armies collapsed in rapid succession ; and by moving only at night, the enemy was able to maintain communications against anything that the American and Chinese air forces were able to fling against them at that time.

Whole tracts of country fell into the hands of the enemy who, with their specially-prepared political agents, immediately set about mobilising rich rice-producing supply bases for their forces of occupation.

By the first few days in December Chungking was seething with wild rumours, many of which were fantastic results of natural wishful thinking. According to one, the Americans had already landed on the coast of Fukien, and the Japanese would shortly have to withdraw from Kweichow. Another said that the Americans had put some twenty thousand men into Kweiyang, while a less optimistic one had it that the Japanese were by-passing Kweiyang and striking directly at Chungking itself.

We had it on " good authority " that the Generalissimo had personally gone to Yenan to sign an agreement with the Communists, and that General Hu Tsung-nan's Army had been seen on the way to Kweiyang. On the other hand, the Bank of China was said to have reserved its fleet of eight buses in readiness for the evacuation of its staff from the capital towards the north-west, while the Kansu Oil Administration was holding its fleet of trucks in Lanchow for fear they should fall into the hands of the Japanese ; and a still richer rumour than all : the road from Lanchow to Mongolia had been thoroughly mined against the possible advance of a Russian Army, should the latter decide to intervene in civil war in favour of the Communists.

One outstanding fact remained clear. The Chungking regime was facing its most serious military and political crisis of the whole war.

Militarily this was obvious enough. Never before had the Japanese been able to advance beyond Changsha, now they were striking into the heart of Chungking's own mountain bastions of defence.

Politically the crisis was not so obvious, but it was equally real and equally serious. By its failure to fulfil the earlier promise of industrial reconstruction, by the financial collapse of the national monetary system, by its hesitancy in introducing democratic local self-government, and by its foolish tactics in opposing the Communists while preaching United Front, the Kuomintang had lost the confidence even of the progressive educated groups who had initially supported it. On top of this failure to hold the confidence of its own best followers, the Kuomintang had not won the support of the local population ; their plans for rural reconstruction had merely served to increase the hostility of the Szechuan gentry without appreciably improving the livelihood of the peasants. Should any real military threat to the province of Szechuan itself develop, the position of the Chungking Government would become exceedingly precarious. There was no real guarantee that the local population would not, at the lead of its wealthier representatives, go over, lock, stock and barrel, to the enemy. Only a revolutionary change in the Chungking policies would save them from complete disaster : a swing over towards real co-operation with the Communists would become inevitable.

The announced changes in government personnel appeared to be a clearing of the decks as a precaution should the emergency demand a complete change-over. At the same time, so long as the crisis did not reach such a head, no complete change-over need be expected.

The crisis passed. And by February 1945 it was again announced that the Communist-Kuomintang negotiations had broken down.

Nevertheless, with the inevitable defeat of the Japanese, and the victory of democratic nations throughout the world, the strength of the Fascist cliques in China must become gradually more feeble. There can be no doubt that, under pressure from progressive non-party individuals throughout the country, the Kuomintang will finally succeed in ridding itself of its worst Fascist elements, elements that have up to date been thriving on hopes of building up a New Order in co-operation with the Japanese. It is certain that, with the Chinese supreme genius for compromise, some way will be found when the time comes for co-operation in the reconstruction of the country on democratic lines.

Chapter XIX

COLLEGE LIFE IN FREE CHINA

CULTURAL HISTORY

Dr. Sun Yat-sen and his colleagues in conspiracy started a capitalist democratic revolution in Canton in 1911 under direct stimulus of imported cultural weapons. He and his generation had been brought up on Darwin, Adam Smith, Montesquieu, the classical physical sciences and technology; the industrial revolution in the West was their pattern to be adapted for the modernisation of China, freed by revolution from the bonds of feudally established reactionary authority of the Manchu Dynasty.

Politically this revolution was a failure, but it did succeed in replacing China's classical educational system by Western types of teaching methods and Western curricula.

But the October Revolution in Russia, the revolution in Germany and Austria, all stimulated China's intellectuals to revive the struggle against the forces of reaction. Dr. Hu Shih's literary renaissance started at Cornell in 1916, and was very soon taken up with great enthusiasm in his home country.

This cultural renaissance is sometimes called the May Fourth Movement, after the date, in 1919, when the radical youth organisations succeeded in prodding their country's government into refusing to sign away Shantung to the Japanese at the Versailles Treaty. The movement had worked out no systematic ideology, but under its stimulus great progress was made in literary reconstruction. Militant ideas were imported from Europe and Russia, releasing the reading public from habitual acquiescence in the pseudo-feudal authority of their government and its social injustices.

By 1924 the revolutionary movement had built up a clear body of ideas sufficient for a practical political programme to be presented to the whole nation. This programme was presented at the First People's Congress under Dr. Sun's presidency during that year. The Chinese Communist Party had been founded in 1921 by Left-wing members of the revolutionaries, and both groups had been working together in the movement, and were jointly responsible

318

for the 1924 " Sanminchuyi " programme. Since the split between the two parties, both have moved in different directions
away from that programme, both. claim to be interpreting it
correctly. There have been endless arguments between them as
to what was the " real " Sanminchuyi, but into this phase of political
hair-splitting we do not propose to enter.

The 1924 Sanminchuyi, " The Three People's Principles ", were
so popular with the educated classes, that the military campaigns
under their banner succeeded in overcoming the power of those war-
lords who were still associated with the reactionary government ;
and in spite of the later split with the Communists and the colossal
waste of man-power and financial resources that continued for
another ten years of futile civil war, the national revolutionaries
did succeed in giving China her first reasonably stable government
since 1911.

Thanks in great measure to this stability, significant cultural
progress was made during the ten years following 1927 under the
leadership of the Kuomintang. A wholesale Westernisation took
place among the national educational institutions, through which
was imported vigorous cultural material from America and Britain.
This constituted a rebirth and modernisation of the abortive revolution of 1911. The intelligentsia, or young scholar-gentry, were
being brought up on Ibsen and Shaw ; Keynes, Lipman and League
of Nations literature ; James and Freud ; Haldane and Huxley,
Eddington and Jeans, Whitehead and Bertrand Russell. The old
philosophy and the old culture were well-nigh drowned in a fresh
flood of intense Nationalist enthusiasm coupled with a youthful
impatience with the procrastinating tactics of the government
itself.

We have already described the effects of this awakening among
the students of Peiping. In spite of undue Westernisation, perhaps
an over-emphasis on things foreign to the Chinese heritage, nevertheless it was upon this popular awakening among the students
of the national schools and colleges that China's successful resistance
to Japan has had to be built. Without a strong and healthy
Nationalist movement behind them, neither the militarists co-
operating with the Nationalists' Government, nor the Communists
with their proletarian-peasant masses, would have been able to
resist the cunning strategy of the Japanese.

It was from the ranks of these very " bourgoisie " students

that the Communists attracted most of their enthusiastic and patriotic local workers in their mass movement for democratic reconstruction behind the enemy's rear ; and it is from the ranks of the same Western-minded students that the Kuomintang must rely for its vast structure of local government service and, be it remembered, even for its nation-wide secret service organisation. The backbone of the country, whichever way you look at it, is the student body ; and because the students have American and British ideas, neither the extremist tendencies of the Communists, nor the reactionary policies of certain of the Kuomintang cliques can do as much harm as they might otherwise.

The so-called " bourgoisie " culture has also made significant contributions to technical science in China. Chinese science students have proved themselves at least the equal of Westerners in scientific and technical ability. They have mastered the Western curricula of Western educational systems, made important research contributions both in pure science and in science applied to local problems in their own country.

Nor was this purely a high-brow affair among college students and professors of the old scholar-gentry class. In pre-revolutionary times, the scholar-gentry succeeded in keeping hereditary control of government because the children of the poor and middle classes could not afford the expense of a thorough training in the classics ; while the system of public examination for government office was theoretically open to all, it was in practice one of the most effective devices for maintaining class privilege. The modern system of state-subsidised education introduced by the Kuomintang shattered this barrier, and was perhaps the most significant single revolutionary step taken in the early days by the Kuomintang.

Coupled with this revolutionary educational policy, great schemes of rural reconstruction were set afoot. Model counties were organised, and first-rate projects in agricultural and sociological research were begun. Dr. James Yen's great " Tinghsien Experiment ", and his continued campaign for mass education and agrarian reform secured epoch-making results. All technical problems were essentially solved ; the way was clear along which China's peasant population should be guided towards prosperity. Yet the application of these results on any considerable scale was frustrated time and again by the vested interests of local officialdom. In one model county a university professor was appointed magis-

rate in order to overcome such hindrances, but such a solution of
the problem was obviously not of universal applicability. Real
enemy of progress was no longer ignorance, or lack of an agreed
programme of reform, but direct opposition from the reactionary
sections of the landlord-cum-war-lord class through whose co-
operation the Kuomintang was trying to administer the country.

The Communists claimed from the start that rural reconstruction
and mass education were in themselves futile unless accompanied
by a thorough-going land reform to eliminate exploitation by the
landlords, and the farming-out of taxation rights by corrupt
government officials. The Kuomintang preferred the more gradual
process of reform under the guidance of the scholar-landed-gentry
classes, even though this meant a direct compromise with the
landlords and war-lords who wielded power under the old regime.

The Kuomintang have paid a heavy price for the advantages of
this compromise policy. It has meant that the cultural movement
under the nationalists has been confined to less than twenty per
cent. of the population of the country. Even mass education and
rural reconstruction, and, still later, industrial co-operation, have
touched only the minority, and have in general suffered frustration
at the hands of local authorities. Over eighty per cent. of the
people have remained almost untouched by the capitalist democratic
ideas surging in the minds of the offspring of wealthy families associated with Western trade.

But the real crisis for the Kuomintang came in 1936 and 1937.
The appeasement policy forced upon the National Government
and the Kuomintang by the military situation between 1935 and
1937 lead inevitably to a lack of confidence and misunderstandings
on the part of patriotic intellectual youth ; almost all Kuomintang
efforts relating to patriotic youth were of necessity repressive.
The Communists were astute enough to make political capital
out of this situation. Following the Sian Incident, thousands of
eager patriots were ready to sacrifice their lives in a national effort
to resist Japan under the banner of a United Front ; and if the
Kuomintang had been alive to the need for popular mobilisation
for war, they would have had at least the machinery for enlisting
the co-operation of patriotic youthful volunteers for national
service. As it was the Communists, not tied down by any
compromise with conservative elements, did have such machinery,
and did have work for young patriots to do.

While the Nationalists issued vague proclamations about the duties of youth to serve the supreme interests of the State, the Communists had already set up colleges for the training of volunteers in mass education and anti-Japanese propaganda among the peasants, using, in fact, the methods already well established in the rural reconstruction and mass education institutes of the national "bourgoisie" and Western mission institutions. The Communists sent young scientists and young sociologists to the front as important officers in a total warfare against the Japanese of so thrilling a nature that enthusiasm among the volunteers knew no bounds.

There is no doubt that the progressive sections of the Kuomintang would have done precisely the same, but their conservative associates held them back. Instead, probably to disparage the Communists' success, the Kuomintang began prating about conserving intellectual youth and protecting them from the demoralising influence of war ; it was the duty of the student to stick to his books and his laboratory, preparing himself rather for reconstruction after the war. Through the years 1937 to 1939, therefore, Yenan became a romantic centre of patriotism, and a large per centage of idealist youth migrated there as an escape from the tendency towards cynicism and disillusion that began to undermine morale in the rest of Free China.

In the early days of the war with Japan, the college students, as we have recorded, were the backbone of China's heroic resistance. What was their position now ?

During the first years of the war when the national universities were migrating out of the fighting zones, the Kuomintang Government allocated generous sums of money towards the building of temporary accommodation on new sites in the interior of the country. But to the general demand for special adaptation of college curricula to war-time needs, Kuomintang reaction was typical of the worst form of obstruction. One of the leading party representatives is reported to have made reply to this demand : " I have studied many years abroad, and never have I heard of special education in war-time! If you insist in this unreasonable demand, we do not know how to help you."

Instead of introducing shortened training courses for technical workers, the Ministry of Education set about forbidding students from taking on extra-curricular activities connected with the war. Technical students were dissuaded from reading material outside of strictly technical literature ; topics like the social responsibility of the scientist were regarded as dangerous, even the reading of daily papers was discouraged. The technical student must concentrate upon his normal peace-time technical education, and on that alone.

From the point of view of general strategy for the long-range building up of the country's reserves of trained personnel, this policy was probably correct, but the government's tactics led to much misunderstanding. The Kuomintang Government also spent good money in strengthening technical training centres and in subsidising students in science and engineering. But unfortunately the party's sincerity in these praiseworthy efforts was overshadowed by various political moves which we must here describe.

EDUCATIONAL FIFTH COLUMN

Minister Chen Li-fu rightly stressed that in the previous few years China's new educational system had emphasised the mere accumulation of knowledge to the neglect of moral training. He presented a new policy designed to correct this deficiency, modelled after the tutorial systems of Oxford and Cambridge. In 1938 a complete set of regulations to this end were drawn up and published. From among these it is worth while to quote a few extracts :

" (vii) Tutors are held responsible for students' thought and behaviour. Honour will be given to former tutors whose students win distinction in study or their later careers. Blame will be laid upon tutors whose students show incorrect thought and behaviour in later life."

We wonder what college don would accept a tutorship in Oxford or Cambridge under such conditions. But the next regulation changes the situation completely :

" (viii) Any tutor may demand dismissal of a student from his group ; the student may then select another tutor, but a second dismissal will mean the end of his college career."

" (xi) Upon graduation a student's certificate must be signed by his tutor with a detailed statement giving an estimate of the student's thought, behaviour and academic standing."

All tutors were placed under the direction of Deans of Discipline appointed by the Ministry of Education, one for each institution, from among members of the Kuomintang. The same system permeated, or was intended to permeate the whole educationa[l] system from colleges down to the primary schools.

It is perfectly easy to understand how this system rapidly became dominated, if not completely controlled, by a gang of unscrupulous wire-pullers. Their methods of proselytisation for the party cliques, at first crude as we saw in the story of our student-teacher Liu Shuang, in Chapter VI, could now afford to become more refined. Any individual could be dismissed from his social position if his thoughts were regarded as dangerous to the regime. If this repressive machinery had been used only as a means of strengthening the position of the Kuomintang in its struggle with reactionary elements, all might have been well ; but in fact it was the Fascist elements who got themselves into the position of control operating the machinery to consolidate their own position and to frustrate efforts on the part of the progressive educated public.

By about 1940, in spite of proverbial Chinese inefficiency, the machinery of repression had been pushed into energetic operation, and produced widespread disapproval from liberal-minded college teachers. The end of academic freedom was deplored on all sides. But this opposition was unorganised, and came too late : the Kuomintang had already established its gestapo system, and with this, opposition was effectively crushed.

These gestapo agents were planted in every class, listening even to private conversations between a professor and his students. Censorship of private reading matter and personal correspondence went along with the moral guidance administered by the tutors. No one was secure, economically, unless he maintained " correct " relations with the dominant Kuomintang cliques.

Japanese fifth columnists, working through pro-Japanese sympathisers, eventually appear to have succeeded in influencing the whole structure. Through the Deans of Discipline, they were able to exert a strong anti-war pressure upon impressionable students. Spread about among the youth of the nation were ideas of this kind : " China is a peace-loving nation, who ever talks of war are the real traitors ", and " The real duty of a student is to study, it is a waste of time for a student to worry about how to save the country." Many tutors openly praised Hitler and Mussolini, criticised Russia and the United Front programme of resistance to Japan.

In fact the whole educational system, with some notable

exceptions, was distorted into an organised effort to undermine democratic culture, and substitute a twisted form of Fascism. Every student in every school was provided with a copy of " China's Destiny ", that unfortunate pamphlet upon the publication of which the Japanese gleefully remarked that Chungking's attitude now differed in no material respect from that of Wang Ching-wei, the Puppet of Nanking.

CENTRES OF LIBERAL THOUGHT

But it takes more than a political clique to suppress the Chinese scholar class. Centres of liberal thought remained loyal to their traditions ; notably at Kunming, the South-Western Associated University. Against these centres the Ministry of Education could at any time have resorted to economical and political discrimination : in the matter of rice-grants, endowments and other privileges given generously enough where recipients pretended to " toe the party line ". It would hardly be fair to assert that such discrimination actually took place, although it would be easy to find people who believed that it had. The reputation of all these centres in academic circles both at home and in the West, put them into a very strong position so long as the democratic powers were not yet defeated by the Axis ; and with the change in the tide in international affairs in favour of the democracies, the liberal centres weathered the threatened storm and remain to assume once again their cultural leadership of the country.

This whole position came to public notice in the West only when the Ministry of Education began sending special party officials to Britain and America with the express purpose of watching the thought, behaviour and studies of Chinese students studying abroad. These " thought controllers " raised a furore of protest from educational circles in America, although British comment was more diplomatic. These espionage agents—for that is what in fact they were—were a part of a larger system of control over China's students wishing to go abroad for study. The control began with a selection of the candidates for scholarships : in addition to the purely academic examinations, there was the additional requirement that every candidate must pass through a special training school in Chungking set up for the preparation of Chinese going abroad. Here the candidates received military training and a series of lectures on political principles from the point of view of the Kuomintang, and a prescribed form of instruction in " correct behaviour " while abroad.

As a method of controlling the thought of young men and women going out of the country, the system was probably a farce. As a system of blocking the exit of students with wrong party connections, it worked fairly efficiently. But the whole thing exposed the Kuomintang authorities to so much ridicule from abroad that it did more damage to their cause than anything that could have been done by their political opponents getting out of the country.

HARDSHIP AND WANT

Apart from these political troubles and their gallant stand for freedom of thought, the Chinese scholar class has had a grim struggle with hardship and want. Almost all cultural institutions in Free China were in fact refugees from coastal cities since occupied by the enemy. Their libraries, equipment, stocks and personnel have been transported thousands of miles over mountainous country into the comparative safety but deadening isolation of the far western provinces.

Even in peace time, to import into these provinces an insignificant quantity of scientific supplies was a major problem involving immensely disproportionate expense, appalling waste of time, and even loss of life. War-time blockades multiplied these handicaps a thousand-fold. For nearly eight years China's intellectuals have been fighting both against these forces of nature, and against misunderstandings with the local population who regard all " down river " folk as foreign barbarians. In these battles they have won a series of brilliant victories. But the fight against financial uncertainty, even hunger and want, is still in progress.

Inflation has brought real suffering to all salaried groups. University professors cannot afford to buy clothes, it costs them a month's salary to buy a pair of cheap shoes, even though salaries have been increased ten-fold since the beginning of the war. They go to class in faded gowns that hide an embarrassing multitude of deficiencies in their under-garments. Their wives take on outside clerical work, and grandparents mind the children. The men do most of the household chores, and many teachers hold concurrent posts in several colleges, each nominally full-time, in order to make ends meet. Free rice allowances are made by the government to national institutions, and special rates are allowed to private institutions, but even with this, the average living standard of the college teacher was lower than that of any ricksha coolie on the streets of Chungking.

No other section of salaried employees suffered quite so much : bank clerks, office workers in government departments, shop assistants, even unskilled labourers in government-owned factories, had their salaries hooked more or less faithfully to a fairly accurate living index. As a direct result of this, in spite of official efforts to increase the numbers of college students, young people were being prepared by their families, not for college careers, but for government and party jobs and merchant business where comparatively easy money was to be had.

There was one fantastic interview that Bill had with a young college teacher in this connection. It began in the usual way with general talk about college work, and then, when we were alone, the boy began to talk in whispers. We were sitting in the windows of a private residence overlooking the front garden, when he suddenly got up and looked through the window and drew Bill over to the inner side of the room.

" One's life is in danger these days!   It is really! " he whispered.

" No!   Surely! " Bill had tried to reassure him.

" But it is!   The Sanminchuyi Youth Corps is nothing but a gestapo.   The Kuomintang Government is stamping out all freedom of thought and action.   Our private conversations are spied upon, and those guilty of careless words disappear mysteriously.   I tell you, the Old Fellow is out to eliminate the educated class ; he fears the intellectual revolutionary movement, and he is deliberately starving us out of existence.   His son is being trained in Kiangsi, after a Moscow education, and after the intellectuals of the older generation have been effectively silenced, the Old Fellow will go over to the Communists and will produce this young fellow as candidate for the position of China's Stalin to lead the new China in a totalitarian dictatorship."

Of course one can meet cranks in any country, but this one was symptomatic in quite an interesting way. He had accepted the Kuomintang's claim to actual leadership at its face value, and imputed ulterior motives to lines of action or inaction where in fact there was neither motive nor leadership at all. The Kuomintang is to blame for this entirely, simply because it has so persistently claimed to itself the credit for all progress and consolidation going on in Free China, and so consistently tried to cover up failures and deficiencies even where these have really nothing to do with their own political responsibilities. The Kuomintang has made the strategic mistake of identifying the nation with itself, when in fact it is nothing of the kind.

It is particularly easy for Westerners to slip into the same error ; we must be more than careful to realise that there are immense forces in China that have no relation with politics or political parties. There are evils in China which are hang-overs from the past, and there are progressive forces which reach out to the future, and none of them accept the politicians as their leaders. The politicians are in fact more like puppets on the stage ; they may wave the banners and recite the slogans, but the real creative work goes on quietly behind the scenes.

After our " decontamination " had been going on for a month, we felt it safe to pay a visit to the Christian Universities in Chengtu. It did our souls good to come again among our old friends, many of whom had escaped from Peiping after Pearl Harbour. In the light of all the difficulties with which these people were faced, we were amazed at the constructive work which they were able actually to achieve.

Although Chengtu is by no means the only centre where first-class academic work was going on in war-time China, their work may be taken as typical. Similar work was going on in many other places, notably in and around the centres of Chungking, Kunming and Kweiyang, and at other places like Kiating (Szechuan), Tali (Yunnan), Hanchung and Chengku (Shensi), and even in the provinces of Kwangsi, Kwangtung and Fukien, right under the noses of the Japanese. Quiet, unpublicised liberalising influences were at work, continuing heroic loyalty to the cause of higher learning in spite of physical and economic hardships that would have crushed any but the most enthusiastic devotees.

To a considerable extent deficiencies in individual possessions have been alleviated by a pooling of resources. But in general the precarious nature of inland travel facilities effectively blocks any comprehensive programme of co-operation. Even in Szechuan where the best motor highway has been constructed between the national and the provincial capitals, fuel shortage and lack of spare parts for repairs prevents all but the most essential traffic. The post office cannot handle sufficient mail to make long distance book-parcels service a possibility. If, therefore, for example, a biologist in Chengtu wishes to consult reference material in the National Libraries in Chungking, he would have to be prepared to spend at least two weeks on the trip, and two months' salary for a return ticket.

There were many things that forcibly reminded us in Chengtu that it is one thing merely to keep alight through periods of dark-ness a torch of learning that has been handed down for generations by an intellectually alert population, quite another to create from less than nothing, as these Chinese scientists and their Western colleagues have done, the proper atmosphere for advanced scientific work among a people almost completely isolated from and alien to such fields of endeavour.

Chapter XX

JOURNEY HOME AND RETROSPECT

In contrast with our thousand miles on foot, the journey home was all by air. Fourteen hundred miles in an American Douglas air liner from Chungking to Calcutta ; first stop Kunming, lend-lease supplies pouring in out of the sky ; we had to wait, all strapped in ready for the take-off, three-quarters of an hour for a turn on the runway ; three miles high over Mitkyina and down again for supper at a military airport in Assam. Only ten hours' flight in all to cover even a greater distance than had taken us months to march.

In Calcutta, crowded to bursting point with Allied troops, we spent five pleasant weeks waiting for transport, and were fortunate to include a week-end at Kalimpong in the Himalayas as guests of the St. Andrews' Homes for Anglo-Indians : we caught a splendid vision of the eternal snows over Kinchinjunga.

Then a huge four-engined Sunderland flying boat with thirty passengers, in six hops to England. Camel carts of Karachi, an oil pipe-line through the desert of Iraq, the deep Dead Sea and Palestine, a carrier fleet oozing through the Suez Canal ; the pyramids from above the rich green valley of the Nile ; and Cairo—Cairo with the best stocks of luxury goods of any city in the world.

El Alamein and the remains of that great tank battle upon which the fate of the world had hung ; Benghazi and the desert isle in the Little Gulf of Sydra ; Oran and Gibraltar ; how the world swung beneath us with smoothly satisfying ease.

The Rock gave us our only jolt. There was a wind storm brew-ing, and the seas were too rough to bring the ship down outside the harbour. Manœuvring to get into position for a harbour landing, the skipper had to take the flying boat close down over the edge of the Rock. We were already strapped in, ready for the exciting moment when she would strike water. One young R.A.F. boy returning home on sick leave was standing by the window gazing out at Gib. Suddenly an air-pocket sucked the huge plane down, down for a breathless three seconds. There was a crash above our heads from the crew upstairs before the thing bumped at the bottom of the pocket, and the R.A.F. boy knocked his head on the ceiling and was thrown to the floor. We had no idea that air could be so hard.

We waited in breezy little Gibraltar for two days for the ice and snow to abate on the South Coast, with a patience fortified by reports of air crashes in Italy and the Crimea ; and at last, after a week of super luxurious travel we were disgorged upon bomb-scarred London in the small hours of the morning ; shared a taxi with an American soldier, a British business man, and two cockney girls who chatted excitedly about two men with black masks over their eyes who had been their fellow-passengers earlier in the night. Then six hours' wait in Euston station before dawn in the bitterest cold wave that had struck the country in years.

But we were home again. Home, and the comfort of being able to use one's mother tongue in the normal routines of everyday life ; to feel inconspicuous in a crowd ; to know that there is no one snooping round the corner interested in one's political opinions ; there is something about England's freedom for the loss of which no amount of Oriental glamour or continental efficiency can ever compensate. And now a glorious spring climaxed by Victory in Europe.

So we come to the appropriate place and time for retrospect, to look back over the last fifteen years covered by our story.

CHINA'S PROBLEMS

Of China, land of paradox, we can fairly claim a many-sided experience. Seven years in her cultural capital before the Japanese attacked ; four and a half years in Peiping under occupation by the enemy ; two years among the peasants liberated from the invaders by the Chinese Communists behind the Japanese Front fighting lines ; and finally a year with the Kuomintang in the country's war-time capital, Chungking. We have lived with Chinese scholars, farmers, soldiers and politicians ; dwelt for a time in more than eighty different cities, towns and villages in almost every part of the country. As connoisseurs of comfort we have obviously been guilty of unduly tempting Providence ; and yet it has been all overwhelmingly worth while.

We have often been asked to summarise our attitude to China's problems, and we shall here attempt to do so in the light of these different points of view.

In the first place we must remind ourselves that China is not just a country, but a Continent, and her problems should be thought of in relation, say, with the problems of Europe ; her geographical area and her population are both greater than those of the whole of Europe, and her ethnological characteristics are equally as varied.   Is it surprising that the people of Szechuan are not wholly in sympathy with the Chungking Government when we remember that its European analogue would be a British Government in Bucharest or Belgrade ?   Is it at all a slur on China's unity that there should be border clashes between the Communists and the Kuomintang round the Shensi Border Region, when even in our own small Kingdom we have an acute Irish problem ?

The wonder of it is, not that " China should be still disunited ", but that there should exist so great a measure of real agreement between her leaders throughout the whole nation of four hundred and fifty millions.

For in fact, except for superficial shades of opinion the Communists and the Nationalists have practically the same fundamental programme for the building of a New China based upon the broad general outline of Dr. Sun Yat-sen's " Three People's Principles " : national unification, political democracy, and economic reconstruction.   The real differences between the two opposing groups in China have arisen almost entirely from fortuitous circumstances —not that either the Communists or the Nationalists would agree with such a statement, but we believe nevertheless that it is true.

MORALITY AND DISCIPLINE IN THE COMMUNIST ARMY

Both parties agree on the need for moral rejuvenation, and in this the Communists have achieved a more practical success with far less hypocrisy.   Cultural leadership of a vigorous farming community can never be consistent with moral flabbiness.   In all our experience we have never seen a more spartan group than the Communist Armies.

What would the normal young recruit to any Western Army feel if he were presented with the certainty that he would be completely deprived of his beer and his girl friends for a period expected to be anything between five and ten years ?   Yet that is the certainty for every boy in the Eighth Route Army ; and they are all volunteers.

These boys are not angels, and they are not abnormal.   Possibly their meatless diet has something to do with it, they are too poor to afford better. Probably the shock of seeing Japanese bestiality has had its sobering effect.

We ourselves, since December 8th, 1941, living as we were actually among the men of the Chinese Armies, and marching a thousand miles with different units during that time, never once saw a drunk or disorderly Chinese soldier. In fact through all our fifteen years in China we have seen less disorderly conduct among the Chinese of whatever political complexion than anyone could see in a single day among our own troops in Calcutta : and our boys would only be behaving normally under the circumstances at that.

But the greatest contrast is between the Chinese scene and the other side of the Oriental picture. Apologists for the Japanese have tried to account for the holocaust at Nanking in December 1937, as a pardonable exception. But the same kind of ugly business has been repeating itself continually in the Border Regions of North China ; it is apparently a normal phenomenon among Japanese troops, and no doubt has its basic psychological causes. The Japanese leaders have deliberately debased the morals of their fighting men, and they fight like wild beasts.

Against these horrors the Chinese have reacted in what is in fact a puritan revival, with a political instead of a theological rationalisation.

Had the Chinese attempted to send a mere fighting machine into guerrilla areas they would have had to compete with the most efficient fighting machine in the Orient ; they could not afford either to treat the men as well, nor to provide them with such excellent equipment as the Japanese and their puppets had. They would have had to fight the war on their enemy's terms, on the enemy's own grounds. Instead, against the enemy's fighting machine, the Chinese have sent a crusading army of spiritually conscious warriors, and the battle has been fought on China's own terms. The guerrilla struggle in North China has been one of the essential parts of the over-all strategy in the national resistance movement.

Inefficiency, carelessness, armoured weakness, yes, all these defects can be tolerated, in fact have to be endured to a degree that exasperates many Western observers. But moral courage, faith in their leaders, a clear understanding of the meaning of their struggle, pillars of their precious morale, one slight defect there, and the whole structure of the guerrilla war bases would collapse. Instead, through eight long years of ever more intense struggle their strength has grown rather than diminished. If we measure efficiency as the quotient of fighting value divided by military equipment times expense to the people, there is probably no more efficient army in the world than the Chinese army in general; and the Chinese Communist Army in particular.

Having said all this, we still do not agree that Communism would be the best system by which to organise for human prosperity in times of peace, not even in China; indeed less in China than elsewhere. Chinese laziness and inefficiency are proverbial. Lin Yu-tang has done his best to interpret this national characteristic in a pleasant philosophical light, and although he has written more specifically of the scholar-gentry class, laziness is still not an unknown thing among the peasants, hard-working though they have to be; and in this we have seen that the Communists are a hundred per cent. Chinese. The fighting units were superb, their officers on the tips of their toes through all emergencies. In contrast to this, at base headquarters, the men were normally lazy, and wherever there was perfect safety, there was more laziness and inefficiency than in pre-war Peiping. Nothing short of a machine-gun would move many of the men to more than the absolute minimum of effort.

The Chinese are more inert than we Westerners. As a general rule they have no perpetual "itch to be at something"; yet if compelled to by circumstances, they can produce an effort surpassing ours. This is really a matter of physiology rather than psychology. Their normal metabolism is lower, they burn less energy during repose, they are more relaxed; in consequence they are not so alert, they are more peaceful. But once aroused, they have more reserves for hardship than we have, or would have on the same supply of fuel.

If a Western soldier had to fight on the same diet as the Chinese guerrilla, he would be an hospital case inside a few weeks, yet the Chinese guerrillas have thrived for years and still go on fighting.

But with this background, one can see that Communism, by removing all the normal stimuli to activity, would leave the Chinese a hopelessly plastic material waiting for the next imperialistic invader. That the Communists themselves seem to be aware of this weakness in their own ideological position would appear from the fact that their great productive campaign in Yenan is not based upon the ideals of Communism at all, but upon direct application of the profit stimulus through simple capitalist democracy.

Both parties agree on the necessity for building up a republican form of democracy, both plan to industrialise the nation's economy, both have almost identical programmes of agrarian reform, neither party wishes to let China remain dominated by foreign imperialist powers.

The Kuomintang has done an excellent job of liberalising the capitalists and the landed gentry, and it is hardly surprising that they have at times come near to being dragged under by the dead weight of reaction to which they were necessarily tied. No bloodless revolution could have done better with the material at hand.

The Communists have for their part worked miracles among the farmers, made golden opportunities for the common people out of calamitous adversities inflicted upon them by the enemy : they have carried through a fundamental part of the Three People's Principles with tremendous success, and liberated a grand total of something like eighty million people in an area of Occupied China no less than twice the area of Great Britain.

There is no essential contradiction here ; the two sides have been working on complementary aspects of the same general programme. If only their mutual suspicions—which again are natural consequences of past history—could be dissolved, the two groups could become, instead of warring factions, opposing parties in a progressive democratic constitution.

Since this book was written, the atom bomb has ended the war but destroyed the peace ; after a brief truce, China's civil conflict has confounded our optimism by flaring up again with ever greater violence. Having failed in their war-time effort to attract Western support, the Chinese Communists have reverted to their original reliance upon Soviet Russia. The civil war now has a new international flavour, and while it may still be possible for the United States so to administer its aid as to compel the Nationalists along more liberal lines, both Chinese parties have read the American political barometer quite otherwise and are busy trying to capitalise on the U.S.-Russian conflict.

Just one more word about China's future democracy. The Kuomintang has been trying to wage war against Japan on the basis of temporary dictatorial powers, to build up an industrial structure by national edict, and to postpone democratic constitutional reform until peace-time conditions permit a calm and careful approach to the problems of such a reform.

On the other hand the Communists, in their areas, have been waging their type of war against the Japanese on a basis of immediate democratic reconstruction. This, as we have pointed out in former chapters, was actually a matter of life-and-death for the Communists; in no other way could they succeed in holding out against the Japanese in the areas they have liberated from the enemy. By this courageous and aggressive policy the Communists have made, on their part, a brilliant contribution to the nation.

The Kuomintang are tied to a policy of gradual introduction of popular representation under their own party's tutelage, while the Communists have gone ahead with popular representation in a revolutionary manner. But they still have not eliminated the " tutelage " : the party workers who started the peasants off in self-government were Communists, the colleges where local government civil service officials receive their training under Communist Party influence and guidance, the armies in North China, while voluntarily financed by popular government resources, remain under the control of the party in the same way as the Nationalist Armies are under the control of Kuomintang members. There is no organised opposition in the Communist areas, any more than there is in the Kuomintang areas, although the local coalition is far more effective in Communist areas than elsewhere.

Neither side can be blamed for this situation. We must remember, before passing judgment, that democracy is far more than a mere system of popular representation. It is a way of life in a community with a background of experience and tradition in living liberally. Democracy is a mode of functioning of a trained and experienced society.

This being so, how can one expect a democracy to emerge within a community with almost no experience of democratic life and all of whose traditions have been semi-feudalistic for several generations ?

Of course the Chinese masses have a genius for self-government, they are as culturally ripe for democracy as any other race on earth ; but their actual experience has been practically nil.   The overthrow of an occasional tyrant is not practical democracy, it is an essential crisis within a feudal society.   The Chinese peasant certainly has an instinct for group action when faced by a common threat.   But this cannot honestly be dignified by the term " democratic experience " ;   it is at most 'the raw basis upon which a democratic experience can eventually be built.

To build a democracy in the full sense of the word surely requires some form of " tutelage ", whether by one political party, or by a coalition of parties.   In China the Communists have introduced a skeleton " system " of democracy first, in as perfect a form as can reasonably be worked out in advance, and are in fact giving the " masses " experience in handling it.   Personally we believe this to be, from an educational point of view, the wisest course. But the opposite procedure may just as sincerely be regarded as correct ;   and under the circumstances in which the Nationalists have had to operate, their method of tutelage may have been the only practical one for them.

Now an organised opposition is a most important dialectical component in a fully experienced democracy ;   its absence in China (as in Russia) is one of their most glaring departures from the dialectical materialism that the Communists pretend to accept as their gospel.   But even in Britain during times of crisis we resort to coalitions and " national governments " ;   and surely the nurturing of an infant democracy during a period of national rebirth is a crisis of the first magnitude, calling for a coalition more than at any other time.   It is some move towards such a coalition or compromise between the Communists and the Nationalists that all sincere well-wishers for China are now looking for to-day.

A WORD OF CAUTION

There are several special points which should be borne in mind by all Western observers of the Chinese scene.   First is the Chinese genius for creating a good impression—it is their greatest concern in their relation with foreigners.   Second is their regard for smooth courtesy rather than blunt frankness, and their respect for propriety rather than for uncomfortable truthfulness, both in their dealings with each other and with foreigners.

The reader will have gathered from our story that the

Communists are as characteristically Chinese in these particulars as the Nationalists. On the whole they are very pleasant characteristics ; they make for happiness in daily life, and soften the crude angles that make life so hard in a mechanical age. But if we wish to understand the Chinese people, these characteristics necessitate a more objective approach than one realises at first contact.

The casual observer, even the trained critic, is most easily misled into believing he has the true facts of the situation. The enthusiasm of the foreign journalists who spent a month or so in Yenan on a flying visit from Chungking during the summer of 1944 was quite amusing in this respect ; and on the other side of the fence, of particular importance is the fact that a considerable proportion of official information from Chinese sources, including the few Western writers employed by the National Government, is propaganda for political purposes and therefore, no matter how acceptable as entertainment towards the establishing of mutual good-will, it remains unreliable as information upon which to form sound judgments. So long as the country remains under the one-party dictatorship this situation will naturally continue, and Westerners will have to rely upon their own direct observations for the truth, no matter how hard it is to come by.

For ourselves, we were far more confident in our judgments about China during our first five years in the country than we were after ten years ; and now, after fifteen, we have at last come to realise that description is a safer goal than explanation ; if the Chinese themselves cannot agree on an explanation of their own troubles how much less can we ?

CHINA'S REAL STRENGTH

China is a land of contrasts and extremes, of dialectical paradoxes and seeming contradictions : childishness and maturity, culture and crudeness, wealth and poverty, honesty and insincerity, reliability and deceitfulness, violence and reasonableness, indolence and energy, wisdom and stupidity, and through all this diversity a real and powerful unity.

It is perhaps this very diversity that has been China's real strength : through all the vagaries of influence from the rest of the changing world, China has possessed herself ; no matter what force may threaten, she has had the appropriate elements within herself with which to counteract. Her human and spiritual resources are inexhaustible and unsurpassed, and as the crises of her history have called these hidden potentials into action, now this, now that great figure rises into prominence in the human scene.

Historians, journalists and diplomats watch these prominent figures, and calculate with care and skill in an effort to predict the future ; but China's destiny is not to be found in this man or that, this or that political programme or military power. The real life of the Chinese people cannot be understood in terms of mere conspicuous personages, political parties and publicity campaigns. Political turmoil is a mere froth upon the outer surface of the seething fluid underneath ; it is within the fluid mass of China's people that the real forces can be felt, silently and persistently pressing on with irresistible momentum.

As one eminent Chinese scientist put it in private conversation one day in November 1944 :

"There are many men in China working quietly and constructively. I do not believe in publicity and splash. If you are in the public eye, the authorities must interfere and try to control you. I keep as quiet and inconspicuous as possible, and they can do nothing to me. It is the solid personal contacts with the youth of China that will count in the long run, and no government authority can do much to spoil that work.

"This kind of Sino-British co-operation programme, as worked out by the various cultural relations associations, committees, commissions and administrations, and all the rest, are all right in their way ; but they are all superficial in their impact on Chinese life compared with the steady long-term work of individual scientists among the youth. The basis of any rebirth of civilisation is the educated youth ; it is not the big noises and the governing classes. These are merely ornaments and trappings, the necessary encumbrances that drag us down. The struggle is won at the foundations, and it is we who work quietly and struggle silently without publicity who really influence the course of events."

It is only by living among them that one can even begin to understand what these silently struggling forces are ; and in that understanding which we can but dimly grasp, we believe that we shall discover essentially the same spiritual powers that are at work among ourselves.

Although the Chinese peasant is poles apart from us in language, creed, race and class, yet there exists a real basis of human understanding between us in terms of which all such barriers can eventually be broken down. The Chinese peasant is very far from the primitive human type that superficial observation might lead one to suppose. He may live close to nature, but he is not its slave ; he lives close in order to keep control over his surroundings. For a hundred generations he has maintained a continuous battle for existence, and not only for existence. His achievement of a rare jollity, a zest for life in the face of adversity, demands a truer philosophy for practical purposes than the verbose systems of abstract definitions, axioms and theorems, emanating from the luxurious chairs of higher learning.

The human brain is undoubtedly the climax of nature's evolutionary process, and creative intellectual activity the greatest of all human achievements. But our own comfortable way of life, playing about with processes of abstract thought, maintaining our physical health through the repetition of meaningless gymnastic antics, certainly gives no valid reason to feel superior.

For our part we have been jerked down off our balcony seat, pushed out of the professorial chair, and forced against our inclinations, among a virile people on the rough mountain trails of real life. It has been a revelation to us. We hope that at least it has purged us of that unpleasantly common disease of modern civilisation : intellectual snobbery.

But neither has it produced the reverse extreme reaction. In moments of despair for the future of our modern scientific civilisation it is often a temptation to look wistfully into the past and long for the simple life, the life of the family that lives off its own land, and wins a triumphant and significant conquest over nature in producing the daily needs of the human race. Ah, yes! We have seen them. The men work themselves out before they are forty ; their wives bear children once a year for fifteen years ; they die like flies from pestilence and famine ; they suffer untold agonies of mind through the harsh uncertainties of fate ; the price for a simple self-sufficient life is too high.

Enlarge the simple community to improve the diet? But for that there must be good roads and transport facilities, to build which there must be modern industry. Improve your health services? Ask the medical worker to produce results without the help of modern implements and drugs, none of which would be possible without modern scientific technology. Even such simple matters as providing the peasant with a better plough or a better spade to lighten the load of his daily work, where would it come from without modern steel and therefore modern heavy industry? Modern industry can and will lighten the load for the ancient art of agriculture, and the lot of the peasant will improve, but not by a wholesale return to primitive simplicity.

If one is anxious for the simple life, it will of course be perfectly possible to turn modern farmer and accept all the aids which modern science can give. But can we expect a whole continent deliberately to say to itself:

" We shall remain a continent of peasants, and rely upon the industry of other peoples to provide for us the best tools and techniques so that our lot may not be so harsh as that of our ancestors?"

The idea is absurd. And the Chinese are never absurd altogether; above all the Chinese are realists. They are going all out for modernisation in its totality.

Differences in achievement between sections of the human race are not due to essential differences of racial type. Just as a complex grouping of ordinary " non-living " atoms into organic molecules permits them to function as living things, so the complex structure of modern society has accompanied the emergence of new human powers. It is a more efficient organisation of society developed under favourable circumstances that has permitted the emergence of modern scientific culture in the West; it is not any particular Western racial " flair " for science. The Chinese peasants represent an abundance of human material as rich in wisdom, skill and strength as any other community; they are now already beginning to evolve a new social structure of immense potentiality.

We have been watching them take these first steps towards a great synthesis through which their potentialities will be released for still nobler cultural contributions to humanity. We have tried to draw a picture of this metamorphosis from close at hand. Perhaps we have been too close for a broad view. We have seen only a few of the facets of the whole crystal, measured only a fraction of the forces that are building up the great superstructure which will be the New China. We hope, however, that this account will be of interest to all readers with a concern for the evolution of human society towards forms that will allow individual men and women to rise to higher moral and intellectual levels of achievement.

INDEX